Nietzsche, German Idealism and its Critics

Nietzsche Today

Volume 4

Nietzsche, German Idealism and its Critics

Edited by
Katia Hay and Leonel Ribeiro dos Santos

DE GRUYTER

ISBN 978-3-11-055472-4
e-ISBN (PDF) 978-3-11-030818-1
e-ISBN (EPUB) 978-3-11-038290-7
ISSN 2191-5741

Library of Congress Cataloging-in-Publication Data
A CIP catalog record for this book has been applied for at the Library of Congress

Bibliographic information published by the Deutsche Nationalbibliothek
The Deutsche Nationalbibliothek lists this publication in the Deutsche Nationalbibliografie;
detailed bibliographic data are available in the Internet at http://dnb.dnb.de.

© 2017 Walter de Gruyter GmbH, Berlin/Boston
This volume is text- and page-identical with the hardback published in 2015.
Typesetting: Lumina Datamatics
Printing and binding: CPI books GmbH, Leck
♾ Printed on acid-free paper
Printed in Germany

www.degruyter.com

Acknowledgements

Many of the papers in this volume are revised and expanded versions of papers first presented at an International Conference on "Nietzsche and German Idealism" at the University of Lisbon in 2012. We would like to thank the authors and those who have written texts specifically for this volume for engaging in this project. Texts by Danielle Cohen-Levinas, Thomas Kisser and Eike Brock were translated from French and German into English; we would like to thank James Pearson and Herman Siemens for their help in the translations and revisions. We also would like to express our gratitude to Christoph Schirmer for his patience and support.

This project was made possible by the generous support of the Centro de Filosofia from the University of Lisbon and the FCT (Fundação para a Ciência e a Tecnologia).

Contents

References and Abbreviations —— IX

Katia Hay
Introduction —— 1

Part One: Nietzsche and German Idealism (Hegel, Fichte, Schelling)

Frederick Neuhouser
Hegel and Nietzsche on Spirit and its Pathologies —— 11

Herman W. Siemens
'Punishment by Fate' as a Cypher for Genealogy: Hegel and Nietzsche on Immanent Law —— 35

João Constâncio
Struggles for Recognition and Will to Power: Probing an Affinity between Hegel and Nietzsche —— 66

Maria João Branco
The Song of the Sirens: Nietzsche and Hegel on Music and Freedom —— 100

Thomas Kisser
The Reality of the Will: On the Problem of Individuality in Nietzsche and Fichte —— 115

Carlos João Correia
Schelling and the Death of God —— 154

Katia Hay
Understanding the Past in Nietzsche and Schelling: *Logos* or *Mythos*? —— 167

Part Two: After Idealism: Nietzsche and the Critics of German Idealism

Eike Brock
Life is Suffering: On Schopenhauer's and Nietzsche's Philosophical Engagement with Suffering —— 189

Razvan Ioan
Philosophical Physiology: Schopenhauer and Nietzsche —— 208

Philipp Schwab
Critique of 'the System' and Experimental Philosophy: Nietzsche and Kierkegaard —— 223

Elisabete M. de Sousa
Musical Controversies in Nietzsche and Kierkegaard —— 246

José Miranda Justo
Time and Freedom in Kant and Kierkegaard: Towards a Better Understanding of the Affinities between Kierkegaard and Nietzsche —— 258

Danielle Cohen-Levinas
A Critique of the Aesthetics of German Idealism: Reflections on Nietzsche's Rupture with Wagner —— 271

Leonel Ribeiro dos Santos
The 'Will to Appearance' or Nietzsche's Kantianism According to Hans Vaihinger —— 282

About the Authors —— 297

Index —— 301

References and Abbreviations

References to works *other* than those by Nietzsche, Kant, Fichte, Hegel, Schelling, Schopenhauer, Kierkegaard and Heidegger are given as follows: (author date, pages). A bibliography for these references is given at the end of each article.

For works by Nietzsche, Kant, Fichte, Hegel, Schelling, Schopenhauer, Kierkegaard and Heidegger references and abbreviations used by the authors are given below. Each section is concluded by a list of English translations of German texts that have been used (but also modified) by the authors of this volume. Unless specified otherwise translations into English of other texts are from the authors and/or editors themselves.

Friedrich Nietzsche

BAW	Friedrich Nietzsche, *Frühe Schriften 1854–1869*. Hans Joachim Mette/Carl Koch/Karl Schlechta (Eds.). [photomechanical reprint of: Friedrich Nietzsche, *Werke und Briefe. Historisch-kritische Gesamtausgabe. Werke* (terminated after five vols.). Munich: C.H. Beck'sche Verlagsbuchhandlung, 1933–1940]. Munich: DTV 1994.
KGB	Friedrich Nietzsche, *Briefwechsel. Kritische Gesamtausgabe*. Giorgio Colli/Mazzino Montinari et al. (Eds.). Berlin, New York: De Gruyter 1975ff.
KSA	Friedrich Nietzsche, *Sämtliche Werke. Kritische Studienausgabe*. 15 vols. Giorgio Colli/Mazzino Montinari (Eds.). Munich, Berlin, New York: DTV/De Gruyter 1980.
KSB	Friedrich Nietzsche, *Sämtliche Briefe. Kritische Studienausgabe*. 8 vols. Giorgio Colli/Mazzino Montinari (Eds.). Munich, Berlin, New York: DTV/De Gruyter 1986.

English abbreviations used:

A	*The Anti-Christ*	
BGE	*Beyond Good and Evil*	
BT	*Birth of Tragedy*	
	BT Attempt	"Attempt at a Self-Criticism"
CW	*The Case of Wagner*	
D	*Daybreak*	
EH	*Ecce Homo. How One Becomes What One Is*	
	EH Books	"Why I Write Such Good Books"
	EH BT	"The Birth of Tragedy"
	EH Smart	"Why I am so Smart"
	EH WA	"The Case of Wagner"
	EH Wise	"Why I am so Wise"
GM	*On the Genealogy of Morality*	

GS	*The Gay Science*
GSt	*The Greek State*
HC	*Homer's Contest*
HH	*Human, All Too Human*
HL	(UM II) "On the Use and Disadvantage of History for Life"
NCW	*Nietzsche Contra Wagner*
RWB	(UM IV) "Richard Wagner in Bayreuth"
SE	(UM III) "Schopenhauer as Educator"
SGT	*Socrates and Greek Tragedy*
TI	*Twilight of the Idols or How to Philosophize With a Hammer*
TI Errors	"The Four Great Errors"
TI Fable	"How the 'True World' Finally Became a Fable"
TI Maxims	"Maxims and Arrows"
TI Morality	"Morality as Anti-Nature"
TI Skirmishes	"Skirmishes of an Untimely Man"
TL	*On Truth and Lie in an Extra-Moral Sense*
UM	*Untimely Meditations*
WS	(HH II) *The Wanderer and His Shadow*
Z	*Thus Spoke Zarathustra*
Z I Creator	"On the Way of the Creator"
Z I Despisers	"On the Despisers of the Body"
Z I Metamorphoses	"On the Three Metamorphoses"
Z I Virtue	"On the Bestowing Virtue"
Z II Redemption	"On Redemption"
Z II Self-Overcoming	"On Self-Overcoming"

For the references to Nietzsche's published/titled texts: Authors have used the English abbreviations and the section/aphorism number/or abbreviation, KSA volume, and page number (e.g. GM I 16, KSA 5, p. 285; Z II Redemption, KSA 4, p. 179).

References to the *Nachlass* are as follows: NL Year, KSA volume, the notation in KSA, and page number (e.g. NL 1887, KSA 12, 9[86], p. 380).

References to *Nietzsche's letters* include the volume and page or letter number in KSB or KGB.

Quotes from Nietzsche: Passages emphasised by letter-spacing in the original have been rendered in italics by the authors.

Translations used:

The Anti-Christ, Ecce Homo, Twilight of the Idols, and Other Writings. Aaron Ridley/Judith Norman (Eds.). Translated by Judith Norman. Cambridge: Cambridge University Press 2005.

Beyond Good and Evil. Prelude to a Philosophy of the Future. Translated by Walter Kaufmann. New York: Vintage Books 1966.

Beyond Good and Evil. Rolf-Peter Horstmann/Judith Norman (Eds.). Translated by Judith Norman. Cambridge: Cambridge University Press 2002.
The Birth of Tragedy and The Case of Wagner. Translated by Walter Kaufmann. New York: Vintage Books 1967.
Daybreak: Thoughts on the Prejudices of Morality. Maudemarie Clark/Brian Leiter (Eds.). Translated by Reginald Hollingdale. Cambridge: Cambridge University Press 1997.
Ecce Homo. In: Friedrich Nietzsche: *On the Genealogy of Morals. Ecce Homo*. Translated by Walter Kaufmann/Reginald Hollingdale. New York: Vintage Books 1989.
Human, All Too Human: A Book for Free Spirits. Translated by Reginald Hollingdale. Cambridge: Cambridge University Press 1986.
The Gay Science. With a Prelude in Rhymes and an Appendix of Songs. Translated by Walter Kaufmann. New York: Random House 1974.
The Gay Science. Bernard Williams (Ed.). Translated by Josefine Nauckhoff. Cambridge: Cambridge University Press 2001.
On the Genealogy of Morals. In: Friedrich Nietzsche: *On the Genealogy of Morals. Ecce Homo*. Translated by Walter Kaufmann/Reginald Hollingdale. New York: Vintage Books 1989.
On the Genealogy of Morality. Keith Ansell Pearson (Ed.). Translated by Carol Diethe. Cambridge: Cambridge University Press 1994.
Nietzsche Contra Wagner. Translated by Walter Kaufmann. In: *The Portable Nietzsche*. Walter Kaufmann (Ed.). New York: Penguin Books 1976.
Selected Letters of Friedrich Nietzsche. Translated by Christopher Middleton. Indianapolis: Hackett 1969.
Thus Spoke Zarathustra. A Book for All and None. Translated by Graham Parkes. Oxford, New York: Oxford University Press 2005.
Thus Spoke Zarathustra. A Book for All and None. Adrian Del Caro/Robert Pippin (Eds.). Translated by Adrian Del Caro. Cambridge University Press 2006.
On Truth and Lie in an Extra-Moral Sense. Translated by Walter Kaufmann. In: *The Portable Nietzsche*. Walter Kaufmann (Ed.). New York: Penguin Books 1976.
Twilight of the Idols. Translated by Walter Kaufmann. In: *The Portable Nietzsche*. Walter Kaufmann (Ed.). New York: Penguin Books 1976.
Untimely Meditations. Translated by Reginald Hollingdale. Cambridge: Cambridge University Press 1997.
The Will to Power. Translated by Walter Kaufmann/Reginald Hollingdale. New York: Vintage Books 1968.
Writings from the Late Notebooks. Translated by Kate Sturge. Cambridge: Cambridge University Press 2005.

Immanuel Kant

AA	*Kant's gesammelte Schriften*. 29 vols. Ed. the Royal Prussian, subsequently German, then Berlin-Brandenburg Academy of Sciences. Berlin: Reimer, subsequently De Gruyter 1900ff.
KrV	*Kritik der reinen Vernunft*
KU	*Kritik der Urteilskraft*

Translations used:

Critique of Judgement. Translated by. J.H. Bernard. London, New York, Toronto: Macmillan 1914.
Critique of Pure Reason. Translated by Norman Kemp Smith. London: Macmillan 1929.

Johann Gottlieb Fichte

F SW	*Fichtes sämmtliche Werke.* 8 vols. I. Hermann Fichte (Ed.). Berlin: Veit & Comp. 1845/46.
F SW IV	*Das System der Sittenlehre nach den Prinzipien der Wissenschaftslehre*
GA	Johann Gottlieb Fichte, *Gesamtausgabe der Bayerischen Akademie der Wissenschaften.* 42 vols. Reinhard Lauth/Erich Fuchs/Hans Gliwitzky/Peter K. Schneider (Eds.). Stuttgart- Bad Cannstatt: Frommann Holzboog 1962–2012.
GA I/2	*Grundlage der gesamten Wissenschaftslehre (1794/95)*
GA II/3	*Nachgelassene Schriften 1793–1795*
GA IV/4	*Kollegnachschriften 1794–1799*

Other German abbreviations/references used:

BdM	*Die Bestimmung des Menschen.* Berlin: Vossische Buchhandlung 1800.
StA-2/ SWV-2	"Wissenschaftslehre 1811". In: *Die späten wissenschaftlichen Vorlesungen II.* Stuttgart-Bad Cannstatt: Frommann Holzboog 2003.
UI	*Ultima Inquirenda. J.G. Fichtes letzte Bearbeitungen der Wissenschaftslehre Ende 1813/Anfang 1814.* Reinhard Lauth (Ed.). Stuttgart- Bad Cannstatt: Frommann Holzboog 2001.
WL-1801/ 02	*Darstellung der Wissenschaftslehre (1801/1802).* Reinhard Lauth/Peter K. Schneider (Eds.). Hamburg: Meiner 1997.
WL 1804-II	*Die Wissenschaftslehre. Zweiter Vortrag im Jahre 1804.* Gereinigte Fassung. Reinhard Lauth/Joachim Widmann/Peter Schneider (Eds.). Hamburg: Meiner 1986.
WLnm-K	*Wissenschaftslehre nova methodo. Kollegnachschrift K. Chr. Fr. Krause.* Erich Fuchs (Ed.). Hamburg: Meiner 1994.

Translations used:

Early Philosophical Writings. Translated and edited by David Breazeale. Ithaca, New York: Cornell University Press 1988.
The Science of Ethics as Based on the Science of Knowledge. William T. Harris (Ed.). Translated by Adolph E. Kroeger. London: K. Paul, Trench, Truebner & Co. 1897. (Available online: https://archive.org/details/scienceofethicsa00fichrich. Accessed 30 April 2015).
The Science of Knowledge. Edited and translated by Peter Heath and John Lachs. New York: Cambridge University Press 1982.
The Vocation of Man. Translated by William Smith. London: John Chapman 1848.

Georg Wilhelm Friedrich Hegel

TWA   Georg Wilhelm Friedrich Hegel, *Werke in zwanzig Bänden. Theorie-Werkausgabe*. New edition on the basis of the Works of 1832–1845. Eva Moldenhauer/Karl Markus Michel (Eds.). Frankfurt a.M.: Suhrkamp 1969–1971.

English abbreviations used:

Ae III	*Lectures on Aesthetics* (III) [TWA 15]
E III	*Encyclopedia of the Philosophical Sciences* (III) [TWA 10]
FS	*Frühe Schriften* [TWA 1]
JW	*Jena Writings* [TWA 2]
PhR II	*Philosophy of Religion* (II) [TWA 17]
PhS	*Phenomenology of Spirit* [TWA 3]
PR	*Elements of the Philosophy of Right* [TWA 7]
SC	"The Spirit of Christianity and its Fate" [TWA 1]
SL II	*Science of Logic* (II) [TWA 6]

For the references to Hegel's works: Authors have used the English abbreviations, the section or paragraph, TWA volume, and page number (e.g. *PhS* §18, TWA 3, p. 23).

Translations used:

Elements of the Philosophy of Right. Allen W. Wood (Ed.). Translated by H.B. Nisbet. Cambridge: Cambridge University Press 1991.
Phenomenology of Spirit. Translated by A.V. Miller. Oxford: Oxford University Press 1977.
The Science of Logic. Translated and edited by George di Giovanni. Cambridge: Cambridge University Press 2010.

Friedrich Wilhelm Joseph Schelling

SW	Friedrich Wilhelm Joseph Schelling, *Sämmtliche Werke*. Division I: 10 vols. (= I–X); Division II: 4 vols. (= XI–XIV). Karl Friedrich August Schelling (Ed.). Stuttgart, Augsburg: Cotta 1856–1861.
WA I/II	Friedrich Wilhelm Joseph Schelling, *Die Weltalter. Fragmente, in den Urfassungen von 1811 und 1813*. Manfred Schröter (Ed.). Munich: Beck 1946.

Translation used:

Philosophical Investigations into the Essence of Human Freedom. Translated by Jeff Love and Johannes Schmidt. New York: SUNY 2006.

Arthur Schopenhauer

Werke   Arthur Schopenhauer, *Sämtliche Werke*. 7 vols. Arthur Hübscher (Ed.). 3rd ed. Wiesbaden: Brockhaus 1972.
Nachlass   Arthur Schopenhauer, *Philosophische Vorlesungen. Aus dem handschriftlichen Nachlass*. 4 vols. Volker Spierling (Ed.). 2nd ed. Munich: Piper 1987–1990.

German abbreviations used:

E   *Die beiden Grundprobleme der Ethik* [Werke IV]
HN I   Handschriftlicher Nachlass. Vol. I [Nachlass I]
PuP I/II   *Parerga und Paralipomena, kleine philosophische Schriften I/II* [Werke V/VI]
WN   *Über den Willen in der Natur* [Werke IV]
WWV I/II   *Welt als Wille und Vorstellung I/II* [Werke II/III]

Authors have used the German abbreviations followed by section, and page number (e.g. WWV II, p. 404).

Translations used:

On the Fourfold Root of the Principle of Sufficient Reason, and On the Will in Nature; Two Essays. Translated by Karl Hillebrand. New York: Cosimo Classics 2010.
The World as Will and Representation. Vol. 1. Translated and edited by Judith Norman, Alistair Welchman and Christopher Janaway. Cambridge: Cambridge University Press 2010.
The World as Will and Representation. Vol. 2. Daniel Kolak (Ed.). Translated by David Carus and Richard Aquila. London: Pearson 2010.

Søren Kierkegaard

SKS   *Søren Kierkegaard Skrifter*. Vols. 1–28, K1–K28. Niels Jørgen Cappelørn/Joakim Garff/Jette Knudsen/Johnny Kondrup/Alastair McKinnon/Finn Hauberg Mortensen (Eds.). Copenhagen: Gads Forlag 1997–2003.
     Not   Notesbog 1-15 [SKS vol. 19].
     NB   "Notabene" [SKS vols. 20–26].
     Papir   Papirer [SKS vol. 27].

English translations and abbreviations used:

CA   *The Concept of Anxiety*. Translated by Reidar Thomte in collaboration with Albert B. Anderson [KW VIII]
CUP1   *Concluding Unscientific Postscript* [KW XII,1]
EO1/2   *Either/Or I/II* [KW III/IV]
JP   *Søren Kierkegaard's Journals and Papers*. Vols. 1–7. Translated by Howard V. Hong/Edna H. Hong, assisted by Gregor Malantschuk. Bloomington, London: Indiana University Press 1967–1978.

KJN	*Kierkegaard's Journals and Notebooks*. Vols. 1–11. Niels Jørgen Cappelørn/Alastair Hannay/David Kangas/Bruce H. Kirmmse/George Pattison/Vanessa Rumble/K. Brian Söderquist (Ed.). Princeton, Oxford: Princeton University Press 2007ff.
KW	*Kierkegaard's Writings*. Vols. I–XXVI. Translated by Howard V. Hong/Edna H. Hong. Princeton, Oxford: Princeton University Press 1978–1998.
PC	*Practice in Christianity* [KW XX]
PF	*Philosophical Fragments or a Fragment of Philosophy / Johannes Climacus, or De omnibus dubitandum est* [KW VII]
PV	*The Point of View* including *On my Work as an Author* and *The Point of View for My Work as an Author* [KW XXII]
R	*Repetition* [KW VI]
TA	*Two Ages: The Age of Revolution and the Present Age. A Literary Review* [KW XIV]

Authors have indicated both the Danish and English references: SKS volume, page number; English abbreviation, page number (e.g. SKS 4, p. 273; PF, p. 73).

Martin Heidegger

GA	Martin Heidegger, *Gesamtausgabe*. Frankfurt a.M.: Klostermann 1975ff.
Heidegger GA 5	*Holzwege*, 1977 [1935–1946]
Heidegger GA 6.1	*Nietzsche I. Der Wille zur Macht als Kunst*, 1996 [1936–1939]

Translations used:

Off the Beaten Track. Edited and translated by Julian Young and Kenneth Haynes. Cambridge: Cambridge University Press 2002.
"The Will to Power as Art". In: Martin Heidegger: *Nietzsche. Vol 1 and 2*. Translated by David F. Krell. New York: Harper Collins 1991.

Katia Hay
Introduction

In *Daybreak* 190, Nietzsche accuses Schelling and Hegel of having converted the Germans into something "obnoxious" and "pitiful" and refers to their Idealism as a "soft, sweet-natured, silver, glistening idealism" that tries to embellish the "cold" and "dry" reality of things (D 190, KSA 3, p. 162f.). In a way, this aphorism reflects Nietzsche's generally dismissive attitude towards the German Idealists (including Schopenhauer and Kant, though not always for the same reasons). And although it does not reflect Nietzsche's more positive statements about his German predecessors, it may explain why it is that Nietzsche has largely been considered to be a severe critic of, if not radical opponent to German Idealism. However, the general idea that there is an unbridgeable opposition between Nietzsche and German Idealism is also due to a tradition within philosophical research, which with a few exceptions has had the tendency to either disregard the possible relations between them or, in the best case, underline the differences.[1]

In this volume we have intended to explore new ways of addressing and new ways of interpreting the relations between Nietzsche and the German Idealists. It has been our underlying assumption that, in spite of the obvious differences (which in many cases have to do with the radically different conceptual vocabularies and presuppositions), there are also compelling affinities between them. This does not mean that we have neglected the differences, but it does mean that the reality of these differences has not impeded a fruitful analysis of the way in which Nietzsche's texts can be put in dialogue with Hegel, Fichte or Schelling. For it is only within or through this dialogue that we can gain any clarity as to where to locate and how to define both the similarities and the differences with precision. In addition, in order to better understand the particularity of Nietzsche's position *vis-à-vis* German Idealism, we have considered it important to take into account his relation to other authors, such as Schopenhauer or Kierkegaard, who are also well known for their criticisms of German Idealism.

---

[1] For studies on Nietzsche and Hegel see for instance: Robert R. Williams: *Tragedy, Recognition, and the Death of God: Studies in Hegel and Nietzsche* (OUP, 2012), William Dudley: *Hegel, Nietzsche and Philosophy: Thinking Freedom* (CUP, 2004) or Stephen Houlgate: *Hegel, Nietzsche, and the Criticism of Metaphysics* (CUP, 1986). Comparative studies on Nietzsche and Schelling and/or Fichte are less common: see for instance John E. Wilson: *Schelling und Nietzsche: Zur Auslegung der frühen Werke Friedrich Nietzsches* (De Gruyter, 1996).

This double focus, so to say, is also reflected on the structure of the book, which is divided into two parts: (1) "Nietzsche and German Idealism (Hegel, Fichte, Schelling)" and (2) "After Idealism: Nietzsche and the Critics of German Idealism".

This second perspective or second movement – mainly focused on Nietzsche's relation to Schopenhauer and Kierkegaard – enables us to assess the ways in which Nietzsche's critical response to German Idealism may be similar to that of Kierkegaard, Schopenhauer and other later authors of the twentieth century. But it also raises important questions about the way in which we should understand the affinities/differences between Nietzsche and the German Idealists in relation to other topics, such as for instance the problem of Nihilism. Indeed, the realisation that Nihilism is a problem and a concern that Nietzsche *shares* with Schopenhauer and Kierkegaard, gives us a new perspective from which to understand a number of topics dealt with in the first part of the volume, such as the 'pathologies of the spirit' or the sentence regarding the 'death of God'. Thus, we can ask whether Nihilism is not a problem and a question that Nietzsche shares with the German Idealists as well. To what extent is Nietzsche's diagnosis of Modernity similar to Hegel's? And to what extent does Schelling's thought express the encounter with Nihilism? In a similar way, we may ask: to what extent is Nietzsche's and Kierkegaard's critique of the 'system' different from Schelling's?

This volume does not respond to all these questions, but it does help to raise them, to formulate them and to clarify the very complex relations between these authors on a *conceptual* level. Indeed, for the most part, the focus has been placed, not so much on Nietzsche's actual reception of his predecessors (Schopenhauer, Kierkegaard, Hegel, Schelling, Fichte and Kant), nor on their possible influence on him, but rather on a conceptual analysis that tries to bring out the profound interrelatedness of their thinking. Each paper considers one particular aspect of Nietzsche's thought (such as his notions of 'life', 'law', 'will to power', 'drives', his critique of morality or his aesthetics) in relation to one or more of the authors mentioned. This much more systematic or conceptual approach has not only revealed surprising affinities between Nietzsche and the German Idealists, but has also generated new angles from which to understand, reinterpret and evaluate different aspects of Nietzsche's thought.

***

This volume collects selected papers from leading specialists on Nietzsche, Kant, Hegel, Schelling, Fichte and Kierkegaard. Most of the articles included in this volume are considerably revised and expanded versions of the papers presented at the International Conference "Nietzsche and German Idealism", held at the University of Lisbon in 2012. A number of invited articles, however, have been written specifically for this occasion. An overview of the articles is provided in the following:

In his paper **Frederick Neuhouser** considers the affinities between Hegel and Nietzsche in their conceptions of life, spirit (*Geist*) and spiritual pathology. Neuhouser first addresses Hegel's notion of spirit as 'sublated' life (*aufgehobenes Leben*) in the *Phenomenology*. Central to this section is an analysis of the way in which, for Hegel, the 'pathologies of the Spirit' are related to the internal division (*Entzweiung*) or contradiction that is characteristic of self-conscious life. The second section begins with an examination of Nietzsche's conception of life (understood in terms of processes of self-overcoming) and his conception of spiritual illness and health. For this analysis, Neuhouser focuses on Nietzsche's account of the bad conscience and the aesthetic ideal in the *Genealogy*. This analysis enables Neuhouser to point out differences but also unexpected similarities between Hegel and Nietzsche in the way in which they define 'spiritual life' in contrast to 'animal' life, and in their more or less explicit claim that 'great spiritual health' involves a constant engagement with inner contradictions; i.e. it only is possible through 'illness'.

Herman Siemens compares the critique of law in Nietzsche and the young Hegel and the ways in which they respond to it. Siemens argues that, for both thinkers, the problem of law lies in its radical opposition, contradiction or conflict with life, and shows how they both respond by searching for life-immanent and life-affirming forms of law. For Hegel, Siemens concentrates on the writings from the Frankfurt period (1797–1800) and the text "Der Geist des Christentums und sein Schicksal". For Nietzsche, he focuses on the concept of 'law' throughout Nietzsche's published texts and the *Nachlass*. In this way, Siemens is able to trace the affinities between Nietzsche's and Hegel's attempts to delineate a new form of law that addresses their critique, but without losing the differences. While Nietzsche will inscribe the problem of law in his overall project of self-overcoming or self-transformation, understood as an ongoing evaluation and questioning of normativity, the response of the young Hegel will involve a form of reconciliation and realisation that relations to others are internal to our self-relation.

João Constâncio analyses the affinities between Hegel's and Nietzsche's psychological and sociological descriptions of interpersonal and social relationships. His strategy to develop this analysis is to focus on the structural similarities between Hegel's notion of recognition (and the dynamics of the so called 'struggles for recognition' from the *Phenomenology*) and Nietzsche's notion of 'the will to power' (and the dynamics associated with it). While the first section is dedicated to Hegel's description of the so called master-slave relation, in the sections dedicated to Nietzsche, Constâncio questions the ways in which the 'will to power' has been interpreted as an egoistic drive to dominate. Engaging with prominent Nietzsche and Hegel scholars, Constâncio shows how a more nuanced interpretation of Nietzsche's concept of the 'will to power' can help us understand in a new light or re-describe the (Hegelian) intersubjective dynamics of failed-recognition or domination. The question raised in this paper is precisely how fruitful this re-description can be for further interpretations of Nietzsche and the structural or conceptual affinities between Nietzsche and Hegel.

Maria João Branco examines Hegel's and Nietzsche's views on music and its relation to and implications for philosophy. She begins by drawing attention to a problem that has been central for philosophical theories on music, namely its seductive and potentially 'dangerous' effects, in the sense that the listener is deprived of any control over what he or she is listening. Analysing key texts from Nietzsche's GS, BGE, D and HH, Branco argues that Nietzsche's critique of German Idealists (such as Hegel) has to be understood in the light of his critique of a process of desensualisation (*Entsinnlichung*) that goes hand in hand with a rejection of non-conceptual sources of knowledge. This leads Branco to revise Hegel's ambivalent thoughts on music and his critique of 'absolute music' on the grounds of its abstractness and because of the 'threat' it represents to reason. Interestingly, her analysis shows that the opposition between Hegel and Nietzsche is not as clear-cut as one might expect. Branco then uses this as a cue for interpreting the complexities of Nietzsche's critique of Wagner.

Thomas Kisser invites us to rethink the problem of individuality or what he calls 'the drama of existence' in Nietzsche and Fichte. Kisser's starting point is to show that there are important affinities between both philosophers, which have to do with their dynamic understanding of reality and the importance, for both authors, of the relation between will and representation. In order to develop his argumentation, Kisser focuses on the distinction and the relation between the Dionysian and the Apollinian, i.e. between unity, multiplicity, individuation and art in *The Birth of Tragedy*. The result of this analysis enables him to connect some of the most interesting philosophical movements in Nietzsche's early texts to the project of the *Genealogy of Morality*. For this, he focuses on the notion of 'interpretation'. In the last sections of his paper, Kisser continues by analysing some of the key movements in Fichte's *Vocation of Man* and other later texts. In this way, he not only shows the similarities between Fichte and Nietzsche, but also addresses some of the most important differences, which follow precisely from their opposed ways of interpreting the dynamic character of reality. Presented as a preliminary work for further investigations into the relation between Nietzsche and Fichte, this close reading of some key passages from Fichte's texts already indicates what might be seen as the 'shortcomings' of Nietzsche's philosophical position.

Carlos João Correia takes the thought of the 'death of God' (typically considered a Nietzschean motive) as the starting point for his paper. Correia's purpose, however, is not only to clarify the meaning that the 'death of God' has in Nietzsche's thought. Rather, his intention is, in the first instance, to show the extent to which the 'death of God' is not an uncommon image in the history of philosophy, nor in Western and non-Western religions and mythologies. Indeed, Correia's claim is that the 'death of god' should be seen as a universal mytheme or cosmogonic principle. In addition and parallel to this line of investigation, Correia shows how an analysis of the meaning that Schelling gives to the 'death of God' will help us decipher the very intricate logic that structures his thought (especially in his later works). The death of God is thus revealed as the condition of the genesis of the world: it constitutes an intrinsic part of the entire process of mythology, which, as Correia shows, is to be understood as the process of self-awareness of the world.

Katia Hay focuses on the similarities between Schelling and Nietzsche in their understanding of, and writing about the past. In the first section of her paper, she analyses the affinity between Schelling's and Nietzsche's projects for a future philosophy and the way in which, for both authors, the problem of the future is related to the problem of the past. In the second section she examines the ways in which, for both Schelling and Nietzsche, our history and *pre*-history is to be understood and explained in terms of the movements and developments of the relation between two wills (in Schelling) or drives (in Nietzsche). In this section, Hay also addresses the question of the nature of these terms ('wills', 'drives') and their role in enabling us to create or re-create the past in a way that is not pre-determined or fixed. In the last section, she analyses further points of convergence between these authors that result from the way in which they both conceive of the will, not as a unitary force, but as the result of a plurality of forces.

Eike Brock examines the differences and affinities between Schopenhauer and Nietzsche in relation to their understanding of life and suffering, or more precisely: in relation to the claim that 'life is suffering'. In the first section, Brock describes the way in which, for Schopenhauer, the ultimate ground of suffering is the 'will'. He then passes to Nietzsche's *Birth of Tragedy*, in order to show how Nietzsche finds a justification and source of affirmation of life and suffering in art (in contrast to Schopenhauer, for whom the only possible form of redemption lies in the negation of will). In the second section and sub-sections, however, and following Bernard Reginster's interpretation of Nietzsche, Brock considers the way in which the 'will to power', the idea of the 'transvaluation of all values' and, finally, the notion of *amor fati* all constitute different ways in which Nietzsche continues to address the problem of suffering in his later works.

More importantly, though, these last considerations enable Brock to claim that through the notion of *amor fati*, Nietzsche comes closer to Schopenhauer than one might expect.

Razvan Ioan focuses on the analogies between Nietzsche's and Schopenhauer's understandings of (philosophical) physiology. Ioan argues that, in spite of the well-known differences, there are interesting similarities regarding the problem of unity and multiplicity. More precisely, his claim is that there are points of connection between Schopenhauer's notion of 'Platonic Ideas' (and their manifestation in 'natural forces') and Nietzsche's conception of the drives. These affinities reverberate in the way in which they both regard reason or the intellect as a product of the body. Intertwined with the consideration of the similarities regarding the 'multiplicity' of drives/forces, however, Ioan also analyses the different ways in which both Schopenhauer and Nietzsche account for the 'unity' of the individual. While Schopenhauer uses the metaphor of a monarch, representing a metaphysical will that provides for unity and harmony, for Nietzsche the unity can only be understood as the result of a complex relation of tension between forces.

Philipp Schwab presents a meticulous study of the similarities and differences between Kierkegaard and Nietzsche and their critique of German Idealism, and more precisely their critique of the 'system'. Schwab argues that in both cases this critique goes hand in hand with a new (existential) way of thinking about the individual and also a new (experimental) way of pursuing philosophy. Schwab first analyses the notion of 'indirect communication' in Kierkegaard, focusing on how it reflects and also emerges from his critique of systematic thought. In the second section of his paper, Schwab shows the ways in which Nietzsche's critique of traditional thought can be understood in terms of a 'critical' and at the same time 'affirmative' experimental philosophy. In this way, Schwab shows how both Kierkegaard and Nietzsche are constantly engaging in forms of critique that are always self-critical and therefore, in one way or other, self-undermining. The indirect or experimental form of their discourses responds to the apparently paradoxical nature of their critique.

Elisabete M. de Sousa analyses the differences and similarities between Nietzsche's and Kierkegaard's approaches to music as well as the possible influence that Kierkegaard may have had on Nietzsche. Following the work done by Brobjer, Sousa first argues for the need to re-evaluate the mediating role played by Georg Brandes in Nietzsche's reception of Kierkegaard. Sousa then discusses in detail certain passages and aspects from Kierkegaard's writings on Mozart's Don Giovanni (in *Either/Or*) that Nietzsche may have read and points towards similarities between these and Nietzsche's own writings on (Wagner's) music. However, these similarities, as Sousa later observes, sometimes seem to be mere coincidences. Thus, in the last section of her paper, Sousa suggests two lines of research for determining more precisely the relation between Nietzsche's and Kierkegaard's writings on music: the figure of Schopenhauer and his reception in Scandinavia in the late 1830s, and the study of the German musical periodicals, which could have been read by both Kierkegaard and Nietzsche.

José Miranda Justo's paper is intended as a preliminary remark to a further study on the relation between Nietzsche's 'eternal recurrence' and Kierkegaard's notion of 'repetition'; that is, on Nietzsche's and Kierkegaard's understandings of the relation between time, freedom and necessity. In the first section of his paper, Justo draws on Philonenko's study of Kant's critical texts to analyse the way in which Kant addresses the problem of freedom and necessity in his *Critique of Pure Reason*, emphasising the ways in which this problem is related to the problem of time. In the second section, by referring to key passages from Kierkegaard's *Philosophical Fragments*, Justo underlines the ways in which, for Kierkegaard, the problematic relation between freedom and necessity also involves dealing with the idea of – what he calls – a 'suspension of time': the notion of freedom involves the suspension of any causal *regressus*. And yet, as Justo points out, in Kierkegaard's case this entire discussion will lead him to develop other topics that are not necessarily present in Kant, such as the problem of 'coming into existence', or the notion of 'belief'.

Danielle Cohen-Levinas analyses the consequences of Nietzsche's critique of German Idealism for the history of (musical) aesthetics. Taking his rupture with Wagner as a starting point and drawing on the distinction made by Heidegger between *dichten* and *denken*, she interprets Nietzsche's philosophical project as an engagement with the problem of saying the unsayable and with the relation between art and philosophy. According to Cohen-Levinas, what is important about this new way of understanding the relation between music and thought is that, perhaps for the first time in the History of Aesthetics, it enables us to grasp their profound differences. Music cannot be translated into language. It is precisely from this perspective that we must read Nietzsche's texts and the way in which he introduces musical elements (songs, for instance) into them. In the second part of her article, Cohen-Levinas shows how Schoenberg's musical works, *Moses and Aaron* (in particular), can be interpreted as a realisation, in music, of Nietzsche's critique of, and rupture with Wagner and with the aesthetic models characteristic of German Idealism. Nietzsche is hereby presented as a precursor of authors such as Benjamin and Adorno.

Leonel Ribeiro dos Santos presents some of Hans Vaihinger's (1852–1933) main insights regarding the affinities between Nietzsche and Kant. Dos Santos first considers Vaihinger's book on *Nietzsche als Philosoph*, in which he discusses the coherence of Nietzsche's apparently unsystematic oeuvre and analyses the influence on Nietzsche of Lange, Schopenhauer and Darwin. In the subsequent sections, dos Santos proceeds to show Vaihinger's 'discovery' of the Kantian Nietzsche and the similarities between Kant, Nietzsche and Vaihinger himself. Vaihinger finds these similarities in the importance they give to fiction and its role in all human activities, including science and metaphysics. More importantly, though, is the way in which this reading shows how it is still necessary to re-evaluate the relation between Kant and Nietzsche.

Part One: **Nietzsche and German Idealism
(Hegel, Fichte, Schelling)**

Frederick Neuhouser
Hegel and Nietzsche on Spirit and its Pathologies

Hegel and Nietzsche are not normally thought of as philosophers who have much in common.[1] There are good reasons for this, but it also obscures the respects in which there are important affinities between their positions. One of these affinities resides in their conceptions of spirit (*Geist*) and the conceptions of spiritual pathology, or illness, which follow from what they take spirit to be. In this paper I highlight the similarities between these two thinkers by focusing on the close relation that exists for both between spirit and life, between *Geist* and *Leben*. More specifically, I argue that both Hegel and Nietzsche conceive of spirit in terms of what Hegel calls *aufgehobenes Leben* ('sublated' life), which Nietzsche would be more likely to call 'self-overcoming life'. There are, of course, many respects in which Hegel's conception of Spirit is unlike Nietzsche's – and they should not be forgotten – but these differences should also not prevent us from appreciating their deep similarities in both structure and content.

I

I begin with Hegel. The claim that spirit is *aufgehobenes Leben* suggests that life serves for him as a model for spirit. If life is a teleological process that achieves its ends through activity that possesses a certain characteristic structure, then a living being that fails to achieve those ends, or fails to function in the way that is characteristic of life, will count as diseased, moribund, or in some other way dysfunctional. In other words, a species' failure to reproduce itself, or to organise itself by assimilating and reshaping its environment in accordance with its vital needs, appears, from the perspective of life, as pathological. At the same time, Hegel's conception of spirit provides resources for extending the idea of the pathological beyond the biological realm to include spiritual pathologies

---

[1] I would like to thank Wayne Proudfoot, Herman Siemens, and the participants of three conferences and meetings – "Nietzsche e o Idealismo Alemão" (Universidade de Lisboa 2012), Friedrich Nietzsche Society (London 2011), and the North American Nietzsche Society (Washington, D.C., APA 2011) – for helpful comments on earlier drafts of this paper.

that have no strict analogue in the domain of life. The thought here is that well-functioning forms of spirit, while sharing structural similarities with well-functioning life, would also include functions peculiar to spiritual beings.

It is not difficult to locate the most important respect in which spirit for Hegel goes beyond mere life: although a biological species maintains itself by positing differences internal to itself and then abolishing those differences, as well as by assimilating its external other (inorganic nature) to itself and then remaking it in its own image, life, in contrast to spirit, remains unconscious of itself and of its characteristic activity. Life can exist as what it essentially is only *for another*; its true nature can be realised only *for* a being that, like spirit, is conscious (and, of course, self-conscious). We would not be too far amiss, then, if, as a first approximation, we defined spirit as self-conscious life. In light of this, the question I want to pursue here is: what becomes of life and its essential functions when self-consciousness is added to it? Or, how does thinking of spirit as self-conscious life help to define the well-functioning of a spiritual being and, by extension, to understand what spiritual illness consists in?

Defining spiritual pathology is more complex, of course, than the simple formula 'spirit equals life plus self-consciousness' implies. This quickly becomes apparent when one considers the complications that arise once self-consciousness is introduced into the living. Two of these complications are especially noteworthy. First, the *telos* of life is transformed when self-consciousness enters the picture: in spiritual beings the end of biological reproduction turns into the end of freedom (where freedom is understood such that a certain kind of self-consciousness is essential to it). Second, self-consciousness brings along with it a certain type of *Entzweiung* – an internal division or bifurcation – that is lacking in mere life. Hegel expresses this point by saying that spirit both is and is not identical with life (and that, moreover, it knows itself as both). One could also say that, fully realised, spirit is aware of itself as at once life and more than life (where 'more than life' means above or superior to mere life).

Let us begin with the second of these complications, the 'contradiction' in the conscious relation that spirit adopts to life – the fact that it distinguishes itself from life but also identifies with it. Failures to establish this dual attitude to life, I suggest, count for Hegel as forms of spiritual pathology, disturbances in the proper functioning of the specific activity of subjectivity. One should think here of Hegel's characterization of the subject as "pure, simple negativity", as "the bifurcation of the simple [*Entzweiung des Einfachen*]" and as a doubling (*Verdoppelung*) that first posits difference (or opposition) and then negates that difference by restoring identity between the very opposites it has posited (*PhS* §18, TWA 3, p. 23). The nature of consciousness, according to this claim, is to engage in a distinctive activity – self-negation – that consists in dividing itself in two and subsequently negating this division so as to bring together what it has torn apart in a way that both cancels and preserves that division. This activity of subjectivity is what makes spirit a "*living* substance" rather than a lifeless one. The point here is that with respect to its basic structure the defining activity of spirit mimics the activity characteristic of life (even if the latter lacks the spiritually crucial property of self-consciousness). A biological species, for example, maintains itself over time only by breaking itself up into individual living beings, which, in striving to live and reproduce and even in dying, carry out the vital functions on which the species' survival depends. That the lifelike activity distinctive of spirit is relevant to pathology is indicated by Hegel's identification of this movement of consciousness (in the same paragraph) with the overcoming of alienation. And later, removing any doubt that might remain about the significance of these connections, Hegel characterises the breakdown of consciousness's self-negating activity as a kind of (spiritual) death (*PhS* §32, TWA 3, p. 35–36).

Some of what these abstract characterisations of spirit amount to more concretely is hinted at in the following lines:

> The life of spirit does not shrink from death and [...] devastation but instead tolerates death and preserves itself in it. Spirit wins its truth only by finding itself in its own absolute dismemberment. This power does not [...] turn away from the negative [...] but looks it in the face and abides within it. (*PhS* §32, TWA 3, p. 36)[2]

As I read this passage (and as Nietzsche must have read it, too), the mark of flourishing spirituality is the capacity consciously to tolerate contradiction in a way that avoids denying either of the opposed poles and that for this reason never completely eliminates their opposition.[3] As Nietzsche puts the point, "there is perhaps no more decisive mark of a [...] spiritual nature, than that of being divided in two [...] and of being a genuine battleground of [...] opposed values" (GM I 16, KSA 5, p. 285–286). Although Hegel disagrees with Nietzsche that spiritual tension must take the form of a battle between opposites, they agree on the more fundamental point that spiritual health consists in con-

---

2 "Aber nicht das Leben, das sich vor dem Tode scheut und von der Verwüstung rein bewahrt, sondern das ihn erträgt und in ihm sich erhält, ist das Leben des Geistes. Er gewinnt seine Wahrheit nur, indem er in der absoluten Zerrissenheit sich selbst findet. Diese Macht ist er nicht als das Positive, welches von dem Negativen wegsieht [...]; sondern er ist diese Macht nur, indem er dem Negativen ins Angesicht schaut, bei ihm verweilt."
3 Something similar is true of life: "Something is alive only insofar as it contains contradiction within it; [life] is the power to hold and endure contradiction within itself" (cited in Hahn 2007, p. 29).

sciously negotiating inner contradictions rather than ignoring, denying, or fleeing from them.

Although in this passage Hegel speaks of spirit maintaining a tension-filled relation to death,[4] the spiritual contradiction of interest to me here is that between self-consciousness and life. (Strictly speaking, it is incorrect to call it a contradiction between *spirit* and life because spirit is not to be identified with either of the two poles of this opposition – consciousness or life – but with the activity of holding them together in the appropriate way.) As I have said, spiritual subjects are conscious of themselves both as life and as more than life. If we pursue the suggestion that the absence of a dual consciousness of one's relation to life counts as a way in which spiritual activity fails to carry out its proper function, then the most obvious candidates for spiritual pathology are what the *Phenomenology of Spirit* describes – in the sections on desire, the struggle unto death, and lordship and bondage – as self-consciousness's failure to satisfy itself. In all these forms of self-consciousness, the failure to find satisfaction can be traced back to a subject's inadequate conception of its relation to life, one that either disavows that connection or misconstrues the threat it poses to free subjectivity. The element common to these configurations is an overly exalted conception of subjectivity and its defining characteristic: freedom, or *Selbständigkeit* (self-standingness or self-sufficiency). In each case the essential property of subjectivity, *Selbständigkeit*, is taken to consist in what the *Phenomenology of Spirit* ultimately reveals to be a deficient, one-sided relation to life, in which a subject asserts its *Selbständigkeit* by proving itself *not* to have essential relations to life, thereby demonstrating its elevated status in relation to the merely living through its complete independence from the many ties to the world that living beings rely on in carrying out their vital functions. Similarly, the failures of these configurations lie in ways in which the practices in which subjects engage in order to assert themselves as what they take themselves to be, in fact, require a connectedness to life that belies their self-conception.

It is no accident that in order to say what self-consciousness's well-functioning consists in it has been necessary to invoke the idea of *satisfaction*. This idea is so fundamental to Hegel's conception of spirit and subjectivity that one could define pathology, most generally, as a subject's failure to satisfy itself in its

---

4 By 'death' Hegel seems to mean dismemberment – things being divided up, left lifeless – which also characterises the results of the "negative power" of the understanding (when what the understanding separates is not re-joined by reason); but this metaphorical usage should not prevent us from also taking talk of death literally.

characteristic activity. Defining 'well-functioning' and 'pathology' in terms of satisfaction implies that the distinctive activity of self-consciousness is a kind of striving – an activity that, implicitly or explicitly, is directed at a goal, the achievement of which results in satisfaction and, as the German *Befriedigung* implies, in a state of inner peace. Thus, if Hegel's thought is to supply the resources for a conception of impeded functioning, it is necessary to specify the aim of spirit's distinctive activity. In the *Phenomenology of Spirit* one can find many formulations of what spirit essentially strives for – unlimited *Selbständigkeit*, for example, but also: complete self-knowledge, perfect correspondence between what it is and what it takes itself to be, and the positing of a world that adequately expresses its self-understanding. Alongside these, in "Self-Consciousness", the aim of the subject's activity is described in terms of recognition from other self-conscious subjects.

All these formulations can be understood as aspects of a single aim that guides spirit in each of its characteristic activities. Expressed most generally, spirit's project – its characteristic striving – is self-definition and self-realization. More precisely, a spiritual being always operates, implicitly or explicitly, with a conception of what it essentially is, where the essence in terms of which it defines itself is some version of *Selbständigkeit*, and where *Selbständigkeit* is defined in contrast to what it takes not to be *selbständig*, whether this be a mere thing, another subject that has surrendered its standing as a subject, or – in the case relevant here – life itself, understood as self-consciousness's antithesis. A self-conception of this kind is normative – it invokes a standard for what 'true', fully realised subjectivity consists in – and it is the basis for spiritual striving insofar as a subject is aware that its current existence fails to measure up to what it is essentially. Spirit's striving manifests itself as real activity in which a subject interacts with what it regards as different from itself – the objective world and other subjects – in order to make itself, in its concrete relations with its others, into the kind of free being it takes itself essentially to be. Satisfaction, then, consists in establishing real relations to things and other subjects that give perfect expression to the subject's understanding of its own *Selbständigkeit*, and a pathology in this realm is any state of affairs that systematically impeded satisfaction defined in this way.

If we stick to the simplest of these cases, Desire, its pathology could be described as a subject's systematic inability to satisfy itself – its inability to know and experience itself as free under its own understanding of what freedom consists in. Moreover, this failure is due to Desire's impoverished conception of its own *Selbständigkeit*, according to which being self-standing requires disavowing all dependence on everything outside itself, including the ways it participates in life. The problem here is not that, as a biological being, desiring self-consciousness is in fact involved in life but denies or is unaware of that involvement; the problem, rather, is that because it *defines* its freedom in complete opposition to life, its enactments of its self-conception require it to interact with life (even if purely negatively), thereby refuting its claim to have no essential relation to life and to be for that reason free. The desiring subject's attempts to prove itself above life require it to use life, and hence to depend on it, as a foil in its spiritual quest to realise itself as free. Moreover, its engagement with life – which, as a living being, it cannot avoid – is destined to remain void of spiritual significance, regarded as alien to everything it takes to be essential to it. One could say that Desire's failure lies in its inability to integrate, in both its self-conception and its activity, its dependence on life with its understanding of its own freedom. Its problem is one of uniting two things that appear to it irreconcilably opposed, which is another way of saying that it fails in the spiritual task of negotiating inner contradiction. (And more complicated versions of this failure, including more complicated versions of the subject's alienation from self, can be ascribed to the configurations of self-consciousness that follow Desire, including the struggle unto death for recognition and the relation between bondsman and lord.)

It is important to remember that spirit for Hegel is more than consciousness; its characteristic activities are at once mental (activities of consciousness) and material. Thus, what drives spirit is not merely the urge to *conceive* of itself as free but also to *enact* that self-conception in the world in such a way that its worldly activities bear witness to its actually being what, in consciousness, it takes itself to be. Material practices, then – processes of life – at once express and shape spirit's self-conceptions. In other words, the holding together of opposites that characterises spirit does not occur only within consciousness; material practices, too, can spiritually negotiate contradictions. Moreover, material practices are essential to spirit's goal of achieving a true conception of itself because the only way it has of correcting its self-conceptions is by discovering how those self-conceptions, when enacted in material practices, produce real relations between subject and object – between self-consciousness and life – that belie the very conception of *Selbständigkeit* those practices were meant to express. This means that spiritual pathology must be theorised not simply as false consciousness but also as false material practices – as life processes that embody unsatisfying ways of negotiating the opposition between self-consciousness and life.

The configuration of bondsman and lord offers the sharpest picture of how a subject's relation to self (its self-conception) and its relation to other subjects are at the same time relations to life. First, the social arrangement between bondsman and lord follows from and expresses a specific conception of the freedom appropriate to self-conscious subjects, for both bondsman and lord subscribe to the same one-sided conception of *Selbständigkeit* as complete independence from everything external to the subject, including the part of the world with which a biological organism must interact in order to live. That bondsman and lord subscribe to the same austere conception of freedom explains why the result of the struggle unto death is so thoroughly asymmetric: if *Selbständigkeit* requires absolute independence from everything 'other', then avowing one's ties to life, as the future bondsman does in the struggle, is incompatible with being *selbständig*. The unequal relation between bondsman and lord is merely an expression of this shared all-or-nothing view of subjectivity, conjoined with the fact that, in the face of death, one subject affirms the essential value of life, along with the dependencies that come with it, while the other persists in its exclusive valuation of absolute independence. Thus, the one-sided relation of recognition between bondsman and lord is grounded in a general conception of subjectivity and in the different relations to life that, beginning in their struggle unto death, each takes up in the world. Moreover, bondsman and lord take up relations to life that are just as one-sided as the relations of recognition they are expressions of. The two moments of the material reproduction of life – production and consumption – are torn apart, each ascribed to just one of the relation's poles: the bondsman labours while the lord enjoys, and in doing so each relates to the other in the mode of recognition. For the bondsman, labour is at once a relating to life, a relating to self (an expression of his own attitude to freedom and life), and a relating to another subject (through relations of recognition that define conditions of authority and subjection). Servile labour is a spiritual activity, since it is a way, however primitive and unsatisfying, of negotiating the opposition between self-consciousness and life.

Where exactly, though, does pathology enter this picture? The best answer is that pathology is located in the failure to negotiate the opposition between subjectivity and life in a satisfying way. What this means is that the various ways in which social members participate in life are not, at the same time, expressions of their freedom, and, conversely, the activities they regard as expressions of freedom are not at the same time ways of participating in life. Full spiritual satisfaction requires that life be elevated to freedom and that self-consciousness be filled with the aims of life. On this view, spiritual pathology exists whenever the basic conditions of a society prevent its members – in their self-conceptions, in their recognitive relations to others, and in their material practices – from bringing together their membership in both the realm of freedom and the realm of necessity. Success in doing so would mean that there would be no essential life activity that is not also a site of freedom and no expression of freedom that is not at the same time a material practice.[5]

The relation between bondsman and lord exhibits pathology, then, because rather than negotiating the contradiction between self-consciousness and life, it responds to the problem with a strategy of splitting or dissociation. Life activity gets split in two as production and consumption fall to different, mutually antagonistic social classes. This means that consumption takes place in ignorance of the activity that makes it possible, while production is carried out not with the aim of satisfying oneself or others but because obeying the lord is a prerequisite of staying alive. This division within the activities of life implies a spiritual division: society divides itself into two classes, one of which is absorbed in life but unfree, while the other, as far removed from life as possible, enjoys, precisely for that reason, a kind of freedom. The problem is not only that some are free while others are not but also that both freedom and life remain empty. Labour for the necessities of life becomes a site of domination and self-denial, and enjoyment devolves into luxury consumption that fails to satisfy. Those who labour do so merely in order to survive, while those who consume have a spiritual end in view (proving their freedom) but are moved by a distorted vision of what freedom consists in (complete independence from the ties of life).

In articulating the idea of negotiating contradiction that lies at the heart of Hegel's conception of spirit, I have focused on reconciling subjectivity and life, and in a way that may appear to eradicate rather than preserve the difference between them. To this Hegel's critics object: if every life process becomes the site of freedom and every expression of freedom the carrying out of a life process, is the 'contradiction' between them negotiated or simply done away with? It would be a mistake to deny that Hegel emphasises the reconciliatory moment in the negotiation of contradiction. But it would also be a mistake to conclude that his system omnivorously devours contradictions, digests them, and expels them in a form in which the original ingredients are no longer distinguishable. For if negotiating the contradiction between subjectivity and life resulted in there being no tension at all between them, then spirit would be lifeless and, hence, not spirit at all (*PhS* §32, TWA 3, p. 36). If we take this thought seriously, then relating spiritually to self-consciousness and life requires more than merely dissolving them into one.

---

[5] This claim is correct as long as one restricts oneself to objective spirit; it is less clear, however, whether spirit's highest cultural activities – in the realm of absolute spirit – depend so thoroughly on what I am calling material practices.

One place this issue arises especially acutely is in relation to the biological death of human individuals. It is important to bear in mind that life for Hegel is most fundamentally the life of a species, not of individual living beings. Since the reproduction of the species depends not only on the births but also on the deaths of its members, death is just as essential to life as the strivings of living beings toward self-preservation. A subject that is aware of itself as life, then, is also aware of itself as dying; for a spiritual being, relating to life includes consciously relating to one's death. Hegel understands the problem posed by death in terms of a contradiction between life and self-consciousness. More precisely, the necessity of an individual's biological death stands in conflict with its aspiration to be self-standing. Death imposes itself on living subjects as an absolute constraint on what they can do or make of themselves, and, so, spirituality requires finding some way of reconciling oneself to one's own death.

Once one is alert to the importance of this issue for Hegel, one finds it everywhere in his texts. Apart from the cultural activities of absolute spirit – art, religion, and philosophy – there are many social practices that have the potential to reconcile life (and death) with the subject's aspiration to *Selbständigkeit*: labour, which permanently inscribes one's subjectivity into the world of objects; the bearing of children, which enables parents to 'live through' the generation that survives them; political participation, in which citizens experience themselves as part of a community that, relatively speaking, 'never dies'. Although these practices are ways in which individuals can lessen the constraints their own death imposes, it would be folly to think that they can fully remove death's sting. Life and the finitude intrinsic to it can be made more compatible with the subject's aspirations than it would be without these practices, but, here at least, reconciliation cannot produce a 'differenceless' unity.

II

I turn now to Nietzsche's conception of spiritual illness and health, as articulated in his account of the bad conscience in the *Genealogy of Morality*. As in the case of Hegel, understanding Nietzsche's conception of spiritual illness requires first examining his conception of life, together with its account of what the healthy functioning of a living organism consists in. Life, Nietzsche tells us, is a goal-directed process, a series of activities that aims at power – at ever "*greater* units of power [grössere *Macht-Einheiten*]" – and that pursues this aim through various kinds of pain-inducing activity: "injuring, violating, exploiting, destroying [*verletzend, vergewaltigend, ausbeutend, vernichtend*]" (GM II 11, KSA 5,

p. 312). Readers of Hegel might conclude from this definition that life is a teleological process, but having an aim is not the same as having a *telos*. If 'teleological' implies that the process in question has a determinate end at which it aims, the character of which determines from the outset the course the process takes and the achievement of which brings the process to a satisfying completion – then life for Nietzsche has an aim but no *telos* (GM II 12), and no foreseeable stopping point at which the process is complete and 'satisfaction' is achieved. (And this marks an important difference between Hegel's and Nietzsche's conceptions of life and Spirit, even though, as I have suggested, there are strands of Hegel's thought, according to which, whatever satisfaction Spirit achieves is not eternal but must be continually re-established through the activities of self-bifurcation and the holding together of opposites.)

When Nietzsche says that life seeks ever greater units of power, it can sound like its aim is quantitative, much like the aim Marx finds in the accumulation of surplus value, which, as a purely quantitative aim, explains the restless, unending, infinitely intensified but never satisfied nature of capitalist production. There are, to be sure, aspects of the logic of capitalist accumulation that Nietzsche ascribes to the processes of life. That life seeks the creation of ever greater units of power is meant to signal that Hegelian notions of completion and satisfaction are out of place in understanding vital processes and that those processes are infinitely open-ended and undetermined in ways that the acorn's transformation into an oak is not.

More important, the absence of a *telos* implies that discrete activities of life for Nietzsche are like the economic activities that serve capitalist accumulation in being intrinsically 'meaningless', lacking in themselves the kind of meaning that can be ascribed to the stages of an oak's development, where the specific features of each stage can be explained by reference to the essential characteristics of the end towards which that development tends, an end that 'determines' how the development proceeds. To be more precise, in the case of capitalist accumulation, particular acts aimed at extracting ever greater quantities of surplus value from the circulation of capital have no significance beyond the quantitative aim that governs all such acts. From the perspective of what capitalist accumulation is after, it is a matter of complete indifference whether surplus value is created from the production of shoes or automobiles or luxury yachts, and from that same perspective, production can move, abruptly and with no internal logic, from one sphere into another, depending on where at any particular moment surplus value is to be made. There is, in other words, nothing about the process's aim that determines the specific nature of the movements that make up the process, which means that the qualitative details of the process have no meaning in relation to the overall 'point' of the process itself. The actual course taken by the process has no internal logic that makes sense of its specific moments; it is not a process of development but a series of random, unorganised, intrinsically meaningless events: a "succession of [...] more or less independent [...] processes" (GM II 12, KSA 5, p. 314).

Hence, activities of life for Nietzsche are like those of capitalist accumulation for Marx in that both proceed in the service of one determining aim definable in terms of a quantitative increase in a single good (power, in the case of life, and surplus value, in the case of capital). This is a significant commonality, but it should not blind us to an even more significant difference, one that brings Nietzsche's position closer to Hegel's: life for Nietzsche – including, of course, nonhuman life – seeks something beyond merely quantitative increases. Unlike the capitalist drive to accumulate surplus value, it has, in addition, a qualitative aim in that it also seeks to impose, retrospectively, a coherent form on what at first appear as (and are) random, unrelated events. It is tempting to overlook this aspect of Nietzsche's conception of life, in part because it seems to anthropomorphise nature, ascribing to all living organisms the capacity to *interpret* past events, to impose a coherent order on occurrences that of themselves possess no such order. But it is clearly Nietzsche's intention to ascribe an order-imposing function of this kind to life itself, in all its forms. This can be seen in the fact that he describes life as striving not only for increases in power but also for "perfection [*Vollkommenheit*]" (GM II 12, KSA 5, p. 315).

With this claim Nietzsche introduces into his conception of life the idea of teleological organisation that previous philosophers regarded as life's constitutive feature. For 'perfection' refers to a hierarchical organisation, where higher (or "nobler") functions rule over (or "dominate") lower functions (GM II 12, KSA 5, p. 315–316), making living beings into purposefully ordered wholes – into, in other words, *organisms* in which specialised functions work together to further the ends of the whole. At the same time, Nietzsche's understanding of the purposeful order characteristic of life has two features that distinguish it from more familiar accounts. The first is that, as we have seen, the organism's governing aim is not self-preservation but increasing power (although self-preservation might be a necessary condition of increasing power). The second is that the teleological organisation characteristic of life is not prescribed to the living being in advance, written into its DNA, as it were; instead, it is an organisation that the living being must actively produce and that, once produced, must continually be reproduced, and not merely in the same form but in ever higher forms, which, presumably, are necessary if increasing power rather than static self-maintenance is the aim to be served.

This second feature of Nietzsche's conception of life is bound up with his odd claim that interpretation is a central activity of all life:

every happening in the organic world is an *overpowering*, a *mastering*, and every overpowering and mastering is itself a re-interpreting, a fitting into place, in which previous "meaning" and "purpose" must be obscured or completely extinguished. (GM II 12, KSA 5, p. 313f)[6]

According to this passage, life processes are acts of overpowering and domination in which the assertion of power consists in changing the meaning, or purpose, of that which is overpowered. To change the meaning or purpose of something is to re-interpret it, which in its broadest sense refers to the ordering (*Einordnung*) of "something present – something that has somehow come to be – " "into a system of purposes [*System von Zwecken*]" (GM II 12, KSA 5, p. 313). To interpret, then – to give something a meaning – is to impose a function on what is at first merely 'there' by incorporating it into a system of purposeful activities with which it then cooperates in order to serve a purpose of the organism as a whole: "all purposes are *signs* that a will to power has become master of something less powerful and imposed upon it the meaning of a function" (GM II 12, KSA 5, p. 314). Life strives, then, not merely for greater quantities of power however achievable but, more specifically, for increases in power that result from the imposition of organic order on a given material that, of itself, lacks significance, which it acquires only after having been commandeered by a superior power and forced to play a certain function within that imposed order. Life is essentially interpretation because it assigns a meaning-in-relation-to-the-whole to the intrinsically meaningless. Understood in this way, it is not difficult to see why, after Darwin, life might be construed as essentially 'interpretive': if evolution is a central function of life, then living beings must have the ability to take up random, meaningless variations in their own constitution and employ them for their own vital purposes by assigning them new functions within an already established but now 'readjusted' organic unity.

Focusing on evolution as an essential life activity directs our attention to a further feature of Nietzsche's conception of life, which, though of central importance for Darwin, could equally well have been appropriated from Hegel's treatment of life. The feature in question concerns the fact that (for all three thinkers) the species, not individual living organisms, constitute the basic unit of life, in the sense that certain vital functions can be understood only as processes of the species as a whole and not of individual living beings themselves. In the case of Darwin, for example, what evolves is the species, not individual organisms, and

---

[6] "[A]lles Geschehen in der organischen Welt [ist] ein *Überwältigen, Herrwerden* und wiederum alles Überwältigen und Herrwerden [ist] ein Neu-Interpretieren, ein Zurechtmachen [...], bei dem der bisherige 'Sinn' und 'Zweck' nothwendig verdunkelt oder ganz ausgelöscht werden muss."

even if the species' evolution depends on changes that can take place only in individual organisms, it remains an essentially trans-generational process that, unlike digestion or respiration, cannot be carried out internal to any single living being. For Nietzsche and Hegel, too, life is most fundamentally the life of a species. This may seem to be a controversial claim in the case of Nietzsche – it has implications for whether it is a stronger human species that he hopes for or merely a stronger human specimen – but I regard it as an important, though often overlooked, aspect of his position.[7] That the species, not individual living beings, is the basic unit of life for Nietzsche can be seen clearly in his view that death is a constitutive part of the process of life. If the deaths of individuals belong, as Nietzsche says, "to the conditions of the real *progressus*" (GM II 12, KSA 5, p. 315) of life, then the vital purpose served by those deaths must belong to some living entity larger than the individuals. If 'life' referred primarily to individual living beings, it would make no sense to characterise it as a *progressus* towards greater power since this unidirectional course is not a possibility for individual living beings. Even if much of an individual's life might consist in increasing its own power and complexity, this is clearly not its ultimate destiny.

We are now in a position to say, from the "biological perspective" (GM II 11, KSA 5, p. 312), what health and illness for living beings consist in. If we restrict ourselves to individual organisms, then 'health' refers to an undisturbed carrying out of the life process: the animal's ongoing imposition of organic order on itself in order to create ever greater units of power for the purpose of discharging ever greater quanta of energy through activity. Biological health is equated with an organism's vitality – a "flourishing, rich, self-overflowing" condition, manifested in "powerful physicality" and in "strong, free, cheerful activity" (GM I 7, KSA 5, p. 266) that springs from "plenitude, force, the will of life" (GM Preface 3, KSA 5, p. 250). By the same logic, 'illness' refers to an enduring, premature disruption of the life process, including mere repetitions of the process, in which energy is expended and renewed but sluggishly and at more or less constant levels. Its characteristics are the opposites of those of health: powerlessness, passivity, leadenness, and, perhaps most important, the incapacity to impose order, or meaning, on encountered facts or events.

---

[7] One reason is that, from the beginning of his career, Nietzsche is deeply concerned with the cultural, and not merely individual, conditions under which strength and greatness are achieved (as well as with ways in which cultures, and not merely individuals, can be ill). Even if human greatness is most prominently manifested in great individuals, the latter are never simply self-created; they, too, are the inheritors and appropriators of cultural achievements, and so their greatness depends in some way on the collective greatness of (some subgroup within) the species itself.

The conception of illness I have articulated thus far, from the biological perspective, is insufficient to capture the distinctively human, or spiritual, illnesses Nietzsche is most interested in. In order to understand these, we need to take up a perspective beyond that of (mere) life, one that allows us to grasp spiritual, not merely animal, phenomena. The sense in which the spiritual perspective is beyond that of mere life must not be misunderstood. 'Beyond' does not mean one abandons life in order to take up a wholly different standpoint, that of spirit; what is required, rather, is that one supplement the standpoint of life so as to take account of the fundamental ways spiritual beings differ from mere animals. That is, one introduces into the perspective of life an understanding of what distinguishes spiritual phenomena from purely animal processes – Nietzsche locates the most important difference in reflexivity, or internal division – and one arrives at the idea of spirit by merging the two concepts, life and subjectivity, into one. One asks, in other words, what would life "turned back against itself" (GM II 16, KSA 5, p. 322–323) look like, and how would life thus configured amount to something "higher than" life?

Finally, whatever distinguishing characteristics of subjectivity are introduced into life in order to yield spirit must themselves be continuous with life, or capable of emerging out of life processes alone. In other words, what distinguishes spirit from mere life cannot be such that it divides the two into, as it were, different orders of being – things in themselves and appearances, for example, or free will and mechanically determined nature. Instead, for Nietzsche, the principal distinguishing feature of subjectivity – what makes mere life into spirit – is nothing more than a higher (more complex) organisation of the living, one that develops immanently out of the processes of life themselves.

It is uncontroversial, I believe, that Nietzsche distinguishes the human from the merely animal in this way and that in his account of the origin of the bad conscience he locates the main difference between the human and the merely animal in the acquisition of a "soul" whose chief characteristic is internal division, its being "turned back against itself" (GM II 16, KSA 5, p. 323).[8] This means

---

[8] The instinct of cruelty turned back on itself – the disposition to inflict cruelty on oneself – is crucial to an account of the *origin* of the bad conscience, but it is not yet itself the bad conscience. For the latter, an *interpretation* of the suffering produced by self-inflicted cruelty is required. This point is reflected in Nietzsche's reference here, before interpretation has occurred, to an "animal soul [*Thierseele*]" (GM II 16, KSA 5, p. 323), which is a soul because it is internally divided but is still animal because this remains a mere, un-interpreted disposition. At one point Nietzsche appears to equate the bad conscience with "cruelty turned backwards [*der rückwärts gewendeten Grausamkeit*]" (GM III 20, KSA 5, p. 389), but he is careful to call this the "animal" bad conscience.

that what distinguishes the human from the merely animal is a more complex internal organisation that gives rise to a more-than-animal form of subjectivity – grounded in the capacity to "take sides against oneself" (GM II 16, KSA 5, p. 323) – the source of which is the instinct of cruelty turned back on itself. It is important to distinguish the bare instinct of cruelty turned against itself from the more concrete phenomenon that Nietzsche calls the bad conscience. The main difference is that the former is merely an instinct, a physiological disposition to discharge energy of a certain type in a certain direction. The bad conscience, in contrast, also involves an interpretive apparatus that "hooks onto" this bare disposition and imbues it with meaning. The simplest example of interpretation joining with the disposition to inflict cruelty on oneself to yield the bad conscience is when that instinct latches onto an already present concept – 'debt' – and uses it to give a meaning to action that serves as an outlet for its pent-up energy.

The distinction between interpreted and un-interpreted instincts points to a second feature of subjectivity that plays a role in spirituality, the capacity for interpretation. As we saw above, Nietzsche regards interpretation as a basic activity of all life. In the case of non-human life, interpretation consists in imposing a function on something such that it comes to serve an organism's vital ends. But if interpretation is not distinctive to humans, there is enough of a difference between human and nonhuman interpretive activity to regard the former as distinctive to human subjectivity. Three important differences are: human interpretation is self-conscious (or potentially so); it is mediated by concepts (and hence by language); and it is evaluative in that it assigns, compares, and measures the values of things, employing some version of the concepts 'good' and 'bad'.[9]

My claim is that by virtue of the capacities that distinguish us from other forms of life, humans are vulnerable to spiritual illnesses unknown to mere animals and that these illnesses, while increasing the misery and "danger" of human existence, also create possibilities for higher, more "interesting" forms of spirituality (GM I 6, KSA 5, p. 265–266). The first question to be asked, then, is: what makes the bad conscience a *spiritual* illness? When Nietzsche recounts the origin of the bad conscience, he describes the effect the repressed instinct to

---

9 The last of these is especially important, as evidenced by the emphasis Nietzsche places on "the measuring of values, the contriving of equivalences" as fundamental to civilization, to human existence, and to thought itself, going so far as to call the human being "the creature that measures values, evaluates and measures, as the 'valuating animal as such' [*das 'abschätzende Thier an sich'*]" (GM II 8, KSA 5, p. 306).

cruelty had on its bearers as a "misery, a [...] leaden discontent" brought on by the impossibility of discharging pent-up instinctual energy. While this inhibited vitality is enough to make that condition a sickness, it does not yet make it a spiritual sickness, one that merits Nietzsche's description of it as so "profound [...] *and full of a future* [Zukunftsvolles] that with it the earth's appearance was essentially transformed" (GM II 16, KSA 5, p. 323).

If we return to the distinguishing features of subjectivity, we arrive at a rough conception of spiritual illness: a state of the soul in which interpretation and reflexivity join to produce effects that thwart rather than promote life's aim of creating ever greater units of power by imposing organic form on the initially formless. A spiritually ill being, in other words, has an internally divided soul where one part, making use of concepts that interpret and evaluate, "takes sides" against the other in a way that impedes the external discharge of instinctual energy. A soul divided in this way exhibits what Nietzsche calls the bad conscience.

There are two directions in which this account of the bad conscience needs to be extended, which will lead us to two concepts we have not yet encountered: repression[10] and affirmation. The first is found in Nietzsche's description of the bad conscience as originating in the instinct of freedom being "repressed, pushed back" until, having been "*banished from sight* and violently made *latent*", it is compelled to "release itself on itself" (GM II 17, KSA 5, p. 325),[11] while the consciousness accompanying these events remains ignorant of the instinctual ends they serve. For Nietzsche an instinct that finds no outward discharge and is compelled to turn inward is necessarily distorted in a way that makes it nearly impossible for the desire it seeks to satisfy to be consciously recognised as such. It follows that the conditions under which the human soul develops more or less guarantee that in most cases humans will be in the dark about the content of their souls.

Let us now consider 'affirmation', which appears in the *Genealogy* in two closely related guises, affirmation of self and affirmation of life (GM Preface 5, KSA 5, p. 251–252). (Because of space limitations I will focus on self-affirmation and bracket issues concerning the affirmation of life, including the question of their relative priority.) My claim is that it is necessary to bring in the concept of self-affirmation in order to articulate the reflexivity that defines subjectivity and plays a crucial role in spiritual illness. There can be no doubt that the inability to affirm oneself (and life more generally) occupies a prominent place in

---

10 Reginster 1997, p. 289–290 and 299–300.
11 Emphasis added.

Nietzsche's description of the virulent form of sickness that he takes the bad conscience to have assumed in his own time. Whatever else spiritual health involves, a robust, conscious affirmation of self is central to it. In making reflexive affirmation central to spirituality, Nietzsche might be seen as following Genesis, which locates God's first reflexive deed in his turning around, after six days of Creation, to contemplate himself and his own goodness as exhibited in his worldly activity: "God looked over all he had made, and he saw that it was ... good."[12] To step momentarily outside one's engagement in the world, to look back at oneself and at what one has done, and to find what one encounters good, these are the constitutive moments of spiritually affirming – of saying 'yes' to – one's own being.

Nietzsche makes clear that affirmation in all its forms is a valuing activity that operates, if only implicitly, with evaluative concepts such as good and bad.[13] In order for affirmation to be reflexive,[14] however, it must take place from a position in which immediate, spontaneous self-affirmation has been somehow disrupted (and illness, especially spiritual illness, suggests itself as one possible source of such disruption). Reflexive affirmation involves stepping outside what one immediately is in order to make oneself into the object of one's own "value-positing gaze [*werthesetzenden Blicks*]" (GM I 10, KSA 5, p. 271), and the term 'value-positing' seems to imply that in reflexive affirmation the values in terms of which one assesses oneself are in some sense the product of one's own valuing activity. At the very least, in reflexive evaluation a space is opened up between the subject and its values that makes the subject responsible for them (or able to become responsible for them).[15]

That affirmation in its higher forms is a robustly reflexive phenomenon is suggested by the connection Nietzsche draws, at the beginning of Essay II, between it and the very source of human reflexivity, the bad conscience. In musing about what meaning we might ascribe to the "long history" of the bad conscience – which is also, one should note, "the long history of *responsibility*" (GM II 2, KSA 5, p. 293) – Nietzsche famously hints that the conscience of the spiritually healthy, "autonomous" individual might be regarded as the "ripe,

---

12 Genesis 1:31, New Living Translation 2007. According to the Revised Standard Version 1946: "And God saw everything that he had made, and behold, it was very good".
13 Schopenhauer, for example, is explicitly said to have "*said No* to life and to himself" on the basis of certain values he held (GM Preface 5, KSA 5, p. 252).
14 Presumably the nobles of Essay I (GM I 10) say 'yes' to themselves spontaneously and so without the reflexivity that Nietzsche associates with spirituality. Furthermore, it is doubtful that these unreflective nobles are capable of affirming life more generally, as a whole.
15 This, too, is lacking in the nobles of Essay I.

but also a *late* fruit" of this history, and immediately after this he links conscience with *"the right to say 'Yes' to oneself"* (GM II 3, KSA 5, p. 294f). A few sections later, it is the healthy human being's conscience that is identified as the agency that "heartfully says yes" to its own animal instincts (GM II 6, KSA 5, p. 301). Similarly, when discussing the most dangerous form of spiritual illness that threatens to descend on late nineteenth-century Europe, Nietzsche uses strongly reflexive language to describe the incapacity for affirmation at the heart of that "last illness": the will turns [back] *against* itself in a final act of nihilistic self-denial (GM Preface 5, KSA 5, p. 252). This reflexive denial of self is described as a valuation (GM III 11) of oneself and life that is recognizable both as a form of bad conscience (where cruelty is directed against itself) and (from the perspective of life) as an illness: a condition of exhaustion, depression (GM Preface 5), and disgust with life grounded in "the human's shame at being human" in which "the animal human [has learned] to be ashamed of all his instincts" (GM II 7, KSA 5, p. 302).

It is time now to formulate more systematically how my claims thus far add up to a conception of spiritual illness. In doing so, I will distinguish four features of the bad conscience relevant to understanding it as a spiritual illness. Although in its "most horrifying" form, the bad conscience incorporates all these features, there are also less acute, though still pathological versions of that phenomenon in which some are present but not others. In other words, what we have learned thus far about life and spirit puts us in a position to distinguish gradations of spiritual illness, and recognising this is essential if what Nietzsche says about the bad conscience is to be made coherent. I discuss these four features in ascending order of their pathological significance.

The first – what I will call the measureless drive to make oneself suffer – is especially prominent in the following description of the version of the bad conscience associated with Christianity:

> [the bearer] of the bad conscience has seized on the presupposition of religion so as to drive his self-torture to its most gruesome severity [...] Guilt before *God*: this thought serves him as an instrument of torture. [...] This is a [...] cruelty of the soul without equal: the human *will* to find oneself guilty and reprehensible beyond atonement. (GM II 22, KSA 5, p. 332)[16]

---

[16] "[D]ieser Mensch des schlechten Gewissens hat sich der religiösen Voraussetzung bemächtigt, um seine Selbstmarterung bis zu ihrer schauerlichsten Härte [...] zu treiben. Eine Schuld gegen *Gott*: dieser Gedanke wird ihm zum Folterwerkzeug. [...] Dies ist einer Art Willens-Wahnsinn in der seelischen Grausamkeit, der schlechterdings nicht seines Gleichen hat: der *Wille* des Menschen, sich schuldig und verwerflich zu finden bis zur Unsühnbarkeit".

It is not easy to say why an unquenchable longing for pain should count as pathological for Nietzsche, since suffering – even self-inflicted suffering – is a normal part of life. It is tempting to think that what makes Christian suffering pathological is not merely that the sufferer is the source of his own pain but that he actively seeks it out, and in ever greater quantities, as emphasised in the claim: "one no longer protested *against* pain, one *thirsted* for pain; '*more* pain! *more* pain!'" (GM III 20, KSA 5, p. 390). But even this cannot be the full story because the individual of great spiritual health also welcomes, even seeks out, his own suffering.[17] It is important to remember that the self-inflicted suffering described in this passage is, like all real forms of the bad conscience, *interpreted* self-inflicted suffering. This suggests that the extent to which an unending thirst for pain counts as illness depends on how that suffering is interpreted, which is to say, on what function that pain is made to serve in the sufferer's life and in what relation that function stands to life's aims,[18] including whether the interpretation one gives to one's own suffering allows one to impose a measure on – some limits to – one's self-inflicted pain.

A second feature of the Christian bad conscience is its "mendaciousness [*Verlogenheit*]" (GM III 19, KSA 5, p. 385). As I have treated it here, mendaciousness is a self-imposed self-opacity – a motivated ignorance, achieved through repression, of the underlying instinctual motives of one's deeds and attitudes. If mendaciousness is an aspect of spiritual illness, then one component of spiritual health will be conscious self-transparency. It is important, though, that self-opacity is never the most important part of what makes the various versions of the bad conscience illnesses. This is because repression, with the ignorance of self that accompanies it, is often compatible with significant vitality. Still, other things being equal, self-transparency is, for a spiritual being endowed with consciousness, superior to self-opacity. Or, to put the point in terms that make clear the proximity of Nietzsche's view to philosophies for which alienation is a central category: self-knowledge – an undistorted awareness of who one is and what one wants – is more appropriate to self-conscious beings than the necessary "foreignness to oneself" that Nietzsche attributes to "us knowers" in the first paragraph of his inquiry into the origin of morality (GM Preface 1, KSA 5, p. 247–248).

---

17 Reginster 2006, p. 234–235.
18 Some confirmation of this suggestion can be found in Nietzsche's description of beings that pathologically seek their own suffering as "disgruntled, arrogant and offensive creatures [...] who inflict as much pain on themselves as they possibly can out of pleasure in inflicting pain – probably their only pleasure" (GM III 11, KSA 5, p. 362).

The third feature of the bad conscience (in its acutest form) that is indicative of illness is the most prominent in Nietzsche's texts,[19] and it, too, concerns a spiritual trait: the capacity for self-affirmation. A human who is spiritually ill in this respect says 'no' to himself,[20] a 'no' that expresses a "disgust with life [*Ekel am Leben*]" grounded in a "*shame at the human being* [die Scham des Menschen vor dem Menschen]" (GM II 7, KSA 5, p. 302). Self-denial, then, is bound up with an inability to take pride or satisfaction in oneself as one is, undistorted by the mendacious gaze produced by repression, and it is inseparable from self-hatred and self-contempt. This may be sufficient to explain why self-denial is an illness, but its perversity[21] becomes more glaring when one takes into account the general denial of life that accompanies it. This is seen most clearly in Nietzsche's description of "the *valuation* of [...] life" that underlies the self-denial of the ascetic priest:

> [our life] (along with what pertains to it: "nature", "world", the entire sphere of becoming and transience) is set [...] in relation to a wholly different mode of existence that it opposes and excludes *unless* it turn against itself, *deny itself*; in that case [...] life counts as a bridge to another existence. (GM III 11, KSA 5, p. 362)[22]

Another way of putting this point – one that echoes Marx's characterisation of the alienated relation between life and labour in capitalism – is to say that in self-denial what should be sought for its own sake (life activity in the only world we have) is valued only as a means to something outside it, existence in a "higher" but purely illusory world. As such, self-denial (like self-affirmation) is possible only for a spiritual, reflexive being that can take up a certain perspective on itself and make itself into the object of its own evaluative gaze.

It is tempting to infer from these descriptions of ascetic self-denial that this configuration of suffering, self-opacity, and denial of life is the acutest form of spiritual illness to be encountered among humans. Nietzsche explicitly acknowledges the plausibility of this inference but then just as explicitly rejects it. For he takes the ubiquity and resilience of ascetic self-denial throughout history to indi-

---

19 Already, for example, in GM Preface 5, KSA 5, p. 252.
20 As well as to "nature, naturalness, the facts of his being" (GM II 22, KSA 5, p. 332); also to "'world', the entire sphere of becoming and the transitory" (GM III 11, KSA 5, p. 362).
21 How illness relates to perversity is an interesting question, also in Freud.
22 "[D]asselbe [Leben, FN] wird (sammt dem, wozu es gehört, 'Natur', 'Welt', die gesammte Sphäre des Werdens und der Vergänglichkeit) [...] in Beziehung gesetzt zu einem ganz andersartigen Dasein, zu dem es sich gegensätzlich und ausschliessend verhält, *es sei denn*, dass es sich etwa gegen sich selber wende, *sich selbst verneine*: in diesem Falle [...] gilt das Leben als eine Brücke für jenes andre Dasein."

cate that it has a hidden life-promoting function – that even this life-denying attitude par excellence must, in a highly paradoxical and dangerous manner, be able to be employed by life so as to serve, in however twisted a fashion, its own ends. His thought is that for all the hostility to life expressed in its valuations, the ascetic ideal is still an ideal, and as such it is able to serve – and for large portions of human history actually has served – as a potent stimulus to forceful, world-ordering activity. As Essay III argues, Christianity at the height of its power was capable of truly awesome world-constituting activity, drawing not least on its ability to assign a meaning to human suffering that allowed for an affirmation of self and world (even if, in the latter case, only as a bridge to another world beyond it) and that motivated passionate activity in the very world it disvalued. Even if the values in the name of which Christianity acted are ultimately life-denying, its ordering the world in accordance with those values was an expression of vitality since, as Nietzsche famously claims, *to will nothingness is still to will* (GM III 1, KSA 5, p. 339).

If my claims here are correct, then even at its most vital the ascetic ideal qualifies as spiritual illness. This is because it is marked by a measureless thirst for suffering, self-opacity, and a denial of life. But there is a further feature of the ascetic ideal that makes it an illness (and that points to the possibility of an even acuter form of spiritual illness than Christianity represents). This fourth illness-defining feature of the ascetic ideal is bound up with what Nietzsche calls its great danger, a danger revealed in the self-contradictory (or self-undermining) dynamic on which the ascetic ideal feeds, as described in one of the most important passages of the *Genealogy*. About a third of the way into Essay III Nietzsche claims that there resides at the heart of the ascetic ideal

> an insatiable instinct and will to power that wants to become master not over something in life but over life itself, over its most profound, powerful, and basic conditions; here an attempt is made to use force to stop up the wells of force […] [W]e stand here before a being-divided-into-two that *wills* itself as divided, that *enjoys* itself in this suffering and grows more triumphant and certain of itself the more its own presupposition, the physiological capacity for life, *diminishes*. (GM III 11, KSA 5, p. 363)[23]

---

[23] "[H]ier herrscht ein Ressentiment […], das eines ungesättigten Instinktes und Machtwillens, der Herr werden möchte, nicht über Etwas am Leben, sondern über das Leben selbst, über dessen tiefste, stärkste, unterste Bedingungen; hier wird ein Versuch gemacht, die Kraft zu gebrauchen, um die Quellen der Kraft zu verstopfen […] wir stehen hier vor einer Zwiespältigkeit, die sich selbst zwiespältig *will*, welche sich selbst in diesem Leiden *geniesst* und in dem Maasse sogar immer selbstgewisser und triumphirender wird, als ihre eigne Voraussetzung, die physiologische Lebensfähigkeit, *abnimmt*."

In other words, even when the ascetic ideal functions as a stimulus to activity (and hence as a kind of stimulus to life), the activity it stimulates has as its (unintended) consequence a stopping up of the sources of its own vitality. In this form the ascetic ideal is a manifestation of vitality that, in expressing itself through action, undermines the very conditions of vitality. As I have suggested, this self-undermining dynamic represents the ascetic ideal's greatest danger, as well as the most important respect in which Christianity at the height of its power is a spiritual illness. Moreover, this danger points to the possibility of an even graver condition – something closer to extinction than to illness – that threatens to obtain once the ascetic ideal has played out its self-undermining dynamic to completion and has succeeded in exhausting the wells of its own energy. This extreme of spiritual sickness – nihilism in its most noxious form – may not have yet been reached by contemporary European culture, but Nietzsche senses it lurking on the horizon, the probable if not strictly necessary consequence of the death of God, the final demise of the no longer credible beliefs of Christianity that made its unique vitality possible. For, presumably, that post-Christian aftermath of the ascetic ideal, where the will ceases to will at all, is an even graver violation of life's basic nature than the paradoxical but still vital will that, fuelled by the ascetic ideal, wills nothingness.

Before concluding, I want to consider just one of the implications my account of illness has for Nietzsche's understanding of spiritual health, one that brings out an important affinity with Hegel. It is important to see that this feature of spiritual health is made possible by the spiritual illness I have just described. My point depends on recognising a striking formal similarity in Nietzsche's characterisations of the ascetic ideal at its worst, on the one hand, and of spiritual health, on the other. The former is marked by "a being-divided-into-two [*eine Zwiespältigkeit*]" that "*wills* itself as divided, *enjoys* itself in this suffering", and "in the most paradoxical manner" "becomes more self-confident and triumphant" the more it seeks out the suffering that comes from being internally divided (GM III 11, KSA 5, p. 363). A concrete picture of what it is to seek out and enjoy self-imposed internal division is suggested in Nietzsche's depiction of "the most horrible" form of the bad conscience, where, in language reminiscent of Feuerbach (and of Hegel's account of the Unhappy Consciousness), he portrays the Christian as driven by an insatiable will to "apprehend in 'God' the ultimate antithesis of his own [...] animal instincts" and to "reinterpret these instincts as guilt before God", thereby "stretching himself on the contradiction 'God' and 'devil'" and becoming "palpably certain of his own absolute unworthiness" (GM II 22, KSA 5, p. 332). The main respect in which Nietzsche's account of Christian spirituality goes beyond Feuerbach's is the decisive point here, namely, that the subject of religious alienation actively seeks out, enjoys, and feels himself confirmed in the absolute opposition he posits between himself and the "holy God", the idea of a being shorn of all the properties – especially those bound up with his own creatureliness – that he despises in himself.

That great spirituality is to be located in dividing oneself into two and then negotiating, and enduring, the very contradiction one has created should remind us of Hegel. It is clear that Nietzsche means to incorporate this vision of the fundamental mark of subjectivity into his picture of spiritual health, even if it is not so clear what that is supposed to look like. Rather than try to spell out how Nietzsche envisions this feature of health, I will content myself with pointing out two passages where that intention is clear. The first is the initially surprising remark made in relation to the opposing valuations 'good-bad' and 'good-evil' that:

> there is perhaps no more decisive mark of a "*higher nature*", a more spiritual nature, than that of being divided in two [...] and of being a genuine battleground of [...] opposed values. (GM I 16, KSA 5, p. 286)[24]

The second passage, located in a discussion of the various meanings the ascetic ideal can have, follows on the observation that "the *antithesis* between chastity and sensuality" need not be a tragic one:

> this holds good for all those well-constituted, joyful mortals who are far from regarding their unstable equilibrium between "animal and angel" as necessarily an argument against existence – the subtlest and brightest [...] have even found in it [...] one *more* stimulus to life. (GM III 2, KSA 5, p. 341)[25]

Exactly what it would mean to exist as a battleground for opposing values and self-conceptions is an important question I cannot say much about here. But these passages make clear that, in the exaggerated forms of being-split-into-two that Christianity introduces into subjects, Nietzsche senses the possibility of a great spiritual health, including an affirmation of self and world, which feeds on a love for self-division and a love for holding the opposed parts of this division together without removing their opposition. Far from being "natural" to animal life, this capacity for self-bifurcation and for holding opposites together, so remi-

---

24 "[E]s [gibt, FN] heute vielleicht kein entscheidenderes Abzeichen der 'höheren Natur', der geistigeren Natur [...], als zwiespältig [...] und [...] ein Kampfplatz für [...] Gegensätze zu sein."
25 "Dies dürfte wenigstens für alle wohlgeratheneren, wohlgemutheren Sterblichen gelten, welche ferne davon sind, ihr labiles Gleichgewicht zwischen 'Thier und Engel' ohne Weiteres zu den Gegengründen des Daseins zu rechnen, – die Feinsten und Hellsten [...] haben darin sogar einen Lebensreiz mehr gesehen."

niscent of Hegel, comes into the world only through illness as extreme as the great forms of health they make possible.

References

Hahn, Songsuk Susan (2007): *Contradiction in Motion: Hegel's Organic Concept of Life and Value*. Ithaca, NY: Cornell University Press.

Reginster, Bernard (1997): "Nietzsche on *Ressentiment* and Valuation". In: Ernest Sosa (Ed.): *Philosophy and Phenomenological Research* 57 (2), p. 291–305.

Reginster, Bernard (2006): *The Affirmation of Life: Nietzsche on Overcoming Nihilism*. Cambridge, MA: Harvard University Press.

Herman W. Siemens
'Punishment by Fate' as a Cypher for Genealogy: Hegel and Nietzsche on Immanent Law

In my contribution to the topic of this volume I would like to consider and compare the critique of law in Nietzsche and the young Hegel and how they respond to it. For Nietzsche I will draw broadly on the views on law developed across his work; for Hegel, I will concentrate on a specific period of his early writings, the so-called Frankfurt period of 1797–1800, in which he wrote the well-known text "Der Geist des Christentums und sein Schicksal" ("The Spirit of Christianity and its Fate"; henceforth: *SC*). It hardly needs stating that Nietzsche and Hegel are worlds apart in their philosophical projects, their styles and vocabularies, in their historical moments, philosophical influences and presuppositions. This makes it all the more extraordinary that there are such striking agreements and convergences between them on the problem of law and how to respond to it – at least in this early phase of Hegel's development. This convergence has been put succinctly by Jay Bernstein, who writes:

> Exactly like Nietzsche later, Hegel perceives the moral law as a slave morality that opposes to life an abstract ideal that is in reality a product of life, where the opposition between law and life is logically equivalent to the duality between (rational) universality and (sensuous) particularity. (Bernstein 2003, p. 411)

Condensed in this sentence are four propositions:

1. Law is opposed to life. Yet,
2. Law is a product of life.
3. This relation takes the form of a power relation: a logic of mastery, dependence and (self-)subjection; in short, heteronomy.
4. The logic of mastery works through the opposition of the universal to the particular, reason to sensibility.

To begin with the first two propositions:

1. *Law is opposed to life*: For both thinkers, law stands in radical opposition, contradiction or conflict with life; it is, in Nietzsche's language, life-negating or *lebensfeindlich*; in Hegel's language, law is *ein Fremdes*, alienated from

life. This motivates their shared question: How to overcome the alienation of law from life? What for Nietzsche is the task of *overcoming morality* is for Hegel that of *overcoming positive law*. Yet:

2. *Law is a product of life*: Both thinkers pose this question from a radically immanent standpoint in life or nature, understood as the one and only reality, what Hegel calls Spinozistically "*das Einige*", or "life in the single Godhead [*das Leben in der einigen Gottheit*]" (SC, TWA 1, p. 343).[1] From this perspective law cannot simply be opposed to life, but must be understood naturalistically, as a tension or opposition *intrinsic to nature*; a hostility to life born of life, a deformation of life produced by life itself. Hegel and Nietzsche have very different readings of life and its consequences for a life-immanent understanding of law, but they concur in their *critical diagnosis* of law as installing a logic mastery that divides and fixes the universal against the particular, the rational against the sensuous (propositions 3 and 4). In this regard, they both collapse the self-understanding of morality as transcendent and sovereign onto the plane of immanence, and both respond to this diagnosis by searching for a *naturalistic morality*, a life-immanent and life-affirming form of law. As Hegel puts it: if "law is a power [*Macht*] to which life is subordinate [*untertan*], above which nothing stands, above which not even the deity stands", the task is to find a form of law which is situated "within the domain of life [*innerhalb des Gebietes des Lebens sich befindet*]" (SC, TWA 1, p. 343). Given their very different conceptions of nature, the two thinkers appear to follow different paths here. The task for Hegel is to displace the Kantian *vertical morality* of self-subjection to law with a *horizontal morality* of Sittlichkeit, located in our relations to others. Nietzsche's thought, by contrast, gravitates towards a perfectionist ethics of *radically individual self-legislation*, and it culminates in the question of normativity: How to evaluate different life-forms? What standard of evaluation does *physis*, as the one and only reality, afford? One could say: for Nietzsche the question concerns the *quality of different individual lives*, whereas for Hegel it concerns the *quality of our relations to others*. This contrast certainly accords with the standard view of Hegel as a social thinker, and Nietzsche as an individualist. In order to see to what extent this contrast holds, I shall examine more closely each philosopher in turn, beginning with Nietzsche.

---

[1] "[F]or life is not different from life, because life is in the one divinity [*denn Leben ist vom Leben nicht verschieden, weil das Leben in der einigen Gottheit ist*]" (SC, TWA 1, p. 343). Cf. SC, TWA 1, p. 363: "To love God is to feel oneself in eternity in the all of life [*Gott lieben ist sich im All des Lebens schrankenlos im Unendlichen fühlen*]". For 'das Einige', see SC, TWA 1, p. 338, 374, 390.

I Nietzsche: The Problem of Law

The concepts of law and legislation have a central but profoundly ambivalent place in Nietzsche's 'ontology' of life. They are central, because for Nietzsche life is Becoming (*Werden*) and the character of Becoming is to be an incessant and radically plural *Fest-setzen*, a dynamic and multiple fixing (*Feststellen*) or positing (*Setzen*) of Being.[2] In Nietzsche's vocabulary, *Gesetz* (law) is consistently associated with *das Feste, das Gesetzte*, understood as the result of *Fest-setzen*.[3] Its status is, however, problematic, for, *Gesetz* and *Gesetzgebung* name the positing of the moral law, immutable and universal, in radical contradiction to life. Life, for Nietzsche, is radically plural and dynamic. Life is Becoming (*Werden*), Occurring (*Geschehen*) and Self-Overcoming (*Selbstüberwindung*); a chaos of diverse and particular life-forms in dynamic relations of tension with one another. Law, by contrast, is rigid, static, eternal[4] (as opposed to dynamism and Becoming); law brings unity and order (as opposed to plurality and chaos); law is universal in scope and claims universal validity (as opposed to particularity and nuance), claims Nietzsche links with gestures of subjection, coercion and tyranny (*Unterwerfung, Zwang, Tyrannei*).

For Nietzsche, then, law is life-negating or hostile to life, and one might expect him to take the side of life against law. The problem is, however, complicated by his (negatively derived) one-world hypothesis and the impulse inherited from Heraclitus to interpret law in *monistic* and *immanent* terms. In the first instance, this means to overcome the autonomy of the normative sphere, essential to the self-understanding of morality and law (*Recht*) and to re-think law as an immanent feature of nature.[5] Against the transcendent and sovereign status of law, denounced by Nietzsche as 'Anti-nature', he calls for a "Naturalism of morality": "my task is to translate the seemingly emancipated and de-natured moral values back into their nature – i.e., into their natural 'immorality'" (NL

---

2 E.g. NL 1887, KSA 12, 9[91], p. 385: "[...] Alles Geschehen, alle Bewegung, alles Werden als ein Feststellen von Grad- und Kraftverhältnissen, als ein *Kampf* ...". See also: NL 1884/85, KSA 11, 26[359], p. 244; NL 1885, KSA 11, 34[88], p. 449; NL 1885, KSA 11, 34[89], p. 449; NL 1885, KSA 11, 39[13], p. 623; NL 1885/86, KSA 12, 2[139], p. 135–136; SE 3, KSA 1, p. 360; GS 370, KSA 3, p. 622; A 58, KSA 6, p. 245.
3 See e.g. GS 76, KSA 3, p. 431; NL 1884, KSA 11, 26[359], p. 244; NL 1885, KSA 11, 34[88], p. 449; NL 1885, KSA 11, 39[13], p. 623; BGE 188, KSA 5, p. 108f.
4 For *das Starre, Statische, Feste, Ewige*: NL 1869/70, KSA 7, 3[15], p. 63; HH I 34, KSA 2, p. 55; NL 1883, KSA 10, 15[29], p. 486; A 32, KSA 6, p. 204 with reference to Jesus; cf. NL 1887/88, KSA 13, 11[368], p. 164.
5 See Herschbell/Nimis 1979, p. 17–38; Busch 1989, 271f.; Hölscher 1977.

1887, KSA 12, 9[86], p. 380).[6] As a consequence law cannot simply be opposed to life, and Nietzsche cannot take the side of life against law, because law is an opposition or tension *intrinsic* to life. It is life itself, as multiple and incessant *Fest-setzen*, that constantly produces its opposite, projecting a fixed image of itself that is its counterpart and negation (Being). From a radically immanent standpoint in Nietzsche's concept of nature or life, then, law must be understood and acknowledged as a necessary product and feature of life as *Fest-Setzen*. Yet, as a negation of life, it cannot simply be affirmed in the name of life. So what would be an affirmative law of life, where life depends upon its own negation qua *Festsetzen*? The problem here is how to conceptualise an affirmative form of negation, a form of legislation which, in negating life, affirms and enhances it; a form of law that works not just *against* life, but *with and against* it.

In broad terms, the task is to articulate a space for law in between two extremes: If life is a multiple fixing or positing of Being: *Fest-Setzen*, then there are two ways in which this can go wrong. At one extreme, the processes of fixing or *Fest-setzen* can be reduced to a minimum, so that Becoming descends into a formless, disorganised and unlimited conflict of forces – what Nietzsche sometimes calls the lawless 'war of annihilation' (*Vernichtungskampf*). At the other extreme, Becoming can be arrested through an excess of fixing that subjugates, assimilates and reduces all 'external' difference to the same. At both extremes, life undergoes negation, impoverishment and loss: in the first through a lack of form-giving force and fixation, in the latter through overwhelming force, an excess of fixation, unity and order. The latter is what the young Hegel calls the problem of positivity.

II Hegel: The Problem of Positivity

Under the influence of the events surrounding the French Revolution and the problem of freedom in Kant's philosophy, Hegel's early thought is dedicated to the task of *realising freedom and reason*. The central problem in his early so-called 'theological writings' is not theological at all, but moral. From Kant

---

[6] Cf. NL 1884, KSA 11, 25[309], p. 91. For Christianity as "Antinature of morality" and "antinatural morality" and Nietzsche's counter-conception of "naturalism in morality", see TI Morality 4, KSA 6, p. 85f. For the formulation "Naturalismus der Moral" see NL 1888, KSA 13, 15[5], p. 403 and NL 1888, KSA 13, 16[73], p. 509; cf. NL 1887, KSA 12, 9[8], p. 342: "Vernatürlichung der Moral".

he derives the conviction that "the goal and essence of all true religion, including our religion, is the morality of humans" (*FS*, TWA 1, p. 105) and that the core problem of religion concerns the springs or incentives (*Triebfeder*) for moral action: religion must "interest the heart" and exert "an influence on our feelings [*Empfindungen*] and on the determination of our will" (*FS*, TWA 1, p. 11):

> Thus religion gives morality and its motives a new more sublime sway, it provides a new and stronger dam against the violence of the sensuous pulsions. In sensual men, religion is also sensual, – the religious incentives for doing good must be sensual [...]. (*FS*, TWA 1, p. 12)[7]

The underlying problem is that Hegel, from the very start, rejects the Kantian position that pure Reason can be practical (cf. Geiger 2007, p. 24–32; also *FS*, TWA 1, p. 188). From his teachers at the *Tübinger Stift*, Hegel had been taught that, since morality (i.e. Practical Reason) alone is powerless (*unvermögend*) to assert its primacy over our inclinations, we need help to realise the good, help and support that is provided by God our master upon whom we depend. Moral action, in other words, requires 'positive faith' (*positiver Glaube*); that is, a set of principles vested with absolute authority. While sharing with his teachers the conviction that Reason is practically impotent, he rejects completely the orthodox justification of positivity and looks throughout his early writings for alternative solutions, ways in which to *overcome positive* law and *reconcile* the claims of Practical Reason with our natural drives and inclinations that can actually motivate action.

Without question, it is around the problem of positivity that Hegel's early thought revolves, and in the seven years from the Tübingen fragments of 1793 through to the Frankfurt writings of 1797–1800, his formulation of this problem and his solutions to it undergo several transformations. In the Tübingen fragments, the problem concerns 'objective' religion and how to make it 'subjective', while the Bern fragments concentrate on the figure of Jesus, conceived as a Kantian *Tugendlehrer* in opposition to Christianity, conceived as a religion of authority. Nonetheless, the so-called *Zusätze* to the essay "Die Positivität der christlichen Religion" (1795–1796) give a good indication of what positivity means across the early writings.

---

[7] "Die Religion gibt also der Moralität und ihren Beweggründen einen neuen erhabeneren Schwung, sie gibt einen neuen stärkeren Damm gegen die Gewalt der sinnlichen Antriebe ab. Bei sinnlichen Menschen ist auch die Religion sinnlich, – die religiösen Triebfedern zum Guthandeln müssen sinnliche sein [...]."

The Zusätze on positivity

I. (*FS*, TWA 1, p. 190) A positive faith (*positiver Glaube*) is a system of principles, whose truth is independent of our rational assent (*Fürwahrhalten*) and is grounded instead on irresistible authority: an authority that "subjugates our belief [*unsren Glauben unterwerfen*]". As such, its 'truths' take form of *Sollen* or commandments (*Gebote*). The first commandment is to hold such truths as truths, where the commandment is authorised by its irresistibility: where we cannot but obey (*nicht entschlagen können zu gehorchen*).[8]

II. (*FS*, TWA 1, p. 191f.) In positive faith, God's right over us and our duty to obey are grounded above all in a relation of power, a relation of subjection between master and slave: he is our "powerful lord and commander [*mächtiger Herr und Gebieter*]", we his "creatures and subjects [*Geschöpfe und Untertanen*]", duty-bound to gratitude for his beneficence (*Wohltaten*), and for his truths in our blindness. Since God has overwhelming power (*Übermacht*) not only over "the drives of life" but also over our spirit (*Geist*), positivity signifies not just "the impotence of [our] reason", but the "dependency of our whole being [*Abhängigkeit unseres ganzen Seins*]". As a relation of power that is irreconcilable with the freedom of reason, positivity signifies the collapse of normative validity for the young Hegel. If with Hegel we now ask:

III. (*FS*, TWA 1, p. 193f.) How positive truths can become subjective? How the duty to believe can be satisfied where it transgresses reason? Hegel points to a logic of fear: Fear (of the Almighty Ruler) coerces the understanding (*Verstand*) to extend empirical causality into the supersensory. Fear coerces Practical Reason to demand only those things that can be satisfied with the help of positive religion. Here Hegel's critique of positivity extends to Kant's Postulates of Practical Reason. For Kant, Practical Reason demands the belief in God and the immortality of the soul if we are to have hope that that we can fulfil our duty to realise (part of) the Highest Good. Hegel takes this to mean that Practical Reason, if it is to act as a determining ground for our action, has the need (*Bedürfniss*) to postulate the equation of duty/virtue with blessedness (in the afterlife) and the equation of sin with proportionate punishment (in the afterlife). For Hegel, Kant hereby contaminates the purely *formal* character of Practical Reason and its autonomy with demands that have their source in sensibility; in this amalgam Reason is unable to realise its demands, thereby inviting the alien

---

[8] Cf. *SC*, TWA 1, p. 288; Bernstein 2003, p. 404.

power of positive law and faith to exercise control over our nature and motives or incentives for action. From now on, the young Hegel will reject the belief in God as a false "need of Reason [*Bedürfniss der Vernunft*]" (Pöggeler 1984, 129–130) in favour of a Spinozistic notion of God-in-us, and the project to realise the freedom of reason from a radically *immanent and monistic* perspective in God-or-nature, what he calls 'life' in the Frankfurt writings. Before considering Hegel's Frankfurt writings and how they transform the problem of positivity, an overview of the problem up to that point will be helpful. The problem of positivity can be placed under four headings. Positivity names:

1. the positing of absolute, i.e. *irresistible authority* over and against human *freedom*, an authority that is completely *independent of reason* (our *Fürwahrhalten*), even if its content may accord with reason;
2. a *logic of mastery* or domination: a master-slave power-relation of subjugation and absolute dependence, an irreconcilable hostility to the claims of sensibility (*SC*, TWA 1, p. 276, 282–283, 297);
3. a *devaluation of human nature*: our total dependency and our need for authority under positive law empties human nature of value; what Hegel variously describes as an absolute separation of the human from the divine, and "a resignation which relinquishes any native goodness, nobility, and greatness in human nature" (*FS*, TWA 1, p. 224). Positivity presupposes our "moral impotence [*moralische Kraftlosigkeit*]" or incapacity for spontaneous moral agency;
4. *a logic of fear* (*FS*, TWA 1, p. 117, 193f.; cf. *SC*, TWA 1, p. 276).

Frankfurt writings

In the Frankfurt writings, these four moments recur in sharpened formulations focused on the concept of positive law. Hegel's move to Frankfurt in 1797, however, and his intensive contact with Hölderlin there, brings with it a seismic shift in his understanding of positivity and how to overcome positive law. The change is two-fold. Inspired by Spinoza's God-in-us and Hölderlin's *hen kai pan*, he adopts a radically *immanent and monistic standpoint in life*. This Spinozistic impulse is what brings the Frankfurt writings in the vicinity of Nietzsche's thought. Like Nietzsche, Hegel has a *dynamic* and *pluralistic* understanding of life. It first makes its appearance as an emphasis on the historical diversity of concrete forms of life that Hegel calls 'living nature':

> But living nature is always other than the concept of the same, and hence what for the concept was a bare modification, a pure accident, a superfluity, becomes a necessity,

something living, perhaps the only thing which is natural and beautiful. (*FS*, TWA 1, p. 219)⁹

At the same time, however, Nature or Life is One, *die einige Natur*: "for life is not different from life, since life dwells in the one Godhead [*denn Leben ist vom Leben nicht verschieden, weil das Leben in der einigen Gottheit ist*]" (*SC*, TWA 1, p. 342). From this perspective, the problem of positivity comes to be viewed as a conflict or opposition between law and life. But since life is the one and only reality, this opposition can only be an opposition, separation or diremption (*Trennung, Entzweiung, Zerreißung*) *within life*: "the form of command [*Gebot*] is itself a diremption [*Zerreißung*] of life" (*SC*, TWA 1, p. 327). This brings with it a second shift in Hegel's thought. Under the influence of Hölderlin and the *Vereinigungsphilosophie* in which he was steeped, Hegel reformulates the problem of positivity as a matter of *Vereinigung*: unification and reconciliation of what is split or diremt under positive law into universal and particular, *Sollen* and *Sein*, possibility and actuality (*Möglichkeit, Wirklichkeit*), reason and sensibility (cf. propositions 3 & 4):

> Since the commands of duty presuppose a cleavage [between reason and inclination, HS] and since the domination of the concept declares itself in a "thou shalt", that which is raised above this cleavage is by contrast an "is", a modification of life [...]. (*SC*, TWA 1, p. 324)¹⁰

As this quote indicates, Kant is no longer a resource *against* positive law, but an internalisation of positive law that entrenches, rather than overcomes it:

> Morality is according to Kant the subjugation of the particular under the universal, the triumph of the universal over its opposed particular [...] for the particular or the drives, inclinations, pathological love, sensibility, or however we may call it, the universal is necessarily and eternally something alien, objective; an indestructible positivity remains [...]. (*FS*, TWA 1, p. 299)¹¹

---

9 "Aber die lebendige Natur ist ewig ein anderes als der Begriff derselben, und damit – wird dasjenige, was für den Begriff bloße Modifikation, reine Zufälligkeit, ein Überflüssiges war, zum Notwendigen, zum Lebendigen, vielleicht zum einzig Natürlichen und Schönen." See also *SC*, TWA 1, p. 347: "Weil nämlich die Gesetze nur gedachte Vereinigungen von Entgegensetzungen sind, so erschöpfen diese Begriffe bei weitem die Vielseitigkeit des Lebens nicht [...]". Also *FS*, TWA 1, p. 316 in the context of Jesus' parables: "Es ist in ihnen kein fabula docet, keine Moral kommt aus ihnen, sondern das Geschichtliche, das Werden, der Fortgang des Seienden, des Ewigen, des Lebendigen; – das Werden des Seins ist das Geheimnis der Natur [...]".

10 "Da die Pflichtgebote eine Trennung voraussetzen und die Herrschaft des Begriffs in einem Sollen sich ankündigt, so ist dagegen dasjenige, was über diese Trennung erhaben ist, ein *Sein*, eine Modifikation des Lebens".

11 "Moralität ist nach Kant die Unterjochung des Einzelnen unter das Allgemeine, der Sieg des Allgemeinen über sein entgegengesetztes Einzelnes [...] für das Besondere, Triebe, Neigungen,

Against which Hegel advocates

> rather the elevation of the particular to the universal, unification – *Aufhebung* of both opposites through unification. (*FS*, TWA 1, p. 299)[12]

Or again:

> universality is a dead universality, since it is opposed to the particular, and life is the unification of both, – morality is dependency upon myself, diremption in oneself. (*FS*, TWA 1, p. 303)[13]

Hegel's sharpest analysis of the positivity of law involves a figure of *double-opposition*. Because laws are

> unifications of opposites in a concept, which leaves them as opposites, but the concept itself exists in opposition to reality, hence it follows that the concept expresses an ought. (*SC*, TWA 1, p. 321)[14]

That is to say:

1. (Moral) law generates *oppositions*, e.g. intelligible – natural, universal – particular, prohibition – deed, which it seeks to harmonise in a concept. But since the terms, in order to be what they are (or: mean what they mean), depend upon their opposition to each other, they cannot be harmonised and remain opposed.
2. The concept itself stands in *opposition* to reality. Because the concept expressed by law harmonises what in reality are opposites, the concept is itself opposed to reality, and takes the form (not of Being but) of *Sollen* (cf. Bernstein 2003, p. 408).

In his Frankfurt writings, Hegel draws two kinds of consequence from his concept of life for the overcoming of positive law. *On the one hand* he explores the possibility of *Vereinigung* by way of the concept of love, understood as the

---

pathologische Liebe, Sinnlichkeit, oder wie man es nennt, ist das Allgemeine notwendig und ewig ein Fremdes, ein Objektives; es bleibt eine unzerstörbare Positivität übrig […]."

12 "[E]her Erhebung des Einzelnen zum Allgemeinen, Vereinigung – Aufhebung der beiden Entgegengesetzten durch Vereinigung."

13 "[D]ie Allgemeinheit ist eine tote, denn sie ist dem Einzelnen entgegengesetzt, und Leben ist Vereinigung beider, – Moralität ist Abhängigkeit von mir selbst, Entzweiung in sich selbst."

14 "Vereinigungen Entgegengesetzter in einem Begriff, der sie als Entgegengesetzter lässt, der Begriff aber selbst in der Entgegensetzung gegen Wirkliches besteht, so drückt er ein Sollen aus."

intensification or 'blossom' (*Blüte*) of life. Love, he argues, is not opposed to the content of law, but only to its form,[15] and he tries to show how love can realise the content of law, while overcoming and uniting its opposed terms, thereby making law superfluous: "In love the separate does still remain, but as something unified and no longer as something separate, and life feels life [*In der Liebe ist das Getrennte noch, aber nicht mehr als Getrenntes, [sondern] als Einiges, und das Lebendige fühlt das Lebendige*]" (*FS*, TWA 1, p. 246):

> Love the blossom of life; God's kingdom the whole tree with all necessary modifications, steps of development; modifications are exclusions, not oppositions, there are no laws, i.e. what is thought is the same the real, there is no universal, no relation has become objectively a rule, all relations have emerged living from the development of life, no object is bound to an object, nothing has become fixed [...] Human beings are as they ought to be [...]. (*FS*, TWA 1, p. 308)[16]

On the other side, Hegel also explores the contradiction or alienation of law and life in its most acute form by considering the extreme case of transgression: where the law is broken, and becomes punitive law (*strafendes Gesetz*). If law can be taken up in love, because only its form but not its content is opposed to love, transgression and law can never be reconciled, since the transgression empties the law of reality ("sein Inhalt in der Wirklichkeit aufgehoben ist" (*SC*, TWA 1, p. 338)). Law as punishment, Hegel argues, is "directly, according to its content, opposed to life, because it manifests the destruction of life [*unmittelbar, seinem Inhalt nach dem Leben entgegengesetzt, weil sie die Zerstörung des Lebens anzeigt*]" (*SC*, TWA 1, p. 338).

If punitive law sets itself up over and against life as "a power to which life is subordinate [*eine Macht, welcher das Leben untertan ist*]", Hegel looks to the concept of fate (*Schicksal*) and *punishment by fate* for an alternative form of law which "is situated within the domain of life [*innerhalb des Gebietes des Lebens sich befindet*]" (*SC*, TWA 1, p. 343): an *immanent law* that overcomes the diremp-

---

[15] "Die Entgegensetzung der Pflicht und der Neigung hat in den Modifikationen der Liebe, in den Tugenden ihre Vereinigung gefunden. Da das Gesetz nicht seinem Inhalt, sondern seiner Form nach der Liebe entgegengesetzt war, so konnte es in sie aufgenommen werden, in dieser Aufnahme aber verlor es seine Gestalt [...]" (*SC*, TWA 1, p. 337).

[16] "Liebe die Blüte des Lebens; Reich Gottes der ganze Baum mit allen notwendigen Modifikationen, Stufen der Entwicklung; die Modifikationen sind Ausschließungen, nicht Entgegensetzungen, es gibt keine Gesetze, d.h. das Gedachte ist dem Wirklichen gleich, es gibt kein Allgemeines, keine Beziehung ist objektiv zur Regel geworden, alle Beziehungen sind lebendig aus der Entwicklung des Lebens hervorgegangen, kein Objekt ist an ein Objekt gebunden, nichts ist festgeworden [...] Die Menschen sind so, wie sie sein sollen".

tion and alienation of law from life. The key to a life-immanent law is for Hegel the insight that *any act of mine must be understood as embedded in the thick web of relations and conditions that make my life possible*. On the assumption that life or nature is One, the destruction of the other by the criminal is inseparable from the criminal's self-destruction: "Trespass [*Verbrechen*] is a destruction [*Zerstörung*] of nature, and since nature is One, there is as much destruction in what destroys as in what is destroyed" (*SC*, TWA 1, p. 338). And yet, if Life is One, it cannot actually be destroyed by the criminal act, but only alienated or separated:

> The trespasser thought he had to do with a stranger's life, but he has only destroyed his own; for life is not different from life, since life dwells in the single Godhead; in his arrogance he has destroyed indeed, but only the friendliness of life; he has perverted it into an enemy. (*SC*, TWA 1, p. 343)[17]

The criminal's destruction of the other signifies not the destruction of life, but its diremption (*Trennung*), and with it a loss in the *quality of our relations to others*, what Hegel calls "the friendliness of life". The destruction of the other comes to signify the destruction of ourselves when we come to realise that the other is not external to us, but that our relation to the others is *internal* to our self-relation. With this transformation of self-consciousness, comes what Hegel calls an "infinite gain through the wealth of living relations [*unendlicher Gewinn durch den Reichtum lebendiger Beziehungen*]" (*SC*, TWA 1, p. 327).

At stake in Hegel's naturalistic or life-immanent conception of law, as Bernstein notes, is the displacement of the Kantian 'vertical' morality with a 'horizontal' morality of *Sittlichkeit*. From Kant, he takes over the view that the moral worth of our actions is contingent on our treatment of others. Yet in Kant, others remain external to my private relation to the moral law, a relation of diremption and subjection of my particularity under the universal. For Hegel, naturalising morality means realising that my relations to others are *internal* to my self-relation, so that the moral quality of my action is mediated by the quality my treatment of others. Before considering Hegel's life-immanent counter-concept of law-as-fate, I now turn to Nietzsche with the question: What consequences does *he* draw from his concept of life for a life-immanent and -affirmative conception of law?

---

[17] "Der Verbrecher meinte es mit fremdem Leben zu tun zu haben; aber er hat nur sein eigenes Leben zerstört; denn Leben ist vom Leben nicht verschieden, weil das Leben in der einigen Gottheit ist; und in seinem Übermut hat er zwar zerstört, aber nur die Freundlichkeit des Lebens: er hat es in einen Feind verkehrt."

III Nietzsche on Radically Individual Self-Legislation

For Nietzsche, to adopt an immanent perspective in life or nature as the one and only reality means first and foremost to overcome the autonomy of the normative sphere, essential to the self-understanding of morality and law (*Recht*). His "naturalism of morality" (NL 1885/86, KSA 12, 9[86], p. 38) involves a theoretical project to translate (*zurückübersetzen*) moral terms like 'law' back into the body, the drives, individual and collective *Lebensbedingungen*. On the practical level it means to reformulate the moral law in terms that do not contradict, oppose or ignore life, but articulate in ethical terms the pluralistic, dynamic and conflictual character of life as *Festsetzen*. Ultimately, Nietzsche's naturalism of morality issues in an ethic of radically individual self-legislation, ostensibly at odds with the social/relational naturalism of Hegel's 'horizontal' morality of *Sittlichkeit*. On closer inspection, however, this contrast turns out to be simplistic. A brief reconstruction of Nietzsche's ethic of self-legislation also reveals that it is motivated by criticisms of law that share much with Hegel's critique of positive law.

In his Frankfurt writings, as noted above, Hegel vacillates between the *Aufhebung* of law through love on one side, and the project to reformulate punitive law in life-immanent terms on the other. For Nietzsche, by contrast, an immanent perspective in life as *Fest-Setzen* has the clear consequence that *law is necessary for life* and therefore irreducible. This point deserves some emphasis, since it is insufficiently recognised. In BGE 188, Nietzsche denounces the advocates of *laisser-aller*, who claim to take the side of nature against law, by appealing to what he calls "the moral imperative of nature": " 'Thou shalt obey, someone or other, and for a long time' ['*Du sollst gehorchen, irgend wem, und auf lange*']" (BGE 188, KSA 5, p. 110). But 'Sollen' is not only a "condition for life and growth [*Lebens- und Wachstums-Bedingung*]" (A 25, KSA 6, p. 194) in this sense; it is also what drives and makes possible the Nietzschean project of *overcoming of morality*, or the 'Selbstaufhebung der Moral', as he describes it in the Preface to *Daybreak*. In that book, he writes:

> the confidence in morality is withdrawn – but why? *Out of morality!* Or what else should we call what is going on in it – and in *us*? For our taste is for more modest expressions. But there is no doubt that a "thou shalt" still speaks to us too, that we still obey a strict law set over us – and this is the last morality which can make itself audible even to us, which even we know how to *live*, in this if in anything we too are still *men of conscience* [...]. (D Preface 4, KSA 2, p. 16)[18]

---

18 "[...] wird der Moral das Vertrauen gekündigt – warum doch? *Aus Moralität!* Oder wie sollen wir's heissen, was sich in ihm – in *uns* – begiebt? denn wir würden unsrem Geschmacke nach

There can be no question, then, that the *Selbstaufhebung der Moral* also involves the *Aufhebung* of law or *Sollen*. Ultimately, this is because, as Nietzsche puts it in a *Nachlass* note, *Sollen* is a condition for life:

> Morality is necessary: given that we must act, according to what shall we act? And we must *evaluate* what we have done, according to what? To demonstrate error in the genesis [of moral values, HS] is not an argument against morality. Morality is a condition for life. "Thou shalt" [...]. (NL 1882/83, KSA 10, 4[90], p. 140)[19]

Since the critique of morality does not make morality or legislation dispensable, the question is how the "thou shalt" best meets 'the conditions for life and growth': *What form of law or legislation enhances the quality of human life maximally?* Nietzsche's response involves *radically individual self-legislation* and can be reconstructed around five co-ordinates.[20]

From Nietzsche's middle works on, the problem of law is consistently identified with two phenomena: (1) a logic of self-subjection and heteronomy; and (2) moral universalism, especially the Kantian morality of the universal law.[21] Both are seen to conflict with the character of life: Nietzsche's pluralistic 'ontology' of diverse life-forms implies the uniqueness of each and its particular life-conditions (*Lebens-* or *Existenz-bedingungen*). And as an incessant and multiple *Fest-Setzen*, life involves not just the capacity to obey, but also to command.[22] A life-

---

bescheidenere Worte vorziehn. Aber es ist kein Zweifel, auch zu uns noch redet ein 'du sollst', auch wir noch gehorchen einem strengen Gesetze über uns, – und dies ist die letzte Moral, die sich auch uns noch hörbar macht, die auch wir noch zu *leben* wissen, hier, wenn irgend worin, sind auch wir noch *Menschen des Gewissens*".

19 "Moral ist nöthig: wonach werden wir handeln, da wir doch handeln müssen? Und was wir gehandelt haben, müssen wir *schätzen* – wonach? Irrthum in der Genesis nachweisen ist kein Argument gegen die Moral. Moral ist eine Lebensbedingung. 'Du sollst' [...]".

20 This account is based on the research paper: "(Self-)legislation, Life and Love in Nietzsche's Philosophy" (Siemens 2009).

21 Both objections are often combined, as in NL 1886/87, KSA 12, 7[6], p. 275 and GS 335, KSA 3, p. 562. See also D 108, KSA 3, p. 96; NL 1880, KSA 9, 3[159], p. 98; A 11, KSA 6, p. 177.

22 For Nietzsche, commanding and obeying are not opposites, but intrinsically related to one another (see Gerhardt 1996, p. 231f. on their sociological meaning). Hence Nietzsche criticises obedience as base where it precludes commanding: as a passive self-subjection, slave attitude or fear of commanding (D 108, KSA 3, p. 96; NL 1886/87, KSA 12, 7[6], p. 275; NL 1883, KSA 10, 16[86], p. 530). Instead he pleads for an activistic "nobility in obeying" as freedom under the law (NL 1882, KSA 10, 3[1], p. 97, No. 358); for a self-commanding out of strength, presupposing obedience (NL 1881, KSA 9, 14[20], p. 629; Z II Self-Overcoming, KSA 4, p. 147); for co-commanding (Mit-Befehlen), that is, to interpret duties as self-imposed laws: "ich soll, was ich *will*": NL 1880, KSA 9, 4[111], p. 128); but also for an overcoming of obedience and constraint through love (NL 1882/83, KSA 10, 5[1], p. 201, No. 124).

immanent and -affirmative form of law must therefore oppose these two structural features of law. Insofar as it is opposed to (1) the heteronomy of self-subjection, Nietzschean legislation involves, not just obedience, but also a *sovereign act of commanding* (*Befehlen*). Insofar as it is opposed to (2) moral universalism, it is radically individual or particular, a *radically individual law*; what Gerhardt, borrowing a phrase from Simmel, calls "das individuelle Gesetz" (Gerhardt 1992, p. 41).[23] Another key co-ordinate for understanding Nietzsche's counter-concept of law is his increasing preoccupation over time with (3) *contemporary Nihilism*: with the death of God, all transcendent grounds for the law crumble, throwing the individual back on itself as the source of law. This thought is expressed with extraordinary clarity in a note from 1884:

> [I]n the founders of religion, their "Thou Shalt" has reached them as a commandment of God. As in the case of Muhamed, their legislation of values was for them "inspiration" [*Eingebung*], and that they executed it, an act of obedience. – Now as soon as those ideas have collapsed 1) that of God 2) that of eternal values: then the task of the legislator of values is arises in terrible greatness. (NL 1884, KSA 11, 26[407], p. 259)[24]

Life-immanent law is, then, a matter of *legislation*, a *Fest-setzen* of values. But if it is to be genuinely life-enhancing, that is: radically individual self-commanding (2 + 3), it must be based on individual self-knowledge. Because under Nihilism the individual is thrown back on itself for the sources of law, (4) *the question of self-knowledge* becomes central to the exercise of self-legislation. For Nietzsche, the necessity and profound difficulty of self-knowledge are at the core of free or sovereign self-legislation, and he gives a great deal of attention to the question of self-understanding as the precondition for a radically individual morality.[25] At stake is knowledge of our *physis*, a naturalistic self-understanding stripped of all moralisms, and it is striking how often Nietzsche recurs to the concept of law for this radically individual self-knowledge. He writes of "the

---

23 See also Simmel 1968. The expression "das individuelle Gesetz" also occurs in a note of Nietzsche's where it is opposed to the "ewiges Sittengesetz" (NL 1881, KSA 9, 11[182], p. 512).
24 "[B]ei den Religionsstiftern, ist ihr 'Du sollst' ihnen als Befehl ihres Gottes zugekommen: wie im Falle Muhameds, ihre Gesetzgebung der Werthe galt ihnen als eine 'Eingebung', und daß sie sie ausführten, als ein Akt des Gehorsams. – Sobald nun jene Vorstellungen dahingefallen sind 1) die von Gott 2) die von ewigen Werthen: entsteht die Aufgabe des Gesetzgebers der Werthe in furchtbarer Größe." See also NL 1885, KSA 11, 38[13], p. 612.
25 See: SE 1, KSA 1, p. 340–343; NL 1880, KSA 9, 4[118], p. 130; D 108, KSA 3, p. 95; D 119, KSA 3, p. 111; GS 335, KSA 3, p. 562f.

basic law of your real self [*das Grundgesetz deines eigentlichen Selbst*]" (SE 1, KSA 1, p. 340f.), "the law of one's higher mechanics [*das Gesetz seiner höheren Mechanik*]" (SE 2, KSA 1, p. 343), and, on a physiological level, of "knowledge of one's forces, law of their order and discharge [*Kenntniß seiner Kräfte, Gesetz ihrer Ordnung und Auslösung*]" (NL 1880, KSA 9, 4[118], p. 130) and of the profound difficulty, if not impossibility, of knowing one's drives (*Triebe*): "the laws of their *nourishment* remain wholly unknown to him" (D 119, KSA 3, p. 111; cf. D 108, KSA 3, p. 95). In these contexts, the concept of law often takes on a further, quite specific meaning: it points towards a sense of necessity and constraint (*Notwendigkeit und Zwang*), described variously as a necessity of nature, an inner law of mechanics, a radically individual fate that is fixed (*Granit, Unbildbares*) and absolutely binding on each "self". The claim embodied in this use of *Gesetz* is that there is a necessity, a *Müssen*, which is an irresistible and binding source of *Sollen*. As the standard for evaluating what I truly want it serves as the ground of self-legislation, and it is the business of self-knowledge to lay bare this necessity. To the extent that it succeeds, (5) *the exercise of freedom in self-legislation, makes contact with necessity*.

Bringing these points together, Nietzsche's life-affirmative concept of law is built on the claims that self-legislation (in opposition to the heteronomy of self-subjection) is *sovereign (self-)commanding* (1); self-legislation (in opposition to moral universalism) is radically individual or particular, a form of *moral particularism* grounded in Nietzsche's *ontological pluralism* (2); the need for (self-)legislation becomes urgent in the context of *contemporary Nihilism*, the bankruptcy of transcendent ideals (3); under these conditions, the individual is thrown back on itself for the sources of law, raising in an acute form the problem of *self-knowledge* as the key to exercising self-legislation (4); and as the key to self-knowledge, Nietzsche points to a sense of necessity, a fixed and binding constraint or *Müssen* as the ground of the *Sollen* of legislation (5). Nietzsche's advocates an ethos of radically individual self-legislation, based on knowledge and acknowledgement (*Erkennen/Anerkennen*) of all that is lawful and necessary in (one's) own nature: Life-affirmative law is a *Sollen* grounded in (self-knowledge of) a *Müssen*, an inner necessity or fate (*fatum*).

With the concept of fate (*fatum, Schicksal*) Nietzsche's thought makes contact with Hegel's punishment by fate. But from this account, it is the differences between them, rather than affinities, that stand out: Nietzsche's emphasis on the irreducible *Sollen* or 'oughtishness' of law; on commanding; on Nihilism; on physiology or the body; and above all his *moral particularism*, as against Hegel's horizontal morality of *relations*. In order to examine their relation in greater depth, I will consider a few key texts in Nietzsche's critique of law.

IV Nietzsche's Critique of Law

For Nietzsche, as for Hegel, law contradicts or conflicts with life by installing a logic of mastery that divides and fixes the universal against the particular, the rational against the sensuous (cf. propositions 3 & 4). This diagnosis, and Nietzsche's response to it, can be seen in two texts in which he concentrates his attack on Kant.

I. In *The Anti-Christ* 11, the conflict between law and life is expressed in the charge that the categorical imperative is symptomatic of 'decline', a 'debilitated life', and that universal law is 'damaging', 'a danger' to our life:

> Nothing ruins us more profoundly or inwardly than "impersonal" duty, or any sacrifice before the Moloch of abstraction. – To think that people did not perceive Kant's categorical imperative as a *danger to life*! ... (A 11, KSA 6, p. 177)[26]

Against the sacrifice of sensuous particularity before the universal, Nietzsche appeals to the 'laws of preservation and growth': "The reverse is dictated by the most basic laws of preservation and growth [*Erhaltungs- und Wachsthums-Gesetzen*]: that everyone should devise for himself *his* virtue, *his* categorical imperative" (A 11, KSA 6, p. 177).

Like Hegel, Nietzsche is concerned with the damage to life (*die Zerstörung des Lebens*) that comes from the abstract opposition of universal law to concrete life and the inner needs of my life: "What is more damaging [*Was zerstört schneller*] than working, thinking, feeling without an inner necessity, without a profoundly personal choice, without *pleasure* [*Lust*]? As an automaton of 'duty'?" (A 11, KSA 6, p. 177). As with Hegel, *Zerstörung* here names a loss in the *quality of life*: the loss of *pleasure* and the loss of *personal choice* that comes from the automatism of the universalizability test and acting in conformity with it.

II. In the second text the universal law is opposed to the claims of radically individual self-knowledge. In GS 335, Nietzsche begins by poking fun at Kant: "And now don't bring up the categorical imperative, my friend! The word tickles my ear and makes me laugh despite your very serious presence" (GS 335, KSA 3, p. 562). He then goes on to unmask the universality of the moral law as its opposite: "For it is self-centered [*Selbstsucht*] to consider one's own judgment a uni-

---

[26] "Nichts ruinirt tiefer, innerlicher als jede 'unpersönliche' Pflicht, jede Opferung vor dem Moloch der Abstraktion. – Dass man den kategorischen Imperativ Kant's nicht als *lebensgefährlich* empfunden hat! ..."

versal law". And yet this is a virtually empty kind of self-obsession; one that, in its concern with universalizability, abstracts from one's self, and is bereft of knowledge of one's particular needs and impulses that demand a radically individual law: the creation of one's ownmost ideal.

> What? You admire the categorical imperative within you? This "firmness" of your so-called moral judgment? This "unconditionality" of the feeling, "here everyone must judge as I do"? Admire rather your *self-centeredness* here! And the blindness, pettiness, and facileness of your self-centeredness! For it is self-centered to perceive one's own judgment as universal law, and a blind, petty and facile self-centeredness because it reveals that you have not yet discovered yourself or created for yourself your own, your ownmost ideal – [...] (GS 335, KSA 3, p. 562)[27]

III. In the third text I will consider, the *quality of life* is once again central to Nietzsche's critique of universal law. This time it is expressed as happiness, *Glück*:

> – *Insofar* as the individual wants his happiness, one ought not to tender him any prescriptions regarding the path to happiness: for individual happiness springs from one's own laws, unknown to everyone, and can only be hindered and obstructed by prescriptions from without. – The prescriptions called "moral" are in truth directed against individuals and are in no way aimed at promoting their happiness. (D 108, KSA 3, p. 95)[28]

For happiness, Nietzsche contends, is radically particular and plural: "at every stage of development a particular [*besonderes*] and incomparable happiness can be achieved, neither higher nor lower but rather specific to itself" (D 108, KSA 3, p. 95). The problem is not law as such, but the relation – once again – between law and free choice: Is law posited *above our choice (Belieben)* or does it fall within our choice?

---

27 "Wie? Du bewunderst den kategorischen Imperativ in dir? Diese 'Festigkeit' deines sogenannten moralischen Urtheils? Diese 'Unbedingtheit' des Gefühls 'so wie ich, müssen hierin Alle urtheilen'? Bewundere vielmehr deine *Selbstsucht* darin! Und die Blindheit, Kleinlichkeit und Anspruchslosigkeit deiner Selbstsucht! Selbstsucht nämlich ist es, *sein* Urtheil als Allgemeingesetz zu empfinden; und eine blinde, kleinliche und anspruchslose Selbstsucht hinwiederum, weil sie verräth, dass du dich selber noch nicht entdeckt, dir selber noch kein eigenes, eigenstes Ideal geschaffen hast: – [...]".
28 "Dem Individuum, *sofern* es sein Glück will, soll man keine Vorschriften über den Weg zum Glück geben: denn das individuelle Glück quillt aus eigenen, Jedermann unbekannten Gesetzen, es kann mit Vorschriften von Aussen her nur verhindert, gehemmt werden. – Die Vorschriften, welche man 'moralisch' nennt, sind in Wahrheit gegen die Individuen gerichtet und wollen durchaus nicht deren Glück."

> [U]p to now the moral law was supposed to stand *above* our choice: one did not want to *give* this law to oneself, one wanted to *take* it from somewhere or *discover* it somewhere or *have it commanded to one* from somewhere. (D 108, KSA 3, p. 95)[29]

These concerns clearly echo those expressed in two features of Hegel's concept of positivity: that it posits an *irresistible authority* over and against human *freedom*, an authority that is completely *independent of reason* (our *Fürwahrhalten*); and that it is a *logic of mastery* and subjection.

IV. Further connections with Hegel's critique of positivity are expressed in the last text I will consider. In a *Nachlass* note from 1886/87, Nietzsche develops a critique of 'herd-virtues' under the sign of inertia:

> **Towards a critique of herd-virtues.**
> **Inertia** is active
> 1) in trust, because mistrust makes tension, observation, thought necessary
> 2) in worship, where the difference of power is great and subjugation necessary: to avoid fear, one tries to love, to value and to interpret the power-differential as difference of *value*: so that the relation *no longer breaks out in revolt*.
> 3) in the sense for truth. What is true? Where an explanation requiring a minimum of mental exertion [*geistiger Kraftanstrengung*] is given. Besides, lying is very demanding. [...]
> 6) in integrity: one prefers to obey an existing law rather than to create a law for oneself, rather than to command oneself and others. The fear of commanding – better to subject oneself than to react.
> 7) in tolerance: the fear of exercising rights, fear of judging (NL 1886/87, KSA 12, 7[6], p. 274–275)[30]

It is not just, as Hegel has it, that positive law subjects us to an authority that is completely *independent of reason* (our *Fürwahrhalten*). From points 1)

---

29 "[B]isher sollte das Moralgesetz *über* dem Belieben stehen: man wollte diess Gesetz sich nicht eigentlich *geben*, sondern es irgendwoher *nehmen* oder irgendwo es auffinden oder irgendwoher es *sich befehlen lassen.*"
30 "**Zur Kritik der Heerden-Tugenden./** Die **inertia** thätig/ 1) im Vertrauen, weil Mißtrauen Spannung, Beobachtung, Nachdenken nöthig macht/ 2) in der Verehrung, wo der Abstand der Macht groß ist und Unterwerfung nothwendig: um nicht zu fürchten, wird versucht zu lieben, hochzuschätzen und die Machtverschiedenheit als *Werth* verschiedenheit auszudeuten: so daß das Verhältniß *nicht mehr revoltirt./* 3) im Wahrheitssinn. Was ist wahr? Wo eine Erklärung gegeben ist, die uns das minimum von geistiger Kraftanstrengung macht. Überdies ist Lügen sehr anstrengend.[...]/ 6) in der Rechtschaffenheit: man gehorcht lieber einem vorhandenen Gesetz als daß man sich ein Gesetz schafft, als daß man sich und Anderen befiehlt. Die Furcht vor dem Befehlen – Lieber sich unterwerfen als reagiren./ 7) in der Toleranz: die Furcht vor dem Ausüben des Rechts, des Richtens".

and 3) in the text it is clear that for Nietzsche this is the very appeal of positive law: in its irresistible authority it relieves us of the effort and strain of having to think for ourselves. The appeal of positive law is that it appeals to our inertia. But if we ask: why inertia? Nietzsche's answer is: fear. And here his diagnosis connects with a further feature (4.) of Hegel's concept of positivity, its *logic of fear*. According to Hegel, the authority of positive law derives from our fear of the inescapable power of an almighty master on whom we as slaves are completely dependent in our being (*FS*, TWA 1, p. 193; *SC*, TWA 1, p 276). According to Nietzsche, we prefer to trust rather than question, to *subject ourselves* to an alien law rather than *command ourselves and others* – all in order *to avoid fear*: the slave's fear of destruction at the hands of an almighty master. For both thinkers, what is truly devastating about the command structure of law grounded in fear is how it devalues human nature. According to Hegel, as we saw, positivity, in making our being dependent on its authority, denies our capacity for spontaneous moral action (positivity 3.). According to Nietzsche, we ascribe overwhelming power to the law, so that we cannot but submit and worship it, relieving us of the strain of acting spontaneously or even reacting. Yet we can only secure ourselves against reacting or revolting against this power by interpreting the power-differential as a difference of *worth or value*: we need not revolt, because we are not *worthy* of revolting against the law; we are worth nothing in comparison with the majesty of the law.

All these texts exhibit striking convergences or intersections between Hegel's critique of positivity and Nietzsche's critique of law. Yet there are also clear differences, both in their diagnoses and in the practical consequences they draw from them. For Nietzsche what is in need of explanation is our inertia or passivity, our preference for blind trust over thinking for ourselves, for submission without the urge to revolt, for obedience to pre-given laws over commanding ourselves and others, over creating our own law and exercising rights we claim for ourselves. No doubt this goes back to his diagnosis of Nihilism as a loss of commanding and creative, value-positing power, and as the negation of life as active power; thoughts utterly alien to Hegel. And in line with these differences, he draws very un-Hegelian practical consequences from his critique: *that we should legislate for ourselves, command ourselves (and others?), in response to our particular sources of happiness*. For Hegel, we might say, Nietzsche remains trapped in the command structure of positive law, merely exchanging one side for the other (command for obedience) without breaking through the wrenching isolationism of the moral law. From Nietzsche's point of view, Hegel's aversion to commanding is perhaps symptomatic of his Nihilism, and his aversion to *Sollen*, the oughtish character of law, a denial of life or nature as *Fest-setzen*: an instance of 'Widernatur'.

Yet this characterisation falls short. There are, to begin with, good reasons to question the opposition between Hegel's *relational* or 'horizontal' morality and Nietzsche's moral *particularism*, as opposed versions of naturalised morality. It is important to recall that Nietzsche's theory of power as will to power comes out of a sustained critique of substance ontology and is an attempt to think what Nietzsche calls the "relational character of occurrence [*Relations-Charakter des Geschehens*]" (NL 1884, KSA 11, 26[36], p. 157): it is a *relational* ontology of tension, action-resistance, among forces without substance. In line with this, Nietzsche's moral individualism or particularism is thoroughly relational. The individual has deeply social origins for Nietzsche, and he develops a 'socio-physiology' to describe the formation of the individual through the internalisation of social relations, mores and prohibitions.[31] Human particularity is, moreover, *internally* relational and plural for Nietzsche: each of us, as *unica*, are a "rare coming together [*seltsamer Zufall*]", "a wonderfully colourful multiplicity in one [*wunderlich buntes Mancherlei zum Einerlei*]" (SE 1, KSA 1, p. 337).

But the deepest connection between Hegel and Nietzsche as relational thinkers comes from their shared diagnosis of modernity with sources in Schiller. For both thinkers, the loss of the unifying powers of religious belief and worship brought on by Enlightenment critique has led to an all-pervasive condition of diremption, alienation and disgregation. What the young Nietzsche describes as the period of "atomistic chaos" (see SE 4, KSA 1, p. 367f.) is later radicalised under the sign of Nihilism into a boundless 'war of annihilation' (*Vernichtungskrieg*)[32] among forces and values that threatens not just relations *between* 'atomistic individuals', but the relations that constitute them *as individuals*:

> The dissolution of morality leads as its practical consequence to the atomistic individual and then further to the splitting up of the individual in pluralities – absolute flux. That is why a goal is needed, now and more than ever, and love, a *new love*. (NL 1882/83, KSA 10, 4[83], p. 138)[33]

---

31 On this, see Siemens 2006.
32 For the resemblance between early texts and later texts on Nihilism as a pervasive conflict of force, compare NL 1873/74, KSA 7, 30[8], p. 734: "[...] Jetzt fehlt das, was alle partiellen Kräfte bindet: und so sehen wir alles feindselig gegen einander und alle edlen Kräfte in gegenseitigem aufreibendem Vernichtungskrieg" and NL 1887, KSA 12, 9[35], p. 351: "[...] daß die Synthesis der Werthe und Ziele (auf der jede starke Cultur beruht) sich löst, so daß die einzelnen Werthe sich Krieg machen: Zersetzung".
33 "Die Auflösung der Moral führt in der praktischen Consequenz zum atomistischen Individuum und dann noch zur Zerteilung des Individuums in Mehrheiten – absoluter Fluß. Deshalb ist jetzt mehr als je ein Ziel nöthig und Liebe, eine *neue Liebe*."

These lines clearly resonate with the problem of positivity in Hegel's Frankfurt writings as a condition of *Trennung* or *Entzweiung* between individuals and within each one. More than that, Hegel's appeal to *love* as a unifying force is also echoed by Nietzsche. Indeed, even Hegel's contention that love can take up and sublate (*aufheben*) or replace the moral law altogether, appears to be echoed by Nietzsche in a subsequent note, when he writes:

> *Of the morality of the higher men*
> All that is otherwise morality has here become love.
> But now a new "Thou shalt" begins – knowledge
> of the free spirit – the question of the highest goals. (NL 1882/83, KSA 10, 4[89], p. 140)[34]

The suggestion here is that traditional morality can – in the hands of 'higher men' – be dissolved and replaced by love. And yet, the proximity to Hegel should not blind us to the difference between them. For Nietzsche it is clear that on its own, love will be insufficient: the loss of purpose (*Ziel*) and creative power under nihilistic conditions does not dispense with the need for self-legislation altogether, and Nietzsche's love issues in a new "Du sollst". Yet the appeal to love also indicates that for Nietzsche, *radically individual self-legislation* on its own is also insufficient. On the basis of these notes, the problem of legislation can be formulated as the question: How to conjugate legislation, or rather a *pluralistic* form of self-legislation able to generate a plurality of new 'goals', with the unifying powers of 'a new love'?

V Nietzsche's Agonal Model of Legislation

In a series of notes from the same period, Nietzsche addresses this task by proposing a pluralistic, thoroughly relational model of self-legislation, inspired by the Greek concept of limited antagonism, the *agon* or *Wettkampf*.[35] On this agonal model of legislation, the demand for cohesion (*Vereinigung*) cannot be derived from a Hegelian concept of love that precludes antagonism; instead

---

34 "*Von der Moral der höheren Menschen.*/ Alles, was sonst Moral ist, ist hier Liebe geworden./ Aber nun beginnt ein neues 'Du sollst' – die Erkenntniß des Freigeistes – die Frage nach den höchsten *Zielen.*"
35 For a more detailed treatment of these notes in the context of self-legislation, see Siemens 2009.

Nietzsche looks to derive it from 'a new love', that is, a new concept of love that works through resistance (*Widerstreben*).

In these notes Nietzsche sets himself the task of re-thinking law and law-giving in way that reflects and enhances the *dynamic* and *pluralistic* qualities of life against the rigidity and universalism of the moral law. Nietzsche's agonal solution turns on three key requirements:

1. It is to be a 'law for law-givers', not for passive subjects or 'supplicants': "Law for law-givers/ From *ones who pray, we must* become *ones who bless!*" (NL 1883, KSA 10, 15[58], p. 494).[36]
2. It is to be productive and pluralistic, the creative source of many ideals and not a subjection of many to the ideal or law of One: "I do not want to establish One ideal of the wise man [*Ein Ideal des Weisen*], but a hundred *ideals of the fool!*" (NL 1883, KSA 10, 16[86], p. 530).
3. It is to be law or law-giving that blesses, completes and fulfils 'on every level', not a leveller that demands or pleads that we all 'jump' to One level: "*Main teaching*: to bring it to completeness and **a sense of well-being** on every level – *not* to jump!" (NL 1883, KSA 10, 15[10], p. 482).

As the key to all three requirements, Nietzsche proposes the notion of *a law that can be fulfilled*.[37] A fulfillable law is a law accessible to individual interpretations. Laws that are subject to individual interpretation and fulfilment break, for the first time, our slavish subjection to eternal, immutable laws, what Nietzsche called our "fear of commanding".[38] Fulfillability, in turn, makes self-

---

36 "Gesetz für Gesetzgeber/ Aus *Betenden müssen wir Segnende* werden!"
37 "[D]ie *Erfüllbarkeit größer* als vorher (dem Individuum die Deutung zugänglich)/NB. es **muß erfüllbar** sein und aus der Erfüllung **muß** ein höheres Ideal und dessen Gesetz wachsen!" (NL 1883, KSA 10, 15[19], p. 484). [the *fulfillability greater* than before (accessible to the individual's interpretation)/NB. it **must** be **fulfillable** and from the fulfilment a higher ideal and its law **must** grow!]. Cf. Hegel's comments on πλήρωμα, understood as the unity of inclination and law, of love and reflexion (*SC*, TWA 1, pp. 326, 329, 370).
38 "*Forderung*: das neue Gesetz muß *erfüllbar* sein — und aus der Erfüllung muß die Überwindung und das höhere Gesetz wachsen. Zarathustra giebt die Stellung zum Gesetz, indem er das 'Gesetz der Gesetze', die Moral *aufhebt*./ Gesetze als Rückgrat./ an ihnen arbeiten und schaffen, indem man sie vollzieht./ Bisheriger Sklavensinn *vor* dem Gesetze!" (NL 1883, KSA 10, 16[86], p. 530). [*Demand*: the new law must be *fulfillable* – and from the fulfilment the overcoming and the higher law must grow. Zarathustra gives the attitude towards the law, insofar as he *supersedes* the "law of laws", morality./ Laws as a backbone./ to work on them and create, insofar as one carries them out./ Hitherto slavishness *before* the law!].

legislation possible. For when laws are subject to interpretation and fulfilment, on the model of 'backbone' or provisional framework, individuals are placed in a position to work and re-work them so as to create new and better laws of their own. This is what Nietzsche means by a 'law for law-givers' (1. above). And yet: under nihilistic conditions, creative power – or rather the *incapacity* to "*posit productively a goal for oneself*" (NL 1887, KSA 12, 9[35], p. 350f.) – is precisely the problem, not a solution.[39] This is where the *agon*, or a contest of power, enters the picture: as a *stimulant* to creative self-legislation. When placed in an agonal 'contest for power', law operates as an obstacle, but also a stimulus that provokes others to resist and surpass it with their own, better laws:

> The rights that I have conquered for myself I will not *give* to the other: rather, he ought to *rob* them for himself! like me – and [he] may appropriate them and *wrest* them from me! To this extent there must be a law which emanates from me, as if it wanted to make all into my likeness: so that the singular individual discovers and strengthens itself in contradiction with it. [...]
>
> Whoever *appropriates* a right will not *give* this right to the other – but will be an opponent to him *insofar as he appropriates it for himself*: the love of the father who clashes with his son.
>
> The great educator, like nature: he must pile up *obstacles*, so that they are *overcome*. (NL 1883, KSA 10, 16[88], p. 531)[40]

On the "fear of commanding": " [...] man gehorcht lieber einem vorhandenen Gesetz als daß man sich ein Gesetz *schafft*, als daß man sich und Anderen befiehlt. Die Furcht vor dem Befehlen — Lieber sich unterwerfen als reagiren." (NL 1886/87, KSA 12, 7[6], p. 275)

39 In posthumous notes, Nietzsche writes of a loss of tension (*Spannung*) attending the loss of 'organising power' and its consequences: processes of dissolution (*Auflösung*), exhaustion (*Erschöpfung*) that result in an incapacity to create or "*posit productively a goal for oneself*" and an answer to the question "Why?". NL 1887, KSA 12, 9[35], p. 350f.: "Nihilism [...] ein Zeichen von *nicht genügender* Stärke, um produktiv sich nun auch wieder ein Ziel, ein Warum? einen Glauben zu *setzen*. [...]/ B)) Nihilism als *Niedergang und Rückgang der Macht des Geistes:* der **passive Nihilism**: als ein Zeichen von Schwäche: die Kraft des Geistes kann ermüdet, *erschöpft* sein, so daß die *bisherigen* Ziele und Werthe unangemessen sind und keinen Glauben mehr finden —".

40 "Die Rechte, die ich mir erobert habe, werde ich dem Anderen nicht *geben*: sondern er soll sie sich *rauben*! Gleich mir – und mag sie nehmen und mir *abzwingen*! Insofern muß ein Gesetz da sein, welches von mir ausgeht, als ob es Alle zu meinem Ebenbilde machen wolle: damit der Einzelne sich im Widerspruch mit ihm entdecke und stärke. [...]/ Wer ein Recht sich *nimmt*, wird dies Recht dem Anderen nicht *geben* – sondern ihm Gegner sein, *indem er es sich nimmt*: die Liebe des Vaters, der dem Sohn widerstrebt./ Der große Erzieher wie die Natur: er muß *Hindernisse* thürmen, damit sie *überwunden* werden."

Nietzsche's agonal solution is to raise one's own law as if (*als ob*) it were universally binding, thereby usurping all rights and forcing others to oppose one, to discover and assert their own capacities in re-claiming their rights – like the love of a father who intentionally clashes with his son.

In these notes, Nietzsche's *moral particularism* is emphatically *pluralised* and embedded in a *relational* web of conditions. They show that Nietzsche responds to the task of overcoming of morality by focusing on *relations to others*, no less than Hegel does in his attempt to overcome positive law. *Contra* Hegel, however, these relations are irreducibly antagonistic; Nietzsche's love is 'a new love' mediated by relations of tension and resistance. Tension and antagonism are important for a naturalised concept of law because ('realism') nature or life is relational and conflictual in character. But tension and antagonism are also important as a source of creative power under nihilistic conditions. At the heart of Nietzsche's agonal model of legislation is the claim that resistance need not be a negative, inhibiting force, experienced as loss or a diminution of power. Under conditions of relative parity among powers, resistance can also be a stimulant that one seeks out, an obstacle that provokes one to exercise, extend and measure one's own resources in the effort to achieve mastery.[41] This interpretation of resistance seems to be entirely lacking in Hegel's approach to the task of overcoming positive law, to which I now turn. For Hegel, overcoming positive law means precisely to *overcome hostility*, in favour of 'reconciliation' or the 'friendliness of life'.

VI Punishment by Law, Punishment by Fate and the Law of Life

In the final part of this paper I turn to Hegel's attempt to re-think law in naturalistic or life-immanent terms where the contradiction between positive law and life is at its most extreme: the case of transgression. There are, I submit, significant intersections or convergences between Hegel's life-immanent alternative to punitive law, law-as-fate, and the naturalised concept of law in Nietzsche's writings. In the present context I will focus not on the thematic dimension of Nietzsche's writing, but on its performative dimension, Nietzsche's philosophical *practice*. Genealogy, I will argue, can profitably be reconstructed using Hegel's concept of law-as-fate as a cypher for the problem of law that confronts the genealogist.

---

[41] See HC, KSA 1, p. 789; EH Wise 7, KSA 6, p. 274; cf. NL 1888, KSA 13, 14[173] and NL 1888, KSA 13, 14[174], p. 358–362.

Genealogy, as Nietzsche describes it in the preface to the *Genealogy of Morality*, examines the conditions under which our values emerge and thrive, in order to ask the critical question: What is the value of our values? Like Hegel, Nietzsche presupposes a radically immanent conception of life as the one and only reality, and the task of the genealogist is to adopt an *immanent standpoint in life* and evaluate our values *in the name of life*. But in order to question the value of our values, the genealogist needs a standard of evaluation (*Maasstab*), a standard or rule for evaluating them *in the name of life*. The genealogist must, in short, posit a standard, measure or *law* of life. Yet law, as we know, contradicts life for Nietzsche. Law *qua* law sets itself up over and against life, opposing itself as unity, eternity, universality to the boundless, mobile and chaotic multiplicity of life – of the very life it purports to represent in thought. Genealogy, then, is in need of a *life-immanent law* that (1) allows for an evaluation or transvaluation of values, as a standard of critique in the name of life; yet one which (2) overcomes its alienation – as law – from life, as well as the inherent contradiction in the practice of evaluating things according to the standard or law of life. In what follows, I will argue that Nietzsche's response to this problem can be plotted by following the logic of Hegel's concept of law-as-fate.

For Hegel, punishment by fate offers a way to think a form of separation or *Trennung* that allows for unification or *Vereinigung*, as against the irreconcilable separation created by positive law. Starting out from his Spinozistic concept of life: 'das einige Leben' he is in need, just like the genealogist, of a life-immanent law that overcomes its alienation as law from life. In Hegel's concept of life, as in Nietzsche's, everything is interconnected in a differentiated unity or whole (TI Errors 8, KSA 6, p. 96). The criminal act – and Hegel has the extreme case of murder or the destruction of the other in mind – is motivated by the *false consciousness* or delusion (*Täuschung*) that I can extend my power by destroying an alien or separate life (SC, TWA 1, p. 342). Positive law can certainly punish the offender, but it does nothing to change his false consciousness; indeed, because the law sets itself up as a power over and above life or reality (*Wirklichkeit*), and because the reality of the crime contradicts the law's commandment or *Soll*, it can only be truly satisfied by destroying the criminal (SC, TWA 1, p. 339). In fate, by contrast, law finds itself "within the domain of life [*innerhalb des Gebietes des Lebens*" (SC, TWA 1, p. 343), so that the crime is inseparable from its punishment; indeed, "the crime *is* the punishment in itself" (FS, TWA 1, p. 305). And unlike positive law, it can be reconciled, because fate "is itself one of the limbs, a thing separated, which cannot as separated be destroyed through its opposite, but can through unification be sublated [*durch Vereinigung aufgehoben werden kann*]" (FS, TWA 1, p. 305).

The key to this unification or reconciliation is a transformation of the criminal's false consciousness effected by the 'recoil of law'-as-fate (*rückwirkende*

Gesetz – SC, TWA 1, p. 344 note): his realisation that since life cannot be separated from itself (*Leben ist als Leben nicht vom Leben verschieden*), he is implicated in the same life as the one he injured, what Hegel describes as a "return and rapprochement to oneself [*Wiederkehren und Nahen zu sich selbst*]" (*SC*, TWA 1, p. 345) through his recognition that his relation to others is *internal to* his self-relation.

Hegel's arguments for unification or reconciliation under law-as-fate turn on a series of contrasts he draws between positive law and fate.

I. As a rule or thought (*Regel/Gedachtes*), positive law needs to be opposed to something real or actual in order to exercise its authority. Thus in law, the *Sollen* must be separated from its execution in reality, and its universal claim must be opposed to the human and its inclinations as particulars. In fate, by contrast, punishment is a "hostile power" (*feindliche Macht*), but as *my* fate, it is *individual*, not universal, and inseparable from my act of transgression: from an immanent standpoint in life, "the deed *is* the punishment".

II. In its universality, positive law operates a logic of mastery or domination over the particular human being; and in its eternity, it installs a condition of mastery, opposition or separation (*Trennung*) that precedes any particular act. Hence the criminal act can only be a slave's revolt against his master, a futile attempt to free himself or herself from total dependency. Fate, on the other hand, being my individual fate, is certainly a hostile force, but one to which I am equal and against which I can struggle as a living, struggling power (*kämpfende Macht*) (*SC*, TWA 1, p. 342). Fate does not precede my act of hostility as an eternal law, eternally divided against my particularity. Rather, it is my deed that first creates the law. Before my crime, there is only the differentiated unity of life, what Hegel calls "the one life, which is neither regulated by law nor at variance with law [*dem einigen, weder durch Gesetze regulierten noch gesetzwidrigen Leben*]" (*SC*, TWA 1, p. 342). In punishment by fate, Hegel writes, "the law is later than life" (*SC*, TWA 1, p. 343) and remains within the domain of life: as the law that recoils upon the criminal (*das auf den Verbrecher rückwirkende Gesetz*), fate can be sublated (*aufgehoben*), because *he* himself set it up; the separation, which he created, can be united. This unification, Hegel writes, is love;[42] that is: "the feeling of life that finds itself again [*Dies Gefühl des Lebens, das sich selbst wiederfindet*]" (*SC*, TWA 1, p. 346). Fate kicks in at moment when the criminal

---

[42] "[D]as Schicksal hingegen, das auf den Verbrecher rückwirkende Gesetz kann aufgehoben werden, weil er das Gesetz selbst aufgestellt hat; die Trennung, die er gemacht hat, kann vereinigt werden; diese Vereinigung ist in der Liebe" (*SC*, TWA 1, p. 343n).

realises the falseness of his attempt to go outside life, and feels the connectedness of his life with the life he sought to destroy as a loss of the 'friendliness' or *quality* of life. He is 'punished' by the return of injured life (*verletztes Leben*) in the form of a hostile terrifying ghost, like Macbeth's Banquo.

Much could be said about the proximity of Hegel's *individual* law-as-fate to Nietzsche's ethos of radically *individual* self-legislation rooted in knowledge of one's *fatum*, 'deeper' than life in Hegel's words;[43] or between Nietzsche's attempts to formulate a concept of law that reflects the *dynamic* character of life-as-Becoming and Hegel's law that is born of a deed, comes 'later than life' and returns to it. In the present context, I will restrict myself to Nietzsche's genealogical practice and a certain movement it shares with Hegel's account of law-as-fate. I have in mind a movement that (i) begins with a criminal act of destruction, motivated by the *false consciousness* that the other is completely separate from my life; an act that (ii) *creates a law*, a law that (iii) *recoils upon the agent*, effecting (iv) a transformation of consciousness: the realisation that *he is implicated in the same life* as the one he would destroy. In what follows, these four moments will be tracked to Nietzschean genealogy.

To begin with, it is worth noting that Nietzsche sees his philosophical task as a *fate*, a "hidden force and necessity [...] that rules below and in his singular fates"; as "the future that gives the rule [*Regel*] to our today" (HH I Preface 7, KSA 2, p. 21); and that genealogy promises to discover new possibilities for "the dionysian drama of the 'fate of the soul'" (GM Preface 7, KSA 5, p. 255). It is also worth noting that for Nietzsche the critical task of evaluating, re-evaluating or transvaluating our values (*Umwerten*) places the genealogist in the position of the *criminal*. This is best seen in his concept of *genius*: as a creator of new visions, new works, he is juridically a criminal, since in creating new values, or rather: *a new standard or law of evaluation*, he breaks (with) received laws and values.[44]

The genealogical project *to re-evaluate our values in the name of life* is motivated by the discovery that human civilisation has been dominated by Nihilism, that is, by forms of life that are turned against life: slave morality (Essay I), bad conscience (Essay II) and the ascetic ideal (Essay III). In order to oppose and fight against Nihilism, the genealogist must, then, *take the side of life against life-negating forms of life*, values and ideals – such as the moral law.

---

[43] "Aber bei der Strafe als Schicksal ist das Gesetz später als das Leben und steht tiefer als dieses" (*SC*, TWA 1, p. 343).
[44] See Siemens 2002, p. 86.

The problem is how to avoid repeating Nihilism in opposing it. For in order to evaluate values in the name of life, we need a standard of evaluation or law of life, which, as law, risks repeating the life-negating form of law. How can genealogy oppose Nihilism from a genuinely immanent standpoint in life? How is it to contrive a life-immanent law? Nietzsche's response can, I believe, be read off the narratological structure of GM, which shadows Hegel's story of fate with uncanny precision.

Nietzsche's GM is a *Streitschrift*, a text that wages war on Nihilism and nihilistic values. Like Hegel's criminal, the genealogist begins with an act of destruction, motivated by the *false consciousness* that the other is completely separate from his own life (moment i above). For Nietzsche, as mentioned, the very enterprise to interrogate the value of our values is criminal, since it means to break or break with *received laws and values*. More than that, it is a destruction of life, a *Zerstörung des Lebens* (akin to Hegel's transgression); for it means also to break, or break with life, as it has become (Nihilism). The genealogist takes the side of life against life-negating values and ideals by objectifying them, casting them into the third person as alien and deformed forms of life: slaves, Jews, Christians, free spirits, ascetic priests, philosophers, pessimists, artists etc. are all interrogated, exposed, ridiculed, emptied of value, in short: destroyed – *in the name of life*. One could say: the genealogist wages a philosophical war of annihilation (*Vernichtungskampf*) against life-negating values with the purpose of empowering life and life-affirmation against Nihilism. Like Hegel's criminal, he believes he can extend his power and the power of life he represents by destroying an alien and threatening form of life.

But as Hegel tells us, these acts are motivated by the *false consciousness* that nihilistic values and life-forms are completely separate from the genealogist's own life (moment i above). Since, from a genuinely immanent standpoint, the One life is indestructible (*unzertörbar*), these critical acts achieve not the annihilation of these values, but only separation, diremption, alienation (*Trennung, Verfeindung, Verfremdung*). The genealogist makes part of the totality of life – which includes him, as well as the object of critique – into something alien, an enemy.

In order to question the value of nihilistic values in the name of life, the genealogist must deploy a standard of evaluation; the act of critique itself implies a standard of critique that represents life in some sense, a law of life (moment ii above). This law, in setting itself up against nihilistic forms of life, offers the genealogist a standpoint of critique outside of them, from which to question their value. But if Nihilism has dominated the whole of civilisation, as Nietzsche claims, then there is no standpoint *in life outside of Nihilism*. It seems that "to take the side of human life" against Nihilism, is in fact to take a standpoint *beyond* life; that is, to repeat the life-negating gesture of Nihilism.

But there is only life, as the one and only reality. And the law of life created by the genealogist *recoils upon him*, effecting a transformation of consciousness (moments iii and iv above). Like Hegel's criminal, he is implicated in the very same *"einige Leben"* as his enemy and sees the falseness of his attempt to go outside life. In realising and feeling that he is destroyed to the same degree that he destroys nihilistic values, the genealogist, like Hegel's criminal, effects a "return and rapprochement to himself": an acknowledgement of the life he shares with nihilistic forms of life.

This moment occurs at several points in the GM. At crucial junctures in the text, the standard of critique recoils upon the critic and the genealogist-narrator implicates himself in the traditions, values and figures he is criticising and opposing.[45] These moments undermine his standard of critique, and by robbing him of a standard or standpoint that is free from what he is criticising, they seem to undermine and invalidate the entire project of genealogy. But genealogy, and the need to oppose life-negation, does not stop here. These moments of *auto-implication* are coupled with the demand *to overcome Nihilism from within* in an open-ended movement of (self-)critique. This can be seen in what Nietzsche calls "the law of life" towards the end of the book. With this concept, Nietzsche inscribes the always provisional but interminable positing of law, necessary and impossible at once, within an open-ended movement of "self-overcoming":

> All great things go to ground through themselves through an act of self-sublation: that is the law of life, the law of *necessary* "self-overcoming" in the essence of life, – the lawgiver himself is always already exposed to the cry *"patere legem, quam ipse tulisti"*. (GM III 27, KSA 5, p. 410)[46]

When applied to the philosophical practice of genealogy, this law encapsulates a number of key claims Nietzsche makes. The first is that under nihilistic conditions, we cannot but take the side of life against life-negating forms of life and law. But to engage in an evaluation of values in the name of life requires normative standards, standards whose very form, as law, contradicts the life they purport to represent. They are necessary, but impossible, and must continually be overcome – in

---

45 To cite just one example: Having criticised the free spirits for 'standing too close to themselves', Nietzsche then goes on to say: "[...] in keiner Hinsicht sind sie gerade fester gebunden, im Glauben gerade an die Wahrheit sind sie, wie Niemand anders sonst, fest und unbedingt. Ich kenne dies Alles vielleicht zu sehr aus der Nähe" (GM III 24, KSA 5, p. 399).
46 "Alle grossen Dinge gehen durch sich selbst zu Grunde, durch einen Akt der Selbstaufhebung: so will es das Gesetz des Lebens, das Gesetz der *nothwendigen* 'Selbstüberwindung' im Wesen des Lebens, — immer ergeht zuletzt an den Gesetzgeber selbst der Ruf: 'patere legem, quam ipse tulisti'."

the name of life. Genealogy, then, confronts us with the necessity to engage in the qualitative evaluation different life-forms and values *in the name of life*, and with the inherently problematic nature of doing so. This is not a weakness, but a strength, in my view. To practice genealogy is to be all the time engaged with normative questions of an absolutely fundamental nature: What constitutes the quality, worth or value of a given form of (human) life? By what standard or law can we evaluate different forms of life? What standard or standpoint for evaluating different forms of law does *physis*, as the one and only reality, afford?

In this section I have focused on the philosophical quest for a life-immanent law shared by the young Hegel and Nietzsche of the *Genealogy of Morals*. At stake for both is the worth or *quality* of human life, its ruination under positive law (*die Zerstörung des Lebens*) and its recuperation through life-immanent law. In response to their critiques of positive law from a radically immanent standpoint in life, both thinkers delineate a form of law that is born of a criminal act and recoils upon the agent as his realisation that he is part of the very life he would destroy. This 'return and rapprochement to oneself' takes very different forms in each. For the young Hegel, it involves a form of reconciliation that he calls love: the realisation that relations to others are internal to our self-relation. Nietzsche's genealogist, by contrast, returns to himself with the realisation that he is complicit in life under nihilistic conditions. Under these conditions Hegel's recuperation of the *quality of life* under the horizontal morality of *Sittlichkeit* is no longer available. In its place, Nietzsche proposes an ethos of continuous *qualitative self-transformation* (*Selbst-Überwindung*) through the practice of genealogy, understood as the qualitative evaluation of different forms of life that opens and re-opens the fundamental questions of normativity.

References

Bernstein, Jay M. (2003): "Love and Law: Hegel's Critique of Morality". In: *Social Research: An International Quarterly of Political and Social Science* 70 (2), p. 393–432.
Busch, Thomas (1989): *Die Affirmation des Chaos*. St. Ottilien: EOS.
Geiger, Ido (2007): *The Founding Act of Modern Ethical Life. Hegel's Critique of Kant's Moral and Political Philosophy*. Stanford: Stanford University Press.
Gerhardt, Volker (1996): *Vom Willen zur Macht: Anthropologie und Metaphysik der Macht am exemplarischen Fall Friedrich Nietzsches*. Berlin and New York: De Gruyter.
Herschbell, Jackson/Nimis, Stephen (1979): "Nietzsche and Heraclitus". In: *Nietzsche-Studien* 8, p. 17–38.
Hölscher, Uvo (1977): "Nietzsche's Debt to Heraclitus". In: Robert R. Bolgar (Ed.): *Classical Influences on European Culture Vol III: 1650–1870*. Cambridge: Cambridge University Press, p. 339–348.

Pöggeler, Otto (1984): "Hegel, der Verfasser des ältesten Systemprogramm des deutschen Idealismus". In: Christoph Jamme/Helmut Schneider (Eds.): *Mythologie der Vernunft. Hegels ältestes Systemprogramm des deutschen Idealismus*. Frankfurt a.M.: Suhrkamp, p. 126–143.

Siemens, Herman W. (2002): "Agonal Communities of Taste: Law and Community in Nietzsche's Philosophy of Transvaluation". In: *Journal of Nietzsche Studies* 24 (Special Issue on Nietzsche and the Agon), p. 83–112.

Siemens, Herman W. (2006): "Nietzsche contra Liberalism on Freedom". In: Keith Ansel-Pearson (Ed.): *A Companion to Nietzsche*. Oxford and Malden, MA: Basil Blackwell, p. 437–454.

Siemens, Herman W. (2009): "(Self-)legislation, Life and Love in Nietzsche's Philosophy". In: Isabelle Wienand (Ed.): *Neue Beiträge zu Nietzsches Moral-, Politik- und Kulturphilosophie*. Fribourg: Press Academic Fribourg, p. 67–90.

Simmel, Georg (1968): "Das individuelle Gesetz. Ein Versuch über das Prinzip der Ethik" [1913]. In: Michael Landmann (Ed.): *Das individuelle Gesetz. Philosophische Exkurse*. Frankfurt a.M.: Suhrkamp, p. 174–230.

João Constâncio
Struggles for Recognition and Will to Power: Probing an Affinity between Hegel and Nietzsche

> Struggle is part and parcel of the process of recognition itself ... (Siep 1996, p. 278)

This paper is a first attempt to explore a controversial hypothesis, which can be stated like this: there is a deep affinity – hitherto largely unnoticed – between Hegel's conception of struggles for 'recognition' (*Anerkennung*) and Nietzsche's conception of the dynamics of 'will to power' (*Wille zur Macht*).

This hypothesis is likely to trigger reactions of immediate rejection and scepticism. For recognition seems to be by definition incompatible with any sort of 'will to power', especially if one conceives of recognition as involving reciprocal acknowledgement of rationality (as Hegel does), and hence more than just an affective reciprocity. When two subjects recognise each other as rational and thus interact and communicate with each other as equals (i.e. as equally rational), their relationship seems to cease to be one of power. And if one believes that in dealing with each other in this way – that is, as 'rational' agents –, the two subjects are not deluded, then one cannot at the same time believe that subjects or agents are in fact 'wills to power', or multiplicities of wills to power (i.e. of irrational 'drives'). In addition, the authority of Axel Honneth – the most prominent contemporary philosopher defending the (basically Hegelian) notion of 'recognition' – seems to speak clearly against the hypothesis here at stake. In his book, *The Struggle for Recognition*, Honneth refers to Nietzsche as basically a continuator of Hobbes: in trying to explain all human relations in terms of power, Nietzsche (like Hobbes) did not acknowledge the role of recognition in social relations (Honneth 1995, p. 93). Moreover, in his previous book, *The Critique of Power*, Honneth had already presented Nietzsche's conception of power as incompatible with an intersubjective (or 'recognitive') view of society by assimilating his position to Foucault's. Foucault's project, Honneth had claimed, should be seen as an attempt to "translate the naturalistically informed ideas of Nietzsche's theory of power into the framework of a theory of society" (Honneth 1991, p. 154).

It is, therefore, crucial that the meaning and the scope of my hypothesis of a 'deep affinity' are clearly stated from the start. First of all, my hypothesis is not that Hegel and Nietzsche 'say the same thing', nor that recognition and will to power have the same implications in all respects. My hypothesis concerns the ways in which *struggle, domination, and desire* are implied in the Hegelian notion of recognition, that is: it concerns *the intersubjective dynamics of failed-recognition*. My claim is that (contrary to Honneth's contention) Nietzsche's concept of will to power allows for an adequate description of these intersubjective dynamics of failed-recognition. We shall see that these dynamics are shaped by the recognitive nature of human desire and will, and characterised by what I shall call 'the paradox of domination'. We shall also see how Nietzsche interprets transitions from failed-recognition to reciprocal recognition among equals.

Secondly, it is perhaps important to underline from the start that force, violence, struggle, domination are crucial concepts in Hegel's whole conception of recognition – but they are *operative* concepts, whereas in Nietzsche they become thematic, because the concept of 'power' becomes thematic. Thus, the question raised here is not only whether Nietzsche's concept of power can contribute to clarify how "struggle is part and parcel of the process of recognition itself" (Siep 1996, p. 278), but also whether Nietzsche's notion of power is theoretically superior to Hegel's. If so, then I think that the hypothesis of an affinity between Hegel and Nietzsche regarding the dynamics of failed-recognition becomes highly relevant from a philosophical, theoretical perspective.[1]

Moreover, there should be no doubt that Nietzsche has a concept of recognition – if this means a concept of interpersonal and social relationships in which two or more subjects/persons/agents recognise each other as equals. (Note that, in spite of his professed efforts to de-subjectivise subjects, depersonalise persons, and reduce agents to mere associations of drives, Nietzsche never loses sight of the macroscopic or holistic perspective that considers particular associations of drives as organisms, therefore – broadly speaking – as 'agents', 'persons', 'subjects', even as 'human beings', 'individuals', etc.) For example, in a 'herd' community, Nietzsche believes, agents become really equal to each other, and they rejoice in the reciprocal recognition of their massified equality (the 'last men' – who perhaps 'wink' at each other in bovine contentment – are a particularly relevant case of this).[2] But in aristocratic com-

---

[1] One of the main inspirations of this paper was Brink/Owen 2007. My point is that, in spite of Honneth's dismissal of Nietzsche, the latter is in fact relevant for the debate on recognition and power because of his complex, sophisticated concept of power.

[2] I owe this remark – that perhaps the last men wink at each other – to Prof. Oswaldo Giacóia. I would also like to thank the following friends and colleagues for their criticisms and perceptive remarks on previous versions of this text: Maria João Branco, Herman Siemens, Katia Hay, John Richardson, Marco Brusotti, Christoph Schuringa.

munities, too, noble, aristocratic individuals "treat each other as equals" (BGE 259, KSA 5, p. 207). It should also be clear that Nietzsche emphasises that intelligent, conceptual, i.e. 'rational' communication is crucial for reciprocal recognition (e.g. HH I 446, GS 354, GM II 8). But he also argues that what is recognised as equal is *power*: states of reciprocal recognition are, for him, "equilibria of power" (WS 22, KSA 2, p. 555) in which the parties involved believe to have "approximately equal power" (e.g. HH I 92, D 112, BGE 259, BGE 260, GM I 10, GM II 2, GM II 8). A further question (which I cannot address in this paper), however, is whether Nietzsche may have overemphasised the role of power in all forms of reciprocal interaction and communication (including in the very formation and development of society) and whether Hegel's conception of *rationality* may be 'superior' to Nietzsche's.

Thirdly, what is at stake here is a *descriptive* affinity, not a normative one. It may be true, for example, that it is impossible to reconcile Nietzsche's negative normative assessment of the liberation of 'slaves' in modernity with Hegel's positive assessment – but this is beside the point of my hypothesis. My concern is to examine whether there is an affinity in the way in which Hegel and Nietzsche describe such liberation, and not in their respective normative assessments of it. Both Hegel and Nietzsche describe modernity as a time in which society evolves towards a maximum of equality – but they then assess this differently: as progress towards freedom in the form of reconciliation or reciprocal recognition in Hegel's case, and as *décadence* and weakening of our species' will to power in Nietzsche's case. But this is not the descriptive affinity that I have in mind: my claim is that there is an affinity at a deeper level, an affinity in Hegel's and Nietzsche's psychological and sociological descriptions of interpersonal and social relationships, an affinity in the way in which they describe not so much the final states of achieved recognition, equality or reciprocity, but in the way in which they describe the dynamics of the intersubjective processes and interactions which *fail* to reach reciprocal recognition.

I Hegel's Conception of Recognition

Let us begin by considering Hegel's famous description of a "life-and-death struggle" in the *Phenomenology of Spirit* (*PhS*). This struggle introduces the concept of recognition in the *PhS*, because it is the event which ultimately leads to a first form of one-sided, asymmetrical recognition – or rather failed-recognition, as we shall see: a relationship between a master and a slave, or a lord and his bondsman (*PhS* §187–189, TWA 3, p. 148–150).

The life-and-death struggle is Hegel's version of the state of nature (*Naturzustand*), as he explicitly points out in the *Encyclopedia* (*E III* §432, TWA 10, p. 221). It is a different state of nature from the one involved in social contract theory, particularly from the Hobbesian state of nature. In Hegel's depiction of a time before the existence of any social norms and institutions, there is no 'war of all against all', and the human beings living at that time are already social. For, as Hegel makes particularly clear in his early Jena writings, at the origin of society we should posit collective, communal affects, especially the affect of love among family members, and therefore also a social self, that is, a self (or 'I') already shaped by family ties, especially by pre-contractual ties of love – or, as he later famously writes: "an *I* that is a *We* and a *We* that is an *I*" (*PhS* §176, TWA 3, p. 145).³ And yet, if one wants to understand how society first emerged and gradually evolved from a pre-contractual, pre-institutional state to the present day – i.e. if one wants to understand the whole journey of the 'Spirit' from the primordial times in which human beings lived as nomad, primitive families to the times of the Spirit's (alleged) 'reconciliation' (*Versöhnung*) with itself in the modern world –, one has to conceive of a struggle among at least two of the individuals that lived in those primordial times. That is precisely the 'life-and-death struggle', a duel in which two individuals struggle to death, i.e. risk losing their lives, risk losing their natural, individual embodiment (*Leiblichkeit*), and they do this for the sake of *recognition*. But why should two individuals undertake such a struggle? And what exactly does it mean to struggle for 'recognition'?

According to the *Phenomenology*, each dueller wants to affirm himself, prove his worth, become certain of himself, become independent, and thus achieve consciousness of his freedom. This seems to be the 'desire' of each dueller as a 'self-consciousness' (or as a 'consciousness' that now wants to become conscious of itself). So, each dueller struggles for recognition because "*self-consciousness attains its satisfaction only in another self-consciousness*" (*PhS* §175, TWA 3, p. 144), or, in other words, "self-consciousness exists *in* and *for itself* because and by way of its existing in and for itself for another; i.e. it exists only as recognised" (*PhS* §178, TWA 3, p. 145). In order to affirm himself, prove his worth, become certain of himself, become independent, achieve consciousness of his freedom, each dueller needs to be recognised by the other. His self, his worth, his certainty of himself, his independence, his freedom have to become *intersubjective truths* – that is, facts acknowledged as such not only by

---

3 Cf. On this aspect of Hegel's Jena writings, see in particular Siep 1979, Williams 1992, Honneth 1995, Harris 1996, Williams 1997.

himself, but also by others within an intersubjective network of reciprocal recognition. Otherwise, all of that would continue to be a mere series of 'vanishing moments', Cartesian mental states without any substance, merely subjective, first-personal representations whose reality would remain to be proven. And that is – let us note – what happens to consciousness if its embodied desire only seeks satisfaction in *objects*: each successive object may perhaps satisfy embodied desire, but the moment it does so it is also negated, cancelled, nullified, consumed, and therefore it does not satisfy the *self-consciousness'* desire of self-affirmation, self-certainty, independence, and freedom. Only recognition by another *subject* can give this kind of satisfaction: "*self-consciousness attains its satisfaction only in another self-consciousness*".

On the other hand, the duellers are *from the start* social selves. Before they face each other and start to struggle, they are no Cartesian, solipsistic subjects or isolated self-consciousnesses that still need to prove the existence of other subjects and an outside world. If anything, in their duel they feel they need to prove the opposite, namely that their first-personal certainty *of themselves* is not a subjective illusion. To some degree, this is something they have already confirmed in the context of their family lives. The struggle for recognition in the life-and-death struggle already presupposes a minimal degree of recognition, a previous identification of their 'I' with a 'We', a previously constituted social identity. But this minimal degree of recognition was not struggled for, at least not in the kind of life-and-death struggle that Hegel takes to be paradigmatic of the struggles which lead to social change. Moreover, the self-affirmation that arises from recognition within the context of primitive family life is too parochial: it is not yet the self-affirmation of a self-consciousness as a self-consciousness, even less so as a person, as a citizen, or as a human being. Although the dueller already identifies with a 'We', his sense of self, independence, and freedom is still too weak not to be shaken, unsettled, disturbed, challenged by the presence of an 'other', a 'stranger' that comes from outside of the family. And this is precisely what launches the primordial life-and-death struggle. We can imagine that their self-understanding is that they are fighting for the honour of their respective clans, for example. Note again how different this is from Hobbes' war of all against all.[4]

---

[4] For a summary of the life-and-death struggle, see Williams 2012, p. 34–38 and 46–47. Williams also shows here that Deleuze's subjectivist interpretation of Hegelian recognition in his *Nietzsche* book is flawed (Williams 2012, p. 40–44). Deleuze's mistaken interpretation is probably responsible for many a scholar's presupposition that Hegelian struggles for recognition have nothing to do with Nietzsche. As for Hegel's critique of social contract theory, it must be noted that it goes

I will discuss how Hegel envisions a non-parochial, perfect – and perfectly reciprocal – form of recognition. We shall see how it is based on his conception of reason and rationality. But first, let us consider how the life-and-death struggle ends.

The result of a life-and-death struggle can be simply negative from the perspective of both contenders' aspiration to self-affirmation, self-certainty, independence, and freedom. If neither of the duellers consents at some point to being subjugated by the other, and both struggle to the actual death of one of them; if neither of them at some point *fears death* and prefers to preserve his life to continuing to risk it, then not even a minimal degree of reciprocal recognition will result from the struggle. The duel will have a survivor and a victor, but the former will not be able to continue seeking satisfaction in the other self-consciousness (for the other self-consciousness will have ceased to be a self-consciousness).

In order to conceive of a transition from the state of nature to society, one has to imagine another kind of result; not necessarily a positive result, but at least an *ambivalently* (and hence 'dialectically') negative result, one that involves some sort of progress and, at least, some sort of potential for self-subversion. We are thus invited to envision the possibility that the primordial life-and-death duel ends in a master/slave relationship. What this means, however, is that we are again invited to conceive of a struggle whose true purpose is recognition, but which does *not* end in recognition, especially *not* in reciprocal, perfect recognition (or reconciliation.) For a master/slave relationship is undoubtedly a *failure of reciprocal recognition*, a case of failed recognition: (a) the master does not recognise the other as another self, or as an equal and equally independent will, that is: he has, to some extent, become an 'independent self-consciousness', but he does not acknowledge the existence of the slave as another independent self-consciousness; (b) and the slave becomes a mere instrument of the master's self-consciousness, a 'thing', a 'dependent self-consciousness'. The slave fails to recognise his own self-consciousness as an independent self-consciousness that might acknowledge in the master the existence of *another* independent self-consciousness. Neither the independent self-consciousness of the master nor the dependent self-consciousness of the slave finds "*satisfaction* [...] *in another self-consciousness*" (*PhS* §175, TWA 3, p. 144).

---

well beyond what I say in this paper. For an excellent account, see Patten 2001. On Honneth's critique of "the atomistic, instrumental-rational assumptions concerning human agency" in social contract theory and, in particular, his rejection of the assumption that social conflict is simply based on the self-interested character of human beings, see Brink/Owen 2007, p. 3 ff., and Honneth 1995.

And yet this result is not *simply* negative. Firstly, because it is a relationship between two self-consciousnesses. In the master/slave relationship the slave is 'reified', but this reification is not absolute: the slave's self-consciousness has been negated, but it has not been annulled (as it would have been if the slave had died). The slave remains vulnerable and non-indifferent to the master, and his first-personal, subjective experience of dependence, inequality and alienation is in fact a new way of experiencing the need for recognition, i.e. the need to seek self-affirmation and "satisfaction" in another self-consciousness. (At least potentially, the relationship between the master and the slave remains *inter*subjective, for some room remains for the master to be susceptible, vulnerable, non-indifferent to the will of the slave, even if in a minimal degree. In Hegel's account, however, the burden of the 'dialectical' development of the story falls wholly on the side of the slave.)

Secondly, the master/slave relationship is in fact a first form of social organisation: a first institution and transition to society. The master/slave relationship puts an end to the sheer violence that prevailed in the *quasi*-Hobbesian state of nature of the life-and-death struggle. Undoubtedly, what is now institutionalised is an unequal relationship based on coercion, but the point is that this relationship has become *an intersubjective truth*. It is a social reality, and not a mere 'vanishing moment' in a person's self-consciousness.

Thirdly, the master/slave relationship is a *paradigm*, a *pattern of social change*. The origin and pattern of social change in general is not the 'social contract', but rather the master/slave relationship. Society develops by means of the institutionalisation of the results of struggles for recognition, the development of society is at first and for the most part a succession of struggles that, like the primordial life-and-death duel, lead (if not to destruction and sheer violence then) to successive institutionalisation of one-sided, asymmetrical, coercive, basically failed recognition. But each of these successive institutionalisation has in itself the seeds of its own self-subversion. The reason why, according to Hegel, absence of coercion, equality, and truly reciprocal recognition have slowly appeared and developed across human history is because elemental forms of the master/slave relationship have gradually and very slowly evolved and progressed into institutions of freedom. This progress has eventually made possible a full 'reconciliation' of the 'spirit' with itself in the modern, democratically organised world.

For our ends, the crucial point, however, is that the master/slave relationship is Hegel's way of conceptualising *domination*. And while this means that domination is tantamount to *failed-recognition*, it also means that domination is an asymmetrical, one-sided *power-relationship* in which a human will becomes the master of another human will and thus reifies this other will (or desiring self-consciousness). At the interpersonal level (which Hegel presents as paradigmatic by telling the story of the life-and-death duel), these wills are individual; at the social level they are collective (i.e., they are the 'wills' of classes, peoples, races, genders, etc.). Moreover, it should also be clear that domination as failed-recognition takes many forms, as for instance oppression, marginalisation, social exclusion, literal slavery, etc.

Most importantly, though, the master/slave relationship is Hegel's way of conceptualising the *symbolic mediation* which is involved in domination *qua* failed-recognition. If one of the primordial duellers had died (or if both had died), absolutely no progress would have been made in terms of the satisfaction of the self-affirmation of their self-consciousness, i.e. in terms of recognition. But in the master/slave relationship not only is the self-affirmation of the master mediated by the other (i.e. by the slave), but it is also symbolically mediated. For in the transition from the life-and-death struggle to the master/slave relationship a sheer, brute power-relationship has been transformed into a symbolically mediated power-relationship, i.e. into an interaction between two human wills which now involves intelligent, conceptual communication and indeed reciprocal acknowledgement and understanding of certain norms or rules of conduct. Being a master/slave relationship, the interaction between the two primordial duellers still rests on coercion, it has not become a free relation between them (for it can in no way be said to be *equally* consented by both) – but it has become a regulated interaction, even if only one-sidedly, unequally regulated. The slave has effectively *resigned himself* to being subjugated by the master: in the end, he considered his life to be at least as important as recognition and, unlike the master, preferred being enslaved than continuing to risk death. As Alexandre Kojève puts it, the master/slave relationship is a relationship of "authority" "founded on risk" (Kojève 2014, p. 16–18). Their interaction now presupposes the authority of the master, such that the latter no longer needs (or almost never needs) to use violence in order to be obeyed. Their interaction, though still based on coercion, is now mostly regulated by their identification with their new social roles, which reshape their innermost identities: one of them has indeed become 'the master', the other 'the slave'.

For Hegel, this means that there is *rationality* in the way social (and interpersonal) reality develops (and especially in the way it *progresses* towards freedom). Human social reality involves concepts and the mediation of norms or rules entailed by concepts. In fact, rationality is a crucial issue that concerns recognition already at the most elemental phenomenological level. In Hegel's phenomenology of self-consciousness, the ground of the assertion, "self-consciousness exists *in* and *for itself* because and by way of its existing in and for itself for another; i.e. it exists only as recognised" (*PhS* §178, TWA 3, p. 145), is ultimately the conception of the self-conscious individual as a *rational* subject. One is rational insofar as one is susceptible to reasons and acts in view of certain reasons to act. But in order to be rational one has to inhabit (to borrow Terry Pinkard's Sellarsian expression) a "space of reasons" (Pinkard 1994). And a space of reasons – a normative space – is always already a social space: it is precisely the kind of intersubjective space in which one is *recognised* as rational by other subjects. In such a space one is requested and 'summoned' to *give reasons* for one's actions: one thinks and acts as a being whose commitments and deeds have to have a purpose that fits with the purposes of others; one is confronted with arguments, aspirations, demands, claims that others make, with rules and laws in view of which one has to rationally justify what one has done, is doing or will do. One is, thus, recognised by others as rational while recognising others as rational, and this is how one *becomes* a human agent, a human knower and doer, the *rational* subject of one's thoughts and deeds. Subjectivity is thus made possible by intersubjective recognition.[5]

This is also a crucial part of Hegel's ideal of reconciliation, or perfectly reciprocal recognition and equality. Recognition remains parochial and imperfect as long as it fails to be a relation in which a rational subject recognises itself *in the other*, i.e. recognises the other not only as another subject, but also as a *rational* subject, and at the same time is recognised by the other as an equally rational subject. But in taking the other as a rational subject each rational subject does more than acknowledge a basic equality with the other. For each acknowledges also a difference: each is reciprocally affirmed as an equal, but also as an independent being, an independent self-consciousness. Recognition *qua* reconciliation designates a type of social or interpersonal relation in which each subject is reciprocally posited and affirmed as a universal 'I' (the 'I' of a rational subject), but also as a particular 'I' (an individual subject). In this type of reciprocal recognition, the 'I' of self-consciousness becomes a 'We' in a way that does not *limit* it at all. The other that is included in this 'We' is no longer an impediment or obstacle to the self-affirmation of the 'I', to its sense of worth, its self-certainty, its independence, its freedom. On the contrary, it has now become a *condition* of all that.[6] Indeed, this type of reciprocal recognition between rational subjects *qua* rational is, for Hegel, the ideal type of recognition. It entails an ideal of rational communication and rational *justification* of social norms. In a

---

[5] See especially Terry Pinkard's and Robert B. Pippin's accounts of recognition in: Pinkard 1994 and 2012, Pippin 2008 and 2011.
[6] This is the fundamental difference between Hegelian and Fichtean recognition: see Siep 1979, Pippin 2008, and especially Williams 1992, p. 63–64, 78, 82–83, 88–89.

sense, Hegel's project is ultimately the project of rational justification of the modern world and the modern institutions of freedom. The modern state, the modern institusionalisation of equal rights, democracy, etc. represent, for him, not only the overcoming of domination by means of reciprocal recognition, but also (and most crucially) the justification of such an overcoming in terms of reciprocal recognition of rationality.[7]

The rationality at stake here is not the pure rationality of a Cartesian or a Kantian subject. It is rather the rationality of embodied self-consciousness, and indeed of a desiring self-consciousness ("self-consciousness is *desire* [Begierde]", *PhS* §174, TWA 3, p. 143). Hegelian recognition is primarily a theory of *desire*, and it describes the transition from animal desire to a properly human type of desire. The latter type differs from animal desire for being wholly shaped by intersubjectivity and recognition. As Kojève has famously shown, part of Hegel's point in his phenomenology of self-consciousness is that human desire is "directed toward a non-natural object", namely toward "desire itself" (Kojève 1980, p. 5). Human desire has always *the other's desire* as its object. Human subjects, unlike the other animals, desire to be desired – that is, to be requited and hence properly *recognised* by the other. They seek "*satisfaction* [...] *in another self-consciousness*" (*PhS* §175, TWA 3, p. 144). This drives them to recognise the other, that is, to recognise the other's desire. And this, in turn, changes the nature of every possible object of desire appearing within the social space inhabited by human subjects: objects that would otherwise be "perfectly useless from a biological point of view (such as a medal or the enemy's flag)" (Kojève 1980, p. 6, 3–30) become objects of desire because they are desired by others. In cases of perfect, reciprocal recognition among rational subjects, intersubjective interaction becomes *free*: no one is now being coerced to do anything – coercion magically disappears from the realm of human self-consciousness and desire. Or, in other words, true recognition depends on a *Freigabe*: the parties involved let each other be and thus set each other free from any form of coercion.[8] Thus, human interactions become ethical (*sittlich*), reconciliation is achieved and domination is sublated into freedom.[9]

Let us now move to a first approximation to Nietzsche's hypothesis of the will to power. Most interpretations of this hypothesis take it to imply that in all

---

[7] This is the dimension of recognition highlighted by Pippin throughout Pippin 2008. For Hegel's views on reconciliation and the stages that lead to personal, moral, and social freedom in the modern world, see Hardimon 1994, Neuhouser 2000 and 2008.
[8] See Williams 1997, p. 84–88.
[9] For Hegel's complex views on freedom and the historical stages of the realisation of freedom, see: Hardimon 1994, Neuhouser 2000 and 2008, Losurdo 2004 and Pippin 2008.

forms of human interaction behaviour is motivated by an individualist, egoistic drive to possess or dominate the other, and therefore the occurrence of reciprocal recognition in human interaction is always illusory: even in the case of love, no recognition of the otherness of the other is ever possible. If, however, we look at what Nietzsche has to say precisely about love we may begin to realise how subtle his conception of 'power' and interaction in terms of 'will to power' really is.

II Nietzsche on Love and the Impossibility of 'Possession'

There are many passages in which Nietzsche gives an account of love in terms of power. For example, in *The Gay Science*, particularly in the aphorism *The things people call love*, he presents love as a feeling which cannot be adequately distinguished from greed (*Habsucht*): love, he claims, is about "possession", about assimilating the other "*into ourselves*", and sexual love is most clearly a "craving for new property", a will to gain "unconditional power" over the other's body and soul, a "greedy desire" which is perhaps "the most candid expression of egoism", but which is certainly not "the opposite of egoism" (GS 14, KSA 3, p. 386).

However, the question is, of course, what Nietzsche actually means by 'power' when he writes that love is a will to gain power over the other. The following aphorism from *Beyond Good and Evil*, for example, makes clear that Nietzsche does not conceive of power as tantamount to physical and violent possession of another:

> Human diversity is apparent not only in the variety of tables of goods – which is to say the fact that they consider different goods worthwhile and that they disagree with each other as to the more or less of values, the rank order of common acknowledged goods: –diversity is much more evident in what they think counts as actually *owning* and *possessing* a good. When it comes to a woman, for instance, a more modest person might consider disposal over her body and sexual usage as sufficient and satisfactory signs of possession, of ownership. Someone else with a more suspicious and demanding thirst for possession will see the "question-mark" here, the fact that this is only the appearance of possession; such a person will want to examine more closely in order to be particularly clear as to whether the woman will give not only herself to him, but also give up what she has or wants for the sake of him –: only this will count as "possession" for him. But even *this* would not satisfy the mistrust and possessive desires of a third person, who asks himself whether the woman who gives up everything for his sake is not doing this for some sort of a fantasised version of him. He wants to be thoroughly (even meticulously) well known before he is

able to be loved at all; he does not dare to let anyone figure him out –. He will not feel that he possesses his beloved fully until she harbours no illusions about him, until she loves him just as much for his devilishness and hidden inexhaustibility as for his goodness, patience, and spirituality. (BGE 194, KSA 5, p. 115–116)

Here, Nietzsche conceives of love between a man and a woman in terms of possession and power, and yet he immediately makes clear that he considers physical possession to be merely "the appearance of possession". The second lover in this story – who has "a more suspicious and demanding thirst for possession" than the first and sees a "question-mark" in the idea of possession – worries because he has no proof that he truly possesses the woman. In order to feel that he truly possesses her, he needs her to "give up what she has or wants for the sake of him". He needs a sacrifice from her as a sign of possession because he feels that otherwise he cannot be sure of having power over her. This means that he worries about what is behind her signs of love, in fact that he worries about how he is *perceived* and *desired* by her. In some confused way he realises that in striving to possess her, he is striving to possess her entire being or, more precisely, her "will" – and this would have to involve being perceived by her as the object of her desire. That is precisely the logic of Hegel's conception of human desire as recognitive. Given that human desire has the other's desire as its object, it becomes a desire to be recognised by the other that cannot dispense with also recognising the other, i.e. his or her desire.

The case of the third lover in Nietzsche's aphorism obeys this same logic of recognition, and his is of course the most interesting case. He goes a step further than the second lover because he feels that in order to truly possess the woman he has to reveal to her *his* whole being. Instead of demanding a sacrifice from the woman, he demands a sacrifice from himself. For he forces himself to the painful effort of revealing himself to her without the protection of a social mask: "until she harbours no illusions about him, until she loves him just as much for his devilishness and hidden inexhaustibility as for his goodness, patience, and spirituality". And this is, again, the perfect logic of desire as a struggle for recognition. In order to gain possession of her desire, he feels he must be fully recognised by her – even in his darkest features – and the more he achieves this, the more he recognises *her* in return. What troubles him is the possibility that she might have a "fantasised version of him". So he renounces his pride and makes himself known to her in order to be properly recognised by her, i.e. properly perceived and desired by her. The more he achieves this, the more he can be said to be under her influence – that is to say, the more powerful she has become in relation to him.

And this is not yet the end of the story. The third lover *risks* everything in order to increase his power over his beloved. For the sake of full possession, he risks losing the degree of possession he has already achieved. This accords with Nietzsche's repeated assertion that the dynamic of the 'will to power' – and of desire as 'will to power' in particular – is not a dynamic of *preservation*, but rather of self-overcoming and hence of risk, as we shall see in in the next section.

Thus, just like Hegel, Nietzsche opposes hedonism and especially the thesis that human action is motivated by a homeostatic drive to preserve states of pleasure and avoid states of pain. For Nietzsche, pleasure is basically a collateral effect of the attainment of power. We feel pleasure when we overcome a *resistance* to our will to power, and this explains the psychological fact that we often *seek* pain. As 'wills to power', we often seek to confront ourselves with resistance – painful resistance – in order to overcome our current degree of power and feeling of power.

The case of the third lover in the aphorism from *Beyond Good and Evil* makes clear that love as a "greedy desire" to possess the other is "will to power". In seeking "possession" the lover is led to realise that the other resists possession, but this is precisely what makes him *seek* resistances and risk everything. Because he feels powerless he seeks more power –regardless of the pain that this may bring him. He is caught in the dynamics of the will to power; the dynamic of "growth", "self-overcoming", and the need for more and more power.

What this also implies is that, although a *feeling* of possession is possible, and growing tired of what one *believes* to possess is a common phenomenon (cf. GS 14), *true possession is impossible*. As the third lover's power over the woman augments, her power over him also augments. In such a case as this one, both parties (i.e. both centres of power or force) increase their power over one another. Even if in the process one of them becomes temporarily more powerful than the other and is basically 'commanding' while the other is 'obeying', 'resistance' remains. For resistance, as we shall see in more detail in the next section, is of the essence of power and the feeling of power.

In *Gay Science*, Nietzsche expresses the impossibility of true possession by means of a concept which he borrowed from Ancient philosophy and which, as he was very well aware, played an important role in modern Physics: the concept of 'action at a distance'. Gravity and magnetism are supposed to be instances of this sort of action. In both cases, a physical body attracts another physical body without touching it, as if a force or power within the former were acting upon a force or power within the latter. Roger Boscovich – whose influence on Nietzsche can hardly be overestimated – generalised this idea in

Physics and tried to prove that physical bodies are in reality centres of power or force and all action is 'action at a distance' among such centres of power or force. As Nietzsche's *Nachlass* makes crystal clear, his conception of the 'will to power' incorporates this idea.[10]

Nietzsche uses this concept to describe relations among men and women in §60 of *Gay Science*: "The magic and the most powerful effect of women is, to speak the language of the philosophers, action at a distance, *actio in distans*" (GS 60, KSA 3, p. 425). We should link this to Nietzsche's praise of Stendhal's definition of beauty as *a promise of happiness*. Beauty acts at a distance, as an object of perception that promises something beyond itself, as a perceptual sign of a happiness that appears to be hidden behind it. The lover's drive to possession is, as it were, a drive to break into the other's will and desire, a drive to overcome the resistance that is still preventing him from conquering what he perceives as the possible source of his happiness. The feeling of power emerges from overcoming or expecting to overcome such a resistance. And this means overcoming the *perception* of resistance.

Let us now attempt to systematise the conception of power that is presupposed here and which Nietzsche tries to grasp with the hypothesis of the 'will to power'.

III Nietzsche's 'Will to Power'

Although, as mentioned above, Axel Honneth assimilates Nietzsche's conception of power to Hobbes' and Foucault's and claims that Nietzsche's hypothesis of the will to power is incompatible with recognition, in a footnote of his book on power he makes an important remark: Nietzsche's conception of power, unlike Foucault's, was originally based on a "doctrine of dispositions" (Honneth 1991, p. 322, n. 9), that is, in a doctrine of the *affects*. This is indeed true. The "will to power" is "an affect" (NL 1885/86, KSA 12, 2[151], p. 140), a "*pathos*" (NL 1888, KSA 13, 14[79], p. 259), "the primitive form of affect" (NL 1888, KSA 13, 14[121], p. 300), so that Nietzsche defines his morphology of the will to power

---

10 Cf. NL 1883, KSA 10, 12[27], p. 404; NL 1885, KSA 11, 34[247], p. 503 and NL 1885, KSA 11, 36[31], p. 563: "The physicists cannot eliminate 'action at a distance' from their principles, nor a force of repulsion (or attraction)". See Hesse 1962; Poellner 2000, p. 48–57; Gori 2007, p. 103f.; Branco 2010, p. 258f. and Branco 2011. In his conception of the will to power, Nietzsche accepts Boscovich's critique of materialistic atomism, based on the concept of action at a distance, and intends to use it as a model for his critique of the "atomism of the soul" (BGE 12, KSA 5, p. 26–27).

(*Morphologie des Willens zur Macht*) as a morphology of the affects (*Morphologie der Affecte*).[11] This immediately seems to mark an important difference from what we can find in Foucault. Nietzsche's philosophy is a "psychology" (BGE 23, KSA 5, p. 39), it considers our "soul" (BGE 12, KSA 5, p. 27), our *subjective* life – the *psychē* –, even if, it is a psychology that understands itself as a "doctrine of the affects [*Affektenlehre*]" (NL 1888, KSA 13, 13[2], p. 214) and considers our subjective life from the perspective of how the *body* is *affected*. This is an important fact that is often overlooked. Although Nietzsche is very critical of the concept of subject, and although his philosophy clearly presupposes the possibility of third-person perspectives, he may still be said to preserve the concept of subjectivity because, like Schopenhauer, he also does philosophy 'along the guiding thread of the body' (*am Leitfaden des Leibes*), that is, along the guiding thread of the first-personal, subjective experience of the body – the psychological experience of being a body *from within*.[12]

So, the question is whether Nietzsche's *psychological* approach – his philosophy as psychology, his "physio-psychology" as a "morphology and *doctrine of the development of the will to power*" (BGE 23, KSA 5, p. 38) – implies a conception of power that is fundamentally different both from Hobbes' and Foucault's, as well as whether his conception of power might be helpful for a description and understanding of mutual recognition (instead of being inexorably *opposed* to the possibility of mutual recognition). For this to be so, Nietzsche's conception of power will have to fulfil at least two conditions: (a) it must not entail that power is a function of an egoistic drive for preservation (as in Hobbes' conception), (b) it must not entail that power is tantamount to domination – and least of all to social control as a trans-subjective form of domination (as in Foucault's conception). My argument in the following is that even a brief sketch of Nietzsche's conception of power shows that it fulfils both conditions.

The hypothesis of the will to power concerns, first of all, our *drives* (*Triebe*). It assumes that, in our experience of ourselves, "we cannot get down or up to any 'reality' except the reality of our drives" (BGE 36, KSA 5, p. 54) and, hence, it posits (hypothetically) a multiplicity of such drives as what constitutes what we

---

[11] Cf. NL 1886/87, KSA 12, 6[26], p. 243–244; NL 1888, KSA 13, 12[1], p. 196; NL 1888, KSA 13, 13[2], p. 213–214; NL 1888, KSA 13, 14[72], p. 254 and NL 1888, KSA 13, 14[136], p. 320.
[12] See Constâncio 2011. On philosophising "along the guiding thread of the body" (*am Leitfaden des Leibes*), see NL 1884, KSA 11, 26[374]; NL 1884, KSA 11, 26[432]; NL 1884, KSA 11, 27[27]; NL 1885, KSA 11, 36[35]; NL 1885, KSA 11, 37[4]; NL 1885, KSA 11, 39[13]; NL 1885, KSA 11, 42[3]; NL 1885/86, KSA 12, 2[68]; NL 1885/86, KSA 12, 2[70]; NL 1885/86, KSA 12, 2[91]; NL 1885, KSA 11, 40[21], p. 638–639 ("Ausgangspunkt vom Leibe und der Physiologie"), NL 1886/87, KSA 12, 5[56], p. 205–206.

are. These drives perceive, interpret, build perspectives about themselves, about each other and about the so-called external world (an idea that is already present in D 119 and D 129). Being an elemental perception, interpretation and perspective, each drive is, at the same time, an 'affect'. In as much as it is *perceiving*, a drive is thereby *affected* by what it perceives and how it perceives it. This allows Nietzsche to describe the body as "a society constructed out of many souls" (BGE 19, KSA 5, p. 33), i.e. of many drives and affects that perceive, interpret, build perspectives, and at the same time to conceive of the "soul" as a way of describing the body: the "soul" is conceived as "a society constructed out of drives and affects" (BGE 12, KSA 5, p. 27), i.e. as a "smart body" that perceives, interprets, builds perspectives. Within the context of the hypothesis of the will to power, Nietzsche's conception of what is traditionally called 'soul' and 'body' is *adualistic* and, more than that, it involves a double-aspect theory of body and soul (i.e. it sees body and soul as two aspects, or two possible descriptions, of the same reality).[13]

Drives and affects are not necessarily conscious, and only some of them *become* conscious in the form of thoughts, desires and passions (cf. D 115, BGE 36). Not only conscious desires and passions, but especially conscious thoughts (which involve conceptualisations) are "*only a certain behaviour of the drives towards one another*" (GS 333, KSA 3, p. 559), or "only a relation between these drives" (BGE 36, KSA 5, p. 54). All forms of the properly human consciousness are, in sum, just a "surface" and a "sign" of unconscious drives and affects (cf. D 125, GS 354, BGE 19 and BGE 32, EH Smart 9).

Thus, subjectivity becomes, for Nietzsche, decentred subjectivity. One can only still speak of the "soul" if one understands "soul as subject-multiplicity" (BGE 12, KSA 5, p. 27). That there is no "subject" does not mean that there is no subjectivity (or intersubjectivity): it means, rather, that there is no fixed centre, no unchanging conscious 'I' or ego in our subjective (and intersubjective) lives. We are a multiplicity of drives and affects, an interplay of unconscious relations among "under-souls" (BGE 19, KSA 5, p. 33) and of fragmented conscious expressions of these relations. Assuming that all of the elements of this multiplicity *compete and struggle* with each other, we should conceive of our subjectivity as constructed out of drives and affects (of "under-wills or under-souls", BGE 19, KSA 5, p. 33) that are "wills to power": "*Man as a multiplicity of 'wills to power': each one with a multiplicity of means of expression and forms*" (NL 1885/86, KSA 12, 1[58], p. 25).

According to the hypothesis of the will to power, we can say that a person is *one* person – or that his/her being has *unity* – only if we think of unity as an

---

[13] On Nietzsche's "adualism", see Abel 2001, Constâncio 2011; on Nietzsche's double aspect theory, see Stack 1983, Constâncio 2013a.

"*organisation* and *connected activity*" among a multiplicity of drives and affects, i.e. as "a *formation of rule* which *means* 'one' but *is* not one" (NL 1885/86, KSA 12, 2[87], p. 104–105). Likewise, we can still say that a person has a will or even that a person *is* a will (for example, a "strong will" or a "weak will"), but only if we understand this 'will' as the (always provisional and non-substantial) result of the "*organisation* and *connected activity*" of his/her drives: for example, a 'strong will' will be the result of a well-stabilised – but not unconditionally stable – 'order of rank' among the drives (i.e. a 'formation of rule' built around a 'dominant drive'), a 'weak will' will be the *decadent* result of an 'anarchy of the instincts', etc.

If we take Nietzsche's contention seriously, namely that "the deed is everything" and there is no "indifferent substratum" behind a person's deeds (GM I 13, KSA 5, p. 279), then the unity of a person – *her* 'will', the "*formation of rule* which *means* 'one' but *is* not one" – never exists as such before it is expressed in deeds (and therefore can only be known in retrospect).[14]

Nietzsche's conception of power should, first of all, be understood from the viewpoint of this whole conception of our subjectivity in terms of a multiplicity of drives that struggle with each other but that, in this struggle, are also able to coordinate and establish orders of rank among them. Drives are indeed 'wills to power' ("our drives can be reduced to the *will to power*", NL 1885, KSA 11, 40[61], p. 661); every drive seeks power for itself, "every drive craves domination [*ist herrsüchtig*]" (BGE 6, KSA 5, p. 20)", or, as Nietzsche also puts it: "Every drive is a kind of lust for domination [*Herrschsucht*], each has its perspective, which it would like to impose as a norm on all the other drives" (NL 1886/87, KSA 12, 7[60], p. 315). But the power of each drive depends on its *relation* to the power of the other drives. Power is *relational* – it occurs only *among a multiplicity* of wills to power.

This means that for there to be power, there has to be the kind of reality that perceives, interprets, builds perspectives, and this kind of reality has to be "*efficacious* [wirkend]" (BGE 36, KSA 5, p. 55). Power is the way efficacious wills relate to other efficacious wills; it is a function of the "causality of the will" (BGE 36, KSA 5, p. 55), i.e. of how this kind of causality operates among a multiplicity of wills that relate to each other. If we think of this at the macroscopic level of *persons*, that is, of interpersonal and social relations as relations among 'syn-

---

[14] On Nietzsche's 'expressivism', see Pippin 2010b and 2015. For Hegel, too, "what the subject *is*, is the series of its actions" (*PR* §124, TWA 7, p. 233), and therefore no Cartesian introspection can reveal the subject, i.e. the subject can only be known in retrospect through her deeds (see also, for example, *PR* §343, TWA 7, p. 504: "the history of spirit is its own *deed*; for spirit is only what it does and its deed is to make itself"). On Hegel's 'expressivism', see Pippin 2008. On Nietzsche's critique of introspection (or "self-observation"), see Constâncio 2013b.

thetic' wills, power is the way in which persons are *reciprocally affected* by each other, power is what happens in *intersubjective* relations (each 'subject' being a 'subject-multiplicity'). When Nietzsche writes that "everything is will against will [*alles ist Wille gegen Willen*]" (NL 1886/87, KSA 12, 5[9], p. 187), he means precisely this: from the most elemental forms of organisation of our bodies to the most complex forms of interpersonal and social relationships there are only *subjective and intersubjective multiplicities whose elements affect each other*. That is why the will to power is an *affect* or *pathos*.

Being the effect of relations among wills, power is also *relative*. As Henning Ottmann has put it, a "monopoly of power [*Machtmonopol*]" is impossible: all power is a mixture of power and lack of power or, in other words, power is always a matter of *degree* (Ottmann 1999, p. 358). A will to power is a will to domination (i.e. a will to power wills *auctoritas*, not just *potentia* and not just *possibilitas*), but domination as absolute domination or 'possession' is impossible. What Honneth calls "the reductionist idea of a one-sided rule of force" to be found in Foucault (Honneth 1991, p. 175) is not even a possibility for Nietzsche. At the level of social relations, Nietzsche is not at all interested in describing social control as a comprehensive form of trans-subjective, one-sided domination, but rather in describing intersubjective relations that involve an interplay and mixture of mastery and vulnerability. A crucial case in point is, of course, Nietzsche's own dialectic of the master and the slave in the *Genealogy*. What Nietzsche describes here is how the slave is *affected* by the oppression of the master, and in such a way that the hatred of his impotence – his *ressentiment* – eventually creates new values (i.e. a new *intersubjective* stance), and then, in the end, these values *affect* and defeat the master by instilling a bad conscience in his *intersubjective* relation with the slave.

The reason why, according to Nietzsche, power is relational, intersubjective, and relative is because *resistance* is of the essence of power and the will to power: "A will to power can only express itself against *resistances*" (NL 1887, KSA 12, 9[151], p. 424). A will to power presupposes a multiplicity of forces or spheres of power that *resist* each other. Even the most asymmetrical or hierarchical relations of power presuppose resistance and, indeed, *reciprocal resistance*:

> to dominate is to endure the counterweight of the weakest force, it is thus a form of *continuing* the struggle. To obey is likewise a *struggle*: as long as a force of resistance *remains*. (NL 1884, KSA 11, 26[276], p. 222)[15]

---

15 "*Herrschen* ist das Gegengewicht der schwächeren Kraft ertragen, also eine Art *Fortsetzung* des Kampfs. *Gehorchen* ebenso ein *Kampf*: so viel Kraft eben zum Widerstehen *bleibt*."

This conception of power as a function of reciprocal resistance is also crucial in Nietzsche's *rejection* of the interpretation of the will to power as an egoistic drive for self-preservation. Nietzsche clearly distinguishes the will to power from a Spinozistic 'will to existence' (cf. BGE 13, GS 349) and from a Darwinian 'struggle for existence' (cf. GS 349; NL 1885, KSA 11, 34[208], p. 492), as well as from a Schopenhauerian 'will to live' (cf. Z II Self-Overcoming, KSA 4, p. 147). A will to power is a will that always wants to *overcome itself*, to go beyond itself, to grow or expand its power (cf. GS 349). Nietzsche's hypothesis of the will to power entails the endorsement of a theory of action that emphasises risk and value over prudence and coercion – just like Hegel's. Let's look closer at Nietzsche's notion of risk.

To say that a will to power wants to grow or expand means that it wants to overcome itself, and this means that it wants to *overcome resistances*. For this reason, a will to power will always *seek* resistances that it can try to overcome, and hence, it will often *risk itself*, that is, risk and sacrifice *life itself*, for the sake of more power (i.e. for the sake of an empowerment of what it values):

> To wish to preserve oneself is a sign of distress, of a limitation of the truly basic life-instinct, which aims at the *expansion* of power and in so doing often enough risks and sacrifices self-preservation. (GS 349, KSA 3, p. 585)[16]

One of the main implications of this idea is that, if we understand the concept of an egoistic drive for self-preservation as a homeostatic drive that motivates us to always seek pleasure and avoid pain (i.e. if a theory of action based on the idea of self-preservation entails hedonism), then the hypothesis of the will to power is certainly most opposed to it. In risking itself by seeking resistances that it may overcome, a will to power will often seek *pain* for the sake of self-overcoming (cf. GM III 28; NL 1888, KSA 13, 14[174]). Accordingly, pleasure is merely a collateral effect of the achievement of power, or (more precisely) of the *feeling* of power. Pleasure occurs not because it is what we seek as animals allegedly

---

16 "Sich selbst erhalten wollen ist der Ausdruck einer Nothlage, einer Einschränkung des eigentlichen Lebens-Grundtriebes, der auf *Machterweiterung* hinausgeht und in diesem Willen oft genug die Selbsterhaltung in Frage stellt und opfert." See also Z II Self-Overcoming. Note that all I am trying to establish is that the dynamics of will to power entails risk and is therefore no less at odds with the dynamics of self-preservation than the Hegelian dynamics of a struggle for recognition. It may however be true that Hegel's conception of risk has another implication, which seems to be absent from Nietzsche's conception. Hegel believes that the fact that human beings are capable of risking death for the sake of recognition sets the human species categorically apart from the animal kingdom (i.e. risking death for the sake of recognition is a way of demonstrating one's humanity qua non-animality). I thank Christoph Schuringa for pointing this out to me.

driven by an egoistic drive for self-preservation, but rather because our drives, as wills to power, make us feel an increase in power when they overcome painful resistances. It is perhaps useful to quote just two typical passages in which Nietzsche expresses these ideas very clearly:

> What is a pleasure other than a stimulation of the feeling of power by an obstacle (more strongly still by rhythmical obstacles and resistances) – leading it to swell? Thus, every pleasure includes pain. – If the pleasure is to become very great, the pain must be very long and the tension of the drawn bow prodigious. (NL 1885, KSA 11, 35[15], p. 514)[17]

> The will to power as *life* / Man does *not* seek pleasure and does *not* avoid unpleasure: it will be clear which famous prejudice I am contradicting here. Pleasure and unpleasure are mere consequences, mere accompanying phenomena – what man wants, what every smallest part of a living organism wants, is an increment of power. Striving for this gives rise to both pleasure and unpleasure; out of that will man seeks resistance, needs something to oppose him. Unpleasure, as an inhibition of his will to power, is thus a normal fact, the normal ingredient of everything that happens in the organic world, and man does not avoid it but instead has constant need of it: every conquest, every pleasurable feeling, everything that happens presupposes a resistance overcome. (NL 1888, KSA 13, 14[174], p. 360)[18]

The idea that a will to power is capable of risking itself implies that a will to power is moved by whatever it *values* and not by self-preservation. Drives, as wills to power, are 'estimations of value' (*Werthschätzungen*), a drive differs from another drive for valuing a different goal than the one valued by another drive (that is why, say, the drive for knowledge and the drive for sex are not the same). To say that a will to power is capable of risking its own life while seeking (painful) resistances is tantamount to saying that its striving for more power often leads to a self-destructive, self-sacrificing pursuit *of what it values*. But, more importantly, this implies that a *person* as an association of coordinated

---

17 "[W]as ist eine Lust anders als: eine Reizung des Machtgefühls durch ein Hemmniß (noch stärker durch rhythmische Hemmungen und Widerstände) – so daß es dadurch anschwillt. Also in aller Lust ist Schmerz einbegriffen. – Wenn die Lust sehr groß werden soll, müssen die Schmerzen sehr lange, und die Spannung des Bogens ungeheuer werden."

18 "Der Wille zur Macht als *Leben*/ Der Mensch sucht *nicht* die Lust und vermeidet *nicht* die Unlust: man versteht, welchem berühmten Vorurtheile ich hiermit widerspreche. Lust und Unlust sind bloße Folge, bloße Begleiterscheinung, – was der Mensch will, was jeder kleinste Theil eines lebenden Organismus will, das ist ein plus von Macht. Im Streben danach folgt sowohl Lust als Unlust; aus jenem Willen heraus sucht er nach Widerstand, braucht er etwas, das sich entgegenstellt. Die Unlust, als Hemmung seines Willens zur Macht, ist also ein normales Faktum, das normale Ingredienz jedes organischen Geschehens, der Mensch weicht ihr nicht aus, er hat sie vielmehr fortwährend nöthig: jeder Sieg, jedes Lustgefühl, jedes Geschehen setzt einen überwundenen Widerstand voraus."

and hierarchised drives is capable of risking herself and even sacrificing her own life for the sake of what is valued by her "dominant drive".[19]

Thus, the hypothesis of the will to power does *not* imply that all our actions are *egoistic* – it implies, rather, that the terms 'egoistic' and 'altruistic' are too simple to describe the nature of our actions. Given that a person is an association of drives, given that, as Nietzsche puts it in *Human, All Too Human*, the individuum is in reality a "*dividuum*" (HH I 57, KSA 2, p. 76), what usually counts as an un-egoistic action is in reality an action that results from the fact that a given person "loves *something of herself*, an idea, a desire, an offspring, more than *something else of herself*, that she thus *divides* her nature and sacrifices one part of it to the other" (HH I 57, KSA 2, p. 76). On the one hand, we should say that that action is not really un-egoistic – for it is motivated by the need for satisfaction of the drive that values the idea, desire or offspring at stake (i.e. the action still refers back to the agent).[20] But, on the other hand, the action is also not simply egoistic – for something of the person (some drive or constellation of drives) is really sacrificed *for the sake of* the idea, the desire or the offspring that is valued by the dominant drive. Nietzsche does not deny that self-sacrifice and altruism, at least in some *degree*, are possible. In a posthumous note from 1881, for example, he writes that we live in "a culture of altruism" and "by virtue of habit one thinks of the existence of the other before thinking of one's own (e.g. the prince thinks first of the existence of the people, the mother of the son)" (NL 1881, KSA 9, 11[199], p. 521). Put differently, all human actions are in some sense self-referential and hence 'egoistic', but (a) no human action is 'egoistic' in the usual sense of being motivated by the self-interest and the drive for preservation of a stable, fixed ego and (b) our divided self (the "*dividuum*" that we are) is many times organised around drives that value other people (or even communities of people) and make us act for the sake of other people (or even for the sake of a community, a country, etc.). The ego of ego-ism is, at best, a "synthetic concept" (BGE 19, KSA 5, p. 33) that emerges at the mere surface of our being, and in fact "the great majority [...] do nothing for their ego their whole life long: what they do is done for the phantom of their ego which has formed itself in the heads of those around them and has been communicated to them" (D 105, KSA 3, p. 92–93). On account of the plasticity of our being

---

19 As suggested above *en passant*, Nietzsche believes that a person's drives always organise and coordinate around a (more or less stable) "dominant drive" or "dominant instinct": see GM II 2; GM III 8; CW 8; NL 1885/86, KSA 12, 1[61], p. 26; NL 1887/88, KSA 13, 11[322], p. 136–137; NL 1888, KSA 13, 23[2], p. 600–601.
20 See, for example, HH I 133, HH I 138, D 105, GS 13.

as decentred subjects (or 'subjects-multiplicities', *dividua*), we are prone to value other people as well as goals that we share with them and try to achieve in cooperation with them, so that we are actually prone to develop identities (non-fixed and unstable identities) that are co-determined by the way in which we are affected and changed by other people. (The task of 'setting up a real ego' seems to be a task for the exceptions, for 'higher types' and 'sovereign individuals'.)[21]

As we can see, Nietzsche's assertion that all social and interpersonal relations are power-relations implies the *rejection* of every version of the Hobbesian conception of society as a collection of stable, individual wills seeking their own preservation and pleasure, as well as of any doctrine that assumes that cooperation among individuals must necessarily be motivated by fear, prudence, caution or some similar self-seeking affect. According to Nietzsche, individual wills (or persons as synthetic unities of multiplicities of wills to power) are *divided*, *plastic*, and always already *social* wills that want self-overcoming, not pleasure and self-preservation, and, therefore, they easily become part of collective spheres of power, they easily cooperate with each other, and they easily identify with collective interests in ways that make them risk their pleasure and individual existences for the sake of what they value the most at a given point in time. The best example of this is true friendship as "a kind of continuation of love in which this greedy desire of two people for each other gives way to a new desire and greed, a *shared* higher thirst for an ideal above them" (GS 14, KSA 3, p. 387).

That is not to say that it is impossible for a drive for self-preservation to *ever* become the "dominant drive" in an individual, nor does Nietzsche deny that, in some circumstances, a community of human beings *might* be wholly constituted by subjects that simply struggle for self-preservation and survival. But, as mentioned above, he holds that "the struggle for survival is only an *exception*, a temporary restriction of the will of life" (GS 349, KSA 3, p. 585). The best example of such an exception would perhaps be the life of prisoners in a concentration camp as described by Primo Levi in his book, *If this is a man*. But in any normal form of social life – where there are family ties, communal values, reciprocal rights and duties, and at least minimal levels of security, health, and nutrition – no one is really dominated by a drive for self-preservation.

It can, of course, be argued that in a struggle for self-preservation what comes to the fore is our "animal instincts" (GM II 22, KSA 5, p. 332), the "old instincts" of the hunter-gatherer and "all those instincts of wild, free, prowling

---

21 See Gemes 2006.

man" (GM II 16, KSA 5, p. 322). It should indeed be clear that Nietzsche's hypothesis of the will to power includes the idea that these "bad drives" and the "affects of hatred, envy, greed, and power-lust" are "the conditioning affects of life", they fundamentally and essentially need to be present in the total economy of life, and consequently need to be enhanced where life is enhanced (BGE 23, KSA 5, p. 38). But the hypothesis of the will to power does not *reduce* our psychology to these aggressive, 'bad' drives and affects, nor does it view them as some sort of ultimate core of our being, our 'true', hidden nature. For it is a hypothesis about the *development* (BGE 23, KSA 5, p. 38) of such drives and affects; about how, for example, "everything we call 'high culture' is based on the spiritualisation and deepening of cruelty" (BGE 229, KSA 5, p. 166); and about how human beings become plural and complex beings in such a way that each is indeed a "*multiplicity of wills to power*" (NL 1885/86, KSA 12, 1[58], p. 25), and the modern soul has become "a heap of contradictions" (NL 1887, KSA 12, 9[183], p. 446).

This kind of 'development' (e.g. "spiritualisation and deepening") consists, in part, in the development of new customs, norms, rights, and duties in social life. And these are ways of valuing that involve symbolically mediated interactions at the 'surface' level of consciousness. The instinctive, unconscious values of our drives play a crucial role in shaping the kind of power-relations that are at the basis of all interpersonal relationships and social life, but the "surface- and sign-world" (GS 354, KSA 3, p. 590) of consciousness – particularly of customs, norms, rights, and duties – also plays such a crucial role. For Nietzsche, consciousness is the surface that arises from our ability to formulate concepts and words, for concepts and words (according to this view) express subterraneous relations among the drives, and then also cause changes in these subterraneous relations. Even more importantly, Nietzsche believes that concepts and words (or consciousness and language) do not belong to "man's existence as an individual, but rather to the community- and herd-aspects of his nature" (GS 354, KSA 3, p. 590). Consciousness (together with language) is the "connecting net" that allows human beings to form communities by communicating with each other on the basis of symbols or "communication-signs" (GS 354, KSA 3, p. 590). Customs, norms, rights and duties are, of course, a crucial part of such a net. Therefore, these ways of valuing that involve symbolically mediated interactions are indeed as important for the very existence of society as other forms of valuing that are pre-symbolic and pre-conceptual.

However, even pre-symbolic, pre-conceptual power-relations are in some sense mediated. For, according to Nietzsche, all power-relations presuppose *distance*: 'action at a distance'. For there to be power a will must be able to affect another will at a distance, as the earth seems to affect the moon (while also being affected by the moon) without physical contact or impact. A multiplicity of wills to power is a multiplicity of wills acting and being acted upon (or being affected by) other wills at a distance. Therefore, all power-relations depend on perceptions, perspectives and interpretations – even if these occur merely at the unconscious (or purely affective) level of drives and instincts. Asymmetrical power-relations (e.g. between master and slave) will often result from violence and coercion, but even in such cases the power-relation depends on the *threat* of further violence and, therefore, on the perception of power and the estimate of a superior quantity of power. Moreover, a will may exert power over another will without any violence or coercion, as we saw in the case of sexual love: "The magic and the most powerful effect of women is, to speak the language of the philosophers, action at a distance, *actio in distans*" (GS 60, KSA 3, p. 425).

This is why Nietzsche asserts that the will to power is a 'pathos' or an 'affect', that is to say, a being affected by the perception of resistance and, thus, a being affected at a distance. Even in the relation between a master and a slave, the slave's will is never absolutely owned by the master: for as long as the power-relation is maintained, the slave's will, or his 'will to power', continues to resist the master's will, or his 'will to power', 'at a distance'. The elimination of resistance and of the perception (or recognition) of resistance at a distance would eliminate the power-relation itself. Therefore, absolute possession is impossible and domination is a paradox, for the less resistance there is, the less there is to take possession of and dominate.[22]

Thus, in stating that all social relations are power-relations Nietzsche is implying that all social relations hinge upon a given "equilibrium" (WS 22, KSA 2, p. 555) of "recognised and guaranteed degrees of power" (D 112, KSA 3, p. 101). It is not power as brute force that holds a society together, but rather a multiplicity of symbolically mediated interactions in which reciprocal *recognition* of different degrees of power occurs. Already at the level of purely interpersonal relationships, a minimum of *recognition* of another will *as* another will is part of every power-relation, even of the most asymmetrical, anisotropic power-relations. To put it in terms of the master/slave relation: the master does not take the slave as a person, he does not relate to the slave as an equal at all, but

---

[22] HH I 93 describes a perfect example of this paradox. If a besieged town is utterly destroyed, the conquerors will not be able to exert power over the town. In order to exert power, they need an opposing force over which they can exert power. And since the besieged town is able to threaten with self-destruction, it still has this last threat as a source of resistance and, therefore, of power. This minimum of resistance and power is enough to force a process of *equalisation*, a process from which a certain *equilibrium* of forces emerges.

he *feels* at least a minimum of *resistance* from the part of the slave, that is, he *recognises* a minimum of power on the part of the slave. And the slave, of course, feels forced to resign himself to being subjugated to the master because he estimates the other options as worse than being subjugated to the master and, hence, *recognises* the superior power of the master's position.

Such interpersonal relations as the one between the master and the slave are, however, always already embedded in larger nets of symbolically mediated power-relations, that is, in a society consisting of such relations. As Volker Gerhardt has shown, Nietzsche's theory of society even includes the argument that, since power-relations are mediated by perceptions, perspectives, interpretations, conceptualisations, communication-signs, norms, rights, duties, etc., the equilibrium of power in a society always depends on some sort of "symbolic understanding" or "agreement" among its members,[23] i.e. on a "compact" (HH I 446, KSA 2, p. 290) based on reciprocal *power-recognition*.[24]

At first, the concept of reciprocal "recognition" of different degrees of power within a power-equilibrium seems to be something wholly different from the Hegelian reciprocal recognition of oneself 'in the other', especially since the latter form of recognition involves a change in the status of the other such that he or she ceases to be an obstacle to one's freedom and becomes a condition thereof. But this difference is relativised once we consider that reciprocal recognition of different degrees of power within a power-equilibrium can be understood as an alternative description of recognition of oneself 'in the other' because, as we just saw, it refers to an *intersubjective* equilibrium of power – the difference being that persons are here re-described as 'wills', 'spheres of power', 'subjects-multiplicities' constructed out of drives which are 'wills to power', etc.. (The question raised in this paper is precisely how fruitful this re-description can be.) Moreover, this objection would only be valid if Nietzsche's conception only acknowledged asymmetrical power-relations – but that is not at all the case. He believes that there are *symmetrical power-relations,* equilibria of power in which the parties involved recognise each other as *equals*, that is, in which a will recognises another will as equally powerful and hence a person recognises another person *as an equal*, or *as a person of more or less equal power and standing* (e.g. BGE 259, BGE 260, GM I 10, GM II 2). Thus, just as Hegel describes the

---

[23] Gerhardt 1988, p. 104. The idea of HH I 446, KSA 2, p. 290, is "Ohne Vertrag kein Recht."
[24] This does not preclude Nietzsche from being as critical of the liberal social contract theory as is Hegel: see BGE 257, GM II 17. Note that their reasons for rejecting such a theory are, to a great extent, very similar: they both reject the liberal notion of asocial (or pre-social) "selves" or "subjects". See Owen 1995 and 2008, Siemens 2015.

most elemental and rough forms of reciprocal recognition as instances of *mis*recognition – or failed-recognition – and the most complete and perfect forms of recognition as developments of such elemental and rough forms, so Nietzsche describes asymmetrical and symmetrical relations of power-recognition in a way that makes us question whether every development and transition from failed-recognition and inequality to recognition and equality could and should be re-described in terms of developments and transitions from asymmetrical power-relations to symmetrical power-relations.

In the following section I will summarise this interpretation of Nietzsche's conception of power, making explicit its connection with Hegel's conception of struggles for recognition. I will also briefly outline possible continuations and developments of this research on power and recognition.

IV Will to Power and Recognition

Nietzsche understands power neither in the pejorative sense of control based on violence, nor in the pejorative sense of control based on fraud. Moreover, the de-subjectivised definition of power that Honneth believes he can ascribe not only to Foucault but also Nietzsche – namely "success in a situation of struggle" (Honneth 1991, p. 161, 196–198) – also fails to account for the fact that Nietzsche sees power as power of a 'will' over another a 'will'. For him, "the question" is "whether we believe in the causality of the will" and "*this* belief is really just our belief in causality itself" (BGE 36, KSA 5, p. 55). This makes him develop an *intersubjective* conception of power (although every 'will' is always already a synthesis of a multiplicity of 'under-wills' or drives; each unity of the 'will' is to be seen only as a coordination among 'under-wills' that forms itself at the very moment in which a deed is being done, and never before or independently of that). So, not only does his conception of power involve a "diversity of power relations" and a "multiplicity of competing subjects rather than [...] one subject holding power" (Honneth 1991, p. 155), but it also never entails a model of "trans-subjective" power-relations, i.e. it never ceases to suggest that social and interpersonal relationships are basically intersubjective power-relations, that is, power-relations based on reciprocal perceptions, perspectives, and interpretations. Moreover, these relations are, for Nietzsche, symbolically mediated, and they are often relations of cooperation among equals – which also differentiates Nietzsche's conception of power-relations from Foucault's.

We can thus define power (*Macht*) as *influence* of a 'will' over another 'will', i.e. as *intersubjective influence*. Insofar as power always emerges from an interplay of 'will against will', and in this interplay each 'will' wills domination, power is never just a matter of possibility (*possibilitas*) and capacity (*potentia*), but also of domination (*auctoritas*). Or, put differently, intersubjective influence is always a given *degree of authority* of a will over another will. As Kojève remarks, "authority is necessarily a *recognised* authority" (Kojève 2014, p. 8) or, in Nietzsche's language, authority is 'action at a distance', for relations of authority are "relations of supremacy [*Herrschaftsverhältnisse*]" (BGE 19, KSA 5, p. 34), i.e. relations of command and obedience. And these are necessarily based on reciprocal awareness, i.e. reciprocal perceptions, perspectives, and interpretations.[25] According to Kojève, "authority is the *possibility* that an agent has of *acting* on others (or on another) without these others *reacting* against him, despite being *capable* to do so" (Kojève 2014, p. 8). An agent A has authority over another agent B iff A does not need to use force or violence in order to make B do X, and iff B's awareness of being commanded by A to do X does not make him react against doing X. Nietzsche, I think, would agree – but not entirely. For, although strictly speaking B does not 'react against' doing X, it is still the case, according to Nietzsche, that B, being a 'will', *offers resistance* to A, and hence, sets a limit to the self-affirmation and supremacy of A.

This is a crucial point not only because it entails that domination is never absolute, but also because it explains why domination always contains in itself the seeds of its self-undermining and self-subversion. We saw this in section II. with the example of sexual love. In the stories of the three lovers (BGE 194), the resistance offered by the woman shows, first, that possession is impossible and, second, it shows how the will to dominate can be gradually undermined by that resistance and eventually subverted into some sort of equality between the man and the woman, that is, into a symmetrical power-relation among equals. So, here a relationship of failed-recognition finally leads, in a series of steps and stages, to something at least akin to a state of 'reconciliation' or reciprocal recognition. But we also saw how the social plasticity of our self makes it prone to cooperation, that is, how reciprocal resistance and vulnerability among human subjects makes it easy for them to identify with common, shared goals and cooperate (and even coalesce) with each other in the pursuit of such goals. One of the examples that we considered was how sexual love between two persons becomes a cooperative friendship when it is transformed into "a *shared* higher thirst for an ideal above them" (GS 14, KSA 3, p. 387). Here, again, what

---

[25] Cf. the expression *Herrschaftsverhältnisse*, which Kaufmann rightly translates as "relations of supremacy"; Norman's translation ("power relations") is less literal, and also less precise.

at first was only mutual vulnerability and failed-recognition finally leads to reconciliation (the 'I' becomes a 'We').

But let us finally compare these conclusions with what we saw about Hegelian struggles for recognition:

(i) Both in Hegel's conception of struggles for recognition and in Nietzsche's conception of will to power a dynamics of interpersonal and social interaction is identified which entails risk and breaks with the usual model of interaction motivated by a drive for preservation.
(ii) Both conceptions presuppose an intersubjective space of interaction, indeed of reciprocal self-affirmation and will to dominate. Note that this is not a matter of *one-sided* need for approval. Hegelian struggles for recognition are always reciprocal, that is, truly intersubjective: a struggle for recognition only occurs when *both sides* struggle to see their worth and their very sense of self acknowledged. In Nietzsche, the case of love also showed how such *reciprocal* and *recognitive* struggles for affirmation can be conceived in terms of 'will to power'.[26]
(iii) Both Hegel's conception of struggles for recognition and Nietzsche's conception of will to power presuppose and express (although in different ways) the thesis that the human self is always already social. Indeed, both emphasise the *plasticity* of individuality. (What Nietzsche rejects is Hegel's conviction that 'rationality' is the basic criterion for distinguishing more parochial from more universal identifications of the 'I' with a 'We').
(iv) Both conceptions imply, also, that processes of reciprocal self-affirmation entangle the agents involved in the impossible task of coercing recognition. What I've emphasised in section I. is that, according to Hegel, while a struggle for recognition lasts, there is always an element of *power* (or *force*) – although not necessarily of direct, physical violence – in the intersubjective interaction that is taking place. In the primordial life-and-death duel and in all the struggles that fundamentally repeat its pattern, the parties involved directly use violence to try and coerce recognition from each other. Their will to self-affirmation has become a *will to dominate* the other – a will to find "satisfaction in another self-consciousness" by means of coercion. They behave towards each other in the same way as every desiring consciousness behaves towards a thing, namely in a desire to dominate,

---

26 See again Robert R. Williams's critique of Deleuze's misinterpretation of Hegel on this crucial point: Williams 2012, p. 39. For recognition understood as mere one-sided approval and criticised by Nietzsche for being typical of gregarious natures, see e.g. BGE 206.

even to consume, possess, assimilate the other (i.e., they relate to another subject as if it were an object.) Only a *Freigabe*, only a renunciation to the will to dominate the other, can transform failed-recognition into genuine, reciprocal recognition. Nietzsche, too, describes the dynamics of failed-recognition by conceiving of a dynamics of intersubjective will to dominate (or 'will to power') in which at least one of the parties involved tries to coerce recognition. His analysis of love shows that he, too, believes that only some sort of *Freigabe* can lead to mutual recognition.

(v) What this means is that both Hegel's conception of struggles for recognition and Nietzsche's conception of will to power entail what I have called 'the paradox of domination'.[27] The basis of this paradox is the fact that it is impossible to coerce recognition. This fact means that no absolute stabilisation of a relation of domination is ever possible because as long as the dominated party is still alive and is still a subject (i.e., a self-consciousness, even if only a 'dependent self-consciousness'), the relation of domination contains in itself the seeds of its self-undermining and self-subversion. Or, in Nietzsche's terms, it is of the essence of the dominated party's "will to power" to *resist* being dominated by the other party, and this ensures that their interaction has always in itself the seeds of self-subversion. The paradox itself is that, this being so, the more a subject succeeds in dominating another subject, the less it succeeds in dominating him/her *as a subject*. For the other subject becomes less of a subject if he/she is dominated and, therefore, treated as a "thing", a "slave" deprived of an independent will.[28] Nietzsche's treatment of love in *Beyond Good and Evil* is, again, a very good example of this paradox.

(vi) Finally, both conceptions try to explain not only how failed-recognition works, but also how and why failed-recognition can go through processes of self-undermining and self-subvert into successful, reciprocal recognition (*reconciliation*). As mentioned from the start, this last point is, however, where Hegel and Nietzsche also differ more substantially. For Hegel, the *Freigabe* that makes reconciliation possible consists in the reciprocal recognition of rationality. Nietzsche acknowledges that intelligent communication, symbolical mediation, perhaps even agreement and compromise (which seem to involve reason) are crucial for reciprocal recognition among

---

27 One of the inspirations of this paper was Robert B. Pippin's work on what he calls "the paradoxes of power": see Pippin 2010a.

28 See Benjamin 1996, p. 209: "if I completely control the other, then the other ceases to exist, and if the other completely controls me, then I cease to exist."

equals. But for him, the transition from failed-recognition to reciprocal recognition is a transition from an asymmetrical power-relation to a symmetrical power-relation in which the reciprocal recognition *of rationality* does not seem to play any crucial role – at least not in a Hegelian sense, where the other person ceases to be a limitation to my freedom because I recognise her as a rational subject and she recognises me as a rational subject, etc.

Even so, the main points that I have tried to convey in this article seem to me to sufficiently establish that there is a deep affinity between Hegel's conception of struggles for recognition and Nietzsche's hypothesis of the will to power. If that is true, then there is a whole panoply of Nietzschean themes that need to be revisited in the light of that affinity:

(i) The most obvious case is the Nietzschean "dialectic" of master and slave in *Beyond Good and Evil* (BGE 46, BGE 62, BGE 195, BGE 199, BGE 260, etc.) and, especially, in *On the Genealogy of Morality* (GM I and *passim*). A thorough comparison between Hegel and Nietzsche on the master/slave relationship is yet to be attempted. This should include a consideration of Robert B. Pippin's suggestion that *On the Genealogy of Morality* ought to be read as "something like *The Phenomenology [of Spirit], Part Two*" (Pippin 2008, p. 280–281; cf. Williams 2012).

(ii) Nietzsche's conception of the *agon* should be revisited in the light of the insight that his conception of power entails the conception of domination as potentially self-undermining and self-subverting. This insight seems to me to be particularly interesting for the re-interpretation of Nietzsche's conception of the noble type and aristocratic communities, as well as of other kinds of relationships among equals. Of the 'sovereign individual', for example, Nietzsche says that it is part of its nature to always feel "reverence", "respect" (*Ehrfurcht*) for its "equals" (GM II 2, KSA 5, p. 295), and even of the nobles of the First Essay of the *Genealogy* he says that when they are each other's enemies their reciprocal enmity is "already a bridge to love" (GM I 10, KSA 5, p. 273).

(iii) More generally, the possibility of there being a "deep affinity" between Nietzsche and Hegel on intersubjectivity and recognition (and especially on the intersubjective dynamics of desire, struggle, conflict, and domination, i.e. of failed-recognition) calls for a reinterpretation of Nietzsche's views on society, the state of nature, the social contract, etc. Nietzsche's early conception of society as basically a multiplicity of equilibria of power (WS 22) and his conception of rights and duties in terms of "recognised degrees of power" (D 112) are particularly important for this end. Equally important are his mature views on the 'herd-instinct' and how individuals are 'disciplined and cultivated' by values and norms which promote the interest of the 'herd' (i.e. of the community, society, etc) and not of the individual. If my interpretation of the will to power is correct, then this "discipline and cultivation [*Zucht und Züchtung*]" is still intersubjective and not (like Foucault's 'disciplines') *trans-subjective*. (This is a crucial issue for our view of Nietzsche either as a modern or a postmodern thinker. If he is a modern thinker, then he believes that there could be an individual and collective emancipation from the kind of "discipline and cultivation" that has existed so far, i.e. from "the gruesome rule of chance and nonsense" that "has passed for 'history' so far", as he puts in BGE 203, KSA 5, p. 126; if he is a postmodern thinker, he believes that there is no possible subject, neither individual nor collective, that could carry out such emancipation.)

(iv) Another crucial theme is consciousness and the social nature of our divided, decentred self. There are many passages in Nietzsche that confirm that he conceives of the self as social, but, besides that, the most important text which he actually published on consciousness, namely §354 of *Gay Science*, is focused on the claim that communication among the members of a community is a necessary condition of consciousness, and therefore consciousness is a social, not an individual phenomenon. This clearly calls for a dialogue with Hegel and his intersubjective phenomenology of self-consciousness.[29]

(v) §354 of *Gay Science* seems to treat consciousness exclusively from a third-personal perspective, but, as I have argued elsewhere,[30] Nietzsche's double-aspect approach to the problem of consciousness does not exclude the first-personal perspective. Like Schopenhauer, Nietzsche conceives of the third- and the first-personal perspectives as complementary. For the question on the relationship between his concept of power and the concept of power implied in Hegelian struggles for recognition, it is clearly important to interrogate why and in which sense his hypothesis of the will to power is not only about power considered from a third-personal perspective, but also about *the feeling* of power considered from a first-personal perspective. For this feeling of power seems to be occasioned by social and interpersonal relationships and to be intrinsically intersubjective.

(vi) Finally, and as indicated above, both Hegel and Nietzsche describe modernity as a time in which society evolves towards a maximum of equality. But

---

29 See Siemens 2015, Constâncio 2015.
30 See Constâncio 2011 and 2013a.

Hegel sees this historical development as progress towards freedom as reconciliation, i.e. towards reciprocal recognition, whereas Nietzsche sees it as *décadence*. To a great extent, this development towards equality and *décadence* consists, for Nietzsche, in the fact that the human being has become a "herd-animal"; individuals have become mere "functions of the herd" (GS 116, KSA 3, p. 475). As such, they are 'actors', and modern societies are *societies of actors* (cf. GS 356 and 361) in which each agent tries to identify absolutely with her role in society, i.e. with what she thinks others expect of her. In return, each agent identifies the other with the role the other has in society. As societies of actors, modern societies are *intersubjective spaces of reciprocal misrecognition*. This is certainly part of Nietzsche's conception of the *last man* and the nihilism of *last men*, even more so if we see (as I think we should see) the last man as Nietzsche's nightmarish vision of a future humanity deprived of any sense for the tragic. For Nietzsche conceives of the sense for the tragic not only as a sense for the finitude of the individual, but also as a sort of care for our collective existence and destiny as a species, and particularly as a species marked by finitude. The sense for the tragic unites mankind around the image of "its own imminent shipwreck as *a whole*", and thus, around something "altogether universal and suprapersonal", which is "the human as such" (RWB 4, KSA 1, p. 453). Should we not see in this "sense for the tragic" and care for "the human as such" – which is the opposite of the bovine contentment of the last men and their reciprocal misrecognition – Nietzsche's ultimate positive conception of *reciprocal recognition*?

References

Abel, Günter (2001): "Bewußtsein – Sprache – Natur: Nietzsches Philosophie des Geistes". In: *Nietzsche-Studien* 30, p. 1–43.
Benjamin, Jessica (1996): "Master and Slave: The Bonds of Love". In: John O'Neill (Ed.): *Hegel's Dialectic of Desire and Recognition*. New York: SUNY, p. 209–222.
Branco, Maria João M. (2010): "Arte e Filosofia no Pensamento de Nietzsche". Diss., Lisbon: Faculdade de Ciências Sociais e Humanas, Universidade Nova de Lisboa.
Branco, Maria João M. (2011): "Nietzsche on Metaphor, Musicality, and Style. From Language to the Life of the Drives". In: João Constâncio/Maria J.M. Branco (Eds.): *Nietzsche on Instinct and Language*. Berlin and New York: De Gruyter, p. 35–59.
Brink, Bert van den/Owen, David (Eds.) (2007): *Recognition and Power: Axel Honneth and the Tradition of Critical Social Theory*. Cambridge: Cambridge University Press.
Constâncio, João (2011): "On Consciousness: Nietzsche's Departure from Schopenhauer". In: *Nietzsche-Studien* 40, p. 1–42.

Constâncio, João (2013a): "Towards a 'Morphology of the Will to Power': Notes on Nietzsche's Conception of Philosophy as 'Psychology'". In: M. Filomena Molder/Diana Soeiro/Nuno Fonseca (Eds.): *Morphology: Questions on Method and Language*. Bern, Berlin, Brussels, Frankfurt a.M., New York, Oxford and Vienna: Peter Lang, p. 247–275.

Constâncio, João (2013b): "On Nietzsche's Conception of Philosophy in *Beyond Good and Evil*: Reassessing Schopenhauer's Relevance". In: Marcus A. Born/Axel Pichler (Eds.): *Texturen des Denkens: Nietzsches Inszenierung der Philosophie in "Jenseits von Gut und Böse"*. Berlin and New York: De Gruyter, p. 145–164.

Constâncio, João (2015): "Nietzsche on Decentered Subjectivity or, the Existential Crisis of the Modern Subject". In: João Constâncio/Maria J.M. Branco/Bartholomew Ryan (Eds.): *Nietzsche and the Problem of Subjectivity*. Berlin and New York: De Gruyter (forthcoming).

Gemes, Ken (2006): "Nietzsche on Free Will, Autonomy and the Sovereign Individual". In: *Aristotelian Society Supplementary* 80, p. 321–338.

Gerhardt, Volker (1988): "Das 'Prinzip des Gleichgewichts'. Zum Verhältnis von Recht und Macht bei Nietzsche". In: Volker Gerhardt (Ed.): *Pathos und Distanz. Studien zur Philosophie Friedrich Nietzsches*. Stuttgart: Reclam.

Gori, Pietro (2007): *La Visione Dinamica del Mondo, Nietzsche e la filosofia naturale di Boscovich*. Naples: Edizioni La Città del Sole.

Hardimon, Michael O. (1994): *Hegel's Social Philosophy: The Project of Reconciliation*. Cambridge: Cambridge University Press.

Harris, Henry S. (1996): "The Concept of Recognition in Hegel's Jena Manuscripts". In: John O'Neill (Ed.): *Hegel's Dialectic of Desire and Recognition*. New York: SUNY, p. 233–252.

Hesse, Mary B. (1962): *Forces and Fields. The Concept of Action at a Distance in the History of Physics*. New York: Dover.

Honneth, Axel (1991): *The Critique of Power, Reflective Stages in a Critical Social Theory*. Translated by Kenneth Baynes. Cambridge, MA and London: MIT Press [German edition: Suhrkamp 1985].

Honneth, Axel (1995): *The Struggle for Recognition. The Moral Grammar of Social Conflicts*. Translated by Joel Anderson. Oxford: Polity [German edition: Suhrkamp 1994].

Kojève, Alexandre (1980): *Introduction to the Reading of Hegel. Lectures on the* Phenomenology of Spirit. Assembled by Raymond Queneau, edited by Allan Bloom, translated by James H. Nichols. Ithaca and London: Cornell University Press [French edition: Gallimard 1947].

Kojève, Alexandre (2014): *The Notion of Authority (A Brief Presentation)*. London and New York: Verso [French edition: Gallimard 1942].

Losurdo, Domenico (2004): *Hegel and the Freedom of Moderns*. Durham and London: Duke University Press.

Neuhouser, Frederick (2000): *Foundations of Hegel's Social Theory*. Cambridge, MA: Cambridge University Press.

Neuhouser, Frederick (2008): "Hegel's Social Philosophy". In: Frederick C. Beiser (Ed.): *The Cambridge Companion to Hegel and Nineteenth-Century Philosophy*. New York: Cambridge University Press, p. 204–229.

Ottmann, Henning (1999): *Philosophie und Politik bei Nietzsche*. 2nd improved and extended edition. Berlin and New York: De Gruyter.

Owen, David (1995): *Nietzsche, Politics and Modernity*. London: Sage.

Owen, David (2008): "Nietzsche, Ethical Agency and the Problem of Democracy". In: Herman Siemens/Vasti Roodt (Eds.): *Nietzsche, Power and Politics*. Berlin and New York: De Gruyter, p. 143–167.

Patten, Allen (2001): "Social Contract Theory and the Politics of Recognition in Hegel's Political Philosophy". In: Robert R. Williams (Ed.): *Beyond Liberalism and Communitarianism: Studies in Hegel's Philosophy of Right*. New York: SUNY, p. 167–184.
Pinkard, Terry (1994): *Hegel's Phenomenology. The Sociality of Reason*. Cambridge: Cambridge University Press.
Pinkard, Terry (2012): *Hegel's Naturalism. Mind, Nature, and the Final Ends of Life*. Oxford: Oxford University Press.
Pippin, Robert B. (2008): *Hegel's Practical Philosophy. Rational Agency as Ethical Life*. Cambridge: Cambridge University Press.
Pippin, Robert B. (2010a): "The Paradoxes of Power in the Early Novels of J.M. Coetzee". In: Anton Leist/Peter Singer (Eds.): *J.M. Coetzee and Ethics*. New York: Columbia, p. 19–41.
Pippin, Robert B. (2010b): *Nietzsche, Psychology, & First Philosophy*. Chicago and London: University of Chicago Press.
Pippin, Robert B. (2011): *Hegel on Self-Consciousness. Desire and Death in the Phenomenology of Spirit*. Princeton and Oxford: Princeton University Press.
Pippin, Robert B. (2015): "The Expressivist Nietzsche". In: João Constâncio/Maria J.M. Branco/Bartholomew Ryan (Eds.): *Nietzsche and the Problem of Subjectivity*. Berlin and New York: De Gruyter (forthcoming).
Poellner, Peter (2000): *Nietzsche and Metaphysics*. Oxford: Oxford University Press.
Siemens, Herman (2015): "Nietzsche's socio-physiology of the self". In: João Constâncio/Maria J.M. Branco/Bartholomew Ryan (Eds.): *Nietzsche and the Problem of Subjectivity*. Berlin and New York: De Gruyter (forthcoming).
Siep, Ludwig (1979): *Anerkennung als Prinzip der praktischen Philosophie: Untersuchungen zu Hegels Jenaer Philosophie des Geistes*. Freiburg: Alber.
Siep, Ludwig (1996): "The Struggle for Recognition: Hegel's Dispute with Hobbes in the Jena Writings". In: John O'Neill (Ed.): *Hegel's Dialectic of Desire and Recognition*. New York: SUNY, p. 273–288.
Stack, George J. (1983): *Lange and Nietzsche*. Berlin and New York: De Gruyter.
Williams, Robert R. (1992): *Recognition: Fichte and Hegel on the Other*. New York: SUNY.
Williams, Robert R. (1997): *Hegel's Ethics of Recognition*. Berkely, Los Angeles and London: University of California Press.
Williams, Robert R. (2012): *Tragedy, Recognition, and the Death of God*. Oxford: Oxford University Press.

Maria João Mayer Branco
The Song of the Sirens: Nietzsche and Hegel on Music and Freedom

Nietzsche's criticism of idealism is well-known, as is his hostility towards Hegel and the Hegelian tendency to systematise reality. Nietzsche often declared his rejection of systematic philosophy, and his own works try to put forth an alternative to the philosophic systems conceived by German idealists.[1] Such an alternative way of thinking and conceiving philosophy is closely linked with Nietzsche's suspicions about language and the linguistic formulation of thoughts that seem to be in total opposition to Hegel's praise of the concept and of the philosophical effort of conceptualisation.[2] In this paper I will try to show that such differences between Nietzsche and Hegel can be clarified by paying attention to the interest they both devoted to music. By exploring this affinity, I will try to understand in what way and for what reasons music was important for each of them. Furthermore, I will try to show that their interest in music brings to light a decisive concept in both their philosophies, namely the concept of freedom. More precisely, I will argue that an analysis of their interest and love for music contributes not only for the clarification of Nietzsche and Hegel's understanding of the relation between language and philosophy (or between language and thought), but also – and perhaps even more decisively – that it clarifies a significant aspect of this art, in particular the connection between music and freedom.

As has recently been shown,[3] modern German philosophy from Kant onwards paid special attention to music. It is as if, from early German Idealism to the Critical Theory of the Frankfurt School, most thinkers sensed an affinity between music and philosophy that they would seek to explore with several, and sometimes even opposed consequences for the understanding of philosophy as well as for the understanding of music. Indeed, this attention did not always consist of a mere praise of music, it rather revealed ambivalent considerations about the effects that this art has on its listeners. Thus, if, on the one hand, modern German philosophers stressed the way in which music is free

---

[1] See, for example, TI Maxims 26, KSA 6, p. 63: "I mistrust all systematisers and avoid them. The will to a system is a lack of integrity."
[2] On Nietzsche's critique and use of language, see Constâncio/Branco 2012.
[3] See, especially Bowie 2007 and Hermand/Richter 2006.

from representation and concepts, on the other hand they also focused on the dangers of music, namely that it deprives the listener of his/her independence of and freedom from what he/she is listening to.

This is true for Nietzsche and Hegel's considerations about music. Their *musicophilia* goes hand in hand with the precautions they seem to recommend regarding the experience of listening to music. The great passion that both devoted to that same experience is as well documented as are the different degrees of their musical knowledge. While Nietzsche's musical education allowed him, not only to appreciate, but also to play and even compose music, Hegel was the first to admit the limits of his knowledge of musical theory. On the other hand, while Nietzsche was a deep connoisseur of the history of music and of the most important Western composers, Hegel recognised that he was not very acquainted with great musical works.[4] Nevertheless, and in spite of these differences, both thinkers were devoted listeners and true music lovers.[5] What is more, and so I intend to argue, their experience of listening to music certainly contributed in a significant way to some of their most important philosophical conceptions.

In section 372 of *The Gay Science*, entitled "Why we are not idealists", Nietzsche describes the relation between modern philosophy and music, paying special attention to philosophical idealism. There he writes:

> – Formerly, philosophers feared the senses: have we – perhaps unlearned this fear all too much? Today we are all sensualists, we philosophers of the present and future, *not* in theory but in praxis, in practice ... The former, however, saw the senses as trying to lure them away from *their* world, from the cold kingdom of "ideas", to a dangerous Southern island where they feared their philosophers' virtues would melt away like snow in the sun. "Wax in the ear" was virtually a condition of philosophising; a true philosopher didn't listen to life anymore insofar as life is music; he *denied* the music of life, – it is an old philosopher's superstition that all music is siren-music. Today we are inclined to make the opposite judgement (which could itself be just as mistaken), namely, that *ideas* are worse seductresses than the senses, for all their cold, anaemic appearance and not even despite that appearance – they always lived off the "blood" of the philosopher; they always drained his senses and even, if you believe it, his "heart". [...] Don't you see the spectacle

---

4 On Nietzsche's musical knowledge as well as on Nietzsche's love for music, see Janz 1978–1979 and Safranski 2005. For a discussion of Hegel's own account of the insufficiency of his musical knowledge, see Sallis 2011.

5 If it seems somewhat redundant to support this claim by referring to Nietzsche's biography and philosophy, Hegel's enthusiasm for opera, concerts and *bel canto* – widely documented in the letters he wrote to his wife –, should be underlined, as well as his acquaintance with prominent musical figures of his time, including the most famous German singers. On Hegel's frequency of concerts and his love for opera, see Sallis 2011 and Mallet 2002.

unfolding, this steady *growing paler* – this ever more ideally construed desensualisation [*Entsinnlichung*]? [...] In sum: all philosophical idealism until now was something like an illness, except where, as in Plato's case, it was the caution of an overabundant and dangerous health; the fear of *overpowerful* senses; the shrewdness of a shrewd Socratic. – Maybe we moderns are not healthy enough to need Plato's idealism? And we don't fear the senses because – – (GS 372, KSA 3, p. 623f.)[6]

Nietzsche does not finish the last sentence. However, he seems to indicate that the reason why modern philosophers no longer fear the senses lies less in their lack of courage than in their lack of health and vitality. The text abounds with references to life and its central notion seems to be contained in the enigmatic expression "the music of life".[7] To understand the latter, it is important to recall that the whole passage is meant to clarify its title, that is to say, to explain why those to whom Nietzsche calls 'we' (and he thereby seems to be including himself) – are not idealists or are no longer idealists. He mentions philosophers such as Plato and declares that "today we are all sensualists", suggesting that, at the present time, it is longer possible to find idealists among philosophers. More precisely, he claims that not only "we philosophers of the present" are sensualists, but also that among the future philosophers there will not be idealists. Philosophers, so he argues, are and will be sensualists, "*not* in theory" – he adds – "but in praxis, in practice".

---

[6] "– Ehemals hatten die Philosophen Furcht vor den Sinnen: haben wir – diese Furcht vielleicht allzusehr verlernt? Wir sind heute allesammt Sensualisten, wir Gegenwärtigen und Zukünftigen in der Philosophie, *nicht* der Theorie nach, aber der Praxis, der Praktik ... Jene hingegen meinten, durch die Sinne aus *ihrer* Welt, dem kalten Reiche der 'Ideen', auf ein gefährliches südlicheres Eiland weggelockt zu werden: woselbst, wie sie fürchteten, ihre Philosophen-Tugenden wie Schnee in der Sonne wegschmelzen würden. 'Wachs in den Ohren' war damals beinahe Bedingung des Philosophirens; ein ächter Philosoph hörte das Leben nicht mehr, insofern Leben Musik ist, er *leugnete* die Musik des Lebens, – es ist ein alter Philosophen-Aberglaube, dass alle Musik Sirenen-Musik ist. – Nun möchten wir heute geneigt sein, gerade umgekehrt zu urtheilen (was an sich noch eben so falsch sein könnte): nämlich dass die *Ideen* schlimmere Verführerinnen seien als die Sinne, mit allem ihrem kalten anämischen Anscheine und nicht einmal trotz diesem Anscheine, – sie lebten immer vom 'Blute' des Philosophen, sie zehrten immer seine Sinne aus, ja, wenn man uns glauben will, auch sein 'Herz'. [...] Seht ihr das Schauspiel nicht, das sich hier abspielt, das beständige *Blässer-werden* –, die immer idealischer ausgelegte Entsinnlichung? [...] In summa: aller philosophische Idealismus war bisher Etwas wie Krankheit, wo er nicht, wie im Falle Plato's, die Vorsicht einer überreichen und gefährlichen Gesundheit, die Furcht vor *übermächtigen* Sinnen, die Klugheit eines klugen Sokratikers war. – Vielleicht sind wir Modernen nur nicht gesund genug, um Plato's Idealismus *nöthig zu haben*? Und wir fürchten die Sinne nicht, weil – –"

[7] For an analysis of this notion and a reading of section 372 of *The Gay Science* that I will closely follow here, see Stegmaier 2004.

In this text, idealism is equated with fear of the senses and of the seductive power of sensibility that attracted idealists such as Plato to a dangerous and warm Southern island away from the cold kingdom of ideas. Idealism is no longer possible, Nietzsche suggests, because modern philosophers no longer conceive their senses as being dangerous, i.e. because the senses no longer seduce them. Nietzsche illustrates this situation by referring to the mythical figures of the sirens and to the mythical power of their music that was feared by the Ancients. He writes that, contrary to the sailors of Odysseus' crew, who felt they had to defend themselves from the dangerous and irresistible music of the sirens,[8] modern philosophers stopped putting wax in their ears, implying, thus, that they stopped feeling the need to protect themselves from "the music of life". As I will try to show, Nietzsche's suggestion is less that philosophers learned how to deal with that music, than that they simply became incapable of hearing it. In other words, Nietzsche is not pointing to something like an Odysseus-like courage specific to modern philosophers, but rather to the weakness of their senses and of their ears in particular. So, what seems to be at stake here is their incapacity of hearing, i.e. their deafness.

By mentioning the sirens, Nietzsche combines modern philosophy's sensitive weakness with modern music's impotence for seducing philosophy. But this strange combination results even more so if we look at the relation defined by Nietzsche as "sensualism" between modern philosophers and their senses. In §370 of *Gay Science*, Nietzsche identifies "sensualism" as the philosophy of the eighteenth century, referring explicitly to Hume, Kant and Condillac. But in the Preface to *Daybreak* (§3), the sensualist that Nietzsche has in mind is Kant, insofar as he accepted the senses in his theory of knowledge. In effect, in this passage, sensualism designates a philosophical position that makes all knowledge dependent on the senses, although it does not exclude ideas from thought. Through Kant's example, as a sensualist who does not reject ideas, Nietzsche seems to indicate that, ultimately, a rigid alternative between senses and thought, sensualism and idealism, is not possible, and that throughout the history of philosophy there has only been a difference in the degree between sensualism and idealism. And this is precisely what the text quoted above from *Gay Science* points out, namely that the notion of philosophy may have changed throughout its history, and indeed, as Nietzsche writes, "*not* in theory but in praxis, in practice" (GS 372, KSA 3, p. 623). He seems, hence, to suggest that, today, philosophers may be idealists according to a practice that is lost and sensualists according to a practice that hasn't yet found its theory. And the question

---

[8] *Odyssey* Book x I.

would then be: what does a practice without a theory mean, that is to say, a practice that has not yet been subject to conceptualisation?⁹

In section 188 of *Beyond Good and Evil* Nietzsche gives an indication of what that practice might be. Here, when he speaks about the activity of artists as a practice, he says that their actions obey to "hardness and determinateness" and "defy all conceptual formulation" (BGE 188, KSA 5, p. 108f.). The artist's understanding of his practice dispenses with the need to translate his actions into concepts. According to Nietzsche, it is precisely from practices without concepts that philosophical attempts of conceptualisation come to light. Such not-yet-conceptualised practices are, therefore, something like the opposite of concepts, they are "contra-concepts" (*Gegenbegriffe*), i.e. something that still lacks conceptualisation and therefore constitutes the soil from where conceptualisation can spring.

In the passage from *Gay Science* 372, "the music of life" appears precisely as an example of such *Gegenbegriffe*, and Nietzsche suggests that modern philosophers are no longer sensible to it. It is for this reason that their idealism is no longer that of the healthy Plato, but rather "a soft, good-natured, silver-glistering idealism" which, according to *Daybreak* 190, was practiced by Schiller, Humboldt, Schleiermacher, Schelling and – most significantly for the purpose of the present paper – Hegel, as a "heartfelt repugnance for 'cold' or 'dry' reality" (D 190, KSA 3, p. 163). Modern idealists, we can hence infer, do not feel fear, but "repugnance" for that which is not yet conceptualised. In other words, they are no longer seduced by the music of life that has become "cold" and "dry" ("anaemic", as Nietzsche writes in GS 372, KSA 3, p. 624), i.e. dead to their senses, mute to their ears. Instead of the power of *Gegenbegriffen* what now seduces and attracts them are, in fact, conceptualised ideas.

Kant is not mentioned in this passage from *Daybreak*, most probably because Kant's idealism was moderate; it was still somehow seduced by the senses as providers of sensuous data for knowledge, as the material with which our understanding could work. In any case, of course, Kant's "sensualism" did not dispense with ideas. What is more, in the third *Critique*, ideas become "aesthetic" and very akin to the *Gegenbegriffe* conceived by Nietzsche. Kant defined an aesthetic idea as:

> that representation of the imagination that gives much to think about, but without any determinate thought, i.e. *concept* being able to be adequate to it, which consequently no language can completely attain and make comprehensible. (KU, p. 314)¹⁰

---

9 This question is raised by Stegmaier's reading of GS 372, Stegmaier 2004.
10 "[D]iejenige Vorstellung der Einbildungskraft, die viel zu denken veranlaßt, ohne daß ihr doch irgend ein bestimmter Gedanke, d.i. *Begriff*, adäquat sein kann, die folglich keine Sprache völlig erreicht und verständlich machen kann."

The absence of concepts implies, therefore, that language cannot completely represent these ideas, and this is precisely what led other modern German thinkers, particularly the early Romantics and Schopenhauer, to look for a language that would be adequate for this purpose, namely, the non-conceptual language of music. Music's non-conceptual nature gained, hereby, a meta-conceptual and even a metaphysical value. Nevertheless, if, like these thinkers, Kant considers that music "communicates aesthetic ideas", i.e. ideas that "are not concepts, nor determinate thoughts", quite contrary to them he concludes that music is the lowest form of art because it just plays with feelings (KU, p. 329). Also, by underlying music's constitutive transient character, i.e. the fact that, being made of sounds, musical impressions are *"transitory"*, Kant reinforces his devaluation of music. Therefore and, contrary to the other arts, music does not bring about "a product that serves the concepts of the understanding as an enduring and self-recommending vehicle for its unification with sensibility". In the end Kant argues that music is the art that "leaves us with nothing to meditate about" (KU, p. 329).[11]

Kant's considerations are useful to understand Hegel's views on music. They draw our attention to the fact that, contrary to concepts that fix or determine, that give stability or objectify multiplicity and becoming, music is transient, i.e. it is composed by sounds that simply vibrate and vanish. Hegel also understood music's transience as an important feature of this art. In his *Lectures on the Philosophy of Art* Hegel emphasises the sonorous element of music as an "exteriority [*Äusserlichkeit*] which destroys itself and disappears through its own emergence and existence" (*Ae III*, TWA 15, p. 135). Contrary to words – the meaning of which is sustained by the idealisation of thought – musical sounds do not escape the transient contingency of feelings.[12]

Hegel's idea is that, by eliminating spatiality, music cancels the stability in a persistent material. Consequently, in music, the artwork no longer stands before the subject as a self-reposing, persistent object – a painting, for example –, in which the external, spatial nature is distinguished from the "contemplating I as inner self [*das anschauende Ich als inneres Selbst*]" (*Ae III*, TWA 15, p. 135). Here there is an external object that provokes the inner response. In music, on

---

11 "[S]o hat Musik unter den schönen Künsten sofern den untersten [...] Platz, weil sie bloß mit Empfindungen spielt. Die bildenden Künste gehen ihr also in diesem Betracht weit vor; denn indem sie die Einbildungskraft in ein freies und doch zugleich dem Verstande angemessenes Spiel versetzen, so treiben sie zugleich ein Geschäft, indem sie ein Product zu Stande bringen, welches den Verstandesbegriffen zu einem dauerhaften und für sie selbst sich empfehlenden Vehikel dient, die Vereinigung derselben mit der Sinnlichkeit [...] zu befördern".
12 See Bowie 2007, especially chapter 4, "Hegel, Philosophy, and Music" (p. 105–137).

the contrary, this distinction is lost and "the notes echo only in the deepest soul [*die Noten klingen nur in den tiefsten Seele nach*]" (*Ae III*, TWA 15, p. 136). However, this suppression of spatiality is not a simple negation, a mere cancellation that leaves nothing behind. In fact, spatial objectivity is both cancelled and preserved, hereby constituting the very process of *Aufhebung*. In Hegel's words:

> The *Aufhebung* of the spatial therefore consists here only in the fact that a determinate sensible material gives up its peaceful separateness, turns to movement, yet *so* vibrates in itself that every part of the cohering body not only changes its place but also strives to replace itself in its former position. The result of this oscillating vibration is *tone* [*Ton*], the material of music. (*Ae III*, TWA 15, p. 134)[13]

Hence, music brings about instability as a result of this process of double negation. If, in the first negation, every part of the object is displaced, this displacement is again negated by the striving of the parts to regain their original place. And this is ultimately why, with its process of double negation, music is the most adequate presentation of the inner life, "expressed in its own pure movement as pure movement".[14]

But besides instability or transience, there is something else that, according to Hegel, characterises musical tones or sounds, namely immediacy or abstractness. While sculpture and painting can portray forms of the world of objects, music is a non-mimetic art and it can only express our object-free subjectivity, "the way in which the innermost self is moved in its subjectivity and spirituality" (*Ae III*, TWA 15, p. 135). Thus, if music is the best expression of our inner life, it also leads us to a complete withdrawal into subjectivity, because – contrary to forms and colours – sounds do not represent objects of the world: they only present pure subjectivity to itself. While paintings and sculptures present objective manifestations from which the I who contemplates remains distinct, in music that distinction disappears, and this means that its content is what is subjective in itself or, as Hegel puts it, tone is "in itself without content [*für sich genommen inhaltlos*]" (*Ae III*, TWA 15, p. 223). It is here that Hegel's ambivalence towards music becomes manifest: On the one

---

[13] "Die Aufhebung des Räumlichen besteht deshalb hier nur darin, daß ein bestimmtes sinnliches Material sein ruhiges Außereinander aufgibt, in Bewegung gerät, doch *so* in sich erzittert, daß jeder Teil des kohärierenden Körpers seinen Ort nicht nur verändert, sondern auch sich in den vorigen Zustand zurückzuversetzen strebt. Das Resultat dieses schwingenden Zitterns ist der *Ton*, das Material der Musik."
[14] The expression is from Lydia Goehr in Goehr 2006, p. 34.

hand, music's independence from determinate objects and contents distinguishes it from the other arts and reveals its ideal character, in the sense that it is capable of detaching and going beyond a given content; on the other hand, though, this very freedom from determinacy and content puts forth the danger of a total detachment of any kind of content altogether, i.e. the possibility that music shall become "empty, meaningless [*leer, bedeutungslos*]" (*Ae III*, TWA 15, p. 148). Hegel saw this possibility becoming effective in the music of his time, namely in pure instrumental music that would be known as 'absolute music'.[15] In Hegel's view, this isolation of music within itself was a threat because ultimately it excluded music from the realm of art. Being devoid of words and text, i.e. of any conceptual content, absolute music was devoid of the spiritual content of which art is the sensible expression. Indeed, if art was to be, as Hegel claimed, a sensible manifestation of the Idea, it could not be devoid of content. And this being so, purely formal music, instrumental music manifests nothing, is completely meaningless and risks becoming a mere piece of artifice, which is only for the expert and is untrue to the purpose of art (*Ae III*, TWA 15, p. 145).[16]

---

15 As Carl Dahlhaus shows, the concept of "absolute" or "pure" music" consisted on the association of a music separated from texts, programmes and functions with the expression or the sense of the "absolute". According to Dahlhaus, initially instrumental music that was deprived of words and purposes appeared as empty or devoid of content, for example, for Rousseau, who argued for the model of vocal music recurring to the theory of affects. Afterwards came the tendency to contradict the sentimental characterisation of music or to convert those concrete affects into more diffuse feelings, as in Novalis or Friedrich Schlegel, who reject the utilitarian approach of music. And this is how the principle of music's autonomy appeared. In name of such principle, instrumental music – that until then was considered as deficient version of vocal music – reached the status of musical paradigm and what previously seemed a deficiency (the absence of words and concepts) is then presented as an advantage: instrumental music comes to be considered as a direct expression of the essence of music because it is free from concepts and extra-musical purposes and finalities. See Dahlhaus 1989, especially chapter 1, "Absolute Music as an Aesthetic Paradigm" (p. 1–17).

16 "In neuerer Zeit besonders ist die Musik in der Losgerissenheit von einem für sich schon klaren Gehalt so in ihr eigenes Element zurückgegangen, doch hat dafür auch desto mehr an Macht über das ganze Innere verloren, indem der Genuß, den sie bieten kann, sich nur der einen Seite der Kunst zuwendet, dem bloßen Interesse nämlich für das rein Musikalische der Komposition und deren Geschicklichkeit, eine Seite, welche nur Sache der Kenner ist und das allgemeinmenschliche Kunstinteresse weniger angeht." On Hegel's suspicions about absolute music and particularly about Beethoven's music, see Dahlhaus 1988. Here Dahlhaus claims that Hegel considered that absolute music was "leading on the wrong path, on which the 'universally human interest in art' had to decline" because of its detachment from "a content of feeling that is determinable by concepts" (Dahlhaus 1988, p. 239).

Hence, if, on the one hand, music is the art of the purest feeling, on the other hand it can also become the art of the strictest understanding that appeals only to those who have a technical understanding of it. But even more importantly for what concerns us here, Hegel suspects that music could become a means for arising sensations that are not structured by thought and remain indeterminate. In fact, by referring to no object at all, the inner life that is exemplarily expressed through music is both the form (the continent) and the content of this art, that is to say, there is no distinction, no mediation between form and content, interiority and exteriority. Hence, the same inner life that music should express becomes unattainable through music, i.e. blended with it, obscure. This is ultimately the reason why Hegel considers absolute music to be dangerous: it does not provide the listener with objective, conceptual *Haltpunkte*, thus threatening his or her freedom of thought and independence from the sounds that he or she is listening to. The danger is that the subject can be lost in the abyss of interiority or in pure subjectivity because s/he loses the necessary distance for considering what is happening to him/her while listening to music.[17]

Now we can see how Hegel's distrust of the formalistic tendency in music, that is, his suspicions about pure instrumental music, has something in common with the fear of the siren-music described by Nietzsche in the text we saw above. It is as if Hegel feared the effects of a dangerous sonority that – by resisting rationalisation and conceptual mediation – was depriving the listener from its freedom and independence. Hegel's philosophy, indeed, seems to remain deaf to that very music, in spite of its beauty and charms, as Hegel's silence about Beethoven seems to prove.[18]

To be sure, by escaping representation and linguistic formulation, music seems to be free from any form of conceptual control. This certainly explains philosophers' fear of music, and why music might be considered as the limit of philosophy, as something that escapes and revolts against philosophical, conceptual authority.[19] Music resists being subsumed under a linguistic or conceptual control that would stabilise its constitutive movement and evanescence. However, if sounds are evanescent and without object, it does not necessarily follow from this that sounds are absolutely subjective, because the subject that listens is nevertheless affected by something that is not himself. In other words,

---

[17] In Marie-Louise Mallet's words, "music 'penetrates' the soul, it 'captivates' consciousness, which, 'not having any object to *confront*', is 'taken' by 'the continuous flood of sounds', until it loses its freedom" (Mallet 2002, p. 99).
[18] On Hegel's silence on Beethoven and his preference for Rossini, see Sallis 2011.
[19] See Lacoue-Labarthe 1991, p. 165f.

if the subject is not clearly "distinct" from what s/he listens to, as Hegel suggests, s/he also is not necessarily and totally blended by it. Indeed, the fact that the transience of sounds affects us already means that this transience does not come from within us. Moreover, music does not simply reify our subjectivity because listening to music is not exactly like listening to ourselves or merely recognising ourselves in what we hear. On the contrary, listening to music is more like receiving something that does not spring from us and that we can never fully anticipate, nor conceptually determine. Thus, although music might be a threat to rationality and to philosophical conceptualisation – although it constitutes, as Nietzsche claims, a *Gegenbegriff* –, it also provides us with an experience in which its independence from representation and concepts could never hinder, but rather enhance thought. And it does so, precisely because of the way in which it challenges the categories we have at hand.

But for Hegel, the solution for the problem that arises with purely instrumental music (in contrast to the latter possibility which, as we shall see, is suggested by Nietzsche) is to prevent music from remaining pure, that is to say, from becoming isolated within itself. In other words, music should never submerge the listener in the indeterminacy of sensations, it should not limit itself to the purely musical, that is to say, it should not completely exclude spiritual content. For it must remain art, i.e. the sensible presentation of the spirit. According to Hegel, this possibility depends, not on the divorce, but on the alliance between music and words, because words determine feelings and sensations that, otherwise, would remain as repugnant as the "'cold' or 'dry' reality" mentioned by Nietzsche (D 190, KSA 3, p. 163). Hegel's solution is, thus, to defend the alliance between music and words, i.e. to defend vocal music against pure instrumental music. Hegel's response to the threats and dangers of absolute music could therefore be reformulated as the need to transform siren-music into siren-songs, because, as Sallis writes: "when music becomes song [...] there is added to its subjectiveness the objective subsistence engendered by words and ideas" (Sallis 2011, p. 381). Such response, moreover, is totally in line with Hegel's preference for opera and vocal music, as well as with his praise of Rossini and the "wax in the ear" (GS 372, KSA 3, p. 623) regarding Beethoven. As far as Nietzsche is concerned, though, putting "wax in the ear" was not a solution for the dangers involved in music, especially not in regard to the music of his time.

In order to analyse some of Nietzsche's views on music and to compare them with Hegel's I will start by referring to *Human, All Too Human* 217. Here Nietzsche describes the development of the history of Western music as a process of "*desensualisation* [Entsinnlichung]" (HH I 217, KSA 2, p. 177), analogous to the one he ascribed to the history of philosophy in GS 372. By writing that, as a result of the "evolution of modern music", "our ears have grown more and more intellectualised", Nietzsche argues that, in modern times, our ears "inquire after the reason, the 'meaning', and are no longer content to know that a thing 'is'" (HH I 217, KSA 2, p. 177). For Nietzsche, the consequence of this tendency (the tendency of asking for the meaning of musical sounds, i.e. of asking about the feelings, concepts or ideas that are being expressed by those sounds) is a "bluntness" of the ears. "Our ears become coarser", he writes, they can no longer hear "the subtle distinction between for example C sharp and D flat" (HH I 217, KSA 2, p. 177).

These statements seem to be in complete opposition to Hegel's considerations seen above. The problem, for Nietzsche, is not so much that formal pleasure in music, that is to say, purely musical pleasure, is dangerous, but rather that it is lost; and the proof is that we can no longer hear or recognise what is not yet conceptually determined – *Gegenbegriffe* – because our ears have become deaf to the sheer musicality of sounds. In Nietzsche's view, the danger lies in such deafness inasmuch as it is a symptom of the general enfeeblement of our sensibility, a sign of the modern decline that he named *décadence*. The fact that we have become incapable of distinguishing pure musical notes means that we have become deaf to the subtleness of their nuances. It is as if "we", moderns, and particularly "we", modern philosophers, seduced as we are by the power of ideas, suffer from the results of something like an over-conceptualisation of "cold or dry reality". As far as music is concerned, the result of the general "ever more ideally construed desensualisation [*die immer idealischer ausgelegte Entsinnlichung*]" (GS 372, KSA 3, p. 624) is an intellectualisation of our sense of hearing and of the experience of musical sensations. Thus, when Nietzsche describes the process of the "intellectualisation of the senses" in modernity (HH I 217, KSA 2, p. 177), he refers to it as a disease, an impoverishment that prevents our sensibility and our intellect from complementing each other and from collaborating during the experience of listening to music.

In this sense it seems that Nietzsche defends the legitimacy of absolute music, that is to say, of the music that is exclusively addressed to the sense of hearing. In other words, his criticisms of the progressive desensualisation throughout the history of music and of the intellectualisation of audition apparently support musical compositions that are completely deprived of conceptual meaning and whose conceptual "emptiness" was feared and rejected by Hegel. However, this is not all the case, as his presentation of absolute music makes clear, particularly in *Human, All Too Human*. As is well known, this work is subsequent to Nietzsche's break with Wagner. Some of its texts suggest that this break also entailed a distancing from Schopenhauer's metaphysics of music and they suggest that Nietzsche followed the musical formalism of Wagner's opponent, Eduard Hanslick.[20] Claiming that the beauty or the unity of a musical piece is identical to its form and thus immanent to the work, Hanslick accused Wagner of looking for the beauty and the unity of his works in extra-musical domains such as drama (i.e. the narrative, the words and their meaning) and the realm of emotions and feelings that music arises in its listeners.[21]

Although it is true that this kind of considerations against extra-musical domains are recurrent in *Human, All Too Human*, contrary to Hanslick and in spite of his objections to Wagner, Nietzsche was not a proclaimer of musical formalism, as it becomes clear in his presentation of the concept of absolute music. In HH I 215 Nietzsche distinguishes this latter from "dramatic music", i.e. song and opera where "the tonal art has conquered an enormous domain of symbolic means" (HH I 215, KSA 2, p. 175). On the contrary, "absolute music", he writes, is "either form in itself [...] or symbolism of form speaking to the understanding" (HH I 215, KSA 2, p. 175). But even if Nietzsche was defending a formalistic approach of music, the problem he addresses is that only "men who have remained behind in the evolution of music" would be capable of understanding it "in a purely formalistic way". More precisely, Nietzsche claims that "absolute music" corresponds, not to a musical innovation, but to "a primitive stage of music in which sounds [...] gave pleasure as such" (HH I 215, KSA 2, p. 175). Such stage disappeared a long time ago, so Nietzsche is suggesting, and today we cannot but listen "symbolically" to music because musical forms became "entirely enmeshed on threads of feelings and concepts". In other words, "our intellect introduced significance into sounds" so that we cannot hear "pure" sounds anymore (HH I 215, KSA 2, p. 175). Hence, what our ears give us access to are meanings, ideas, extra-musical contents that somehow function as conceptual or intellectual "wax in the ear", even when we listen to pure instrumental music.

Nietzsche's critique of the 'intellectualisation of the senses', thus, corresponds, not to a defence of the musical compositions feared by Hegel, but rather to a rejection of the tendency, in music as well as in philosophy, to subordinate sensibility to rationality. In what music is concerned, such tendency corresponds to subordinating the sense of hearing to non-musical meanings, especially to metaphysical meanings, as was the case both in Schopenhauer's philosophy of music and in Wagner's late musical works. But if Nietzsche criticises

---

20 This idea is defended, for example, by Éric Dufour, according to whom the notion of musical beauty in HH is "completely Hanslickian". See Dufour 2005, especially "La conception de la musique dans Humain trop humain", p. 197–212.
21 On the polemics between Hanslick and Wagner, see Goehr 2004, p. 88–131.

the subordination of the senses to the intellect (or the subordination of sensations to concepts), it does not necessarily follow that he argues for the opposite tendency. Nietzsche was as much critical of the subordination of sensations to intellectual meaning as he was of the opposite tendency, that is to say, of the tendency to subordinate intellectual meaning to sensations. If he identified a weakening of sensibility by means of the primacy given to the intellect, he was equally suspicious of a weakening of the power of rationality by means of an excessive stimulation of the senses. Thus, both the weakening of the senses and the weakening of the intellect were the dangers Nietzsche feared in the music of his time. Nevertheless, and contrary to Hegel, he didn't put wax in his ears and was, for a period of time, seduced – seduced, indeed, up to "sickness" (CW Preface, KSA 6, p. 12) – by the powerful music of that siren named Wagner. What is more, Nietzsche not only listened to Wagner's music, but he even recommended that philosophers that wished to understand modernity should listen to it. "Wagner *sums up* modernity – he wrote –. It's no use, you need to start out as a Wagnerian ..." (CW Preface, KSA 6, p. 12).

Nietzsche considered that the tendency to introduce extra-musical content in music pervaded Wagner's music. Through the mythological and symbolic dimensions that prevail in his compositions, Wagner gave an extra-musical meaning to his compositions, thereby converting audition into a means of accessing determined contents that had been previously established. By doing so, Wagner gave primacy to the significance of what is being heard over the question of what is there to hear, that is to say, he intellectualised the sense of hearing. He therefore completed the desensualisation of the musical component of music by conceding an excess of significance to musical sounds. In Nietzsche's words, by making use of "great symbols" (CW 6, KSA 6, p. 25), he created the impression that his music was "more meaningful than just music – infinitely more meaningful!" (CW 10, KSA 6, p. 35). But, on the other hand, and at the same time that it intellectualises our listening ears, Wagner's music also does the opposite, namely it stimulates them until the limits of their capacity to listen. Exposed to so much noise, to the Wagnerian "*Sursum! Bumbum!*" (CW 6, KSA 6, p. 25), our ears become deaf, deprived of their capacity to hear. Audition does not become stronger or more refined, but weaker, "coarser" (HH I 217, KSA 2, p. 177). In other words, Wagner's music formal effect, is, paradoxically, anaesthesia: by conquering "the nerves" this music acts as a "narcotic" thus neutralising the capacity to hear. For these reasons Nietzsche considers Wagner as "the artist of decadence", underlining the "sick" nature of its works and the consequences they have on the listeners health (CW 5, KSA 6, p. 21). What is at stake is a music that enfeebles both the sensibility and the intellect of those who hear it, because the massive burden of effects that characterises it hinders the senses as well as the thoughts. Hence, besides promoting the intellectualisation of the senses, it also supresses the capacity to think. As Nietzsche writes, Wagner's music leads the senses to their "exhaustion" and demands from the listener only one thing: "Above all, no thought!" (CW 6, KSA 6, p. 24).

The conclusion is that with Wagner the historical tendency to the intellectualisation of the senses reaches a point where music becomes a negation of the experience of listening to music. Wagner's music is, thus, a negation of itself as music because it denies the very possibility of listening to it. In other words, Wagner's music tyrannises both body and spirit, senses and reason, impeding their free play. According to Nietzsche's final analysis, Wagner's music obstructs the exercise of freedom which, for Nietzsche, music can and should promote. Furthermore, Nietzsche considered that Wagner's music served authoritarian exigencies that prevent a free relationship between the listener and what he is listening to. In contrast to this, an affirmative music is one that "makes the spirit free and fosters "the *pathos* of philosophy" (CW 1, KSA 6, p. 14). And this means that it addresses the senses in order to affirm them as well as the capacity of generating thoughts that emerge from those very affects or sounds. It is a music that seduces the listener without annihilating him, a music that counts on the participation of the listener. And this is exactly what Nietzsche recognised in Bizet's music: being "the opposite" of Wagner's music, it treats the listener as intelligent, even as a musician", it makes him or her "fertile" (CW 1, KSA 6, p. 14). Thus, contrasting Wagner's to Bizet's music, Nietzsche writes the following:

> – Strange! I really do not think about it, or I do not *know* how much I think about it. Because completely different thoughts are running through my head the whole time ... Has anyone noticed that music *makes* the spirit *free*? gives wings to thought? that you become more of a philosopher, the more of a musician you become? – (CW 1, KSA 6, p. 14)[22]

References

Bowie, Andrew (2007): *Music, Philosophy and Modernity*. Cambridge: Cambridge University Press.
Constâncio, João/Branco, Maria J.M. (Eds.) (2012): *As the Spider Spins: Essays on Nietzsche's Critique and Use of Language*. Berlin and New York: De Gruyter.
Dahlhaus, Carl (1988): *Klassische und romantische Musikästhetik*. Laaber: Laaber-Verlag.

---

[22] "– Und seltsam! im Grunde denke ich nicht daran, oder *weiss* es nicht, wie sehr ich daran denke. Denn ganz andere Gedanken laufen mir während dem durch den Kopf ... Hat man bemerkt, dass die Musik den Geist *frei macht*? dem Gedanken Flügel giebt? dass man um so mehr Philosoph wird, je mehr man Musiker wird? –"

Dahlhaus, Carl (1989): *The Idea of Absolute Music*. Chicago: University of Chicago Press.
Dufour, Éric (2005): *L'esthétique musicale de Nietzsche*. Lille: Presses Universitaires du Septentrion.
Goehr, Lydia (2002): *The Quest for Voice. Music, Politics and the Limits of Philosophy*. Oxford and New York: Oxford University Press.
Goehr, Lydia (2006): "*Doppelbewegung*: The Musical Movement of Philosophy and the Philosophical Movement of Music". In Jost Hermand/Gerhardt Richter (Eds.): *Sound Figures of Modernity. German Music and Philosophy*. Wisconsin and London: University of Wisconsin Press, p. 19–63.
Hermand, Jost/Richter, Gerhardt (Eds.) (2006): *Sound Figures of Modernity. German Music and Philosophy*. Wisconsin and London: University of Wisconsin Press.
Janz, Curt Paul (1978–1979): *Friedrich Nietzsche. Biographie*. Vol. 1: *Kindheit, Jugend, die Basler Jahre.*–Vol. 2: *Die zehn Jahre des freien Philosophen.*–Vol. 3: *Die Jahre des Siechtums. Dokumente, Quellen und Register*. Munich: Hanser.
Lacoue-Labarthe, Philippe (1991): *Musica ficta (Figures de Wagner)*. Paris: Christian Bourgois Éditeur.
Mallet, Marie-Louise (2002): *La musique en respect*. Paris: Galilée.
Safranski, Rüdiger (2005): *Nietzsche. Biographie seines Denkens*. Frankfurt a.M.: Fischer.
Sallis, John (2011): "Soundings: Hegel on Music". In: Stephen Houlgate/Michael Baur (Eds.): *A Companion to Hegel*. New Jersey: Wiley-Blackwell, p. 369–384.
Stegmaier, Werner (2004): "'Philosophischer Idealismus' und die 'Musik des Lebens': Zu Nietzsches Umgang mit Paradoxien. Eine kontextuelle Interpretation des Aphorismus Nr. 372 der *Fröhlichen Wissenschaft*". In: *Nietzsche-Studien* 33, p. 90–128.

Thomas Kisser
The Reality of the Will: On the Problem of Individuality in Nietzsche and Fichte

> ... imagine something which distinguishes itself – and yet that from which it distinguishes itself remains aloof. Lightning, for example, distinguishes itself from the black sky but must also trail behind it, as though it were distinguishing itself from that which does not distinguish itself from it. It is as if the ground rose to the surface, without ceasing to be ground. There is cruelty, even monstrosity, on both sides of this struggle against an elusive adversary, in which the distinguished opposes something which cannot distinguish itself from it but continues to espouse that which divorces it. Difference is this state in which determination takes the form of unilateral distinction. We must therefore say that difference is made, or makes itself, as in the expression "make the difference". (Gilles Deleuze, *Difference and Repetition*)[1]

I

Although Nietzsche never engaged in a philosophical discussion with Fichte, the similarity of some of the topics they address could not go unnoticed. These topics concern, of course, morality and its legitimation, and appear to be addressed by both authors in a diametrically opposite way. Indeed, from a Nietzschean point of view, Fichte seems to fulfil in an outstanding way what could be called the predator-prey scheme. For, according to Fichte, morality constitutes the actual content of our self-consciousness, and this self-consciousness, in its turn, is defined as a meaningful process only through its relation to an Absolute that becomes visible primarily within or throughout moral acts.[2] Fichte even claims to be the first to have exposed the structure of practical concepts, and hence, to have understood the phenomenon of an efficacy governed by concepts (*Wirkung nach Begriffen*), i.e. governed by goals (F SW IV, p. 2). For Nietzsche, however, this form of morality always has an ideological character and, in the end, is only the expression of a weakness, which is then supposed to be concealed by that very form of morality. He, who is in the "inevitable position of having to wait", turns patience into a virtue and coercion into free will (GM I

---

1 Deleuze 1994, p. 28.
2 See also Lauth 1965, especially p. 85f.; for the practical structure of self-consciousness see Klotz 2002 and Estes 2002.

14, KSA 5, p. 281).³ In Nietzsche's view, the whole notion of free will and the theory of consciousness related to it inevitably culminate in the conception of purposes as the causes for our actions. And this is, according to Nietzsche, the main error of traditional philosophy; it is because of this that philosophy has been permanently and excessively demanding of man. Morality – that "dragon named 'Thou shalt' " (Z I Metamorphoses, KSA 4, p. 30) – puts life as such under normative demands and blocks any form of spontaneity, provoking a spiral of impotence, which results in *ressentiment* – the real source of our misfortune.

But Fichte constantly introduces counter-positions of his own thought which he then reconstructs and criticises. It is in this way that he reformulates being (*Sein*) as sheer force (*Kraft*); a sheer force that differentiates and expresses itself through individuals, who are consequently understood as force-quanta (*Kraftquanten*). From such a theoretical position, consciousness is only *apparently* primary and cannot guide life through the free expression of the will:

> In *immediate consciousness*, I appear to myself as free; by *reflection* on the whole of Nature, I discover that freedom is absolutely impossible; the former must be subordinate to the latter, for it can only be explained by means of it. (BdM, p. 38)⁴

According to this theory, free will is nothing but a battleground of forces: "A volition is the immediate consciousness of the activity of any of the forces of Nature within us" (BdM, p. 45). As soon as one force or power acquires predominance over the others, we make a decision, which we later, in hindsight, describe as free. But, of course, thought has "nothing to do here, but to watch" (BdM, p. 61). For Fichte, this pure struggle of forces implies the loss of any form of meaning: viewing the world as a super-organism of forces is viewing it as something monstrous, in which our vocation or willpower (*Bestimmung*) cannot possibly flourish:

---

3 This is an idea that Pierre Bourdieu also develops in his social theory (Bourdieu 1977).

4 "Im *unmittelbaren Selbstbewußtseyn* erscheine ich mir als frei; durch *Nachdenken* über die ganze Natur finde ich, daß Freiheit schlechterdings unmöglich ist: das erstere muss dem letztern untergeordnet werden, denn es ist selbst durch das letztere sogar zu erklären." In the first part of *The Vocation of Man* (*Die Bestimmung des Menschen*, 1800), Fichte reconstructs the structure of Spinoza's theory (which at that time was very much discussed). It would go beyond the scope of this paper to discuss the relation between Nietzsche and Spinoza. But observing the fundamental similarities between them (such as the rejection of purposes and the conception of consciousness as having sovereign control over our actions or the conception of happiness as *amor dei intellectualis* or *amor fati*) should be sufficient for us to consider Fichte's interpretation of Spinoza – at least hypothetically – as a possibility for anticipating Fichte's relation to Nietzsche.

To what purpose this ever-revolving circle, this ceaseless and unvarying play, in which all things appear only to pass away, and pass away only so that they may re-appear unaltered – this monster [*Ungeheuer*] continually devouring itself so that it may again bring itself forth, and bringing itself forth only to devour itself again? This can never be the vocation of my being and of all being. (BdM, p. 221)[5]

In opposition to the model of a competition of powers, Fichte takes the experience of consciousness as his starting point, which is viewed as spontaneous and self- determined. Consciousness, however, understands its own spontaneity and self-determination as an image of the Absolute. The Absolute on the other hand, being the true principle which lives from itself (*aus sich selbst lebt*) – i.e. which is truly *absolute* – remains unaffected by its own finite image. Men can and should form their selves according to the image of the Absolute, that is, in accordance with freedom. So, under this moral demand, freedom has an image-like quality. Indeed, the antithesis between Fichte and Nietzsche is clear. However, the question remains as to whether there is any similarity in their positions, since any such convergence would make possible a richer and more creative comparison of their respective philosophies. In what follows I maintain that Nietzsche and Fichte share a dynamic interpretation of reality: reality is the reality of the will. In a sense, Schopenhauer, who defines the world as 'will and representation', probably embodies the most important historical connection between the two philosophers.[6] Indeed, the *title* of his book *Die Welt als Wille und Vorstellung* can be seen as a statement to which both, Fichte and Nietzsche, could have assented.[7] Thus, what I would like to do now is to sketch the ways in which Fichte and Nietzsche develop their understandings of reality. I will then attempt to discuss some of the analogies emerging as a result of this study.

---

[5] "Wozu dieser unabläßig in sich selbst zurückkehrende Zirkel, dieses immer von neuem auf dieselbe Weise wieder angehende Spiel, in welchem alles wird, um zu vergehen, und vergeht, um nur wieder werden zu können, wie es schon war; dieses Ungeheuer, unaufhörlich sich selbst verschlingend, damit es sich wiederum gebähren könne, sich gebährend, damit es sich wiederum verschlingen könne? Nimmermehr kann dies die Bestimmung seyn meines Seyns, und alles Seyns." This monster continually devouring itself is an allusion to Goethe's *Sorrows of Young Wether*, where Werther cries out: "Sky and Earth and all the active powers surrounding me! I do not see anything but a fearful monster, forever devouring, forever regurgitating itself [*Himmel und Erde und all die webenden Kräfte um mich her! Ich sehe nichts, als ein ewig verschlingendes, ewig wiederkäuendes Ungeheuer*]" (Goethe 1774, p. 95; see also GA II/3, p. 260).
[6] Schopenhauer attended Fichte's lectures in Berlin. His notes are published both in his *Nachlass* as in the Fichte-Gesamtausgabe (GA IV/4). See also D'Alfonso 2006.
[7] Nietzsche, by the way, also describes the greatest tendency of German Idealism as a "Liberation from the over-domination of the *anthropos theoretikos* [*Befreiung von dem Überherrschen des ἄνθρωπος θεωρητικός*]" (NL 1869/70, KSA 7, 3[60], p. 77).

But once we interpret reality as an endless dynamic process, we will also be bound to acknowledge that the realisation of this process (as well as the interpretation itself) depends upon finite beings or individuals. The question concerning reality leads us to the question concerning the relation between unity and plurality: how does unity relate to reality? For it is the task of philosophy to be able to identify a unity within the plurality of phenomena that constitute the world. Where is the difference, which, as Deleuze would say, only takes place as a result of the act of its own self-differentiation? How does the 'drama' of differentiation develop in relation to and on the ground of this unity?

II

Nietzsche's conception of the relation between ground (*Grund*) and individuality appears for the first time in his theory on tragedy from 1872. According to this theory, the 'birth of tragedy' results from the encounter of the pure instant of Dionysian, subterranean and formless life (which is considered to be especially dominant within Far Eastern cultures) with the Greek Apollinian tendency of conveying forms and images to everything. In Greek tragedies, the Dionysian instant, or the all-encompassing will, appears as an unlimited and invading power, which, because of its capacity to dissolve all boundaries, threatens individuality. Greek Tragedy, "as the objectification of a Dionysian state, represents not the Apollinian redemption in semblance, but rather the rupture [*Zerbrechen*] of the individual and its becoming-one [*Einswerden*] with the primordial being itself" (SGT, KSA 1, p. 609–610). But what fascinates the individual – who is also always trying to get rid of the concrete burden of his or her concrete existence – is precisely the dissolution of boundaries and the fusion with the primordial being (*Urwesen*), with pure life and sheer intensity. In as much as "tragedy enables us to envisage the redemption of the world [*Welterlösung*], it gives us the most sublime illusion [*Illusion*]: *freedom* from *existence* in general [Freiheit *vom* Dasein überhaupt]" (NL 1870, KSA 7, 5[102], p. 120). Witnessing the downfall of a heroic individual, the ordinary individual is able to reconcile with the transitory and temporal character of life and to recognise life as a force of fundamental and constant renewal.[8]

> The metaphysical joy in the tragic is a translation of the instinctive, unconscious Dionysiac wisdom into the language of images: the hero, the supreme appearance of the will, is

---

[8] See also the beautiful chapter that Hayden White has dedicated to Nietzsche's interpretation of tragedy (White 1973, p. 331–346).

destroyed to our delight, because, after all, he is only an appearance, and the eternal life of the will is not disturbed by his destruction. Tragedy calls out: "We believe in eternal life", while the music is the direct idea of this life. (BT 16, KSA 1, p. 108)[9]

In Greek tragedy pure becoming is made visible as it constitutes the content of the Dionysian. The hero, being the highest expression of individuality, encounters death in order to render visible the eternal and all-dissolving truth of life. But this encounter with death is only successful under very determinate conditions: it is necessary to translate the Dionysian insight into the ground of the world (*Grund der Welt*) – that is, into a vision in the truest sense of the word. For, it is through sight and representation that reality appears to us as being individual and discontinuous, and it is only in this way, through these individual forms, that we are capable of recognising and perceiving things. And yet, the world of boundaries can hardly withstand Dionysus' overwhelming and ecstatic power.

> Now, with the gospel of universal harmony, every man feels himself not only united, reconciled and merged with his neighbour, but also as one with him, as if the veil of maya had been torn apart, so that mere shreds of it flutter before the mysterious primordial One. Singing and dancing, man expresses himself as a member of a higher community: he has forgotten how to walk and talk and is on the verge of flying up into the air as he dances. (BT 1, KSA 1, p. 29f.)[10]

The Dionysian moment of tragedy stands for the ground of the world, where everything is one sole movement. In opposition to this, individuals seem to be only an appearance, a hazy illusion. But the original unity cannot be experienced directly; for this, a mirror imaging in the medium of representation – i.e. of appearance or semblance – is necessary. And this is how the human structure of perception comes into play. "The world of semblance fixes individuation. The world of tone joins together; it must be more closely related to the will" (NL 1869/70, KSA 7, 3[37], p. 70). The visual (*Schein*) is privileged over tone, in other words: it is all about the optic structure of the appearance (*Erscheinung*). We must therefore distinguish between two forms of translating the One into the

---

9 "Die metaphysische Freude am Tragischen ist eine Uebersetzung der instinctiv unbewussten dionysischen Weisheit in die Sprache des Bildes: der Held, die höchste Willenserscheinung, wird zu unserer Lust verneint, weil er doch nur Erscheinung ist, und das ewige Leben des Willens durch seine Vernichtung nicht berührt wird. 'Wir glauben an das ewige Leben', so ruft die Tragödie; während die Musik die unmittelbare Idee dieses Lebens ist."
10 "Jetzt, bei dem Evangelium der Weltenharmonie, fühlt sich Jeder mit seinem Nächsten nicht nur vereinigt, versöhnt, verschmolzen, sondern eins, als ob der Schleier der Maja zerrissen wäre und nur noch in Fetzen vor dem geheimnissvollen Ur-Einen herumflattere. Singend und tanzend äussert sich der Mensch als Mitglied einer höheren Gemeinsamkeit: er hat das Gehen und das Sprechen verlernt und ist auf dem Wege, tanzend in die Lüfte emporzufliegen."

reality of experience. For a start, sensory representations come into play, which, by representing a world of distinct things (including ourselves) maintain the appearance of individuality. Nietzsche sees Greek "epistemology at its peak with the Eleatics" (NL 1869/70, KSA 7, 3[72], p. 79). As is well known, the Eleatics defended the unity and identity of being and thereby excluded difference from being. Accordingly, for Nietzsche, representations of the external world, which determine our everyday life, exemplify the lowest rank of reality, and, in opposition to the philosophical tradition, dream images have a much higher degree of reality. Our dream images give us an immediate feeling of reality, which is not related to or dependent upon dissociative forms of space, time and causality; instead, they express a unique and higher type of coherence. This is how dreams become "the prototype of nature [*das Vorbild der Natur*] for plastic arts" (NL 1869/70, KSA 7, 3[58], p. 76), such as we can see in the first lines of *The Birth of Tragedy*: "The beautiful appearance of the world of dreams, in whose creation each man is a complete artist, is the precondition of all plastic art" (BT 1, KSA 1, p. 26). The way in which dreams are constituted in images grants a certain truth to visibility, which will then become tangible in the plastic arts. Being an art of lines and boundaries, where the individuals stand and remain for themselves, Greek sculpture belongs to Apollo's realm, which is determined by light, boundaries and measure. This originally dreamlike capacity to create images and forms is the material or mediating requirement (*mediale Voraussetzung*) needed for us to be able to convert the meaning of the Dionysian into something we can experience. As far as the shape or configuration (*Gestaltung*) is concerned, the dream-world is to the organism what the work of art is to art itself.

But tone and music are also mediating forms and therefore already constitute a translation. In Greek tragedy the Dionysian shapeless ground (*Untergrund*) *appears* in the form of music. This is to say that it appears as an ecstatic flow, in and by which visions or moments determined and differentiated "through Apollinian influence" (NL 1870/71, KSA 7, 7[127], p. 191) emerge in the form of figures and actions.[11] However, the reality of images is not the only means by which a tangible translation of the *One* reality is generated; music – i.e. the tragic chorus – also possesses a representational character. Both music and images convey the mediating structure of tragedy, which enables the encounter with absolute life. Thus, in tragedy we are

> on the one hand *pure intuition* [reine Anschauung] (i.e. projected images from a purely entranced being [*Wesen*], which in this intuition itself remains in the highest quietude),

---

[11] See also *The Dionysian Worldview* and chapter 4 of *The Birth of Tragedy*.

on the other hand we are the one being itself. Thus, we are only totally real suffering, wanting, hurting: as representations we have no reality, although we do have another form of reality. When we feel ourselves as the *one* being we are immediately elevated to the sphere of the pure intuition, which is totally without pain; even though we are at the same time pure will, pure suffering. As long as we are merely "represented" we do not participate in that relief of pain, whereas the one representing enjoys [this lack of grief, TK] fully.

In art, however, we become the "representing" ones, and this explains the rapture. (NL 1870/71, KSA 7, 7[201], p. 214–215)[12]

What enables us to recognise and to accept both the terrifying and the beautiful truth about the overwhelming flow of life is precisely the mediating structure of tragedy. By connecting harmony and disharmony, the artist makes sheer intensity visible.[13] Representation, in as much as it is a means for the *relief of pain*, will therefore become the medium of art, where grief is beheld but not suffered anymore. Indeed, from a physiological point of view, this entire representational process is already a cathartic strategy of the body. For, what we can see and keep at a distance does not affect us. The Apollinian side of the artistic act uses representation to create distance. The artistic form constitutes, thus, a shield against the simultaneity of absolute life and death within individuality. In this way, the intensity is made present but at the same time it is bound with pleasure as it is converted into an object for our contemplation. Also, we become both the vivid flow and the formal vision. But the content of the tragic vision, the downfall of the hero, leads individuality to dissolution, and hence, threatens to dissolve the mediating form or representation itself. Tragedy not only stages the downfall of one particular individual, it also directs this destructive power against itself, i.e. against itself as a form. In other words, it "negates itself and its Apolline visibility" (BT 21, KSA 1, p. 139),[14] and at this precise moment, rea-

---

12 "[E]inerseits *reine Anschauung* (d.h. projicirte Bilder eines rein entzückten Wesens, das in diesem Anschaung höchste Ruhe hat), anderseits sind wir das eine Wesen selbst. Also ganz real sind wir nur das Leiden, das Wollen, der Schmerz: als Vorstellungen haben wir keine Realität, obwohl doch eine andre Art von Realität. Wenn wir uns als das *eine* Wesen fühlen, so werden wir sofort in die Sphäre der reinen Anschauung gehoben, die ganz schmerzlos ist: obwohl wir dann zugleich der reine Wille, das reine Leiden sind. Solange wir aber selbst nur 'Vorgestelltes' sind, haben wir keinen Antheil an jener Schmerzlosigkeit: während das Vorstellende sie rein genießt./ In der Kunst dagegen werden wir 'Vorstellendes': daher die Verzückung."
13 This is a notion that, via Schiller (2004 [1792]), refers to Kant's Judgment on the Sublime, which always needs a part of "negativer Lust" (KU, p. 75).
14 As Nietzsche says, the Apollinian drama penetrates the sphere of Dionysian wisdom: "where it negates itself and its Apollinian visibility" (BT 21, KSA 1, p. 139).

lises the unity between subject and object. "*The tragic myth* [...] leads the world of appearances to its limits, where it negates itself and seeks to flee once again into the womb of the true and single reality" (BT 22, KSA 1, p. 141).[15] Within the unity of what is representing and what is being represented we are able to understand the pain and overcome it through the image. In so doing, we also realise the unity of the (vanishing) form and the unity of the ground of the world. But this entire process would remain incomprehensible to us if we were to see here only a form of art, i.e. a form of theatre. For, what is exposed in tragedy is the will itself, it is exposed as appearance (*Erscheinung*), as the projection of the primordial One (*Ur-Eine*), which, in its turn, becomes visible to itself and achieves its fulfilment through the integration of pain and contemplation (*Schmerz und Anschauung*). Indeed,

> the entire comedy of art is certainly not performed for us, neither for our edification nor our education, just as we are far from truly being the creators of that world of art. We are, however, entitled to assume this about ourselves: for the true creator of that world, we are already images and artistic projections, and our highest dignity lies in our significance as works of art – for only as an *aesthetic phenomenon* is existence and the world eternally *justified* – although, of course, our consciousness of our own significance in this respect hardly differs from the consciousness which painted soldiers on a canvas have of the battle portrayed there. Hence our entire knowledge of art is basically completely illusory, because, as knowing creatures, we are not one and identical with the essential being which gives itself eternal enjoyment as the single creator and spectator of that comedy of art. Only insofar as the genius during the act of artistic creation is fused with that primordial artist of the world, does he know anything about the eternal nature of art; for in that state he resembles, miraculously, that uncanny image of fairy tales, which may turn its eyes and contemplate itself. Now he is simultaneously subject and object, simultaneously poet, actor, and spectator. (BT 5, KSA 1, p. 47–48)[16]

---

15 The example Nietzsche has in mind is Isolde's death.
16 "Denn dies muss uns vor allem, zu unserer Erniedrigung und Erhöhung, deutlich sein, dass die ganze Kunstkomödie durchaus nicht für uns, etwa unsrer Besserung und Bildung wegen, aufgeführt wird, ja dass wir ebensowenig die eigentlichen Schöpfer jener Kunstwelt sind: wohl aber dürfen wir von uns selbst annehmen, dass wir für den wahren Schöpfer derselben schon Bilder und künstlerische Projektionen sind und in der Bedeutung von Kunstwerken unsre höchste Würde haben – denn nur als *aesthetisches Phänomen* ist das Dasein und die Welt ewig *gerechtfertigt*: – während freilich unser Bewusstsein über diese unsre Bedeutung kaum ein andres ist als es die auf Leinwand gemalten Krieger von der auf ihr dargestellten Schlacht haben. Somit ist unser ganzes Kunstwissen im Grunde ein völlig illusorisches, weil wir als Wissende mit jenem Wesen nicht eins und identisch sind, das sich, als einziger Schöpfer und Zuschauer jener Kunstkomödie einen ewigen Genuss bereitet. Nur soweit der Genius im Actus der künstlerischen Zeugung mit jenem Urkünstler der Welt verschmilzt, weiss er etwas über das ewige Wesen der Kunst; denn in jenem Zustande ist er, wunderbarer Weise, dem unheimlichen Bild des Mähr-

Tragedy is thus not a spectacle done for men by men, for the sake of artistic enjoyment; but rather the real enjoyment is only possible when the primordial being (*Urwesen*) appears as pure intensity and at the same time embodies both the threat and the redemption. It is here that the actual drama of existence, the unity between a primordial suffering and its redemption becomes comprehensible. Tragedy bears the primordial paradox of life, namely that the primordial One needs to manifest itself in individuals, thereby experiencing a painful fragmentation. The grief of the One lies in the fact that it cannot remain as one. This grief is also at the core of every individual; on the one hand, it expresses the conflict between individuality and self-preservation, and, on the other, the longing for the unity of life. In this sense, tragedy represents the metaphysical structure of the world. The primordial One is at the base of all individuals and their behaviour, although its origin is not recognisable as such. Indeed, we only become aware of its origin through the reflection of the artist, and this is also how the primordial One achieves self-awareness.

> The *visions of the primordial One* can only be *adequate* reflections of *being*. Contradiction is the essence of the primordial One; in this sense it can be both the highest pain and the highest pleasure. The highest pleasure is to submerge in the appearance: it is then that the will becomes totally externalised. It achieves this in genius. The will is at all times both the highest ecstasy and the greatest pain: to think of the ideality of dreams in the brain of one drowning – an endless time is condensed in a second. Appearance [*Die Erscheinung*] as that which is *becoming*. The *primordial One* contemplates the genius, who sees the appearance purely as appearance: this is the peak of ecstasy of the world. But, in as much as the genius [...] is an adequate reflection of the primordial One, he is the image [*Bild*] of the contradiction and the image of the pain. Each appearance is now simultaneously the primordial One itself: all feeling of suffering is the *primordial suffering* [Urleiden], only that it is seen, localised, in the net of time through the appearance. *Our pain is a represented one*: our *representation* remains always a *representation*. Our life is a *represented* life. [...] Thus, the genius' creativity is also *representation*. These reflections in the genius are *reflections of appearance*, no longer of the primordial One: as *copies* [Abbilder] of the *copy*, they are the purest moments of calm for Being. The truly non being – the work of art. The other reflections are only the *outer side of the primordial One*. Being satisfies itself in the complete semblance (Schein). (NL 1870/71, KSA 7, 7[157], p. 199f.)[17]

---

chens gleich, das die Augen drehn und sich selber anschaun kann; jetzt ist er zugleich Subject und Object, zugleich Dichter, Schauspieler und Zuschauer."

17 "Die *Visionen des Ureinen* können ja nur *adäquate* Spiegelungen des *Seins* sein. Insofern der Widerspruch das Wesen des Ureinen ist, kann es auch zugleich höchster Schmerz und höchste Lust sein: das Versenken in die Erscheinung ist höchste Lust: wenn der Wille ganz Außenseite wird. Dies erreicht er im Genius. In jedem Moment ist der Wille zugleich höchste Verzückung und höchster Schmerz: zu denken an die Idealität von Träumen im Hirn des Ertrinkenden – eine unendliche Zeit wird in eine Sekunde zusammengedrängt. Die Erscheinung als *werdende*. Das

We can see how the artist is the one who actually provides a reflection of reality: artistic imagination uses the ability to create images through the work of art in a special way. The genius mirrors the unreal or illusory nature of reality and thereby creates, through the work of art, the image of the image, the appearance of the appearance. But that very ability to create representations already enables us in our daily life to observe the world from a distance; it protects us from the insight into our very fragile nature. Thus, insofar as

> the primordial pain is broken through representation, *our existence* itself is a continuous artistic act. The creation of the artist is therefore *imitation of nature* in the most profound sense. (NL 1870/71, KSA 7, 7[196], p. 213)[18]

Ordinary representations already disrupt this primordial grief. But, through the reduplication of the appearance, the artist is able to make the internal side of the primordial One visible, whereas everyday reality is only the 'outer side of the primordial One'.

> With the Greeks the "will" wished to gaze upon itself through the transforming power of genius and the world of art; in order to glorify itself, its creatures had to sense that they themselves were worthy of being glorified; they had to see themselves again in a higher sphere, without this complete world of contemplation affecting them as an imperative or as a reproach. (BT 3, KSA 1, p. 37)[19]

This reflection within the appearance itself, through which the chorus is then able to see itself within the scene, is the true creative act. Nietzsche himself

---

Ureine schaut den Genius an, der die Erscheinung rein als Erscheinung sieht: dies ist die Verzückungsspitze der Welt. Insofern aber der Genius [...] eine adäquate Spiegelung des Ureinen ist, ist er das Bild des Widerspruchs und das Bild des Schmerzes. Jede Erscheinung ist nun zugleich das Ureine selbst: alles Leiden Empfinden ist *Urleiden*, nur durch die Erscheinung gesehen, lokalisirt, im Netz der Zeit. *Unser Schmerz ist ein vorgestellter*: unsre *Vorstellung* bleibt immer bei der *Vorstellung* hängen. Unser Leben ist ein *vorgestelltes* Leben. [...] Also ist auch das Schaffen des Genius *Vorstellung. Diese Spiegelungen im Genius sind Spiegelungen der Erscheinung*, nicht mehr des Ureinen: als *Abbilder des Abbildes* sind es die reinsten Ruhemomente des Seins. Das wahrhaft Nichtseiende – das Kunstwerk. Die anderen Spiegelungen sind nur die *Außenseite des Ureinen*. Das *Sein befriedigt sich im vollkommenen Schein*."

18 "[D]urch Vorstellung der Urschmerz gebrochen wird, ist *unser Dasein* selbst ein fortwährender *künstlerischer* Akt. Das Schaffen des Künstlers ist somit *Nachahmung der Natur* im tiefsten Sinne."

19 "In den Griechen wollte der 'Wille' sich selbst, in der Verklärung des Genius und der Kunstwelt, anschauen; um sich zu verherrlichen, mussten seine Geschöpfe sich selbst als verherrlichenswerth empfinden, sie mussten sich in einer höheren Sphäre wiedersehn, ohne dass diese vollendete Welt der Anschauung als Imperativ oder als Vorwurf wirkte."

clearly emphasises the metaphysical character of the artistic act by alluding to theodicy when he says that "only as an *aesthetic phenomenon* is existence and the world eternally justified" (BT 5, KSA 1, p. 47).[20]

> The more I become aware of those all-powerful artistic drives in nature, and of a fervent longing in them for semblance, for their redemption and release in semblance, the more I feel myself driven to the metaphysical assumption that that which truly exists, the eternally suffering and contradictory, primordial unity, simultaneously needs, for its constant release and redemption, the ecstatic vision, intensely pleasurable semblance. (BT 4, KSA 1, p. 38)[21]

The metaphysical dimension of the tragic understanding of the world exposes the fact that both our daily life and our most basic self-understanding are nothing but mere illusion. Nietzsche thematises the function of representations as empirical perceptions within the structure of human action most especially in his notes from 1870 to 1875:

> The world of representations is the means to bind us in the world of deeds and to compel us to actions in the service of instinct. The representation is the motive to deeds, although it does not alter [*berührt*] the essence of the action. The instinct that compels us to a certain deed and the representation that enters our consciousness as a motive are completely separate. Freedom of will is the world of representations that have been slipped in between; it is the belief that motives and actions necessarily condition one another. (NL 1870/71, KSA 7, 5[77], p. 110)[22]

Representations, thus, help us to structure individual life and to organise the practical aspects of existence. Consciousness, understood as the capacity for having representations and the possibility of formulating motivations for actions,

---

20 This has been considered to be a key sentence in Nietzsche's *Birth of Tragedy*. See for instance Schmidt 2012, p. 162f.
21 "Je mehr ich nämlich in der Natur jene allgewaltigen Kunsttriebe und in ihnen eine inbrünstige Sehnsucht zum Schein, zum Erlöstwerden durch den Schein gewahr werde, um so mehr fühle ich mich zu der metaphysischen Annahme gedrängt, dass das Wahrhaft-Seiende und Ur-Eine, als das ewig Leidende und Widerspruchsvolle, zugleich die entzückende Vision, den lustvollen Schein, zu seiner steten Erlösung braucht."
22 "Die Welt der Vorstellungen ist das Mittel, uns in der Welt der That festzuhalten und uns zu Handlungen im Dienste des Instinkts zu zwingen. Die Vorstellung ist Motiv zur That: während sie das Wesen der Handlung gar nicht berührt. Der Instinkt der uns zur That nöthigt und die Vorstellung die uns als Motiv ins Bewußtsein tritt liegen auseinander. Die Willensfreiheit ist die Welt dieser dazwischen geschobenen Vorstellungen, der Glaube daß Motiv und Handlung nothwendig einander bedingen." Nietzsche is obviously referring to Schopenhauer with this conception of the will as a non-reality and of the individual will as appearance. (Cf. Schopenhauer 1991, p. 36f. et passim).

is an interruption of the continuous and dynamic character of reality; i.e. of the reality of the absolute Will, which is now taken to be the true reality of the world. While we understand everyday reality as if there were a connection between our representations and the actions they motivate, actual reality takes place in secret. Sovereignty of everyday consciousness or what we could call first-order consciousness is based on the idea of a purpose (*Zweck*), according to which consciousness itself precedes and subjugates reality through its actions. But, as the young Nietzsche already made clear when he talked about the genesis of purposes, this sovereignty is actually based on an illusion, for these purposes originate entirely in the past.

> The separation of will and representation is quite simply a fruit of necessity in thought: it is a reproduction, an analogy of the experience that when we want something, we visualise the purpose, hovering before our own eyes. But this purpose is nothing but a past being reproduced: it is in this fashion that the will's urge makes itself understood. But the purpose is not the motive, the agent of the action: even though this may seem to be the case. (NL 1870/71, KSA 7, 5[80], p. 113)[23]

The distance that we place between will and representation and which constitutes the individual's sovereignty, stems from the experience in which we predetermine the action with a purpose. But the determination of the purpose originates in the past, for it is through the past that we interpret our present. Nietzsche thinks on the assumption that the organism's actual and true movements take place totally unconsciously and that our representations of these movements always appear to us in a distorted form. Whenever we want something, this will is preceded by a drive to which we give an object by means of an image, and this is how we rationalise the movements in our body, for our own understanding of it. In this respect Nietzsche proves to be a *Supercartesian*; in effect, for him there can be no connection between our representations and the body's true effective forces, because there is not such a corresponding causality. We misunderstand the indeed paradoxical appearance of the will or the primordial One and take the realm of representations and consciousness to be the true reality; although these merely constitute occasional causes for the primordial will to express itself. More precisely, the motives or conscious purposes are occasional causes, in an inverted sense. It is not the Absolute that acts on the

---

[23] "Die Trennung von Wille und Vorstellung ist ganz eigentlich eine Frucht der Nothwendigkeit im Denken: es ist eine Reproduktion, eine Analogie nach dem Erlebniß, daß wenn wir etwas wollen, uns das Ziel vor Augen schwebt. Dies Ziel aber ist nichts als eine reproduzirte Vergangenheit: in dieser Art macht sich die Willensregung verständlich. Aber das Ziel ist nicht das Motiv, das Agens der Handlung: obwohl dies der Fall zu sein scheint."

occasion of certain human actions – as occasionalism would typically have it; rather, we introduce occasional causes as an appearance on the occasion of the actions of the One Will, and we do so in order to make these actions ordinarily comprehensible and to place them under the sign of individuality. That is to say, we simulate images of purposes in order to render our actions plausible, but these take place completely independently of this whole process. In this sense, Nietzsche is pointing towards a primordial intellect, which not only steers things, but also arranges the process of individuation itself as it arranges the mechanism that constitutes the world of appearances whilst simultaneously hindering its being recognised as such, i.e. as appearance.

> Representation is the merest of all powers: *as agens*, it is only deceptive, for it is only the will that *acts*. But individuation is based on representation, so that if the latter is merely a deception, if it is only an illusion that helps the will to act – the will acts – in untold multiplicity for the unity. Its cognitive organ and the human's coincide in no way: that belief is naïve anthropomorphism. Cognitive organs in animals, plants and humans are only the organs of conscious cognition. The terrific wisdom of its construction is already the activity of an intellect. Individuation is thus never the work of a conscious cognition, but of that primordial intellect [*Urintellekts*]. The Kantian-Schopenhauerian Idealists never acknowledged this. Our intellect *never* takes us further than to conscious cognition: but to the extent that we are still intellectual instinct, we may dare to say something more about the primordial intellect. Beyond these limits we cannot go.
>
> Human instincts come into their own in large organisms like state church, even more so in people, in society, in humanity; much larger instincts in the history of a star:
>
> there are myriad representations, foreground delusions, in state, church etc., whereas here the overall instinct is already creating.
>
> From the standpoint of conscious thinking, the world appears as countless individuals nested in one another: whereby the concept of the individual is superseded. The world a monstrous organism birthing and preserving itself: multiplicity lies in things because the intellect is in them. Multiplicity and unity the same – an unthinkable thought. Above all important to see that individuation is *not* the birth of conscious spirit. That is why we may speak of delusions on the presupposition of the reality of individuation. (NL 1870/71, KSA 7, 5[79], p. 111f.)[24]

---

24 "Die Vorstellung ist von allen Mächten die geringste: sie ist *als Agens* nur Trug, denn es *handelt* nur der Wille. Nun aber beruht die individuatio auf der Vorstellung: wenn diese nun Trug ist, wenn sie nur scheinbar ist, um dem Willen zum Thun zu verhelfen – der Wille handelt – in unerhörter Vielheit für die Einheit. Sein Erkenntnißorgan und das menschliche fallen keineswegs zusammen: dieser Glaube ist ein naiver Anthropomorphismus. Erkenntnißorgane bei Thieren Pflanzen und Menschen sind nur die Organe des *bewußten* Erkennens. Die ungeheure Weisheit seiner Bildung ist bereits die Thätigkeit eines Intellekts. Die individuatio ist nun jedenfalls nicht das Werk des bewußten Erkennens, sondern jenes Urintellekts. Dies haben

Thus, while we think that we are acting according to our representations, these are rather the means by which we create an illusory multiplicity. Through these single representations we virtually create our temporal existence; we create the illusion of multiplicity. From the standpoint of the primordial intellect everything is a real unity, but we cannot grasp this with our own individual understanding. The organisation of this primordial intellect is only visible to us through the great constructions of history and society, which we always already conform to. If we seek to grasp reality in its isolated individuality – that is to say, in the form of subjectivity – we are bound to go astray. And yet, the insight into the illusory character of subjectivity cannot be easy for us. It is, hence, indeed understandable why art and tragedy constitute for Nietzsche the true means by which we attain understanding of the world. For sciences, being so eager to expose the illusory aspect of our autonomy and to destroy, through their analyses, our entire self-understanding as individuals, would lead us to utter hopelessness and apathy. Any will to act would completely die away. What remains is

> The only possibility of life: art. Otherwise aversion from life. The drive of sciences is the total destruction of illusion: if there were no art, quietism would follow. (NL 1869/70, KSA 7, 3[60], p. 76)[25]

Only art is capable to grasp the actual reality of life without falling into nihilism. Only art can move us to the affirmation of life. But how does this artistic framework between the primordial One and individuality address our initial question? In effect, artists know and transform everyday activities, and while they bring to

---

die kantisch-schopenhauerischen Idealisten nicht erkannt. Unser Intellekt führt uns *nie* weiter als bis zum bewußten Erkennen: insofern wir aber noch intellektueller Instinkt sind, können wir noch etwas über den Urintellekt zu sagen wagen. Über diesen trägt kein Pfeil hinaus./ In den großen Organismen wie Staat Kirche kommen die menschlichen Instinkte zur Geltung, noch mehr im Volk, in der Gesellschaft, in der Menschheit; viel größere Instinkte in der Geschichte eines Gestirns:/ in Staat Kirche usw. giebt es eine Unzahl Vorstellungen, vorgeschobenen Wahn, während hier schon der Gesammtinstinkt schafft./ Vom Standpunkte des bewußten Denkens erscheint die Welt wie eine Unsumme ineinander geschachtelter Individuen: womit eigentlich der Begriff des Individuums aufgehoben ist. Die Welt ein ungeheurer sich selbst gebärender und erhaltender Organismus: die Vielheit liegt in den Dingen, weil der Intellekt in ihnen ist. Vielheit und Einheit dasselbe – ein undenkbarer Gedanke./ Vor allem wichtig einzusehn, daß die Individuation *nicht* die Geburt des bewußten Geistes ist. Darum dürfen wir von Wahnvorstellungen reden, unter der Voraussetzung der Realität der Individuation."

25 "Einzige Möglichkeit des Lebens: die Kunst. Sonst Abwendung vom Leben. Völlige Vernichtung der Illusion ist der Trieb der Wissenschaften: es würde Quietismus folgen – wäre nicht die Kunst."

light the illusory nature of appearances, they also resolve the foundational metaphysical conflict in a positive way. The individual is now able to feel life and to affirm its dissolution – at least in its mediating rupture (*in der medialen Brechung*). And yet, although this deed may seem to be illusory (*scheinhaft*), it is nevertheless realised by the primordial One.

> For brief moments we are truly the primordial being itself and we feel its unbounded lust and joy in existence; the struggle, the agony, the destruction of appearances, all this now seems necessary to us given the uncountable excess of forms of existence thrusting and pushing themselves into life, given the exuberant fertility of the world-Will. We are pierced by the raging sting of these pains at the very moment when, as it were, we become one with the immeasurable, primordial delight in existence and when, in Dionysian ecstasy, we sense the indestructible and eternal nature of this joy. In spite of fear and pity, we are fortunate vital beings, not as individuals, but as the *one* living being, with whose procreative joy we have been fused. (BT 17, KSA 1, p. 109)[26]

Both pain and contemplation are integrated in the psychic economy of tragedy so that the tragic process makes the world process visible.

> The will is the most general form of appearance: i.e. the alternation between pain and pleasure: the presupposition of the world as the continuous healing of pain through the pleasure of pure contemplation. The *universal one suffers* and projects the will in order to heal, in order to achieve pure contemplation. Suffering, longing, lack as primordial source of things. (NL 1870/71, KSA 7, 7[165], p. 202)[27]

It is therefore not so much about "imagining [*Vorstellung*] that man should redeem himself – as if it wasn't the world-essence that is redeemed in us!" (NL 1870, KSA 7, 6[5], p. 131). In other words, artists cannot distinguish themselves from the One either; on the contrary, by breaking with the daily, individual reality, they enable the Absolute to achieve self-consciousness and redemption.

---

26 "Wir sind wirklich in kurzen Augenblicken das Urwesen selbst und fühlen dessen unbändige Daseinsgier und Daseinslust; der Kampf, die Qual, die Vernichtung der Erscheinungen dünkt uns jetzt wie nothwendig, bei dem Uebermaass von unzähligen, sich in's Leben drängenden und stossenden Daseinsformen, bei der überschwänglichen Fruchtbarkeit des Weltwillens; wir werden von dem wüthenden Stachel dieser Qualen in demselben Augenblicke durchbohrt, wo wir gleichsam mit der unermesslichen Urlust am Dasein eins geworden sind und wo wir die Unzerstörbarkeit und Ewigkeit dieser Lust in dionysischer Entzückung ahnen. Trotz Furcht und Mitleid sind wir die glücklich-Lebendigen, nicht als Individuen, sondern als das *eine* Lebendige, mit dessen Zeugungslust wir verschmolzen sind."
27 "Der Wille ist die allgemeinste Erscheinungsform: d.h. der Wechsel von Schmerz und Lust: Voraussetzung der Welt, als der fortwährenden Heilung vom Schmerz durch die Lust des reinen Anschauens. Das *All-eine leidet* und projicirt zur Heilung den Willen, zur Erreichung der reinen Anschauung. Das Leid, die Sehnsucht, der Mangel als Urquell der Dinge."

The difference that constitutes individuality not only appears here for the first time, but is dissipated as the tragedy proceeds. In other words: the scenario in which we find ourselves now could not be more metaphysical. True knowledge of reality annihilates reality because it annihilates the difference and reality itself is merged into the Absolute. The "appearance of appearance" (*Erscheinung der Erscheinung*) takes the Absolute (which suffered from the process of its differentiation) back to its true wholeness. The Dionysian drama of the disjointed God ends with the self-affirmation of absolute unity, in the recuperated wholeness of the God.

III

In his work on tragedy, Nietzsche criticises our everyday consciousness with its teleological view of the world and, in so doing, already points towards the genealogical method. Although he does not develop its relation with the genealogical form of critique, he already uses the notion of interpretation in the *Birth of Tragedy*.

> We indicated earlier that the Homeric epic is the poetry of Olympian culture, with which it sang its own song of victory over the terrors of the fight against the Titans. Now, under the overwhelming influence of tragic poetry, the Homeric myths are re-born to new life, and in this metempsychosis they show that since then the Olympian culture has also been overcome by an even deeper world view. [...] Dionysian truth takes over the entire realm of myth to symbolise *its own* insights, and it expresses these partly in the public cult of tragedy, and partly in secretly conducted dramatic mystery-festivals, but always in the disguise of the old myths. What power was it that liberated Prometheus from his vultures and transformed the myth into a vehicle of Dionysian wisdom? It was the Herculean power of music, which having attained its supreme manifestation in tragedy, is able to interpret myth in a new and most profoundly significant way; we have already characterised this as the mightiest deed of which music was capable. (BT 10, KSA 1, p. 73f.)[28]

---

[28] "Es ist früher angedeutet worden, dass das homerische Epos die Dichtung der olympischen Cultur ist, mit der sie ihr eignes Siegeslied über die Schrecken des Titanenkampfes gesungen hat. Jetzt, unter dem übermächtigen Einflusse der tragischen Dichtung, werden die homerischen Mythen von Neuem umgeboren und zeigen in dieser Metempsychose, dass inzwischen auch die olympische Cultur von einer noch tieferen Weltbetrachtung besiegt worden ist. [...] Die dionysische Wahrheit übernimmt das gesammte Bereich des Mythus als Symbolik *ihrer* Erkenntnisse und spricht diese theils in dem öffentlichen Cultus der Tragödie, theils in den geheimen Begehungen dramatischer Mysterienfeste, aber immer unter der alten mythischen Hülle aus. Welche Kraft war dies, die den Prometheus von seinen Geiern befreite und den Mythus zum Vehikel dionysischer Weisheit umwandelte? Dies ist die heraklesmässige Kraft der Musik: als welche, in der

Music, hence, "interprets" the Homeric myth and generates the tragedy. In Greek tragedy, indeed, even the Gods succumb to the power of fate – music has gained power over them. The term 'interpretation' cannot be understood here as the way in which the Greek tragedians were transmitting Homer's texts, but rather as the power of the whole process of interpretation, such as would be the case ten years later in his *Genealogy of Morality*. In this text, the notion of interpretation designates the fundamental process (*Kerngeschehen*) of the world. The actual history of the world is the history of its successive interpretations; the history of the overcomings, in which

> every purpose and use is just a *sign* that the will to power has achieved mastery over something less powerful, and has impressed upon it its own meaning of a use function; and the whole history of a "thing", an organ, a tradition can to this extent be seen as a continuous chain of signs, constantly revealing new interpretations and adjustments, the causes of which do not even need to be connected to each other – in some circumstances they rather follow and take over from each other by chance. Consequently, the "development" of a thing, a tradition, an organ is certainly not its *progressus* towards a single goal, even less is it the logical *progressus*, taking the shortest route with least expenditure of energy and cost – but rather it is the sequence of more or less profound, more or less mutually independent processes of subjugation exacted on the thing, together with the resistance encountered every time, the attempted transformations for the purposes of defence and reaction, as well as the results of successful counter-measures. Form is fluid; the "meaning" [*Sinn*], however, is even more so ... Even within each individual organism things are no different: with every essential growth in the totality, the "meaning" of the individual organ also shifts – sometimes the partial destruction of organs, the reduction in their number (for example, through the obliteration of intermediate structures) can be a sign of increasing power and perfection. What I wanted to say is this: even the partial *loss of utility*, decay and degeneration, the loss of meaning, and functional purpose, in short, death, also belong to the conditions of true *progressus*, which always appears in the form of a will and a way to a *greater power* and always establishes itself at the expense of a huge number of smaller powers. (GM II 12, KSA 5, p. 314f.)[29]

Tragödie zu ihrer höchsten Erscheinung gekommen, den Mythus mit neuer tiefsinnigster Bedeutsamkeit zu interpretiren weiss; wie wir dies als das mächtigste Vermögen der Musik früher schon zu charakterisiren hatten."

29 "Aber alle Zwecke, alle Nützlichkeiten sind nur *Anzeichen* davon, dass ein Wille zur Macht über etwas weniger Mächtiges Herr geworden ist und ihm von sich aus den Sinn einer Funktion aufgeprägt hat; und die ganze Geschichte eines 'Dings', eines Organs, eines Brauchs kann dergestalt eine fortgesetzte Zeichen-Kette von immer neuen Interpretationen und Zurechtmachungen sein, deren Ursachen selbst unter sich nicht im Zusammenhange zu sein brauchen, vielmehr unter Umständen sich bloss zufällig hinter einander folgen und ablösen. 'Entwicklung' eines Dings, eines Brauchs, eines Organs ist demgemäss nichts weniger als sein progressus auf ein Ziel hin, noch weniger ein logischer und kürzester, mit dem kleinsten Aufwand von Kraft und Kosten erreichter progressus, – sondern die Aufeinanderfolge von mehr oder minder tiefgehenden,

The notion of interpretation, thus, sets the basis for the methodology of the genealogy and points towards both the true and terrifying processes of the world. Interpretations refer to an existing reality, but only in order to incorporate that very reality. And what is more, the incorporation (*Einverleibung*) is itself a form of creation, a creation of something new. The Homeric myth invents the Olympic Gods and designs the Apollinian world, in which the chthonian powers will be overcome. The tragic myth interprets these figures, in order to take them to their limit and make the Dionysian ground of life (*dionysische Lebensgrund*) in them visible. The history of thought should also be understood in this sense. Whenever we talk about progress, we are always projecting from "men to nature – grotesque shadow projections of man onto nature, just like mountains" (NL 1872/73, KSA 7, 19[134], p. 462). Thus, the Pythagoreans use numbers, Democritus matter, Heraclitus "the plastic power of the artist [as, TK] a primordial one" (NL 1872/73, KSA 7, 19[134], p. 461) and others use yet other ideas as explanatory principles of nature. None of them, however, are doing anything but interpreting nature; and nature, in its turn, actually first emerges out of the interpretation itself. Nevertheless, interpretation is not merely a 'spiritual' principle. The body also "*interprets*: what takes place in the formation of an organ is an interpretation; the organ delimits, determines degrees, power differences" (NL 1885, KSA 12, 2[148], p. 139). Where other philosophers have found essences or at least types, Nietzsche sees degrees of power, which take the form of 'interpretations'. Each and every development manifests itself in a certain degree of power. Organic bodies develop a hand as an interpretation of reality. The result of this is the grasping-world (*Greifwelt*); such a world does not exist before the emergence of the hand. The hand is what first turns the world into a grasping-world. "The *degree of power* determines which *being* [Wesen] will have the other degree of power: under which form, violence or needfulness it is effective or it resists"

---

mehr oder minder von einander unabhängigen, an ihm sich abspielenden Überwältigungsprozessen, hinzugerechnet die dagegen jedes Mal aufgewendeten Widerstände, die versuchten Form-Verwandlungen zum Zweck der Vertheidigung und Reaktion, auch die Resultate gelungener Gegenaktionen. Die Form ist flüssig, der 'Sinn' ist es aber noch mehr ... Selbst innerhalb jedes einzelnen Organismus steht es nicht anders: mit jedem wesentlichen Wachsthum des Ganzen verschiebt sich auch der 'Sinn' der einzelnen Organe, – unter Umständen kann deren theilweises Zu-Grunde-Gehn, deren Zahl-Verminderung (zum Beispiel durch Vernichtung der Mittelglieder) ein Zeichen wachsender Kraft und Vollkommenheit sein. Ich wollte sagen: auch das theilweise *Unnützlichwerden*, das Verkümmern und Entarten, das Verlustiggehn von Sinn und Zweckmässigkeit, kurz der Tod gehört zu den Bedingungen des wirklichen progressus: als welcher immer in Gestalt eines Willens und Wegs zu *grösserer Macht* erscheint und immer auf Unkosten zahlreicher kleinerer Mächte durchgesetzt wird."

(NL 1888, KSA 13, 14[93], p. 271). When the grasping-world emerges as such, it emerges as a function of the hand. The stronger power has created a functional form for itself. The necessity within this process can only be briefly indicated here, but what is clear is that the passage from aquatic to terrestrial creatures implies both a need and a necessity:

> to either become land animals or perish [...] suddenly all instincts were devalued and "suspended". From this point on, these animals were to go on foot and "carry themselves", whereas previously they had been carried by water: a terrible heaviness bore down on them. (GM II 16, KSA 5, p. 322)[30]

From the standpoint of the difference of power, the will to power appears as a subject:

> Mere power differences could not perceive themselves as such: there must be something there wanting to grow, something that every other something wanting to grow interprets with regard to its value [...] In truth, *interpretation is itself a means to become master over something. (The organic process presupposes constant **interpreting***. (NL 1885, KSA 12, 2[148], p. 139–140)[31]

In this sense, power degrees, which confront us concretely in the form of a hand or a grasping-world, point towards an underlying dynamic, which constantly craves new forms and ever increasing degrees of power. The will to power is the actual subject of the interpretations in as much as they are understood as processes of overpowering, constituting both organic and social life. But we must not mistake this concept of the will to power with our own experience of wanting:

> Let us stay with the feeling of the will! What do we become aware of as "will"? We recognise here that the will is only a hypothesis. It could be true – or not.
>
> There is no more "will" than what we are aware of. I.e. we have added the will to certain appearances of consciousness; just as we have added "matter" to others. (NL 1883, KSA 10, 12[30], p. 405–406)[32]

---

30 "... entweder Landthiere zu werden oder zu Grunde zu gehen [...] – mit Einem Male waren alle ihre Instinkte entwerthet und 'ausgehängt'. Sie sollten nunmehr auf den Füssen gehen und 'sich selber tragen', wo sie bisher vom Wasser getragen wurden: eine entsetzliche Schwere lag auf ihnen."

31 "Bloße Machtverschiedenheiten könnten sich noch nicht als solche empfinden: es muß ein wachsen-wollendes Etwas da sein, das jedes andere wachsen-wollende Etwas auf seinen Werth hin interpretirt. [...] – In Wahrheit ist *Interpretation ein Mittel selbst, um Herr über etwas zu werden. (Der organische Prozeß setzt fortwährendes **Interpretiren** voraus*."

32 "Bleiben wir doch stehen beim Willens-Gefühl! Was wird uns als 'Wille' bewußt? Da erkennen wir, daß Wille nur eine Hypothese ist. Sie könnte wahr sein — oder auch nicht./ Es giebt nicht

The individual will itself proves to be an interpretation, an illusion for the sake of life, which is obviously produced by the will to power itself. In this sense, we are dealing with the most general dimension of being – one that is unconsciously effective in every being. It is therefore not incorrect to associate Nietzsche's will to power with Darwin's formal concept of a 'struggle for life' (cf. Darwin 1859 and Engels 2009, p. 30). But we can see how this conventional and outdated evolutionary theory, which presupposes the existence of a yet to be discovered ecological niche, is overcome by Nietzsche and his constructivist theory of interpretation. Interpretation, thus, also replaces the notion of truth. Truth does not emerge as the copy of something given, but rather as a creation.

> "Truth" is thereby not something that would be there to be found and discovered, – but rather something *that is to be created* and that designates a *process*, or what is more it designates a will to overpower that has no end in itself. To ascribe truth as a process in infinitum, an *active determining, not* a becoming aware of something ⟨that⟩ would be fixed and determined in itself. It is a word for the "will to power" (NL 1887, KSA 12, 9[91], p. 385)[33]

Everything emerges from the dynamic of interpretation, nothing is given. On the whole, our exterior world must be understood as an interpretation. In fact, our drives "don't do anything else but interpret nervous stimuli and, according to their requirements, posit their 'causes'" (D 119, KSA 3, p. 113). This is how the world of things first emerges.

> *Stimulus* and the thing that *triggers it* mixed up from the beginning! The sameness of the stimuli was the origin for the belief in "*equal* things": the *continuously equal* stimuli created the belief in "things", "substances".

> The *life preserving principle* must be sought in the way in which the first organic formations felt the stimuli and evaluated exteriority: the belief that wan, the belief that survived was the one *that made further living possible, not* the belief closest to truth, but the most useful. "Subject" is the condition of life for organic existence, therefor not "true", but rather the feeling of subjectivity *can* be essentially false, but the only means to survive. *Error, father of the living!* (NL 1881, KSA 9, 11[270], p. 544f.)[34]

---

mehr 'Wille' als was uns davon bewußt wird. D.h. zu gewissen Erscheinungen des Bewußtseins haben wir den Willen hinzugedichtet: wie 'Materie' zu anderen."

33 "'Wahrheit' ist somit nicht etwas, was da wäre und was aufzufinden, zu entdecken wäre, – sondern etwas, *das zu schaffen ist* und das den Namen für einen *Prozeß* abgiebt, mehr noch für einen Willen der Überwältigung, der an sich kein Ende hat: Wahrheit hineinlegen, als ein processus in infinitum, ein *aktives Bestimmen, nicht* ein Bewußtwerden von etwas, ⟨das⟩ 'an sich' fest und bestimmt wäre. Es ist ein Wort für den 'Willen zur Macht'".

34 "*Reiz* und *veranlassendes* Ding von Anbeginn an verwechselt! Die Gleichheit der Reize gab dem Glauben an '*gleiche* Dinge' den Ursprung: die *dauernd gleichen* Reize schufen den Glauben

Essences or types emerge from detecting similarities in our perceptions and are not to be attributed to external forms. Interpretations do not measure themselves against things (this is not about correspondence), but against their own usefulness. And this generates, in its turn, stable forms; forms which are related to our actions, and not to 'things in themselves'. We can now see how Nietzsche's interpretation theory is not only directed against traditional thought, but is also able to incorporate it or to explain it within its own interpretative paradigm. Reality cannot be explained through its relation to truth or purposes; it rather emerges in the midst of a battle of forces, in the form of interpretations, and then leads these forces to form structures. The result is then

> that the apparent *purposes* are not intended, but at the moment in which supremacy over a lesser power is reached and the latter works as a function of the greater [power, TK], the order of rank, the order in the organisation must give the impression of an order of means and purposes. (NL 1887, KSA 12, 9[91], p. 386)[35]

Purposes appear only when the struggle has already taken place and the forces have already found their order. One can say that the purpose of the Homeric Gods was to suffer the power of fate in tragedies, or, as the Christian historians pretended, that the Roman Empire achieved such a great expansion in order to make the Christian Mission possible. In any case, whatever needed to comply with the interpretation, will become clear once we consider the purposes themselves. Also, what follows from the interpretation is not only the concept of things and the notion of purposefulness (*Zweckhaftigkeit*), but also a theory of the subject.

> The emergence of "things" is entirely due to the work of the ones representing, thinking, willing, inventing. The concept "thing" itself as well as all its attributes – even "the subject" is such a product, a "thing", like all others: a simplification in order to designate the *force* that posits, invents, thinks, as such, as distinct from all particular instances of positing, inventing, thinking. That is to say, it designates the *capacity* as distinct from all other particulars: at bottom, [it is] the doing together with the view towards all still

---

an 'Dinge', 'Substanzen'./ In der Art, wie die Erstlinge organischer Bildungen Reize empfanden und das Außer-sich beurtheilten, muß das *lebenserhaltende Princip* gesucht werden: derjenige Glaube siegte, erhielt sich, *bei dem das Fortleben möglich wurde*; *nicht* der am meisten wahre, sondern am meisten nützlichen Glaube. 'Subjekt' ist die Lebensbedingung des organischen Daseins, deshalb nicht 'wahr', sondern Subjekt-Empfindung *kann* wesentlich falsch sein, aber als einziges Mittel der Erhaltung. Der *Irrthum Vater des Lebendigen!*".

35 "[D]aß die anscheinenden *Zwecke* nicht beabsichtigt sind, aber, sobald die Übermacht über eine geringere Macht erreicht ist und letztere als Funktion der größeren arbeitet, eine Ordnung des Rangs, der Organisation den Anschein einer Ordnung von Mittel und Zweck erwecken muß."

expected doings (the doing and the likeliness of similar doings). (NL 1885/1886, KSA 12, 2[151], p. 141)[36]

Analogous to the notion of things, as being the unity of a function, we construct the notion of subjects, as the unity of functionalisation. What is crystallised in the subject is not a moral instance or an object of moral determinations, but the future dimension of the activity, in the form of hope. But this conception of the subject is as illusory as the notion of purpose and the notion of truth.

> – Is it still necessary to put the interpreters behind the *interpretation*? That is already poetry, hypothesis.
>
> The world is knowable as long as the word "knowledge" bears a meaning: yet the world is to be interpreted differently, it does not have a meaning behind itself, but rather has countless meanings "perspectivism".
>
> It is our needs that interpret the world: our drives and their for and against. Each drive seeks some kind of domination; each of them has its perspective, which it would like to impose as a norm for the other drives. (NL 1886, KSA 12, 7[60], p. 315)[37]

This is why the origin and purpose of things are divided, and history presents itself in such a way:

> that anything in existence, having somehow come to its present state, will again and again be interpreted from a new perspective, appropriated in a new way, reorganised for and redirected to new purposes by a power superior to it; that all events in the organic world involve *overpowering*, *dominating* and that, in turn, all overpowering and dominating involve a re-interpretation, a readjustment, in which their former "sense" and "purpose" must necessarily be obscured or entirely erased. (GM II 12, KSA 5, p. 313–314)[38]

---

36 "Die Entstehung der 'Dinge' ist ganz und gar das Werk der Vorstellenden, Denkenden, Wollenden, Erfindenden. Der Begriff 'Ding' selbst ebenso als alle Eigenschaften – Selbst 'das Subjekt' ist ein solches Geschaffenes, ein 'Ding', wie alle Andern: eine Vereinfachung, um die *Kraft*, welche setzt, erfindet, denkt, als solche zu bezeichnen, im Unterschiede von allem einzelnen Setzen, Erfinden, Denken selbst. Also das *Vermögen* im Unterschiede von allem Einzelnen bezeichnet: im Grunde das Thun in Hinsicht auf alles noch zu erwartende Thun (Thun und die Wahrscheinlichkeit ähnlichen Thuns) zusammengefaßt."
37 " – Ist es zuletzt nöthig, den Interpreten noch hinter die *Interpretation* zu setzen? Schon das ist Dichtung, Hypothese./ Soweit überhaupt das Wort 'Erkenntniß' Sinn hat, ist die Welt erkennbar: aber sie ist anders deutbar, sie hat keinen Sinn hinter sich, sondern unzählige Sinne 'Perspektivismus'./ Unsre Bedürfnisse sind es, die die Welt auslegen: unsre Triebe und deren Für und Wider. Jeder Trieb ist eine Art Herrschsucht, jeder hat seine Perspektive, welche er als Norm allen übrigen Trieben aufzwingen möchte."
38 "[D]ass etwas Vorhandenes, irgendwie Zu-Stande-Gekommenes immer wieder von einer ihm überlegenen Macht auf neue Ansichten ausgelegt, neu in Beschlag genommen, zu einem neuen Nutzen umgebildet und umgerichtet wird; dass alles Geschehen in der organischen Welt ein

What is central to the project of the Genealogy is the fact that the will to power remains active even if it is reversed, i.e. in its own re-activity. As can be seen in Zarathustra's first speech about *On the Three Metamorphoses* of the spirit and from the whole historical structure of the *Genealogy of Morality*, Nietzsche's notion of the will to power proves to be successful for the analysis of this reversal or deformation, however paradoxical this might be. For it is through the *Genealogy of Morality* that it becomes clear how the weak have defeated the strong, how the slaves have subjugated the masters. *Ressentiment* takes over (*überwindet*) the original spontaneity, the priests defeat the "original noblemen", morality begins to dominate the world. But what does this process mean?

> While all noble morality grows out of a triumphant yes saying to itself, slave morality says no from the start to everything that is "outside", "other", "non-self". And *this* no is its creative act. This reversal of the evaluating glance – this *essential* reorientation towards the outside instead of back onto itself – is a feature of *ressentiment*: in order to arise, slave morality first requires an opposing, external world. Psychologically speaking, it needs external stimuli in order to act at all, – its action is basically a reaction. The opposite is the case with the noble method of valuation: this acts and grows spontaneously. It seeks its opposite only to affirm its own self even more thankfully and exultantly, – its negative concept "low", "common", "bad" is merely a pale contrast created after the event compared to its positive basic concept, saturated with life and passion, "we the noble, the good, the beautiful, and the happy!" (GM I 10, KSA 5, p. 270f.) [39]

Reactions defeat actions, powerlessness prevails over true sovereignty. This victory is attained through the spirit, which arises as the perverted form of the will to power. The *Genealogy of Morality* is also a genealogy of reason, for it is

---

Überwältigen, Herrwerden und dass wiederum alles Überwältigen und Herrwerden ein Neu-Interpretieren, ein Zurechtmachen ist, bei dem der bisherige 'Sinn' und 'Zweck' nothwendig verdunkelt oder ganz ausgelöscht werden muss."

39 "Während alle vornehme Moral aus einem triumphirenden Ja-sagen zu sich selber herauswächst, sagt die Sklaven-Moral von vornherein Nein zu einem 'Ausserhalb', zu einem 'Anders', zu einem 'Nicht-selbst': und *dies* Nein ist ihre schöpferische That. Diese Umkehrung des werthesetzenden Blicks – diese *nothwendige* Richtung nach Aussen statt zurück auf sich selber – gehört eben zum Ressentiment: die Sklaven-Moral bedarf, um zu entstehn, immer zuerst einer Gegen- und Aussenwelt, sie bedarf, physiologisch gesprochen, äusserer Reize, um überhaupt zu agiren, – ihre Aktion ist von Grund aus Reaktion. Das Umgekehrte ist bei der vornehmen Werthungsweise der Fall: sie agirt und wächst spontan, sie sucht ihren Gegensatz nur auf, um zu sich selber noch dankbarer, noch frohlockender Ja zu sagen, – ihr negativer Begriff 'niedrig' 'gemein' 'schlecht' ist nur ein nachgebornes blasses Contrastbild im Verhältniss zu ihrem positiven, durch und durch mit Leben und Leidenschaft durchtränkten Grundbegriff 'wir Vornehmen, wir Guten, wir Schönen, wir Glücklichen!'"

the *ressentiment*-man who first starts calculating and rationalising the world.⁴⁰ The first noble men, the ones who lived at the beginning of the historical process described by Nietzsche, interact with their environment with such spontaneity and immediacy that they do not withhold any negativity within themselves, and hence, do not feel the need for an organised regime. In effect, that inner, negative energy that urges one to dominate is far more characteristic of the Judeo-Christian religion, which, by proclaiming the slave-revolt, perverts all genuine power relations. For morality, too, is nothing but an interpretation of reality: "*My main principle: there are no moral phenomena, but only a moral interpretation of these phenomena. This interpretation itself has extra-moral origins*" (NL 1885/86, KSA 12, 2[165], p. 149). Morality is also an interpretation whose main utility lies in its functionality and capacity for overpowering. As we can see, there is nothing outside the will to power. Through the genealogical method any apparently objective knowledge as well as all social structures, especially those that seem to be opposed to it, are seen as forms of the will to power.

How could the genealogy be anything other than a form of the will to power? In fact, the will to power becomes aware of itself through the genealogy. This awareness has a purely scientific side to it, but also an affective one. As self-awareness, the will to power says yes to itself in the genealogy and becomes a gay science. By fully recognising itself and accepting itself in the form of *amor fati*, the will to power reconciles itself with the course of the world. Numerous book-projects from later years illustrate in different ways this same model, where the will to power loses and finds itself anew.

  I.   Decadence values
  II. The countermovement and its fate.
  III. The problem of modernity.
  IV. The great *noon*.
       (NL 1888, KSA 13, 15[102], p. 467)⁴¹

---

40 See Habermas 1988, p. 119: "The nihilistic rule of a subject-oriented reason is understood as the result and expression of a perversion of the will to power". However, contrary to Habermas, we do not believe that the process of the genealogy is situated "beyond the horizon of reason"; but rather that this process is in some sense completed. This is at least the way in which Nietzsche sees it.

41 "I. Die Niedergangs-Werthe/ II. Die Gegenbewegung und deren Schicksal./ III. Problem der Modernität./ IV. Der grosse *Mittag*."

We can now begin to understand how, just as the underlying Dionysian life goes through its own fragmentation, the will to power goes through its own perversion, and that this precise process constitutes Nietzsche's philosophy. The will to power rediscovers its original self-affirmation by traversing all the different perspectives, Judeo-Christian religion, morality, science and philosophy. And now this new self-re-affirmation has a reflective form. To be sure, the fact that life achieves its true being by first undergoing its own downfall (*Selbstverlust*) is a metaphysical fate. But, for Nietzsche, the actual agent of the entire process is this very being.

We can now see how, according to the notion of the will to power, although individuals are the ones who deal with the many different situations, by doing so, they do not realise anything else than the will to power itself, which is this very dynamic of self-overcoming. This realisation, however, has to be understood in a direct and ontological sense. Indeed, the question that always remains is: to what extent can we recognise this, to what extent are we strong enough to accept or incorporate this knowledge? Through this realisation we become the self-awareness of the will to power. We recognise that the principle is absolute and that it does not allow anything to remain outside or unexplained by it. In the end there is no definitive difference between us and the will to power. In the genealogy, such as in tragedy, individuality and subjectivity are proved to be merely superficial and illusory moments; moments that must be overcome, but that do not provide any form of autonomy.

IV

For Fichte, too, the representation of the world is never a copy of an objective reality, but a construction. During his time in Jena (from 1794 to 1800), Fichte's thought is especially focused on the inner necessity of this construction. The maxim of his thought is: the constitution of the I takes place in its opposition and interaction with the not-I. There is nothing outside this interaction. As we can see from the three axioms in the *Foundations of the Entire Science of Knowledge* (1794), the act of self-positing underlies this interaction (which also manifests itself in our concrete relations with the world). The I that is "absolutely posited, and founded on itself" is the ground of all activity of the human mind, "and thus of its pure character, of the pure character of activity as such" (GA I/2, p. 258–259). Yet this pure activity can only become real within 'difference'. Thus, the second axiom posits the negation or contradiction which is just as underivable as the identity or the original positing, and also just as necessary for understanding what the I is. But these axioms need a unity or synthesis in order to produce the I. This synthesis is exposed in the principle of sufficient reason (*Satz des Grundes*) and:

> [o]nly then can we say from both that they are *something*. The absolute I of the first principle is not something (it has and can have no predicate); it is simply *what* it is, and this can be explained no further. But now, by means of this concept [of the ground, TK], consciousness contains the *whole* of reality; and to the not-I is allotted that part of it which does not attach to the I, and *vice-versa*. Both are something; the not-I is what the I is not, and *vice-versa*. (GA I/2, p. 271)[42]

We are dealing with the possibility of concrete facts (*Gegebenheiten*) in the world. For this purpose, the principle of sufficient reason posits a unity of I and not-I. Fichte finds this unity in reality understood as substantiality (*Sachhaltigkeit*), which is the first category of quality. Substantiality itself is constituted from the principle of identity: thing-contents (*Sachgehalte*) are identical to themselves. Substantiality however becomes concrete through a negation; a negation that – once it takes place – amounts to a delimitation of a concrete content, such as that of an animal or a desk. Negation is delimitation, and leads us to the category of quantity: the I and the not-I share reality in reciprocity. That is why the "the not-I is what the I is not, and *vice-versa*". Therefore, although the not-I's content always comes from the I, it can only be materialised through a process of delimitation, namely through the not-I. In other words, although the I is ground for the not-I, it always needs its negation in order to posit itself.

The formal structure of reality is thus developed from the grounding principles. But, in as much as they are merely theoretical, these principles do not refer to any existing fact, so that the demonstration of the grounding acts always bears a hypothetical character. The argument is valid in cases where there is knowledge, and it consequently also claims that if there is knowledge then it must take place according to these three principles. Indeed, the factual existence of knowledge or of finite rational beings cannot be deduced *a priori*, for this would presuppose an *a priori* knowledge of the positing of the I, and most importantly, of the not-I. But how can one prove *a priori* that there must be an *a posteriori?* Conversely, the abstraction from the given reality could not provide a construction with its inner necessity. Theory constructs the necessary structure

---

[42] "Erst jetzt [...] kann man von beiden sagen, sie sind *etwas*. Das absolute Ich des ersten Grundsatzes ist nicht etwas; (es hat kein Prädikat, und kann keins haben), es ist schlechthin, *was* es ist, und dies läßt sich nicht weiter erklären. Jetzt vermittelst dieses Begriffes [des Grundes, TK] ist im Bewußtseyn *alle* Realität; und von dieser kommt dem Nicht-Ich diejenige zu, die dem Ich nicht zukommt, und umgekehrt. Beide sind etwas; das Nicht-Ich ist dasjenige, was das Ich nicht ist, und umgekehrt."

of our knowledge of reality, but this structure, as such, is merely virtual. Fichte therefore follows the transcendental separation (introduced by Kant) of an *a priori* theory with its structural claims from the positing of existence. There is, however, something substantial in the theory that follows this separation of structural claims and the positing of existence, for reality needs the positing to be undertaken by something that posits.[43] Our self-awareness points towards the power of this positing: we only experience our own activity (*Selbsttätigkeit*) while we carry it out (and with inner evidence) because

> there is something else besides in the representation of my activity which cannot be externally given, but must lie in me, which I cannot empirically perceive or learn, but which I must know immediately, namely, that *I myself* am to be the last ground of the change which is to occur.
>
> I am the ground of this change signifies: – that that which *knows* of the change is that which effects it; the subject of consciousness and the principle of causality are one. But that which I assert, at the origin of all knowing, of the subject itself of this knowing, or, in other words, that which I know because I know at all; this I can have derived from no other knowing; I know it immediately; I posit it absolutely. (F SW IV, p. 3)[44]

The concept and awareness of my own activity is not given to me externally, for I cannot learn the original relation to myself by reproducing, so to say, my relation to others. My experience about myself is based on an original self-relation. Fichte crystallises the structure of the process of positing, negating and delimitating through the notion of drive (*Trieb*). As we have already seen, the knowledge of something is altogether a specification of something (*etwas überhaupt*) and therefore presupposes a process of delimitation or determination (*Begrenzung*) which is undertaken by the subject. A potentially infinite intentionality is thereby halted, as it reflects upon itself by coming up against a boundary, and hence distinguishes two opposite realms: an external reality, i.e. the world of objects, and an internal reality, namely the drive. The ideal genesis of the subject takes place in this way. It is central for Fichte that the boundary or

---

43 Cf. Stolzenberg 1994.
44 "[Es liegt etwas, TK] in der Vorstellung von meiner Wirksamkeit, was mir schlechthin nicht von aussen kommen kann, sondern in mir selbst liegen muss, was ich nicht erfahren, und lernen kann, sondern unmittelbar wissen muss; dies, dass *ich selbst* der letzte Grund der geschehenen Veränderung sein soll./ Ich bin der Grund dieser Veränderung, heisst: dasselbe und kein anderes, welches um dies Veränderung *weiss*, ist zugleich auch das Wirkende: das Subjekt des Bewusstseyns, und das Princip der Wirksamkeit sind Eins. Was ich aber beim Ursprunge alles Wissens vom Subjecte des Wissens selbst aussage, was ich weiss, dadurch, daß ich überhaupt weiss, kann ich aus keinem anderen Wissen gezogen haben; ich weiß es unmittelbar, ich setze es schlechthin."

impact may not be attributed to the I itself, for this would mean that we fall into pure idealism. On the other hand, though, the boundary must be understood as a fully formal structure, so that what determines the content of reality comes from the I. Otherwise we would, epistemologically, fall into pure realism. For Fichte, what this means, is that the subject is an intermediate or middle point, but in such a way that it produces its own extremities or sides.[45] The world is thus an interpretation generated by the I according to its own structure, but the world itself only appears to the I within this reality. As a consequence, the I is the absolute potency of self-positing which needs to be presupposed for any other positing.[46] But the particular self-positing can only take place in the form of a limitation from some inexplicable boundary, which henceforth makes the nature of reality possible. At this moment, the absoluteness of the I, the pure activity, appears as the idea of the I; the idea through which the I understands itself and everything else. That is to say: the determining contents of reality are I-ish (*ichhaft*). The fact that we see the world as a collection of singular things or substances, the fact that we think of it as a causal interaction of forces, and that we recognise other free willing beings, is all the result of the I's projections (*Übertragungen*) on to the world (which is a notion that Fichte introduces into epistemology). These projections take place in accordance with the I's consciousness of the activity and the resulting principle of sufficient reason, on the one hand, and the I's consciousness of passivity, i.e. of sensation, on the other. The sensation must be grounded on something; that is why there is an object. The object must have some kind of autonomy – an autonomy that we ascribe to it, in order to constitute it as an object of knowledge.

> My immediate consciousness is composed of two elements: – the consciousness of my passivity, i.e. the sensation, and the consciousness of my activity in the production of an object according to the law of causality; the latter consciousness connecting itself immediately with the former. My consciousness *of the object* is only a yet unrecognised *consciousness of my production of a presentation of an object*. I am only cognisant of this production because I myself am the producer. And thus all consciousness is only immediate consciousness, a consciousness of myself and therefore perfectly comprehensible. (BdM, p. 121)[47]

---

45 Cf. already the first pages of "Eignen Meditationen" from winter 1793/94 (GA II/3, p. 3–181). See also Henrich 2003, p. 174 f.
46 Cf. Stolzenberg 1994.
47 "Mein unmittelbares Bewußtseyn ist zusammengesetzt aus zwei Bestandtheilen, dem Bewußtseyn meines Leidens, der Empfindung; und dem meines Thuns, in Erzeugung eines Gegenstandes nach dem Satze des Grundes; welches letztere sich an die erstere sich unmittelbar anschließt. Das Bewusstseyn *des Gegenstandes* ist nur ein nicht dafür erkanntes *Bewußtseyn*

This is how we construct reality as reciprocal limitations according to our experience of passivity and activity, thereby projecting syntheses of activity and passivity to the external world. This is why reality for Fichte, as for Nietzsche, is formed out of degrees of power. Each experience and each time reality is assigned to an object is the expression of a certain degree of power: a specific degree of activity, which at the same time constitutes a certain degree of passivity. According to Fichte, it is only in this interaction with the not-I that man achieves his or her own reality. Here, Fichte is thinking of the relation to other people or free beings. Indeed, we cannot really talk about a limitation or restriction given to us by things. What really imposes a limitation on us in a very powerful way are not things, but other people with their own will. Once the dynamic acquires this interpersonal quality – i.e. when freedom bumps into freedom and searches for recognition – the human form of reality, the interpersonal realm is both invoked and accessed. Only then does the idea of the I as such acquire a form (*Gestalt*) for us. This is how the boundary or limitation becomes the condition for actual, social life. The I seeks for recognition rather than unconditional expansion.

For the philosophers themselves this boundary also constitutes the condition for speech. It is a boundary that cannot be surpassed; furthermore, the boundary itself and what lies beyond it appear as the problem and the task of life, which we can now address with the idea of an interaction among free beings. In this sense, Fichte is excluding all boundary theories that take the form of an objective theory of individuality, such as the theories put forward by classic metaphysics. It is not possible to say anything about the structure of individuation itself; we can only accept the condition that we are always already an individuated being which is only able to see its boundary from one side. In the end, the ground for boundary-positing, and hence, for individuality itself, remains undisclosed to us, although it still constitutes the absolute precondition of our very existence. But, just as Nietzsche believes, *qua* philosophers we are expected to come to terms with this situation. And yet, we can see how Fichte conceives his perspectivism in a different way than Nietzsche.

Fichte never identifies the concrete I with the absolute I; nor does he fail to present the sobering process that is involved in this constructivist epistemology. For, if all external occurrences happen to be a construction of the subject, to what extent are we entitled to talk about reality, i.e. reality taken in the strongest

---

meiner Erzeugung einer Vorstellung vom *Gegenstande*. Um diese Erzeugung weiß ich schlechthin dadurch, daß ich es selbst bin, der da erzeugt. Und so ist alles Bewußtseyn nur ein unmittelbares, ein Bewußtseyn meiner selbst, und ist nunmehr vollkommen begreiflich."

sense, a reality which can guarantee the meaningfulness of life? Or must we fall pray of nihilism, such as the nihilism that Nietzsche takes to be the actual goal of science? In fact, and quite unexpectedly, according to this conception the I becomes the only possible reality, for

> there is no other thing than that of which you are conscious. You yourself are the thing; you yourself, by virtue of your finitude – the innermost law of your being – are thus presented before yourself and projected out of yourself and all that you perceive out of yourself is still – yourself only. (BdM, p. 136–137)[48]

But in this way, the I itself becomes a "mere presentation, without meaning and without purpose" (BdM, p. 164). The I cannot maintain an absolute scepticism against itself. Some well-known passages from Fichte's *Vocation of Man* define the most external boundary of thought as one which can only recognise itself in its own dissolution. Constructivism, understood as the claim that brings dynamism to the process of knowing and takes away the stasis of reality, also dissolves the consistency of the act of knowing itself: the I becomes an appearance (*Schein*).

> There is nothing enduring, either out of me, or in me, but only a ceaseless change. I know of no being, not even of my own. There is no being. *I myself* absolutely know not, and am not. *Images* [Bilder] are: – they are the only things that exist, and they know of themselves after the fashion of images: – images which drift by without there being anything by which they drift; images, which, are connected with each other through images: – images without anything which is pictured in them, without significance and without aim. I myself am one of these images: – nay, I am not even this, but merely a confused image of the images. All reality is transformed into a strange dream, without a life which is dreamed of, and without a mind which dreams it; – into a dream which is woven together in a dream of itself. *Intuition* is the dream, *thought*, – the source of all the being and all the reality which I imagine, of my own being, my own powers, and my own purposes – is the dream of that dream. (BdM, p. 245)[49]

---

48 "[E]s giebt kein anderes Ding, als das, dessen du dir bewußt wirst. Du selbst bist dieses Ding; du selbst bist durch den innersten Grund deines Wesens deine Endlichkeit, vor dich selbst hingestellt, und aus dir selbst herausgeworfen; und alles, was du außer dir erblickst, bist immer du selbst."

49 "Es gibt überall kein Dauerndes, weder ausser mir noch in mir, sondern nur einen unaufhörlichen Wechsel. Ich weiss überall von keinem Seyn, und auch nicht von meinem eigenen. Es ist kein Seyn. – *Ich selbst* weiss überhaupt nicht, und bin nicht. *Bilder* sind: sie sind das Einzige, was da ist, und sie wissen von sich, nach Weise der Bilder: – Bilder, die vorüberschweben, ohne dass etwas sey, dem sie vorüberschweben; die durch Bilder von den Bildern zusammenhängen, Bilder, ohne etwas in ihnen Abgebildetes, ohne Bedeutung und Zweck. Ich selbst bin eins dieser Bilder; ja, ich bin selbst dies nicht, sondern nur ein verworrenes Bild von den Bildern. – Alle Rea-

As we see, any material construct from the part of the subject is also dissolved in Fichte's account. The I is never the object of objective knowledge; for it cannot be determined. Indeed, this extreme scepticism, introduced here by Fichte, cannot be resolved on an epistemological level. In other words, Fichte's dynamic and constructivist view of things also opens up the possibility of an utter lack of sense and reference. Knowledge can never legitimise itself; it is always dependent upon a dynamic which confers meaning to it; direction and coherence. It is at this very point that Fichte brings morality into play:

> Not merely to know, but to *act* according to your knowledge, is your vocation: – thus is it loudly proclaimed in the innermost depths of my soul, as soon as I recollect myself for a moment, and turn my observation upon myself. Not for idle contemplation of yourself, not for brooding over devout sensations; – no, you are here for action; your action, and your action alone, determines your worth. (BdM, p. 182–183)[50]

Just as for Nietzsche, the value or worth of life triggers the practical value of our agency. For Fichte this value is grounded on the notion of self-activity (*Selbsttätigkeit*) itself:

> There is within me a drive to absolute independent self-activity. Nothing is more unbearable to me, than to be merely by another, for another, and through another; I must be something for myself and by myself alone. I feel this drive along with the perception of my own existence; it is inseparably united to my consciousness of myself.
>
> I explain this feeling to myself, by reflection; and add to this blind drive the power of sight, by thought. According to this drive I must act as an absolutely independent being: – thus I understand and translate the drive. I must be independent. (BdM, p. 184)[51]

---

lität verwandelt sich in einen wunderbaren Traum, ohne ein Leben, von welchem geträumt wird, und ohne einen Geist, dem da träumt; in einem Traum, der in einem Traume von sich selbst zusammenhängt. Das *Anschauen* ist der Traum, das *Denken*, – die Quelle alles Seyns und aller Realität, die ich mir einbilde, *meines Seyns*, meiner Kraft, meiner Zwecke – ist der Traum von jenem Traume."

50 "Nicht bloßes Wissen, sondern nach deinem Wissen *Thun* ist deine Bestimmung: so ertönt es laut im Innersten meiner Seele, so bald ich nur einen Augenblick mich sammle und auf mich selbst merke. Nicht zum müßigen Beschauen und Betrachten deiner selbst, oder zum Brüten über andächtigen Empfindungen, – nein, zum Handeln bist du da; dein Handeln und allein dein Handeln bestimmt deinen Werth."

51 "Es ist in mir ein Trieb zu absoluter, unabhängiger Selbstthätigkeit. Nichts ist mir unausstehlicher, als nur an einem andern, für ein anderes, und durch ein anderes zu seyn: ich will für und durch mich selbst etwas seyn und werden. Diesen Trieb fühle ich, so wie ich nur mich selbst wahrnehme; er ist unzertrennlich vereinigt mit dem Bewußtseyn meiner selbst./ Ich mache mir das Gefühl desselben durch das Denken deutlich, und setze gleichsam dem an sich blinden

Yet at this point, a further doubt is introduced; a doubt similar to the one we have already seen in Nietzsche. For our own inner activity, the drive or the will, is also communicated to us through the structure of consciousness.

> Since it is I who feel this drive [*Treiben*], and since I cannot pass beyond myself, either with my whole consciousness or in particular with my capacity for sensation, – since this I itself is the last point at which I can grasp this drive, it certainly appears to me as a drive founded in myself to an activity also founded in myself. But might it not be, however, that this drive, although unperceived by me, is in reality the drive of a foreign power invisible to me, and that notion of independence merely a delusion, arising from my sphere of vision being limited to myself alone? I have no reason to assume this, but just as little reason to deny it. I must confess that I absolutely know nothing, and can know nothing, about it. (BdM, p. 189)[52]

Can we draw the conclusion with certainty that we *are* self-acting from the fact that we *feel* that we are? We consider it to be certain when we feel this way, but quite obviously this gives us no evidence at the level of reflection. We cannot exclude the possibility that we might be unconsciously steered by forces and laws alien to our conscious will. On the other hand, though, the latter does not imply the falsehood of this consciousness and that we recognise another instance moving us. We are, thus, confronted with an undecidable dilemma. The resolution is only possible in relation to its unresolvable character. This is how Fichte approaches the problem:

> I want to freely accept the vocation [*Bestimmung*] which this drive assigns to me, and in this resolution I will at once lay hold of thought, in all its reality and truthfulness, and on the reality of all things which are pre-supposed therein. I want to restrict myself to the position of natural thought, in which this drive places me, and cast from me all those over-refined and subtle inquiries, which alone could make me doubtful of its truth. (BdM, p. 193)[53]

Triebe Augen ein, durch den Begriff. Ich soll, zufolge dieses Triebes, als ein schlechthin selbstständiges Wesen handeln; so fasse und übersetze ich jenen Trieb. Ich soll selbstständig seyn."

52 "Da Ich es bin, der dieses Treiben fühlt, und da ich über mich selbst, weder mit meinem ganzen Bewußtseyn, noch insbesondere mit meinem Gefühle hinaus kann, da dieses – Ich selbst das letzte bin, wo ich jenes Treiben erfasse, so erscheint es mir freilich als in mir gegründetes Treiben zu einer in mir selbst gegründeten Thätigkeit. Könnte es nicht aber doch, nur von mir unbemerkt, das Treiben einer mir unsichtbaren fremden Kraft, und jene Meinung von Selbstständigkeit lediglig Täuschung meines auf mich selbst eingeschränkten Gesichtkreises seyn? Ich habe keinen Grund dies anzunehmen: aber eben so wenig einen Grund, es zu läugnen. Ich muß mir bekennen, daß ich darüber schlechthin nichts weiß, noch wissen kann."

53 "Ich will jene Bestimmung mir freiwillig geben, die der Trieb mir anmuthet; und ich will in diesem Entschlusse zugleich den Gedanken an seine Realität und Wahrhaftigkeit, und an

Fichte, thus, decides to block the reflection to a certain extent and to affirm the natural and immediate consciousness within the reflection. This consciousness consists in the recognition of a free will which guides our life and expresses itself through purpose-type concepts, i.e. concepts which anticipate the reality of our deeds. In this way, independence will become the most authentic aim of all our actions. Reflection is hence abandoned within reflection and action is set as the original activity. At this point, we can accomplish that process of self-positing (up to the boundary) as a form of openness towards the other and towards others:

> The I posits itself absolutely, and is thereby complete in itself and closed to any impression from without. But if it is to be a self, it must also posit itself *as* self-posited; and by this new positing, relative to an original positing, it opens itself, if I may so put it, to external influences; simply by this reiteration of positing, it concedes the possibility that there might also be something within it that is not actually posited by itself. Both types of positing are conditions for an operation of the not-I; without the first, there would be no activity of the self to undergo limitation; without the second, this activity would not be limited for the I, and the latter would be unable to posit itself as limited. Thus the I, as such, is initially in a state of reciprocity with itself, and only so does an external influence upon it become possible. (GA I/2, p. 409)[54]

The subject posits itself, thus, as a union of unity and difference, as an interconnection of *closedness* and openness. This openness of experience is not the result of a deduction, but comes from the act of self-positing as an open being; i.e. one which affirms its own activity as well as its openness to experience, and realises that there could not be one without the other. The interaction is, thus, borne by the I's reflective ability or its ability to posit itself *as* I. In this way, the

---

die Realität alles dessen, was er voraussetzt, ergreifen. Ich will in dem Standpunkte des natürlichen Denkens mich halten, auf welchen dieser Trieb mich versetzt, und aller jener Grübeleien und Klügeleien mich entschlagen, welche nur seine Wahrhaftigkeit mir zweifelhaft machen könnten."

54 "Das Ich setzt sich selbst schlechthin, und dadurch ist es in sich selbst vollkommen, und allem äußeren Eindrucke verschlossen. Aber es muß auch, wenn es ein Ich seyn soll, sich setzen, *als* durch sich selbst gesetzt; und durch dieses neue, auf ein ursprüngliches Setzen sich beziehende Setzen öffnet es sich, daß ich so sage, der Einwirkung von aussen; es sezt lediglich durch diese Wiederholung des Setzens die Möglichkeit, daß auch etwas in ihm seyn könne, was nicht durch dasselbe selbst gesezt sey. Beide Arten des Setzens sind die Bedingung einer Einwirkung des Nicht-Ich; ohne die erstere würde keine Thätigkeit des Ich vorhanden seyn, welche eingeschränkt werden könnte; ohne die zweite würde diese Thätigkeit nicht für das Ich eingeschränkt seyn; das Ich würde sich nicht setzen können, als eingeschränkt. So steht das Ich, als Ich, ursprünglich in Wechselwirkung mit sich selbst; und dadurch erst wird ein Einfluß von aussen in dasselbe möglich."

meaningful positing of an exterior reality is justified by its possibility.[55] A project (*Entwurf*) of free life emerges from the connection between the I's activity, the boundary's formal structure and the I's projection (*Übertragung*) of its own contents on to experience.

> Thus, with respect to its existence, the self is dependent; but it is absolutely independent in the determinations of its existence. In virtue of its absolute being, it contains a law of these determinations, valid to infinity, and an intermediary power of determining its empirical existence according to this law. The point at which we find ourselves, when we first set this intermediary power of freedom in play does not depend upon us; considered in its full extension, the series that from this point on we shall traverse to all eternity is wholly dependent upon on ourselves. (GA I/2, p. 411)[56]

The I's commitment, its concrete impulse or the individuality in which we find ourselves, does not depend upon us, for we are born in a very particular perspective. But this perspective does not bind us in any way. By virtue of our inner absoluteness, by virtue of the real idea of ourselves as pure activity, it is possible for us to determine concretely our own course of life. Our intermediary power (*Mittelvermögen*) involves a middle point between the conditions (*Gegebenheit*) that become clear at the very boundaries of man and the absolute I, which, in as much as it is an idea, guides our actions.

V

The I, in as much as it is an instance of reflection and a location for freedom, insists on its being this very I. This self-sufficiency constitutes the pivot point of the whole theory. The I's own insistence creates the intermediate space which

---

[55] This duplexity resulting from the simple positing of the I as I determines the entire project of Fichte's later lectures (his *Nova Methodo*): "once we get to the point of understanding that the I posits itself, as posited by itself, our system will be complete, and this is the case when we will [*Wenn wir dahin kommen, wo wir begreifen, daß das Ich sich selbst seze, als durch sich selbst gesezt, so ist unser System geschloßen, und dies ist der Fall beim Wollen*]" (WLnm-K, p. 64).

[56] "Das Ich ist demnach abhängig seinem Daseyn nach, aber es ist schlechthin unabhängig in den Bestimmungen dieses seines Daseyns. Es ist in ihm, kraft seines absoluten Seyns, ein für die Unendlichkeit gültiges Gesetz dieser Bestimmungen, und es ist in ihm ein Mittelvermögen, sein empirisches Daseyn nach jenem Gesetze zu bestimmen. Der Punkt, auf welchem wir uns selbst finden, wenn wir zuerst jenes Mittelvermögens der Freiheit mächtig werden, hängt nicht von uns ab, die Reihe, die wir von diesem Punkte aus in alle Ewigkeit beschreiben werden, in ihrer ganzen Ausdehnung gedacht, hängt völlig von uns ab."

gives finite being its reality. In Spinoza we can see what happens when the absolute I is related to the object directly, without insisting on this intermediate phase.

> The claim that, *in itself* and *as such*, the pure activity relates to an object, and that no special absolute act of connection is needed for this purpose, would be the transcendental principle of *intelligible fatalism*; the most coherent theory of freedom that was possible before the founding of a Science of Knowledge [...]. (GA I/2, p. 398)[57]

Time and time again we see that Fichte is concerned with finite being's creative intermediate position. It is in this way important to also recognise the other side of limitation. Indeed, Fichte believes that man, as a finite rational being, is also to be distinguished from the Absolute. The way in which the autonomy of both reflection and finite being can harmonise with an absolute being is what constitutes the topic of Fichte's philosophy in the second half of his productive life, that is, from 1800 onwards.

For Fichte, being, understood as a complete self-contained or self-enclosed Absolute is totally opposed to finite beings. This opposition cannot be objectively bypassed; it only becomes obvious in the form of appearance. The One and Absolute remain as such beyond all conceptualisation. The Absolute comes to light as appearance in us, who know something about it. We do not recognise any differentiation within the One, let alone an inner necessity to differentiate itself. Consciousness and self-consciousness are, thus, appearance of appearance (*Erscheinung der Erscheinung*), but only as a factual appearance and an achieved understanding of itself. But it is also in this modality and in this modality alone that the creativity of the finite is visible:

> Thus – according to the *facts* [Faktum], appearance is in itself an absolute, real creative power of something new, something coming thoroughly from nothing; it is its own creative life. The proof of this lies in the following, namely that it *does not* become *this* through the absolute, for the absolute goes only up to the appearance, but never to the appearance of appearance. (StA-2/SWV-2, p. 56)[58]

---

57 "Die Behauptung, daß die reine Thätigkeit *an sich*, und *als solche* sich auf ein Objekt bezöge, und daß es dazu keiner besondern absoluten Handlung des Beziehens bedürfte, wäre der transcendentale Grundsatz des *intelligiblen Fatalismus*; des konsequentesten Systems über Freyheit, das vor der Begründung einer Wissenschaftslehre möglich war".
58 "Also – zufolge des *Faktum* ist die Erscheinung in sich selbst absolute reale Schöpferkraft eines neuen, durchaus aus Nichts, ein eigenes schöpferisches leben. Der Beweiß beruht darauf, daß es *dies nicht* durch das absolute ist, indem dieses nur bis zum Erscheinen dieses, keineswegs aber bis zum Erscheinen der Erscheinung selbst geht."

In this way, the self-positing of the I is set at a distant relation to the Absolute and, at the same time, it is captured in its purest self-sufficiency.

> Knowledge creates selfhood, and it creates itself as being self-creating, and it creates itself purely out of Nothing; and nothing is previously given to it apart from the possibility of creating itself: this possibility, however, is previously given, and this is precisely what pure being is. (WL-1801/02, p. 79)[59]

The *Science of Knowledge* is situated, once again, between facts (which depend upon opposition) and the Absolute (which does not depend upon anything, but rather constitutes the capacity of freedom of appearance). "The form of the Absolute goes up to its appearing, not to its *reflexive* appearing"[60]; "The appearance acquires an *independent* being" (StA-2/SWV-2, p. 56). Reflection, thus, opens up an intermediate space (*Raum des Zwischen*), in which we place ourselves as free beings. This is why reality has to appear as the realisation of a capacity or as self-consciousness, a process which Fichte designates as the schema of schema or the appearance of appearance.[61] In fact, this will become at the same time more and less than the Absolute or being itself, something that Fichte will call the "Ueberseyn" in his last lecture from 1814 (UI, p. 19). For, the finite is only an image or appearance of the Absolute and not the Absolute itself. Fichte rejects the idea of a quantification of the Absolute. And yet, as image or appearance it can also be more than the Absolute itself, because the Absolute is 'only' appearance, but not reflexive and conscious appearance of appearance.

The reference of the finite I to the Absolute must also take place within the finite's inner independence, "the absolute being determines only under certain conditions, but not unconditionally" (WL-1801/02, p. 114). Although the absolute being or substance is totally unlimited, the realisation of the mode or finite being can only come from the mode or finite being itself. Finite realisation is for Fichte always contingent. This is its own condition, and hence, its own unconditionality. That is why the accidental is not in the Absolute, since the Absolute would thereby "lose substantiality"; rather, then,

---

[59] "Wissen erschaft eben selbst, und erschaft sich, als sich erschafend, und erschaft sich rein aus dem Nichts; u. nichts ist ihm vorausgegeben als die Möglichkeit sich zu erschaffen: diese aber ist ihm vorgegeben, und dies eben ist das reine Sein."
[60] "Die Form des Absoluten geht bis zum erscheinen, nicht bis zum *sich* erscheinen."
[61] We can only but hint here towards the creative character of the structure of the appearance of appearance in *The Science of Knowledge* from 1811. For a detailed analysis see D'Alfonso 2005, p. 144f. and Minobe 2006.

it is outside it, in the formally free. And that is how accident and substance are divided and it is possible for them to maintain their meaning. – Being (existence) of knowledge – and only knowledge has existence, and all existence is grounded on and depends merely upon it, except its original determination. (WL-1801/02, p. 114)[62]

This informs the following fundamental character regarding unity and difference in Fichte's *Science of Knowledge*:

> From an ideal point of view it is monistic: it knows that the determining eternal One – beyond all knowledge – is what underlies all knowledge. From a real point of view it is dualistic; knowledge, as something really posited, has two principles: absolute freedom and absolute being. And it knows that the absolute One cannot be attained in any real form of knowledge. (WL-1801/02, p. 114–115)[63]

However, the being that is meant here cannot be understood as a transcendent *quasi* metaphysical being. It is rather so, that "we are it"; in as much as we always bear within us the possibility of reflection as a pure position (*reine Position*), and at the same time are borne by this very reflection (cf. WL 1804-II, p. 154). This being, understood as *actus essendi*, as Fichte puts it, is the ungraspable dynamic that underlies all events and all actions; a dynamic that escapes all attempt at codification. For once we come with our differentiating consciousness, being itself has almost already vanished. In as much as we are previous to all concepts and in as much as we are what first enables any understanding or conceptualising, we remain inaccessible to ourselves. In fact, our whole existence will be fashioned according to the way in which we relate to this pure force of living and being. Fichte calls this the construction of images (*Bilden*) or the becoming of images (*Bildwerden*). In its spontaneity, the absolute and unattainable being becomes a model for us; it becomes object of our affirmation and self-affirmation.

---

[62] "[J]a die Substantialität verlöre, sondern ausser ihm, in dem formaliter freien. Und so erst wird Accidentalität, u. Substantialität geschieden, und in ihrer Bedeutung möglich. – Das Seyn (Daseyn) des Wissens – und nur das Wissen hat Daseyn, u. alles Daseyn ist nur in ihm begründet hängt schlechthin von ihm selbst ab, nicht aber seine Urbestimmung."

[63] "Unitismus ist sie in idealer Hinsicht: sie weiß, daß schlechthin allem Wissen das bestimmende ewige Eine, – jenseits alles Wissens nemlich zu Grund liegt: Dualismus ist sie in realer Hinsicht, das Wissen als wirklich gesetzt, da hat sie zwei Principe, die absolute Freiheit und das absolute Seyn – und sie weiß, daß das absolute Eine in keinem wirklichen Wissen je zu erreichen ist."

VI

We hope that the purpose and significance of the comparison made here between Fichte and Nietzsche is now easier to understand. Without weakening Nietzsche's insights into the ever-present power strategies, i.e. those insights that can help us to overcome our *ressentiment*, it still seems to us that the comparison between Nietzsche and Fichte raises a fundamental philosophical problem; a problem which we have labelled here under a motto related to a quote from Gilles Deleuze, namely the problem of the drama of existence understood as a process of differentiation from everything else, and which constitutes the basis of human life. And it seems that, in this respect, Fichte goes one step further than Nietzsche; surely this is a view that is worthy of further analysis and research.

References

Bourdieu, Pierre (1977): *Outline of a Theory of Practice*. Translated by Richard Nice. Cambridge: Cambridge University Press [French edition: Droz 1972].

D'Alfonso, Matteo (2006): "Schopenhauer als Schüler Fichtes". In: *Fichte-Studien* 30, p. 201–211.

Darwin, Charles (1859): *On the Origin of Species by Means of Natural Selection, or the Preservation of Favoured Races in the Struggle for Life*. London: John Murray.

Deleuze, Gilles (1994): *Difference and Repetition*. Translated by Paul Patton. New York: Columbia University Press.

Deleuze, Gilles (2006): *Nietzsche and Philosophy*. Translated by Hugh Tomlinson. New York: Columbia University Press [French edition: PUF 1962].

Engels, Eva Maria (2009): "Einführung". In: Eva Maria Engels (Ed.): *Charles Darwin und seine Wirkung*. Frankfurt a.M.: Suhrkamp, p. 9–57.

Estes, Yolanda (2002): "Intellectual Intuition, the Pure Will, and the Categorical Imperative in the later *Wissenschaftslehre*". In: Daniel Breazeale/Thomas Rockmore (Eds.): *New Essays on Fichte's Later Jena "Wissenschaftslehre"*. Evanston, IL: Northwestern University Press, p. 209–225.

Goethe, Johann Wolfgang (1774): *Die Leiden des jungen Werthers*. Part 1. Leipzig: Weygand.

Habermas, Jürgen (1988): *Der philosophische Diskurs der Moderne. Zwölf Vorlesungen*. Frankfurt a.M.: Suhrkamp [first edition: 1985].

Henrich, Dieter (2003): *Between Kant und Hegel. Lectures on German Idealism*. Cambridge MA: Harvard University Press.

Klotz, Christian (2002): *Selbstbewußtsein und praktische Identität*. Frankfurt a.M.: Klostermann.

Lauth, Reinhard (1965): "J.G. Fichtes Gesamtidee der Philosophie". In: Reinhard Lauth (Ed.): *Zur Idee der Transzendentalphilosophie*. Munich and Salzburg: Pustet, p. 73–124.

Lauth, Reinhard (1984): *Die transzendentale Naturlehre Fichtes nach den Prinzipien der Wissenschaftslehre*. Hamburg: Meiner.
Schiller, Friedrich (2004 [1792]): "Über den Grund des Vergnügens an tragischen Gegenständen". In: Wolfgang Riedel (Ed.): Friedrich Schiller: *Sämtliche Werke. Erzählungen. Theoretische Schriften*. Vol. 5. Munich: Hanser, p. 358–372.
Schmidt, Alfred (1977): *Drei Studien über Materialismus. Schopenhauer. Horkheimer. Glücksproblem*. Munich: Hanser.
Schmidt, Jochen (2012): *Kommentar zu Nietzsches "Die Geburt der Tragödie"*. Historischer und kritischer Kommentar zu Friedrich Nietzsches Schriften. Ed. Heidelberger Akademie der Wissenschaften. Vol. 1/1. Berlin and New York: De Gruyter.
Schopenhauer, Arthur (1991): *Die Welt als Wille und Vorstellung*. Nach den Ausgaben letzter Hand herausgegeben von Ludger Lütkehaus. Vol. 1. Zurich: Haffmanns.
White, Hayden V. (1973): *Metahistory: The Historical Imagination in Nineteenth-Century Europe*. Baltimore: Johns Hopkins University Press.

Carlos João Correia
Schelling and the Death of God

The philosophical notion of the 'death of God' is typically attributed to the thought of Nietzsche. In the present essay, it will be my purpose to argue that this concept can already be found in the philosophy of Schelling, albeit with a different (and maybe even opposite) meaning from the one we find in Nietzsche's texts.

I

Let us begin by considering how Nietzsche approaches the event of the 'death of God'. Nietzsche uses the 'death of God' as a metaphoric term in order to refer to a civilisation phenomenon or an historical process, of which he considers himself to be the herald or messenger.

The death of God features prominently in two of his published works, namely in *The Gay Science* and *Thus Spoke Zarathustra*. Heidegger points out in his 1943 essay "The Word of Nietzsche: 'God is dead'" (included in *Off the Beaten Track*) that Nietzsche had already set the question in a *Nachlass* note from the 1870s, i.e. two years before the publication of *The Birth of Tragedy*. Quoting from these notes, Heidegger recalls that Nietzsche had written: "I believe in the ancient German saying: 'All gods must die'" (Heidegger GA 5, p. 214).

Although Nietzsche never made any secret of his atheism, his statement about the death of God has a different purpose altogether. If there were a conceptual equivalence between the 'death of God' and 'atheism', one would simply have to admit that the issue has been addressed time and again throughout the history of philosophical thought. It suffices to recall Cicero's work on the nature of gods, *De Natura Deorum* – quite rightly considered by Voltaire to be "probably the best book in all Antiquity" (Voltaire 2005, p. 1124). In this text, Cicero discusses perspicuously arguments concerning atheism.

But Nietzsche's purpose was a different one. To put it simply, he wanted to show that, in Western culture, the Christian representation of God had been erased from the spirit of men. In aphorism 343 from *Gay Science* Nietzsche writes: "The greatest recent event – that 'God is dead', that the belief in the Christian God has lost credence – is already beginning to cast its first shadows over Europe" (GS 343, KSA 3, p. 573). Nietzsche is ambiguous about the way in which we should interpret or feel these 'shadows'. On the one hand, they are associated with a feeling of liberation, for, as he puts it, "we feel [...] as if a new dawn shone on us; our heart overflows with gratitude, amazement, premonitions, expectation" (GS 343, KSA 3, p. 574).[1] On the other hand, though, this cultural event is still felt by Nietzsche as something characterising his own era and, as such, likely to bring about a negative nihilism, linked to the proliferation of anthropocentric values, i.e. values which cannot but be *human, all too human*.

There is, indeed, according to Nietzsche, a sombre aspect to the 'death of God' – one which, in his view, must be overcome. To make his point, Nietzsche produces an interesting comparison with Eastern thought:

> – After Buddha was dead, they still showed his shadow in a cave for centuries – a tremendous, gruesome shadow. God is dead; but given the way people are, there may still be caves for thousands of years in which his shadow will be shown. – And we – we must still defeat his shadow as well! (GS 108, KSA 3, p. 467)[2]

Nietzsche was afraid that quite soon theological values would be metamorphosed into human values, to the point that the human being would merely occupy the place left vacant by the 'death of God'. This is the key to understand the anguish expressed in *Gay Science* – an anguish that becomes patent in the emotional speech of someone who actually understands the meaning of such death and nevertheless is deemed "insane" and is transformed into an object of collective mockery. I am obviously recalling here the well-known §125:

> Where is God? [...] *We have killed him* – you and I! We are all his murderers. But how did we do this? [...] Who gave us the sponge to wipe away the entire horizon? [...] Can't we hear the noise of the grave-diggers who are burying God? [...] God is dead! God remains dead! And we have killed him! How shall we comfort ourselves, the murderers of all murderers? The holiest and the mightiest thing the world has ever possessed, has bled to death under our knives: who will wipe this blood from us? (GS 125, KSA 3, p. 480f.)[3]

---

1 "[W]ir [...] fühlen uns [...] wie von einer neuen Morgenröthe angestrahlt; unser Herz strömt dabei über von Dankbarkeit, Erstaunen, Ahnung, Erwartung".
2 "Nachdem Buddha todt war, zeigte man noch Jahrhunderte seinen Schatten in einer Höhle, – einen ungeheuren schauerlichen Schatten. Gott ist tot: aber so wie die Art der Menschen ist, wird es vielleicht noch Jahrtausende lang Höhlen geben, in denen man seinen Schatten zeigt. – Und wir – wir müssen auch noch seinen Schatten besiegen!"
3 "Wohin ist Gott? [...]*Wir haben ihn getötet,* – ihr und ich! Wir Alle sind seine Mörder! Aber wie haben wir diess gemacht? [...] Wer gab uns den Schwamm, um den ganzen Horizont wegzuwischen? [...] Hören wir noch Nichts von dem Lärm der Totengräber, welche Gott begraben? [...] Gott ist todt! Gott bleibt todt! Und wir haben ihn getödtet! Wie trösten wir uns, die Mörder aller

Authors as prominent as Gilles Deleuze (1962) or George Steiner (1971) have studied the philosophical and cultural meaning of the death of God. However, it is not on the Nietzschean account of the death of God that I will focus here – if for no other reason than that the issue is, as I will attempt to show, far more ancient than Nietzsche suspected it to be.

As rightly pointed out by Heidegger in the essay mentioned above:

> the question remains whether the aforesaid word of Nietzsche [i.e., the death of God] is merely an extravagant view of a thinker about whom the correct assertion is readily at hand: he finally went mad. And it remains to ask whether Nietzsche does not rather pronounce here the word that always, within the metaphysically determined history of the West, is already being spoken by implication. (Heidegger GA 5, p. 213)

To prove his point, Heidegger quotes from Hegel's conclusion to his early work *Faith and Knowledge* [*Glauben und Wissen*], and from the celebrated *dictum* of Plutarch, taken by Pascal: "*Le grand Pan est mort* [*great Pan is dead*]" (*Pensées* 694). Heidegger warns us as follows:

> Hegel's pronouncement carries a thought different from that contained in the word of Nietzsche. Still, there exists between the two an essential connection that conceals itself in the essence of all metaphysics. (Heidegger GA 5, p. 214)

In order to understand the meaning of the 'death of God' in Schelling, let us direct our attention, not towards the Heideggerian reflection on nihilism and the issue of values, but rather towards this unexpected connection between Pascal and Hegel – Schelling's companion in the famous seminar in Tübingen, with regard to which Nietzsche would have voiced the ironical verdict: "One need merely say 'Tübinger Stift' to understand *what* German philosophy is at bottom – an *insidious* theology" (A 10, KSA 6, p. 176).

In the concluding paragraphs to *Faith and Knowledge*, Hegel will in fact take the dominant feeling of the modern period to be the sense of loss of the divine in Nature. Moreover, according to Hegel, "the feeling upon which modern religion rests – the feeling that God himself is dead [*Gott selbst ist tot*]" (JW, TWA 2, p. 432) lends itself to be paraphrased in Pascal's words "Nature is such that she points at every turn towards a *lost God* [*un Dieu perdu*]" (*Pensées* 441). Following Pascal, Nature, in the modern world, is perceived as bereft of divine character. And this, in its turn, is but the logical corollary of the radical separation of the divine from the natural world, for the latter's only claim to the *divine*

Mörder? Das Heiligste und Mächtigste, was die Welt bisher besass, es ist unter unseren Messern verblutet, – wer wischt dies Blut von uns ab?"

lies in the fact that it was created by God. The argument is clear-cut and, as I will endeavour to show later, an important one with respect to our view of Schelling's 'death of God'. If the pagan and animistic view of the natural world as one inhabited by spirits and sacred powers – still conspicuously present nowadays in, for example, the "kami-no michi [*path of the Gods*]" found in Japanese traditional culture – loses its meaning within the Christian view of reality, then the world becomes an inhospitable, hollow universe, divested of essence, the natural grounds of a 'lost God'. Who could ignore the famous cry from Pascal: "The eternal silence of these infinite spaces terrifies me" (*Pensées* 206)? A thought that is nothing more than the logical consequence of Pascal's significant reflection known as the "disproportion of man" (*Pensées* 72), where he describes the status of the human condition as that of one who stands between two abysses: *infinity* and *nothingness*.

Later, in his *Berlin Lectures* on the philosophy of religion, Hegel will pick up the same Pascalian intuition, this time in association with the passion and the death of Jesus Christ. Hegel tells us that, in that instant, nature is agonisingly felt as being bereft of the eternal and divine.

> God died, God is dead – this is the most terrifying thought, that everything eternal and true does not exist, that negation itself is in God; the utmost agony, the feeling of complete and utter loss, the nullification of the highest is, therefore, associated to it. (*PhR II*, TWA 17, p. 291)[4]

This Hegelian view on the death of God – a clear and unequivocal heir to the Pascalian meditation – remains alive today in the sphere of the so-called 'death of god theology', or 'atheist theology', of Thomas J.J. Altizer (2002) and Don Cuppitt (1997). In this sense it also bears a clear correspondence with the account of desacralisation given by the Catholic theologian Joseph Moingt, when he writes:

> In the trial and death of Jesus, I see God exiting from religion and entering into the profane world of men [...] This I hold as the Good News: God leaves the precinct of the sacred where he had been closeted. He is no longer confined to places (the mountain, the temple). [...] God frees us from the burden of religion and the sacred, with all the terrors and all the servitudes resulting therefrom [...] The best way of worshiping Him is paying assistance to your neighbour, loving one another, bringing justice for all. (Moingt 1997, p. 143f.)

---

4 "Gott ist gestorben, Gott ist tot – dieses ist der fürchterlichste Gedanke, daß alles Ewige, alles Wahre nicht ist, die Negation selbst in Gott ist; der höchste Schmerz, das Gefühl der vollkommenen Rettungslosigkeit, das Aufheben alles Höheren ist damit verbunden."

II

Schelling's reflection on the death of God takes place at quite a different level. The well-known rivalry between Schelling and Hegel within the German academic milieus of their day explains much of the vast distance that the former takes from the Hegelian dramatisation of the crucifixion. For Schelling, human death, and therefore that of Jesus, emphasises the essence of the being that has passed away. Death is conceived not as a tragic separation so much as the somewhat paradoxical process of *becoming what one is* – already mentioned by Pindar in his poetry (Pindar 1997, p. 109). "After death", Schelling writes in the 32nd lesson of his *Philosophy of Revelation*, Jesus appears just as he is, in his essence, "in himself" (SW XIV, p. 207).

In his *Erlanger Lectures* (1820/21), Shelling does not hesitate to define the goal of philosophy thus:

> He who wishes to effectively place himself within a genuinely free philosophy must abandon God. For it is in this regard that one should say: he who keeps God will lose Him, and he who renounces to Him will find Him. (SW IX, p. 217)[5]

Schelling then offers us one of the most beautiful accounts of philosophical existence:

> Only he who has reached the bottom of himself and therein recognised the entire depth of life; he who one day abandoned everything and was abandoned by everything; he for whom everything sunk, and who found himself alone in the face of infinity – behold here a decisive step that Plato has compared to death. Dante's inscription above the gates of Hell – "Abandon all hope, ye who enter here" – should be likewise inscribed at the entrance to philosophy. He who truly wishes to pursue philosophy should abandon all hope, all demands and desires; he must yearn for nothing, know nothing, feel absolutely naked and destitute; he must sacrifice everything so as to obtain everything. It is difficult to embark on this journey; it is difficult to leave the last shore behind. (SW IX, p. 217–218)[6]

---

[5] "Also selbst Gott muß der lassen, der sich in den Anfangspunkt der wahrhaft freien Philosophie stellen will. Hier heißt es: Wer es erhalten will, der wird es verlieren, und wer es aufgibt, der wird es finden."

[6] "Nur derjenige ist auf den Grund seiner selbst gekommen und hat die ganze Tiefe des Lebens erkannt, der einmal alles verlassen hatte, und selbst von allem verlassen war, dem alles versank, und der mit dem Unendlichen sich allein gesehen: ein großer Schritt, den Platon mit dem Tode verglichen. Was Dante an der Pforte des Infernum geschrieben seyn läßt, dieß ist in einem andern Sinn auch vor den Eingang zur Philosophie zu schreiben: 'Laßt alle Hoffnung fahren, die ihr eingeht'. Wer wahrhaft philosophieren will, muß aller Hoffnung, alles Verlangens, aller Sehnsucht los seyn, er muß nichts wollen, nichts wissen, sich ganz bloß und arm fühlen, alles dahin-

The Schellingian notion of the 'death of God' can also be traced back to Pascal, particularly to the *dictum* chosen by Heidegger to characterise the death of God. I am referring here to Plutarch's enigmatic phrase mentioned earlier "great Pan is dead" (*Pensées* 695). The expression pertains to an ancient legend, recalled by the classical writer in his *Moralia* (Plutarch 1936, 403). He narrates the tale of a ship's crew that heard an excruciating cry, the origin of which they were unable to pinpoint. This cry announced to them the death of the god Pan. Pascal's intention in repeating this myth can be said to be apologetic, for the French philosopher sees it as a prophecy that foretells the death of the pagan worldview. Incidentally, it should be noted that Nietzsche was not indifferent to this legend; he also recalls the story in *The Birth of Tragedy*:

> Just as the Greek sailors at the time of Tiberius once heard from some isolated island the shattering cry "great Pan is dead", so now, like a painful lament, rang throughout the Greek world, "tragedy is dead! [...] (BT 11, KSA 1, p. 75)[7]

Both Pascal and Nietzsche had in mind the disintegration of the tragic and pagan worldview. In Pascal, this notion is symbolised by the irruption of Christianity; in Nietzsche, on the other hand, it is symbolised by the emergence of the Socratic worldview.

According to Schelling, though, the sad and anguishing lament does not express the nostalgia for something lost, but is rather the pagan manifestation of the conception of the divine. It is the fragmentation of god Pan that embodies and gives life to paganism itself. The fact that it still remains uncertain whether Pan personified one or several deities lends credence to the idea that his death is not merely the death of an individual god. As a deity of fertility and nature, Pan is intimately connected with the figure of Dionysus – a god typically interpreted by Schelling as a "proto-Christ". Pan's dual aspect as both a bucolic and terrifying manifestation – and we find in the latter feature an account for the word 'panic' – renders this deity the incarnation *par excellence* of the tension inherent to the sacred. That being so, the cry "great Pan is dead" gains, even in its Nietzschean context, a new meaning. Indeed, if we look into the etymology of 'tragedy', we will find that this word originally referred to an animal's song of suffering before its death. The animal itself was considered to incarnate the god

---

geben, um alles zu gwinnen. Schwer ist dieser Schritt, schwer, gleichsam noch vom letzten Ufer zu scheiden."

7 "[W]ie einmal griechische Schiffer zu Zeiten des Tiberius an einem einsamen Eiland den erschütternden Schrei hörten 'der große Pan ist todt': so Klang es jetzt wie ein schmerzlicher Klageton durch die hellenische Welt: 'die Tragödie ist todt!'".

Dionysus. *The death of God, as discerned by Schelling and shown by anthropology and the history of contemporary religions, constitutes the vital character of the pagan worldview.*

What we are dealing with here should not in any way be considered a minor issue within Schelling's philosophical system. As I venture to show, once we succeed in understanding the meaning Schelling attributes to the 'death of God', we will be able to recreate the rational logic of his philosophical thought. In other words, it is possible to obtain a complete overview of Schelling's philosophy by combining his steady interest in the philosophy of mythology with his metaphysical doctrine, which is constructed upon his concept of 'potency'. In what follows, we shall see that it is from this same perspective, which brings together his theory of potencies with his account of mythological process, that we may chance upon the crux, not only of the death of God, but also of the internal logic of his philosophy.

Before moving onto Schelling's novel philosophical way of conceiving the notion of potency, it is important first to show the role played by the meaning of mythology (and not so much that of myth) in his philosophical system. Without neglecting the fact that Schelling perpetually re-elaborated his concepts and ideas (in stark contrast with, for instance Schopenhauer's philosophy, whose entire work can be seen as a metamorphosis of one single idea), I sustain the thesis that with his philosophy of mythology Schelling intends to manifest a process both inherent and necessary to paganism, which, in its turn, should also be seen as an "odyssey of consciousness" (SW III, p. 628), to use Schelling's own metaphor. Just as Ulysses returns to Ithaca, to his beloved Penelope and to his faithful dog Argos, so is mythology itself conceived as a necessary process whereby human consciousness totally reconstitutes itself; and it does so to the point where it allows reason to be instituted as that very court which has the ability to acknowledge, albeit not that of establishing, its own groundwork. As noted by Walter Schulz in his illuminating exegesis of Schelling's philosophy, it is *the very history of reason* that is at stake, in the sense that rationality itself requires its own alterity.[8] The philosophy of mythology is thus, in itself, the inverted image, the specular reflection of one single discovery – namely to wit reason's own inadequacy to sustain itself. The inspiration for this notion is ultimately drawn from Kant, particularly if we consider his thesis, found in the *Critique of Pure Reason*, according to which apprehending the "necessary being",

---

[8] "Diese *Selbst*begrenzung der Vernunft ist das Grundgeschehen der Epoche des Deutschen Idealismus, die sich in Schellings Spätphilosophie vollendet." (Schulz 1975, p. 329)

or eternity, of one's being is "human reason's true abyss" (KrV B 641).⁹ It is in this respect, then, that one finds the critical proximity of Kant and Schelling concerning the *ontological argument*. Schelling will argue in his Munich Lectures – which represent, essentially, his own history of modern philosophy – that the ontological argument can only reach the following conclusion:

> *either* God does not exist at all, or, if He exists, He exists always, or He exists necessarily, i.e., not *contingently*; but it is clear withal that His existence is not proved. (SW X, p. 16)[10]

The argument shows, not that God does not exist, but that the notion we have of God is that of a *necessary existence*. Schelling's philosophy of mythology should therefore never be understood as an ontological proof of the existence of God; rather, it should be read as an answer to the following question: if the divine must exist, how is His manifestation processed by human consciousness? This process, intrinsic to one's self-awareness, is what Schelling calls 'mythology', and the goal of the philosophy of mythology is that of apprehending the underlying principles, or potencies, of this process. Among these principles, as we will see, is the idea of God's death.

Schelling's goal is to show how the history of mythologies is the history of the self-awareness of the world, that is to say, the way in which consciousness positions itself – temporally, but also culturally – as self-consciousness. In the same way that Gareth Hill (1992), following Jung, tells us of a series of archetypes that animate our imaginary (notably, dual static and dynamic archetypes, simultaneously masculine and feminine), or Gilbert Durand (1969) who will propose two regimes (diurnal and nocturnal) in our imaginary, Schelling also gives us a triadic scheme for the relation between consciousness and the world.

Schelling begins with what he conceives of as being the *first potency*, that is, the first attribute to emerge in the self-constitution of consciousness. His interest in physics and mathematics – ridiculed by Hegel as 'philosophical primitivism' or 'Pythagorism' – lead him to symbolise that first potency as $-A$ or A^1. The difference in notation, between 'minus' and 'exponent' conveys a conceptual distinction: 'minus' indicates potency itself, statically considered, whereas 'exponent' denotes the same principle, but in a dynamic context. The former expresses pure 'possibility of being' (cf. SW XI, p. 289). Insofar as neither of

---

9 "Die unbedingte Notwendigkeit, die wir, als den letzten Träger aller Dinge, so unentbehrlich bedürfen, ist der wahre Abgrund für die menschliche Vernunft." See also Schelling: SW XIII, p. 163f.
10 "Entweder existirt Gott gar nicht, oder, wenn er existirt, so existirt er immer, oder so existirt er nothwendig, d.h. nicht zufällig. Aber damit ist klar, daß seine Existenz nicht bewiesen ist."

them includes *all* forms of being – *i.e.* every possibility – they discriminate none. In its voluntarism – we should keep in mind that Schelling, long before Schopenhauer, posited the will [*Wille*] as 'the original being' – the first potency manifests itself as a "will that wills nothing [*der nicht wollende Wille*]".

In mythological representations, that first potency typically occurs in connection with the gods, *deus otiosus*. However, these gods, whose sole function is to guarantee the undifferentiated unity of all possibilities of being, are not objects of worship. The intuition we find in Brahman's *Upaniṣads* of an undifferentiated and unifying principle of all modes of being is a typical example, another one being that of the heavenly gods invoked in the ancient Chinese civilisation – from *Di* in the Shang dynasty, to *Tian* in Zhou dynasty, frequently invoked by Confucius. In Greek mythology, which was dear to Schelling, the figure of Uranus – similar, one would say, to the Vedic dyad represented by Varuna and Mitra – is a paradigmatic case. The death of Uranus, often portrayed in violent terms, designates the very cosmogonic beginning, for it is from its undifferentiated nature that cosmic order is established. The death of God is, thus, in Schelling's view, the mythological condition of the genesis of the world. The death of God is, thus, not just the beginning of a creative process, for the body of the divine also becomes the body of the world. Let us take a look into a few paradigmatic instances, upon which rests the foundation of several civilisations.

In ancient India, the sacrificial death of the primordial being, Purusha, represents the beginning of the cosmogonic process. Purusha – literally, 'man' – is, in the first Vedic hymn, a gargantuan giant, with a thousand heads, whose body covers the entire universe. The gods sacrifice him and, from his fragmented body, all beings emerge; his dismemberment generates animals, liturgy, the four castes, or *varṇa*, and the celestial bodies: "The moon was born of his consciousness; from his gaze emerged the sun; from his mouth, Indra and Agni; from his breath, the wind" (Doniger 1981, p. 31).

In traditional China, a similar narrative is found in one their most significant cosmogonic myths – that of Pangu, told by Xu Zheng (220–265 AD).[11] Pangu is generated in an egg that contains, in an undifferentiated state, all the world's possibilities. After 18,000 years, Pangu emerges from the egg, creating heaven and earth – metaphors for the principles of *yin* and *yang*. At that time, though, these two principles, while already differentiated, remain united. Pangu is thus forced to use his body to separate them once and for all. Upon completing this scission, he feels tired, goes to sleep and dies. With his death, the second stage

---

[11] See Birrell 1993, p. 25, 29–31, 33 and 190–191.

of creation begins. Following the myth, his body dismembers itself and each of its parts is transfigured into one element of the world: his breathing transmutes into clouds and wind; his eyes, into Sun and Moon; his voice, into thunder; and the flies and parasites covering his body then become human beings.

Now, this universal mytheme – the death of God *qua* cosmogonic principle, mentioned by Schelling – can also be found at the genesis of Western culture. Indirectly, we can detect it in the reference framework of the Judaeo-Christian tradition. In fact, the origin of the vast majority of mythical themes read in the Bible can be traced back to Babylonic culture, which, in its turn, is rooted in the myth of Tiamat.[12] Goddess Tiamat, the primordial mother of all beings, whose name probably means 'sea', was killed and dismembered by Babylonia's hero-God Marduk. In Babylonic New Year festivities, Marduk's victory over the goddess, a triumph that enabled the creation of the universe, was repeatedly celebrated. In the epic poem *Enûma Elish* we are told how Marduk built the world from Tiamat's corpse. The firmament, stars and earth were created from the goddess' blood and bones. It is likewise stated in the Book of *Genesis* that the Wind (or Spirit) of God hovered over the waters of the earth: "The earth was formless and empty, and darkness covered the deep waters. And the Spirit of God was hovering over the surface of the waters" (Gn 1:2).[13] Subsequently, God made the heavens and the dry land by parting the waters (Gn 1:6–7). And from the waters of the great deep (*tehom*) will erupt the deluge that will cover the earth in the time of Noah. The Hebrew word *tehom* is a cognate for the name Tiamat. Evidently enough, what we have here is an indirect influence of the goddess' death in the biblical narrative of creation.

In all these cases we can see that the first potency in Schelling's philosophy of mythology is not just 'pure possibility'; it can also be thought of under a dynamic model. Thus, in A^1 the first potency becomes pure desire ($A=B$), a relentless process of self-searching, but without any concrete object of desire. Schelling considers Persephone's description (in the version of Narcissus' myth told in the Homeric Hymns[14]) as a perfect example of this notion.

The second potency, $+A$ or A^2, conveys, as a counterpoint, the notion of order associated not only with analytical and objective specification, but also with organised hierarchy. The almost oceanic, or nirvanic, fluidity of A^1 gives way to the image of pure entity (*das rein Seiende*). Schelling makes no hesitation in resorting to Aristotle's etiologic, or causal, model to render the relation

---

12 See Bottéro/Kramer 1993, p. 602f.
13 I have used the New Living Translation of the Bible (Tyndale 2007).
14 See the Hymn to Demeter in West 2003, p. 32–71.

between −A and +A intelligible: the former denotes the material cause, the *potentia pura*; the latter, +A, conveys the idea of formal cause, or pure act. Now, if the first potency is an infinite will that wishes nothing, the second potency can be understood as the expression of a being that corresponds, in an act of absolute generosity, to the wishes of all other beings. Schelling's preferred example is, here, Dionysus, especially the version described in the orphic myths: an eternal child whose body is dilacerated by the infinite desire of another, whether this other appears as the titans or the bacchantes; beyond Dionysus, Schelling recalls the figure of Osiris (from Egyptian mythology), whose body, fragmented by Set, is put back together by her sister and lover Isis, or Shiva in the Hindu mythology. Lastly, we find the third potency ±A or A^3, representing actual being; like A^1, it comprehends all possibilities, but it differs from A^1 in that it possesses the additional power of A^2, i.e. the power of self-limitation. The third potency is thus self-consciousness incarnate in the world; one can find it, following Schelling, symbolised in the figure of Hermes, the god of connection and mediation. The figures of Horus in Egyptian mythology, Viṣṇu (particularly as creator or Nārāyaṇa) in Hindu mythology, and even that of Iacchus in the mysteries of Eleusis, provide, in Schelling's opinion, further paradigmatic examples.

The A^1, A^2, A^3 scheme, however, could be considered as being excessively formal and rigid. There is no question that this intuition of potencies runs deep and permeates the length and breadth of Schelling's thought, from its youth right up to the Berlin lectures of the 1840s. For Schelling, *reality is one and the same in all its forms of expression, in all its potencies, only being subsumed in a different fashion in each of these forms*. For instance, art is, for Schelling, the expression of one unique reality, now reproduced under a different form – that difference is what constitutes the artistic universe. The same can be said of mythology or philosophy. What is true of those subjects that make up the scientific system is also true in the different personifications of divinity. There is, however, a risk of immobility and that of failing to bring about a real and effective process which results in a consciousness that manifests itself in the world. Hence Schelling's need to introduce in his scheme that which, in contemporary philosophy of mythology, is known as a *trickster* – the mythological figure of irony and abyss, of the eternal generation of being – a universal figure in the human culture whom Schelling will notate with 'B'.

Its presence is universal and it conveys the notion of an abyssal and chaotic principle (*Abgrund*) without which no system could be free and organically alive:

> For these reasons, Schelling characterizes B variously as the "negating power" *(die verneinende Kraft)*, the "inward-drawing, collapsing power" *(die zusammenziehende Kraft)*, or

the "excluding power" *(die ausschließende Kraft)*. All of these descriptive phrases are more or less equivalent terms. Their main point is to emphasize that real existence begins in chaos. (Beach 1994, p. 133)

Its manifestations are well known: Set, in Egyptian mythology; Cybele, in Phrygian mythology; Moloch, in Phoenician mythology; Loki, in German mythology. Its role is that of processing an inversion on the two first potencies, transforming pure possibility into blind desire, transforming ordering into rigid indifference; hence our sustaining the thesis that, in Schelling, *the 'death of God' bears two distinct, albeit complementary, meanings*. On the one hand it stands for the evanescence of primitive monotheism, thus allowing for the cosmogonic process. On the other hand, the assumed and willing death of the second potency – such as one finds in the death of Dionysus, or Shiva drinking all the poison and avoiding the destruction of the worlds – is the inclusion of the blind and abyssal principle (B) in A^2's process of self-destruction. Tolkien's tale of Frodo Baggins immediately springs to mind: his carrying the One Ring to the abysses, so that, with his (Frodo's) death, the ring itself may be destroyed. *For Schelling, the death of God is, ultimately, nothing more than restoring B to its status as the foundation of being and, thus, to its nullification as actual being.*

This being said, Schelling will struggle with a particular enigma throughout his work – namely, the issue of self-consciousness. In his view, any genuine concept of self, of *Selbst*, must show us how it is possible that consciousness, that is to say, one's consciousness of him/herself, finds itself detached and split, not only from all other consciousnesses, but also from the world that appears before our eyes as *Other*. "Far from being true that man and his activity render the world intelligible", Schelling writes, "man is, in actual fact, the most unintelligible [...]. It is man that leads me to ask the last desperate question: 'Why is there being? Why not nothingness?'" (SW XIII, p. 7).[15] The issue of self-consciousness' privacy is, for Schelling, a dreadful puzzle, for he flatly refuses to compromise with any kind of dualism. In his thought, spirit and nature, body and soul, life and matter, are one and the same thing. He often reiterates that nature is the visible aspect of spirit and spirit the invisible aspect of nature. How, then, are we to feel ourselves as different from others, with our own private and unique self-consciousness, objectifying an external nature? In the face of this puzzling question, Schelling's answer will be, from Munich

---

[15] "Weit entfernt also, daß der Mensch und sein Thun die Welt begreiflich mache ist er selbst das Unbegreiflichste [...] Der Mensch treibt mich zur letzten verzweiflungsvollen Frage: warum ist überhaupt etwas? warum ist nicht nichts?".

onwards, constant: it is not possible to rationally understand this condition, for life is not a system; it is not entirely reason; it is also desire, at times violent and brutal desire, as manifest in potency B. That, however, does not entail that the process by which consciousness reveals itself is irrational, so much as that there always remains a residue, something unfathomable in our life, in our existence, that cannot be fully systematised. The only prospect we are left with is to follow the history of reason through those mythic and symbolic narratives that embody the history of self-consciousness in the world since it is these very narratives that express the dramas, tensions, treasons, and desires that give true meaning to life.

References

Altizer, Thomas J.J. (2002): *The New Gospel of Christian Atheism*. Aurora: The Davies Group.
Beach, Edward A. (1994): *The Potencies of God(s). Schelling's Philosophy of Mythology*. Albany: SUNY.
Birrell, Anne (1993): *Chinese Mythology. An Introduction*. Baltimore and London: JHU Press.
Bottéro, Jean/Kramer, Noah (1993): *Lorsque les dieux faisaient l'homme. Mythologie mésopotamienne*. Paris: Gallimard.
Correia, Carlos J. (2003): *Mitos e Narrativas. Ensaios sobre a experiência do mal*. Lisbon: CFUL.
Cuppit, Don (1997): *After God. The Future of Religion*. London: Weidenfeld & Nicolson.
Deleuze, Gilles (1962): *Nietzsche et la philosophie*. Paris: PUF.
Doniger, Wendy (1981): *The Rig Veda*. London: Penguin.
Durand, Gilbert (1969): *Les Structures anthropologiques de l'imaginaire. Introduction à l'archétypologie générale*. Paris: Bordas.
Hill, Gareth S. (1992): *Masculine and Feminine. The Natural Flow of Opposites in the Psyche*. Boston and London: Shambhala.
Moingt, Joseph (1997): "Le Dieu des chrétiens". In: H. Monsacré/J.L. Schlegel (Eds.): *La Plus Belle Histoire de Dieu. Qui est le Dieu de la Bible? Essai*. Paris: Seuil.
Pascal, Blaise (1976): *Pensées*. Léon Brunschvicg (Ed.). Paris: Garnier-Flammarion.
Pindar (1997): *The Odes and Selected Fragments*. Richard Stoneman (Ed.). London: JM Dent.
Plutarch (1936): *Moralia V*. Frank C. Babbitt (Ed.). Cambridge, MA and London: Harvard University Press.
Schulz, Walter (1975): *Die Vollendung des Deutschen Idealismus in der Spätphilosophie Schellings*. Pfullingen: Neske [first edition: 1955].
Steiner, George (1971): *In Bluebeard's Castle. Some Notes Towards the Re-Definition of Culture*. London and Boston: Faber & Faber.
Voltaire (2005): "Fin du Monde". In: Louis Moland (Ed.): *Œuvres complètes de Voltaire. Le Dictionnaire Philosophique. Édition Intégrale*. Mazères: Le Chasseur abstrait éditeur.
West, Martin L. (Ed.) (2003): *Homeric Hyms. Homeric Apocrypha. Lives of Homer*. Cambridge and London: Harvard University Press.

Katia Hay
Understanding the Past in Nietzsche and Schelling: *Logos* or *Mythos*?

Just before Socrates uses a myth to explain the complex nature of the soul in Plato's *Phaedrus*, he justifies his narrative approach or mythological "manner of discourse", by saying that only a God would be able to tell the truth about the soul (*Phaedrus* 246a).[1] We humans, with our limited and finite knowledge, cannot *say* what the nature of the soul *is*, but we might be able to show what it *resembles*. Without wanting to initiate a discussion about the role that mythological narratives play in Plato's works, I would like to underline Plato's recourse to a form of knowledge and discourse that only offers us an *approximate* account of the truth through images, in opposition to a divine, although impossible form of knowledge that can say how things truly are; that is, his justification of *mythos* over *logos*. I would like to use this as a tool with which to examine the ways in which Schelling and Nietzsche address the problem of the past. To put it differently, the question guiding my reading of Nietzsche and Schelling is the following: to what extent are they producing *logos*, to what extent are they actually 'saying' anything 'true' about the past and about our most deepest and ancient nature? And furthermore: to what extent does this matter, to what extent is this 'truth' relevant to the kind of knowledge their texts seek to convey?

To be sure, *if* the truth or falsity of their claims proves to be irrelevant, *if* what they are doing can, at least to some degree, be identified more as a myth or narrative than as a scientific description, the question that we will need to address is whether there are any reasons – any *good* reasons – for this to be the case. For, we must not neglect the fact that both Schelling's and Nietzsche's philosophical writings are the result of a rigorous, rational and also *scientific* (in the sense of *wissenschaftlich*) endeavour. In other words, whatever form this parallel reading of Nietzsche's and Schelling's philosophical investigations into the past may take, we need to be able to remain true to their philosophical projects and the way in which they carry these out. It is for this reason that I shall begin by considering the ways in which Nietzsche and Schelling conceive of philosophy; what it is and what it should be. And as we shall see, this will also constitute our first confirmation regarding the affinities between the two thinkers.

---

[1] I am following the translation by R. Hackforth, Cambridge University Press.

However, it seems important to note that by focusing mainly on the analogies between Schelling and Nietzsche, it is not my intention to deny the fundamental differences between them, but rather to bring them together in a way that might enable us to create new, different, perspectives that might enrich our reading both of Nietzsche and Schelling.

I The 'Sailor- Philosopher' and the 'Philosophy of the Future'

The title of an essay from 1825 "Über die Natur der Philosophie als Wissenschaft" ("On the Nature of Philosophy as Science"), already gives us a clear indication that, for Schelling, philosophy is – or should be – understood as science (*Wissenschaft*). According to Schelling, however, this implies, on the one hand, that philosophy is a process, and on the other, that error (*Irrthum*) is fundamental and necessary for its development. In this context, Schelling describes his own trajectory and considers the figure of the philosopher-scientist (the one who seeks the truth) through the image of a sailor on the open sea. Schelling does this in order to distinguish the *real* philosopher from the others: those who do not dare to leave the harbour, he argues, will not encounter any dangers, they will not commit any errors, but they will never enable philosophy to fulfill its task either, that is to say: they will not enable it to become true philosophy.

> Whoever wants to wander [*irren*], must – at the very least – be on his way; but he who has not even hit the road and remains sitting at home instead, he cannot go astray [*irren*]. Who ventures to go out into the ocean might lose his way or be cast away due to storms or to his own clumsiness, but he who does not even leave the harbour, whose entire effort consists rather in not leaving, and by eternally philosophising about philosophy impeding it to become philosophy, he has, indeed, no dangers to fear. (SW IX, p. 211)[2]

Like a hero (or heroine), the philosopher has to leave everything behind: "Alles lassen" (SW IX, p. 211), says Schelling. In other words, if we want to

---

[2] "Wer irren will, der muß wenigstens auf dem Wege seyn; wer aber gar nicht einmal sich auf den Weg macht, sondern völlig zu Hause sitzen bleibt, kann nicht irren. Wer sich in die See wagt, kann durch Stürme oder eigne Ungeschicklichkeit freilich vom Wege abkommen und verschlagen werden, wer aber gar nicht aus dem Hafen ausläuft, dessen ganzes Bestreben vielmehr darin besteht, nicht auszulaufen, sondern durch ein ewiges Philosophiren über Philosophie zu verhindern, daß es gar nie zur Philosophie komme, der hat freilich keine Gefahren zu befürchten."

pursue our tasks as true philosophers, we must abandon all 'truths', fixed ideas and presuppositions: "even God, for God is from this standpoint also only a being [selbst Gott, denn auch Gott ist auf diesem Standpunkt nur ein Seyendes]" (SW IX, p. 211).

The image of the philosopher as a sailor or philosophy and knowledge as a ship on the open sea is certainly not an unusual metaphor.³ But it is interesting to see the extent to which Nietzsche also uses it to describe a similar trajectory and a similar vision. In the last paragraph of the section entitled "On the prejudices of philosophers" of *Beyond Good and Evil*, Nietzsche refers to his own philosophy as the realisation or inauguration of a "colossal [*ungeheueren*] and almost new domain of dangerous knowledge [*gefährlicher Erkenntnisse*]" (BGE 23, KSA 5, p. 38). And in a similar way as he had already done in §124 of *The Gay Science*,⁴ Nietzsche describes our task – as true and honest philosophers – as the task of a sailor on the open sea, who is forced to sail and to leave the shore behind:

> On the other hand, once one has drifted up to here with one's ship, well then! courage! [...] our eyes wide open and a firm hand at the helm! – we sail *away* right over morality [*wir fahren geradewegs über die Moral* weg], we crush out, we destroy perhaps the remains of our own morality by daring to make our voyage over there, – but what do *we* matter! Never yet did a *profounder world* of insight reveal itself to daring travelers and adventurers [...]. (BGE 23, KSA 5, p. 38–39)⁵

For Nietzsche, as for Schelling, true philosophers have to be courageous enough to leave all certainties behind and to question all assumptions, even those that are closest to us and determine our mode of being in the world: we have *to sail away over our morality*. And, as for Schelling, the individual philosopher himself

---

3 Bacon famously used the image of a ship to illustrate his *Novum Organum* in 1620. One might attempt to compare this image with the Romantic ship-wreck version that we can find in some of Caspar David Friedrich's paintings.
4 "We have forsaken the land and gone to sea! We have destroyed the bridge behind us [...] Woe, when homesickness for the land overcomes you, as if there had been more *freedom* there – and there is no more 'land'!"(GS 124, KSA 3, p. 480) ["Wir haben das Land verlassen und sind zu Schiff gegangen! Wir haben die Brücke hinter uns, [...] Wehe, wenn das Land-Heimweh dich befällt, als ob dort mehr *Freiheit* gewesen wäre, – und es giebt kein 'Land' mehr"].
5 "Andrerseits: ist man einmal mit seinem Schiffe hierhin verschlagen, nun! wohlan! jetzt tüchtig die Zähne zusammengebissen! die Augen aufgemacht! die Hand fest am Steuer! – wir fahren geradewegs über die Moral *weg*, wir erdrücken, wir zermalmen vielleicht dabei unsren eignen Rest Moralität, indem wir dorthin unsre Fahrt machen und wagen, – aber was liegt an uns! Niemals noch hat sich verwegenen Reisenden und Abenteurern eine *tiefere Welt* der Einsicht eröffnet".

is less important ("what do *we* matter!") than the task of creating or developing a new philosophy and a new form of knowledge. Indeed, this form of self-sacrifice and courage seems to be, for both thinkers, the only way we will be able to deal with and address what Nietzsche in this text calls the real *Grundprobleme*, which both authors seem to identify with the problem of our drives or, to put it in more Schellingian terms, the problem of the will.[6]

Both in Nietzsche's *Gay Science* and *Beyond Good and Evil*, this insight about the real *Grundprobleme* goes hand in hand with and initiates a new form of doing and understanding philosophy. It is a new *psychology* or *physiology*, which, among other things, will lead him to question the whole concept of the will to knowledge (*Wille zur Erkenntnis*), and to *suggest* that the true origin of philosophy, the impulse moving us to philosophise, lies not so much in a hypothetical drive to knowledge (*Trieb zur Erkenntnis*), but rather in the desire to dominate (*herrschen*): "For all drives are eager for power: and *as such* they try to philosophise [*Denn jeder Trieb ist herrschsüchtig: und als solcher versucht er zu philosophiren*]" (BGE 6, KSA 5, p. 20). Or, as he also puts it, this new form of knowledge is dangerous and painful, because it works with an almost sickening[7] hypothesis about the nature of life, namely, that all 'good' drives can be derived from 'bad' (*schlimm*) ones, and that:

> even the emotions [*Affekte*] of hatred, envy, the greed for possession and the greed for domination [should be seen, KH] as life-conditioning emotions, as factors which must be present, fundamentally and essentially, in the general economy of life [...]. (BGE 23, KSA 5, p. 38)[8]

At this point, one could argue that all similarities between Schelling and Nietzsche come to an end. For, the concept of philosophy defended by Schelling in all of his texts, but especially in his essay from 1825, seems to be the very opposite of what Nietzsche is doing with his new *physiology* or *psychology* of the drives. In effect, in his text about the *Nature of Philosophy as Science*, Schelling develops the concept of the 'true principle' of philosophy and claims that the "one subject" running through all the different and opposed philosophical systems, the *one subject* that, in spite of this, always avoids being fixed into any

---

6 See also Norman 2004.
7 Nietzsche uses the term 'seasickness' (*Seekrankheit*).
8 "Gesetzt aber, jemand nimmt gar die Affekte Hass, Neid, Habsucht, Herrschsucht als lebenbedingende Affekte, als Etwas, das im Gesammt-Haushalte des Lebens grundsätzlich und grundwesentlich vorhanden sein muss, folglich noch gesteigert werden muss, falls das Leben noch gesteigert werden soll, – der leidet an einer solchen Richtung seines Urtheils wie an einer Seekrankheit."

of these systems [*jenes Eine Subjekt, das durch alles geht, und in nichts bleibt*] (SW IX, p. 216), is freedom. Eternal freedom (*ewige Freiheit*) is the true subject and object of philosophy and our *goal* is the (immediate) knowledge of it (SW IX, p. 240).[9] Moreover, Schelling claims that eternal freedom should be understood as eternal, pure potentiality (*das ewige, lautere Können*), as a force, a desire that does not desire anything: it is "the will in as much it does not will [*Der Wille, inwiefern er nicht will*]" (SW IX, p. 222). A concept, which seems to be diametrically opposed to Nietzsche's notion of the will, which always wants something, and in its *horror vacui* always has a goal: the will to maintain itself, the will to be, the will to dominate, or if nothing else, as Nietzsche repeatedly writes in the *Genealogy of Morality*: the will to nothingness (GM III 1, KSA 5, p. 339). And yet, Schelling's almost inconceivable notion of a 'will that does not will' (a freedom that escapes all forms) and its implications for the problem of knowledge and of understanding philosophy, as we shall see, does not necessarily preclude the convergences between the two philosophers.

To be sure, Schelling (in contrast to Nietzsche) does not seem to be suspicious about the will to knowledge being the origin of philosophy *qua* knowledge, but he does, nevertheless, question whether the particular kind of will that has ruled in the history of philosophy, namely a will that wants a total system, i.e. a system in which all former theories and all former truths are to be annihilated, or at the very least *explained, understood, subsumed*, will ever be capable of grasping or representing anything thoroughly. Considering the intrinsic opposition and mutual exclusion of the different theories throughout the history of philosophy, or what he calls the "*bellum intestinum* in human knowledge" (SW IX, p. 209), Schelling argues that one must give up hope on the possibility of ever finding "a sole perspective [*eine einzelne Ansicht*]" (SW IX, p. 210) that would permanently overrule the others. This form of truth and mastery, so to speak, will always of necessity be temporary:

> A system might become master over another, however, only apparently and for a certain time; not in reality and in the long run. The fact that this is impossible – the fact that all systems have the same right, the same validity claim – this is the insight that must precede the idea of a system in the great sense, the system par *excellence*. (SW IX, p. 211)[10]

---

[9] "Das *Ziel* also ist das unmittelbare Wissen der ewigen Freiheit" (SW IX, p. 240).
[10] "Also allerdings scheinbar und für eine Zeit kann ein System des andern Meister werden, wirklich und in die Länge nicht, und daß dieß unmöglich sey – daß an sich jedes System gleiches Recht habe, gleichen Anspruch zu gelten – dieß ist die Einsicht, welche der Idee des Systems im großen Sinn – des Systems par *excellence* – vorausgehen muß."

In other words: if there is such a thing as the unity (*Einheit*) of philosophy, and if it makes sense at all to talk about philosophy as one unitary science or quest, this unity can only be represented or materialised through a 'System' (i.e. a science, a discourse) in which all other systems, i.e. all *perspectives* do not exclude one another. This is Schelling's idea of a system *par excellence*. As he later writes: "The task is namely that they [the systems, KH] really *coexist* [*die Aufgabe ist eben, daß sie wirklich* zusammenbestehen]" (SW IX, p. 213). Thus, according to Schelling, the main error of all former philosophical positions has been (to put it in Nietzschean terms) their 'will to truth', in the sense that this *will* has always been a 'will to overrule' the other systems.

In his 1811 version of *The Ages of the World*, we find a similar line of thought, when Schelling writes that: "in relation to living sciences [*lebendige Wissenschaft*], one can say that all sentences [*Satz*] are false, from the very fact that they are expressed [*ausgesprochen*] as such" (WA I, p. 48). The problem, as we can see here too, is not so much the fact that all systems are necessarily limited, but the fact that they necessarily present themselves as being the 'one truth' and impose themselves over the whole – in the same way a sick organ imposes itself over the rest of the body, hereby impeding the body from functioning as a whole. This comparison (which Schelling also used in his *Freedom Essay* to explain the idea of the 'possibility of evil') will lead Schelling to refer to those systems as 'illnesses' (SW IX, p. 212f.) – an image, which inevitably reminds us of Nietzsche's preface to *Gay Science* where he refers to the history of philosophy as a history of illnesses (GS Preface 2, KSA 3, p. 347f.). For both authors, philosophy only makes sense within the history of philosophy.[11] We can only ever understand philosophy if we understand it as a process, a historical process, for which diversity, error and sickness are not only inevitable, but also absolutely necessary for its own realisation. Nietzsche goes a step further by affirming that the lack of error would mean the total death or absence of life. And although this idea is not totally alien to Schelling (who in many different ways argues that the absolute eradication of errors or sickness is only possible through death, cf. SW VII, p. 371), he does not defend it in such a polemical or radical way as Nietzsche does when he affirms that the underlying *will to life* is the *will to error* (cf. BGE 24, KSA 5, p. 41f.).

What is important, however, is that for both Schelling and Nietzsche, this long history of *illnesses* or the existence of conflicting theories is not *per se* negative. Quite on the contrary, it is necessary for the development of philosophy, and each individual philosopher will have to go through all the inevitable errors

---

11 Cf. BGE 6, KSA 5, p. 20, where Nietzsche even refers to philosophy as an evolving *plant*.

and failures; s/he will have to go through all those 'illnesses'. And yet – and here we have the argument which explains why Schelling introduces the notion of an eternal freedom – philosophy itself has never remained and will never remain in any of these positions: it has taken many forms and gone through all of them, but it has always remained, so to say, untouched, pure, *lauter*. And it has done so, in spite of the 'will to dominate' underlying all individual theoretical efforts.

It is precisely in this sense that Schelling conceives his own position to be liberating and the true subject of philosophy to be 'eternal freedom'. For the one who has achieved this point of reflection is free from the logic of exclusion, he is: "free from all systems – *above* all systems [*frei vom System – über allem System*]" (SW IX, p. 212). In other words: leaving all our truths behind, leaving God behind, this form of exposing oneself to the dangers of the unknown seas, far from intimidating and overwhelming us, should liberates us. And it is also on this level that we can see similarities with Nietzsche; especially if we think of Nietzsche's notion of the great *Loslösung*[12] (cf. HH I Preface 3, KSA 2, p. 15f.), which is necessary for us to become 'free spirits' and which, one could argue, infuses all of Nietzsche's writings.[13] In any case though, both for Schelling and Nietzsche this 'liberation' or '*Loslösung*' can never be fully attained, it is never final, but rather must be repeated time and again and must be understood as part of an ongoing, *eternal* process.[14]

Conversely, both Schelling and Nietzsche consider that this new way of understanding the history of philosophy as a history of necessary mistakes, this new way of understanding one's own position within the history of philosophy as one that must be able to address the plurality of systems in a way that does not negate them, and is hence somehow able to affirm them, is the only way in which philosophy can be open to the future. In fact, what is at stake, for both Nietzsche and Schelling, and what they are trying to construct is not only *a future philosophy*, but something more like *a philosophy of the future*, i.e. a form of philosophy that is able to conceive, prepare, open up and in a certain sense *create* something radically new: a philosophy that is able to *conceive* the future. Indeed, without wanting to ascribe to Nietzsche anything like a desire to create

---

[12] The English translation for '*Loslösung*' is very often 'liberation', but this word does not contain, like the German does, the root from the verb 'lassen', 'to leave'.
[13] We can also see this structure in BGE: the second section entitled "The Free Spirit" is preceded by §23 where, as we have seen above, Nietzsche describes the 'dangerous' knowledge he is inaugurating as a process whereby we 'sail *away* from' our former truths and believes.
[14] The great *Loslösung* is only the *first victory*, a victory that must be conquered and re-conquered, again and again. Cf. HH I Preface 3, KSA 2, p. 16.

a unified, ultimate philosophical 'System' (as one might find in Schelling), it is important to see how they both share a similar worry and a similar aim insofar as they are both trying to understand philosophy in a way that it remains radically open to the future, open to change.

More interesting for us now, though, is the fact that for both Nietzsche and Schelling this openness towards the future is only possible if we acknowledge the radically unknown and impenetrable character of the past: An open and undetermined future is only possible if we accept an open and undetermined past, because if we were to find a fixed, unchanging past, it would not be possible to postulate any real future. To put it briefly: Schelling's and Nietzsche's engagement with the past, with our history and prehistory needs to be understood as a result of their engagement with the problem of the future and the necessity of transforming our notion of philosophy and philosophical discourses. For Nietzsche most certainly, and in a sense for Schelling too, this form of philosophical engagement with the past will not only affect the practice and development of philosophy as such, but should also enable us to transform, or at least influence the transformation of humankind.[15] Indeed, it is important that we understand what is at stake before we begin examining the ways in which both Nietzsche and Schelling attempt to reconstruct the past, which (this we know at least) can only be *a radically open, i.e. indeterminate past.*

II Understanding the Past and Movements of the 'Two Wills'

Both Schelling and Nietzsche give great importance to the engagement with and the *study* of the past. To a large extent, this concern is related to the belief in the constant evolution of things. In Schelling's words: "Everything is but the working of time and only through time does it achieve its specificity and meaning" (WA I, p. 12), or as Nietzsche puts it in *Gay Science*: "Lightning and thunder need time; the light of the stars needs time; deeds need time, even after they are done, in order to be seen and heard" (GS 125, KSA 3, p. 481). This idea is also depicted in *Beyond Good and Evil* when Nietzsche refers to humanity, as "the plant 'man' [*die Pflanze 'Mensch'*]" (BGE 44, KSA 5, p. 61). In fact, already

---

[15] Although we will not find a figure like the *Übermensch* in Schelling, he does make it clear in his *Ages of the World*, that the real 'future' is only possible if we think of it as a radical *change* and *rupture* with the present.

in *Human, All Too Human*, where he criticises the lack of historical sense in philosophy, he affirms that:

> Everything has become; there are *no eternal facts*, nor are there any absolute truths. Thus *historical philosophising* is necessary from now on and the virtue of modesty too. (HH I 2, KSA 2, p. 25)[16]

We have already seen how, for both Nietzsche and Schelling, philosophy must be conceived as a historical process, so that: to understand philosophy means to understand this very process. The consequence of this will be (in both cases) that philosophy will always necessarily become in some way or other an investigation into and an account of the past, that is to say: a *historical philosophising*, or, to use a more Schellingian term: a *narration*.[17] On the other hand, the ever evolving character of all things means that, whenever we investigate the past, we are also investigating ourselves, our deepest self. As Schelling puts it in his essay "On the Divinities of Samothrace": "what is first is at the same time the deepest [*das Erste ist zugleich das Unterste*]" (SW VIII, p. 353). The study of the most remote past is always the study of something within us, something that still has some form of presence in our being: "that spinning wheel of birth, that auto-destructive frenzy is still, right now, at the core of all things [*jenes drehende Rad der Geburt, jener wilde sich selbst zerreißende Wahnsinn [ist] noch jetzt das Innerste aller Dinge*]" (WA I, p. 43). Or, as Nietzsche writes in BGE: "the past of every form and mode of life, and of cultures which were formerly closely contiguous and superimposed on one another, flows forth into us" (BGE 224, KSA 5, p. 158). Or in *Gay Science*: "you still carry likes and dislikes of things [*Schätzungen der Dinge*] with you which have their origin in passions and loves from centuries ago!" (GS 57, KSA 3, p. 421).

But, whereas it is easy to identify a text dedicated specifically to the problem of the past in Schelling's writings (namely the three versions of his *Ages of the World*, from 1811–1813 and 1815), in Nietzsche we find that his *Auseinandersetzung* with the past is present in almost all of his works: from the *Birth of Tragedy* to his later texts. In *Human, All Too Human,* for instance, he conceives his work as the realisation of the "history of the origin of thought" (HH I

---

[16] "Alles aber ist geworden; es giebt *keine ewigen Thatsachen*: sowie es keine absoluten Wahrheiten giebt. – Demnach ist das *historische Philosophiren* von jetzt ab nöthig und mit ihm die Tugend der Bescheidung."

[17] In the introduction to the three versions of his Ages of the World, Schelling says explicitly that the past is to be narrated (cf. WA I, p. 2).

16, KSA 2, p. 37) and the "study of the origin and history of moral feelings" (HH I 35, KSA 2, p. 57). In fact, one could argue that all these approaches should be seen as a prelude to his *Genealogy*, where Nietzsche 'studies' the past most consistently; and yet, I will focus primarily on some of his remarks from *Beyond Good and Evil: Prelude to a Philosophy of the Future*. For it is here that (like Schelling) he analyses the present in terms of ancient forces, wills or drives. For both authors, our *history* and *pre-history*, our very 'essence' is to be understood and explained in terms of the movements and developments of the relation between these forces.

In effect, contrary to what one might expect and in sharp contrast to Schopenhauer, in Schelling there is never *one* will alone. At the very instance in which Schelling addresses the notion of a unitary and primordial being (*Urwesen*) in terms of an original will, at the moment in which he examines the *history of the development* of the *Urwesen* (cf. WA I, p. 10), he is forced to think of it, not as a single will, but as a relation between forces, a relation between 'two wills'. In Schelling there is never *one* will, but *two*: the pure, expansive will (*lauterer Wille*) and the contractive will or contractive force (*contrahirende Kraft*). In this sense, it is my thesis, that the true 'predecessor' of Nietzsche's philosophy of the will (as a multiplicity of wills or drives) is not Schopenhauer, but Schelling. Moreover, this duality or 'plurality of forces'[18] constitutes perhaps the central point of convergence between the two philosophers. For, far from leading Schelling to develop an atomistic view of reality, this duality of forces will lead him to redefine the way in which we should understand ourselves, namely as a complex unity, a living unity, or as he also names it a "living bond [*lebendige Band*]" (SW VII, p. 362) between opposing forces. We find an analogous idea in Nietzsche when he suggests, for instance in BGE, that *we **are** a war* (BGE 200, KSA 5, p. 120; cf. BGE 19).

Already in his *Freedom Essay* (1809) Schelling describes the entire process of becoming (i.e. the becoming of being, but also the becoming of reason, the becoming of consciousness and the becoming of freedom) as a struggle between two forces. This struggle will be a recurrent theme in the *Ages of the World*, in which Schelling attempts to describe the movements that took place – or must have taken place – at the very origins of existence (and which still inform our present, or at least certain aspects of our present selves). Even the origin of corporeal matter (*körperliche Materie*) is described as the result of a struggle

---

18 Although in his *Ages of the World*, Schelling refers specifically to two different wills, in his *Freedom Essay* Schelling seems to refer more loosely to a multiplicity of 'forces'.

between two opposed forces or wills. For, according to Schelling, at the very beginning, there is no difference between matter and spirit, nature and thought: physical and spiritual matter are the same. It is only through the process of becoming that they separate and become different from one another (WA I, p. 31–36). According to Schelling this means that the "first matter [*erste Materie*] cannot be opposed to spirit [*dem Geist entgegengesetzte*], but must be a spiritual matter [*geistige Materie*]" (WA I, p. 32), or as he explains in the second version of the *Ages of the World*: matter is "in itself spiritual and non-corporeal [*in sich geistig und unkörperlich*]" (WA II, p. 151–152).

However 'metaphysical' or anti-Nietzschean this may appear, we find in Nietzsche a very similar idea when he suggests in §36 of BGE, that "thought is only a relation between drives [*Denken ist nur ein Verhalten dieser Triebe zu einander*]", and conversely: that it is only 'logical' to consider that the "so called mechanical (or 'material') world" possesses "the same degree of reality [*vom gleichen Realitäts-Range*] as our emotions" (BGE 36, KSA 5, p. 54). In the end, he suggests that matter be considered as "a *primary form* [Vorform] of life" (BGE 36, KSA 5, p. 55), which he describes as:

> a more primitive form of the world of emotions, in which everything still lies locked in a mighty unity [*in mächtiger Einheit beschlossen*] which afterwards branches off and develops itself [...] (BGE 36, KSA 5, p. 54–55)[19]

In other words, what Nietzsche seems to be suggesting is that 'matter' as such cannot be understood as being essentially different from organic life, from affect or from thought, but rather must be seen as a prior form of life: what is differentiated in organic life (affect and thought) is undifferentiated in matter. And this is exactly the same view that we find in Schelling, when he explains how everything evolves from a division (*Scheidung*) and "separation of forces [*Auseinandergehen der Kräfte*]" (WA I, p. 36):

---

[19] "Gesetzt, dass nichts Anderes als real 'gegeben' ist als unsre Welt der Begierden und Leidenschaften, dass wir zu keiner anderen 'Realität' hinab oder hinauf können als gerade zur Realität unsrer Triebe – denn Denken ist nur ein Verhalten dieser Triebe zu einander –: ist es nicht erlaubt, den Versuch zu machen und die Frage zu fragen, ob dies Gegeben nicht *ausreicht*, um aus Seines-Gleichen auch die sogenannte mechanistische (oder 'materielle') Welt zu verstehen? Ich meine nicht als eine Täuschung, einen 'Schein', eine 'Vorstellung' (im Berkeley'schen und Schopenhauerischen Sinne), sondern als vom gleichen Realitäts-Range, welchen unser Affekt selbst hat, – als eine primitivere Form der Welt der Affekte, in der noch Alles in mächtiger Einheit beschlossen liegt, was sich dann im organischen Prozesse abzweigt und ausgestaltet (auch, wie billig, verzärtelt und abschwächt –) [...] – als eine *Vorform* des Lebens?"

> The forces that split up (but are not fully dispersed [*auseinandergetreten*]) in this division [*Scheidung*] are the material [*Stoff*] from which the body is subsequently configured; the vital bond which arises as the center of forces in this division [...] is the soul. (SW VII, p. 362)[20]

Schelling describes this process of differentiation as a process towards *light*: "All birth is birth from darkness into light" (SW VII, p. 360). Creation itself is understood in terms of an "inner transmutation or transfiguration [*Verklärung*] of the initial principle of darkness into light" (SW VII, p. 362). Nietzsche, however, seems to be more suspicious in his evaluation, when he describes the process of differentiation as a process that weakens (*abschwächt*) and softens (*verzärtelt*) (cf. BGE 36, KSA 5, p. 55). And yet, granting that it would be wrong to oversee this important difference, it would also be wrong to ascribe to Schelling a naïve optimism regarding the becoming and progress of reason, light or freedom. For the process described by Schelling also involves a process of becoming more and more delicate or fragile, in the sense that it is a process that will finally confront us with the possibility of choosing between good and evil, life-affirmation and life-destruction. So, in a sense, the closer we come to reason, freedom and 'light', the more 'fragile' we are, and the easier it is for us to fall (back) into chaos and (self)-destruction, as he points out in his *Freedom Essay* (SW VII, p. 359–360).

On the other hand, and also in contrast to Nietzsche, the struggle between the two wills does not constitute Schelling's 'absolute' starting point. So, in a certain sense, it would be wrong to say that his starting point lies in the *co-existence* of two opposite wills as was suggested above. Strictly speaking, this duality constitutes only the beginning *of reality* or the beginning of the *coming into existence*. But before this – Schelling argues – there must be something like a *beginning before the beginning*. Schelling identifies this pre-beginning or primordial beginning (*Uranfang*) as the *Lauterkeit* (limpidness or pureness)[21]; it is the will that does not will, but before it even knows itself as such. Thus, the key question that Schelling needs to answer now is: Where does the 'other' will come from, the second one: the 'will to existence' (*Wille zur Existenz*), the 'contracting will' or, as Schelling also explains, the 'hunger for being' that will initiate, so to say, the 'real' beginning? And Schelling's answer is that this second will "engenders itself [*erzeugt sich selbst*]" (WA II, p. 137; cf. WA I, p. 17) within

---

20 "Die in dieser Scheidung getrennten (aber nicht völlig auseinandergetretenen) Kräfte sind der Stoff, woraus nachher der Leib configurirt wird; das aber in der Scheidung [...] als Mittelpunkt der Kräfte entstehende lebendige Band ist die Seele."
21 Also called 'lauterer Wille', 'Liebe', 'Wille der Liebe', etc.

the pure *Lauterkeit*, which henceforth becomes its matrix; and it does so: "in the same way a will engenders itself in the human soul, unconsciously, without its intervention [*wie sich ein Wille im Gemüt des Menschen, bewusstlos, ohne sein Zutun erzeugt*]" (WA II, p. 137).

From this point onwards, says Schelling, begins a new *epoch* (cf. WA I, p. 22). Through its auto-creation, the contracting will (*zusammenziehender Wille*) awakens (within the first will) the longing for being or becoming 'real', that is: the longing for becoming sensitive and the longing for feeling itself. This means that before the contracting force had awakened, the *Lauterkeit* did not know itself. It had everything, but in the same sense it had nothing; in its sheer perfection it was insensitive (*fühllos*) (WA I, p. 29). Thus commences a first phase in which there is no struggle or discord between the two wills: they are both involved in a process of mutual perception and recognition. Schelling calls this moment a *holdes Wechselspiel* (lovely interplay) in which the *Lauterkeit* is pleased to discover its reality, and the contracting will is content, because its insatiable desire and craving-to-possess seems to have calmed down (WA I, p. 30). Of relevance for us now, however, is the philosophical claim underlying Schelling's poetical and dense writing, namely that true existence is not possible without the *feeling* of existence and that this feeling always involves (at least at the beginning) a moment of intense joy and plenitude (*Überfluss*): it is affirmative (cf. WA I, p. 32). The first feeling of the will is not a feeling of lack, as in Schopenhauer, but a feeling of plenitude or excess, as we can find in Nietzsche.

But because of the very structure of its emergence, the pure form of the will, the *Lauterkeit*, which has now become sentient, will also become fundamentally insatiable. The initial playfulness between the two wills gradually evolves into a fight and a struggle (WA I, p. 34ff.). And this struggle will become more and more virulent until the two forces manage to separate themselves – although only to fall back into a similar process (cf. WA I, p. 55). This is the "eternal wheel" (WA I, p. 43) I referred to before. But it also constitutes the birth of the desire to become free. The now awakened and sensitive *Lauterkeit* wants to be, but it wants to be free from the contracting will, which it now perceives as an alienating force. The entire process of becoming seems, hence, to be constructed as a constant process of identity and differentiation; unity, separation and transformation, which can be understood both as an ongoing process of liberation and as the process of *becoming what one is*.[22]

---

[22] The intriguing question concerning 'how one can become who one is' is also important for Nietzsche as is evident from the subtitle of his book *Ecce Homo*: "How one becomes what one is [*Wie man wird was man ist*]" KSA 6, p. 255). On the question of 'becoming who you are'

III Broader Analogies between Nietzsche and Schelling

In the section above I have outlined what Schelling describes in the *Ages of the World* as the 'initial movements' between the two wills that emerge from the primordial will or *Lauterkeit*. In addition, through this brief description, we have seen that some of the essential elements in Schelling's thought are also present in Nietzsche. But the question that we need to answer now is: how to address these somewhat punctual similarities? Are they indicative of deeper similarities? Where should we situate them? – Addressing these questions is all the more urgent, because, from a certain Nietzschean perspective, one might be tempted to take Schelling's texts as *bad metaphysics*. Indeed, from the idea of an *Urwesen* and the very ambiguous notion of a beginning before the real beginning (*Lauterkeit*), it might seem that Schelling is trying to reconstruct the past by establishing a fixed and unitary origin or ground, which would determine everything that exists.

And yet, quite the opposite is the case. First of all, because what determines our existence is not the *Lauterkeit* itself, but rather the *relation* and the movements between the two wills. With these movements, Schelling is not only describing the beginning or the coming into existence of reality; these movements not only reflect the structure of reality and the process of becoming; but more importantly, they also reflect the most ancient structure of our most present and lively desires, which (as we have seen) is always characterised by a struggle, a process of differentiation and separation. And this seems to be exactly Nietzsche's point when he describes how everything that we do, everything that we think and feel is a result of the relation of drives doing, thinking and feeling within us (cf. BGE 23).[23] Moreover, once we acknowledge that Nietzsche also conceives of the drives as being *prior* to our own existence and constituting the 'true' origin or spring of our actions and identity, we can see that the 'nature' of Nietzsche's drives is less clear than what might appear. Although he seems to refer to them *as if* they were clearly identifiable and even countable forces working within us,[24] they remain rather mysterious – if not

---

in Nietzsche see Babich 2003, Acampora 2013 (especially p. 151–198) and Löwith 1986 (esp. 127–141), who also establishes analogies between Nietzsche and Schelling.

23 See also the analysis of willing in BGE 19, KSA 5, p. 32, which is described not only as "a complex of feeling and thinking, but also [as, KH] an affect".

24 In his *Genealogy of Morality*, for instance, Nietzsche seems to "draw up a list of the particular drives" of the philosopher, and distinguishes "his drive to doubt, his drive to deny, his drive to 'metaphysical'. In other words: Nietzsche's 'theory of drives' (just like Schelling's 'theory of the two wills') cannot be taken as a biological or physicalistic account of human nature and life in general, but rather, needs to be interpreted, as I will argue further, as an 'experiment', a tool, a possibility.[25]

Secondly, Schelling does not present the primordial being *Urwesen* or *Lauterkeit* as something fixed. In a similar way as the 'ground to existence' in his *Freedom Essay* (that very something that enables every form of existence to be and become what it is), the *Lauterkeit* or first will is totally indeterminate. But this means also that it is unfathomable, impossible to grasp, impossible to think, impossible to put into words; something that constantly escapes us. Our deepest past is absolutely ungraspable and slips through our fingers the very minute we try to conceptualise it. And it is precisely because of this that Schelling needs to create a new language to refer to it, i.e. to *create* or *re-create* it in a way that does not disavow its indeterminacy. Only by showing and reinforcing its elusive and arcane character, can he remain true to the idea that the past is never closed and fixed, but radically open. Schelling's poetical narrative and almost mythological reconstruction of the past (highly problematic from an *empirical* point of view) is a necessary consequence of the fact that he is talking about and referring to something that he cannot refer to. Regarding Schelling's great narration of the past, the relevant question is not whether it is 'true' or 'false' in an empirical or factual sense, but whether it is capable of grasping and saying something *real* about the past, and most importantly about our most deepest selves.

However much we try, we will never be able to 'see', 'measure' or 'weigh' one of Schelling's 'wills'. And this is also the case for Nietzsche's 'drives', which cannot be understood within the logic of a referential or apophantic language, but as "concepts, that is to say, as conventional fictions" (BGE 21, KSA 5, p. 36).[26] Neither Schelling's nor Nietzsche's philosophies of the past and of our deepest nature can be taken as 'empirical knowledge'. And yet, this does not invalidate their theories, but it does indicate the way in which they must be addressed and interpreted. By referring to notions that necessarily remain unfathomable (will and/or drives), both authors are inviting us to take them not as dogmas, but as *tools*: tools for knowing and discovering ourselves and our

---

prevaricate (his 'ephectic' drive), his drive to analyse, his drive to research, investigate, dare, his drive to compare and counter-balance" (GM III 9, KSA 5, p. 357).
25 For a more positivist approach to Nietzsche's theory of drives see Richardson 2004.
26 Although this claim is in reference to the concepts of cause and effect, I believe that this idea can be generalised to all concepts.

(most remote) past in ways that are almost impossible, and yet immensely fruitful. For both Schelling and Nietzsche the origin of things is always (already) created in the present; our most remote past always has its origin in the present, because it is only in the present that we first refer to the past *as such*. Furthermore: it is only *for the sake of the present* (and the future), that the question of the past becomes relevant. This is clear in Nietzsche's *Genealogy*, for instance, which can only be understood as motivated by the crisis of nihilism in the present – and the desire to overcome it.

In other words, what is important about their 'reconstructions' of the past is the way in which they make us 'reconstruct' ourselves in the present and think about ourselves in ways that enable us to transform ourselves and create new possibilities for the future. To be sure, the kind of knowledge that we gain about ourselves will not be a knowledge solidly founded on unquestionable truths; what we learn, rather, is to re-interpret, question and hereby re-determine and re-invent ourselves in new ways. In what follows, I will describe further points of convergence between Schelling and Nietzsche that are a direct consequence of interpreting ourselves (our origin and our past) and our relation to our desires in terms of a struggle between two wills and a multiplicity of drives respectively.

One of the most striking results of the dynamic described by Schelling between the two wills is that it breaks with the normal way in which we conceive of agency and of the relation between subject and desire: agent/subject and object are always the will. In Nietzsche's terms: "Naturally, 'will' can only operate on 'will', and not on 'matter' [*'Wille' kann natürlich nur auf 'Wille' wirken – und nicht auf 'Stoffe'*]" (BGE 36, KSA 5, p. 55). Conversely, for Schelling, the joy experienced by the (first) will – thanks to the self-generated activity of the second will – turns out to be nothing more than the will's joy in feeling *itself*. The *Lauterkeit* is not only 'pleased' to discover the other, but to discover its very own being, its own desire or love. Or as Nietzsche writes: "One loves ultimately ones desires [*Begierde*], not the thing desired [*Begehrte*]" (BGE 175, KSA 5, p. 103). On the other hand, problematising the relation between subject and object of desire leads both Schelling and Nietzsche to question the idea that we might be the 'owners' or the origin/cause of our own will or desires. As we already saw in Schelling's description: a will arises within our soul "unconsciously, without its intervention" (WA II, p. 137). Or in Nietzsche's words: "we learn to despise when we love, and precisely when we love best: – but all of this unconsciously [*unbewusst*], without noise, without pomp" (BGE 216, KSA 5, p. 152). This does not mean, for Nietzsche or Schelling, that we have no autonomy or that we are mere puppets of our desires, but rather that our sense of autonomy and freedom needs to be reinterpreted in terms of the interaction between wills or drives. Understanding ourselves (understanding our sense and our desire of freedom) involves understanding the structure of our desires. And this involves, first of all, realising that a will is never isolated, but always operates in relation to another will, other forces or drives.

For Schelling, as well as for Nietzsche, it is impossible to conceive of any will as a straightforward, unidirectional, singular flow of desire. This becomes clear when we analyse the complexities the *Lauterkeit* goes through before it is able to separate and affirm itself as an independent 'being'; or perhaps we should rather say, before it feels the longing for this independence. The *Lauterkeit* or expansive force always remains, in one way or other, in tension, i.e. in relation to the second will, the will to existence or the contracting force, and vice versa.[27] As we have seen above, the will's first longing for independence and freedom emerges as the result of a gradual process of differentiation and conflict between the two wills. For, although the first 'feeling' that Schelling ascribes to the encounter between the two wills is an affirmative, innocent feeling of joy, this positive feeling is soon disturbed. The *Lauterkeit* suddenly feels threatened by the presence of the contracting will and wants to separate and liberate itself from the latter.

On the other hand, this means that the longing for separation first emerges as a will to return to a previous state: the longing for freedom takes the form of a will or longing (*Sehnsucht*) for the past. Immediately after having experienced the pleasure of becoming sensitive and graspable (*fasslich*), the *Lauterkeit* gradually wants to go back to a past which it could only be aware of *in the present*, i.e. once that previous state had been left behind. Schelling describes this moment as the "the fate of all life [*das Verhängnis alles Lebens*]": it is the desire to go back to "quiet nothingness [*das stille Nichts*]" (WA I, p. 34) – an impossible return, because it would imply the end of its new born life; life would have to give up life.

In this sense, one could say that the will to freedom is unmasked by Schelling and exposed as a pernicious and self-destructive desire, because it is fixated on returning to a past that is unreal or at the very least irretrievable, and ultimately involves willing one's own annihilation. And, although I cannot develop in more detail here, it is important to note the similarity between Schelling's analysis of freedom and diagnosis of modernity and Nietzsche's analysis and critique of the process of 'nihilism' and '*ressentiment*' in his *Genealogy*: in a

---

[27] This seems to be at least one of the points that Nietzsche makes when he writes in BGE 19 that "willing" seems to be "above all something complicated, something that is a unit only as a word" and that "in all willing there is, first, a plurality of sensations", which he describes as the "sensation of the state, *away from* which" and the "sensation of the state *towards* which" (BGE 19, KSA 5, p. 32).

sense, both criticise the way in which we tend to seek for freedom in self-negation. As I suggested above, however, this does not mean that Schelling and/or Nietzsche reject the idea of freedom altogether (although they both reject the idea of freedom as a mere form of 'freedom of the will'). But it does mean that we need to distinguish between different forms of freedom and learn to pursue one that does not fall into the same pattern of self-destruction over and over again. In fact, what Schelling seems to be suggesting is that we learn to will differently. 'True' freedom cannot be rooted in a desire to return to the past. On the contrary: it must be able to overcome it. The (natural) longing for the past must be transformed into a desire for the future. For this, however, it is essential that we learn to break with the past – to break with the past, in a radical but *constructive* way, i.e. in a way that enables us to overcome ourselves and to affirm and redefine our own temporality: our past, our present and our future. Only in this way will be able to construct our freedom, which is a freedom for the future, as Nietzsche writes: what is important is not *wovon* (from what) we free ourselves, but *wozu* (what for) (cf. Z I Creator, KSA 4, p. 81). Indeed, we cannot go back to the past and we cannot change or negate it either, but we can learn to love it, to affirm it, to incorporate it in a way that is 'liberating', such as when Zarathustra says that we must transform all forms of "it was" into "thus I wanted it! [*so wollte ich es!*]" (Z II Redemption, KSA 4, p. 179); or when Schelling introduces the idea in his *Freedom Essay* that, in order to be able to explain our freedom, we must assume that 'we' made a choice before time, by which we 'freely' chose our character.[28]

For both Schelling and Nietzsche the problem of future realisations of freedom is directly related to the problem of the past and how we understand the past.[29] However, the rupture with the past and pursuit of freedom in the form of the creation of a new future does not mean a mere negation of the past, it is not a merely destructive rupture, but one that enables us to situate ourselves in the present in a way that is open to the future; a rupture that enables us to engage with the past without falling into a negative and self-destructive dynamic, i.e. without falling pray of *ressentiment*. In a sense, the process of becoming free is born from a reinterpretation and re-appropriation of the past. For this process to be truly liberating, however, it is crucial that we are able to

---

[28] I have developed this idea in length in Hay 2012.
[29] I believe that the engagement with the past in a way that may enable us to reconfigure and create a truly new future is the case in almost all, if not all, of Nietzsche's books. It is particularly strong in *Zarathustra*, *Beyond Good and Evil* and in the *Genealogy*, but also in *Gay Science*, where he explicitly talks about a future philosophy which will have overcome the tragedy of existence (GS 1, KSA 3, p. 369–372).

create ways of thinking of the past that do not fix the past, but are able to maintain its indeterminacy. In my view this is exactly what both Schelling and Nietzsche achieve through their very particular way of re-defining or creating concepts such as 'wills' and 'drives'. This was their way of 'leaving all certainties behind' and their attempt to think of human existence as being radically indeterminate and free *as well as* necessarily unfree.

Finally, it seems important to add one last thought, which is present in both philosophers; namely, that however liberating this whole process may be, it is an extremely painful and difficult process. To learn to see ourselves as a result of the movements of indeterminate, unfathomable forces; to understand that there is always a certain contradiction or tension between being and freedom; to grasp that our freedom lies only in our capacity to reinterpret ourselves – none of this is exactly reassuring. As Schelling writes: "pain [*Schmerz*] is something necessary and general, the unavoidable passageway to freedom [*Durchgangspunkt zur Freiheit*]" (WA I, p. 40). Or in Nietzsche's words:

> We oppose men [*Wir Umgekehrten*], having opened our eyes and conscience to the question where and how the plant "man" has so far grown most vigorously, we think that this has happened every time under the reverse conditions, that to this end the dangerousness of his situation had to first grow to the point of enormity, his power of invention and simulation (his "spirit") had to develop under prolonged pressure and constraint into refinement and audacity, his life-will had to be enhanced into an unconditional power will. We think that hardness, forcefulness, slavery [...], that everything evil, terrible, tyrannical in man, everything in him that is kin to beasts of prey and serpents serves the enhancement of the species "man" as much as its opposite does [...] (BGE 44, KSA 5, p. 61–62)[30]

References

Acampora, Crista D. (2013): *Contesting Nietzsche*. Chicago: Chicago University Press.
Babich, Babette E. (2003): "Nietzsche's Imperative as a Friend's Encomium: On Becoming the One You Are, Ethics, and Blessing". In: *Nietzsche Studien* 33, p. 29–58.

---

[30] "Wir Umgekehrten, die wir uns ein Auge und ein Gewissen für die Frage aufgemacht haben, wo und wie bisher die Pflanze 'Mensch' am kräftigsten in die Höhe gewachsen ist, vermeinen, dass dies jedes Mal unter den umgekehrten Bedingungen geschehn ist, dass dazu die Gefährlichkeit seiner Lage erst in's Ungeheure wachsen, seine Erfindungs- und Verstellungskraft (sein 'Geist' –) unter langem Druck und Zwang sich in's Feine und Verwegene entwickeln, sein Lebens-Wille bis zum unbedingten Macht-Willen gesteigert werden musste: – wir vermeinen, dass Härte, Gewaltsamkeit [...] dass alles Böse, Furchtbare, Tyrannische, Raubthier- und Schlangenhafte am Menschen so gut zur Erhöhung der Species 'Mensch' dient, als sein Gegensatz".

Hay, Katia (2012): *Die Notwendigkeit des Scheiterns. Das Tragische als Bestimmung der Philosophie bei Schelling*. Freiburg and Munich: Alber.
Löwith, Karl (1986): *Nietzsches Philosophie der ewigen Wiederkehr des Gleichen*. Hamburg: Meiner.
Norman, Judith: "Schelling and Nietzsche: Willing and Time". In: Judith Norman/Alistair Welchman (Eds.): *The New Schelling*. London and New York: Continuum, p. 90–105.
Plato (1952): *Plato's Phaedrus*. Translated with an Introduction and Commentary by Reginald Hackforth. Cambridge: Cambridge University Press.
Richardson, John (2004): *Nietzsche's New Darwinism*. New York and Oxford: Oxford University Press.

Part Two: **After Idealism: Nietzsche and the Critics of German Idealism**

Eike Brock
Life is Suffering: On Schopenhauer's and Nietzsche's Philosophical Engagement with Suffering

> Hello cruel world, do you know that you're killing me? I don't mind, but I could use a little sympathy.
>
> (Bad Religion, *Hello Cruel World*)

> He, who has never accepted in a moment of firm resolution – yes, even rejoiced in – what has struck him with terror, he has never taken possession of the full, ineffable power of our existence. He goes along the edge; when things play out, he will have neither been alive nor dead.
>
> (Rainer Maria Rilke, *Letter to Margot Sizzo*)[1]

Life is suffering. Apparently there is no doubt about that. Luckily, though, this not very edifying equation is not quite correct. It should really be: Life is always *also* suffering. That means that life and suffering are not identical, life is not made out of suffering alone, but suffering is an integral part of life – and there is presumably no doubt about that. However, if suffering is part of the *conditio vitae*, if it represents a vital fact that affects human beings in a particular way (since as self-reflective beings we are susceptible to suffering not merely physically but also spiritually); and if, furthermore, this fact notoriously plays into the question of the good life, then the problem of suffering becomes indisputably a philosophical *topos*. More than that: as Arthur Schopenhauer affirms, suffering could even be the starting point and engine, in short: the *agens* of philosophical thought.

In Schopenhauer's philosophy at least, suffering is not just the starting point, but also that upon and around which everything turns. Against this background it is unsurprising that suffering also occupies an exceptional place in the philosophical worldview of Schopenhauer's stellar pupil Friedrich Nietzsche. To begin with, there is the biographical background: the young Nietzsche runs into Schopenhauer's magnum opus *The World as Will and Representation* when he is in the throes of an existential crisis that cries out for orientation and spiritual guidance (cf. BAW 3, 297).[2] It is precisely in a situation of personal adversity

---

[1] English translation based on: *A Year with Rilke: Daily Readings from the Best of Rainer Maria Rilke*, trans. and ed. by Joanna Macy and Anita Barrows. New York: Harper Collins 2009, p. 88. (Quotes from Rainer Maria Rilke translated by Anita Barrows.)

[2] See also Ross 1997/98, p. 156–167.

that he discovers Schopenhauer's philosophy of suffering. And although in *The World as Will and Representation* Schopenhauer depicts suffering in the most vivid colours, so that one would think that it would plunge Nietzsche – already groping in the dark – even deeper into the maelstrom of psychic gloom, the opposite is the case: the sombre work has a salutary effect on the despairing youth. Nietzsche himself explains this *prima facie* surprising effect as follows:

> Here [in *The World as Will and Representation*, EB] I saw a mirror in which I beheld the world, life and my own temperament in dreadful magnificence. Here, the full disinterested eye of art looked upon me. Here I saw sickness and healing, banishment and asylum, hell and heaven. (BAW 3, p. 298)

In short: Nietzsche felt himself understood. His sombre mood, his suffering and nausea at existence, also the contempt for the average man and above all, the manifold and vehement invocation of the meaninglessness of existence linked with the hope for a creative renewal of meaning through art – Schopenhauer's words promised all of this to him. In addition, he prized Schopenhauer's uncompromising and unflinching manner as well as his stylistic genius. Nietzsche is, then in complete agreement both with the philosopher's headstrong work and with the headstrong philosopher himself, so that he chooses Schopenhauer to be his teacher, or to be his "first and only educator" (NL 1886/87, KSA 12, 6[4], p. 232–233).

Nietzsche is a very gifted as well as receptive pupil – nonetheless he is also exceptionally critical. Zarathustra's words: "One repays a teacher badly if one remains a pupil forever" (Z I Virtue 3, KSA 4, p. 101), describe accurately Nietzsche's attitude towards his revered teacher Schopenhauer. At the same time Schopenhauer's and Nietzsche's philosophies each advance "a tragic vision" in their "disclosure of the world". They show us without fear "the terrifying and cruel ground of our existence" (Colli 1982, p. 28). They are in agreement when it comes to emphasising the overwhelming part played by suffering in life. All in all, they offer the same diagnosis of life. Yet they part ways regarding the question of how to engage with this diagnosis philosophically. The evaluation of suffering is to an extent the watershed between them, from which their thought flows into two different systems.[3] Whereas Schopenhauer, starting out from the irreducibility of suffering takes the path of life-negation (at least from a theoretical point of view), Nietzsche takes it upon himself to affirm life in a decisive manner. To that end, he falls back on two strategies, both of which are anti-Schopenhauerian. On the one hand, there is the attempt at an aesthetic justifica-

---

3 In contrast to Schopenhauer, Nietzsche does not present a philosophical 'system'.

tion of life, which the young Nietzsche undertakes in *The Birth of Tragedy*; on the other, the later attempt to give a positive turn to the negative experience of suffering through the philosophical conception of the 'will to power'. But, towards the end of his productive life, through his *amor fati*, Nietzsche seems to favour an engagement with the dark side of existence, by which – in a somewhat secret way – he comes closer to Schopenahauer again. It seems as if Nietzsche was striving in *amor fati* for a kind of Buddhistic *ataraxia*; undertaking not to wish anything otherwise than how things are.

In what follows I will present Nietzsche's philosophical attempts at affirmation as moves to break with Schopenhauer's teaching – at least in broad strokes – and at the end as a rapprochement with the teaching of his educator. To begin with, however, the above-mentioned diagnosis of life delivered by both philosophers will be discussed: life is suffering.

I The Diagnosis: Life is Suffering

I.1 Schopenhauer

Standing in the classical metaphysical tradition, Schopenhauer endeavours to develop an overall interpretation of the world. He investigates the essence of things and looks to pursue them to their grounds.[4] Accordingly, he has to look into the depths, seeking philosophical insight into the heart of the world. Instead of perceiving a vein of gold under the surface of things or beholding, as Plato did, a divinely illuminated heaven behind things, Schopenhauer gazes at nothing but darkness. His view into the heart of things is, to speak with Joseph Conrad, a view into 'the heart of darkness', which for Schopenhauer is always to be understood primarily in a moral sense. For the darkness points towards something opaque, and however unknown it may be, we always *know* enough to sense that it is malign, not to say evil. Now: since whoever takes sides with evil acts immorally, and given that the world or life itself is in some sense evil, the mere acquiescence in life, *to live at all* would constitute a fundamental moral transgression. Indeed, as we will shortly see, this corresponds to Schopenhauer's position. In any case, though, the question of how to conduct this life is

---

[4] As a metaphysician Schopenhauer believes that there must be a true Being that is the absolute essence of things. See Rorty, who defines metaphysics as the "search for theories which will get at real essence" (Rorty 1989, p. 88).

not for him *ipso facto* morally indifferent. Rather, the question of *how to live* only becomes more difficult than it already is, because every moral utterance must be made in light of the insight into the general immorality of life. At this point, some remarks on what is usually called the 'Pessimism' of Schopenhauer's worldview are needed.

This nomenclature, not entirely unjustified,[5] has to do with the fact that Schopenhauer always views being or life morally and considers any other way of viewing it as misguided. Looking upon or into the world from a moral standpoint, the world as representation (i.e. the object of knowledge) presents itself as profoundly cruel, insofar as it constantly produces suffering (cf. WWV II, p. 404f.). A person who views this cruel being in any other way than the moral perspective or who denies its moral significance, evinces for Schopenhauer a 'perversity of disposition' (*Perversität der Gesinnung*). The amoral perspective on the world is "the greatest, most ruinous, the fundamental error" (PuP II, p. 214). This flamboyant reproach by his educator must have appealed to Nietzsche, who for his part considers the moral interpretation of the world as the fundamental error, leading him to attempt an *aesthetic* justification of the world. Remaining with Schopenhauer for now: It is the knowing subject, who first brings the moral dimension into the world.[6] Therefore, the idea that one might put the ethical dimension to one side or even consciously reject it in his or her consideration and assessment of the world is – for Schopenhauer – an intolerable thought. Insofar as the knowing subject undertakes a process of abstraction that brackets out the level of morality, he or she makes him or herself particularly guilty. As already mentioned, the mere acquiescence in life by virtue of birth and the subsequent participation in life have already a(n) (im)moral character – so the conscious rejection of morality is the apogee of this immorality. The young Schopenhauer, for whom all living beings *qua* living are sinful, expresses the thought of the fundamental complicity of all living things in guilt

---

5 The label 'pessimist' is accurate at least for the empiricist Schopenhauer. The metaphysician Schopenhauer, however, is closer to an optimist in a Leibnizian sense, as Michael Hauskeller has shown (cf. Hauskeller 2003, p. 85).

6 In general terms, for Schopenhauer Life = being-guilty. And this is also the case for unconscious life forms. On the other hand Life = suffering. Schopenhauer then puts both these equations together in the idea of 'eternal justice' (*ewige Gerechtigkeit*): Everything is guilty, for everything suffers, that is eternal justice (cf. WWV I, p. 415). In this sense, being conscious does not really add anything to the fact of being guilty; even plants are guilty. And yet, there is in Schopenhauer a relation between guilt and knowledge, according to which guilt is bigger, the more knowledge is in play. Thus, Schopenhauer does distinguish between a pure guilt of being and a moral guilt, which would be specific to humans as subjects of knowledge (cf. WWV I, p. 186).

through recourse to the literary *topos* of a 'pact with the devil'. We have all made a pact with the devil so to speak:

> Nothing is more tasteless as laughing off the tales of Faust and others *who gave themselves over to the devil*. The only falsehood in them is that it is told of individuals, whereas we have all made this pact. (HN I, p. 110)[7]

If mere being-in-the-world is already to make a pact with the devil, hell is not something that awaits us after life; life itself is already hell. But is life really as hellish as Schopenhauer would have us believe? What makes life into such a dreadful thing? In other terms: Is Schopenhauer's picture of life as an inferno well chosen? If one understands under hell a place of punishment in the form of uninterrupted suffering, then Schopenhauer could hardly have chosen a better comparison. For it is a fundamental conviction and perhaps the central statement of his philosophy that "*all life* is essentially *suffering*" (WWV I, p. 366).[8] The early Schopenhauer refers this suffering primarily to our inescapable mortality as humans. But it is not the pure fact of transience that is the ground of suffering. Because Schopenhauer cannot afford to believe in a god as guarantor of meaning or in something beyond as goal of our worldly existence; finitude weighs heavy for him. We live and die without any higher meaning. Our life is in the final analysis completely meaningless – and precisely that is what is so bitter: meaninglessness. It is the crux, the thorn in the flesh that makes life such an agony. In this sense, Schopenhauer's remarks about life being a pact with the devil confront us with our finite and meaningless existence without any mitigation: human beings, just as "matter in whichever state" (HN I, p. 110), are delivered unto death. That is our fate and at the same time the punishment for our existence, understood as something that ought not to have been (*nicht hätte sein sollen*) (cf. WWV II, p. 581). As living beings endowed with reason, however, we also have an awareness of this impending fate: we each know that one of these days we will die. Reason brings the fear of death searing into human life. All in all, humans have the dubious honour of being able to designate their lives in comparison with all other living things as the true hell, because when we consider our situation in all seriousness, we must acknowledge that our lives at bottom are 'but a long reprieve'.

---

[7] "Nichts ist abgeschmackter, als die Mährchen zu verlachen vom Faust und Andern, *die sich dem Teufel verschrieben*. Das einzige Falsche an der Sache ist nämlich nur Dies, daß es vom Einzelnen erzählt wird, wir aber Alle in dem Fall sind und das pactum geschlossen haben."
[8] See also WWV I, p. 448, where Schopenhauer uses a comparison that evokes the idea of hell.

Schopenhauer shows his readers – as if they did not know already – that the life we all share resembles that of a "delinquent", who is well cared for with regular last meals, as it were, yet "must still hang" in the end (HN I, p. 110). In *The World as Will and Representation*, Schopenhauer identifies the source of all this misery not as the devil, but as the will. Here, Schopenhauer formulates a metaphysics that reads like a tragedy whose hero is not a king or even someone of high birth, but a blind, onwards-charging, eternally striving loose cannon: an unbridled will. But because this will is all that is, it cannot arrive at any goal – it is always and everywhere already there; there is nothing external to the will that it could reach (cf. Simmel 1907, p. 235). Fatalistically, however, the will is equally denied to come to rest, for such repose is not compatible with its essence: perpetual striving, pure willing that dos not will anything determinate, but at bottom wills only willing itself and can therefore never attain satisfaction – once again meaninglessness shows its face.

In what follows it is worth looking more closely at this protagonist of the tragedy of being, who manifests itself in all tragic heroes and is behind everything tragic, because it plays a central role in Nietzsche's early tragic philosophy, even if under another name than in Schopenhauer. So what exactly is this will? "The world as thing in itself", writes Schopenhauer, "is a great will that knows not what it wills; for it does not know at all, but only wills, precisely because it is a will and nothing besides" (HN I, p. 196). Apart from what was noted above about the blind, purposeless and endless will, this quotation adds that the will as thing in itself is the metaphysical principle of the world. It is what is hidden behind the world of empirical experience, i.e. the world that is our representation.[9] Schopenhauer hereby retains the distinction made by Kant and later rejected by Nietzsche between things for us and the thing(s) in itself.[10] Nevertheless Schopenhauer claims to have discovered what the thing in itself is, which Kant had declared in principle impossible. Schopenhauer believes – and on this point he distances himself from Kant and goes beyond him – that there is for us a privileged and unadulterated access to the thing in itself, only the portal is other than pure thought: We reach the thing in itself through our body. This leads us directly to the heart of the world, because it is given to us not just as an object among objects, i.e. as a representation, but "at the same time in a completely different way, namely as that with which everyone is immediately familiar,

---

9 The World is representation (*only for us*, for we represent the world); and will (both *for us* and *in itself*). (cf. WWV I, p. 3f.).

10 See Nietzsche's distinction between appearance (*Schein*) and being (*Sein*), between it itself (*an-sich*) and for us (*für-uns*), especially in TI Fable, KSA 6, p. 80f.

which the word will signifies" (WWV I, p. 119). Our body is given to us in a twofold manner: from *the outside* we experience ourselves as representation, from *the inside*, we experience that we are will through and through. Hence we are the will become intuitive or representation: "It is the main principle of my philosophy that the body is only the objectivity [*Objektität*], the visibility of the will and hence identical with it" (HN I, p. 180).

According to Schopenhauer, this applies not only to the human being. Nature too has an outer side, in which it is (our) representation, and an inner side, the will.[11] The world *is*, then, representation and *is* nonetheless also will. What makes our situation so miserable is that we are objectifications of the will. This constitutes the core of all suffering. Our mortality, to which the young Schopenhauer had given a central meaning with regard to the suffering of existence, is not the *punctum saliens* for the equation of life and suffering. Rather, that life is *essentially* suffering means that suffering has a metaphysical ground. Our entire agony has a ground, namely the metaphysical ground of our essence, the will itself. I spoke earlier of a tragedy of being, the hero of which is the will. But if in the ground of our essence we all *are* this will, then we are all at the same time tragic heroes. The fate of a tragic hero consists in suffering this fate. And that goes especially for the highest – because reason-endowed – objectification of the will: the human being. He is condemned to continual suffering, because he is will, even if humans suffer in a variety of ways. An essential reason for human agony is seen by Schopenhauer in the fact that as an objectification of the will, human beings cannot enjoy lasting happiness or prolonged contentment.[12] This "metaphysical impossibility of lasting satisfaction" (Lerchner 2010, p. 51) does not alter the fact that we rush from wish to wish, from goal to goal, always borne by the deceptive hope that attaining this one specific goal will finally bring us the longed for peace and contentment. If we are ever granted an extended rest from the consuming business of incessant willing "we are embraced with open arms from the other side by boredom, a torture quite differ-

---

[11] "The point of departure, the bold speculation in Schopenhauer's metaphysics consists in transposing the schema of his own experience of the body – the side of the will and that of the representation – by analogical inference onto the whole of nature. The identity of will and body works as a model for the world." (Spierling 2002, p. 66)

[12] "If the one and only will knows no final satisfaction because of its unicity, then there cannot be such for its highest appearances [the human endowed with reason, EB] either, in whom it manifests itself as blindly striving and who, with their individual wills and their expressions, are the subject of the metaphysics of morals. Its appearance in this domain alters nothing in the per se miserable situation regarding the possibility of happiness – thought as perduring – or enduring satisfaction – contentment" (Lerchner 2010, p. 51).

ent from constantly being driven, yet – no less a torture" (Lerchner 2010, p. 53). According to Schopenhauer, human beings experience – to a greater of less extent consciously – in boredom only the "utter bleakness and emptiness of existence" (PuP II, p. 305). Other than the later Heidegger, who sees in boredom the potential for the human to grasp the radical openness of its existence and as a consequence to seize its life with complete determination (*Entschlossenheit*), Schopenhauer's dull, unproductive boredom is not something one can simply come to grips with by reflecting seriously on one's creative potential. It is psychological in nature but ontological (Lütkehaus 2003, 180), because it is just the expression of the fundamental or essential emptiness of existence. If we were to illustrate life as Schopenhauer sees it, it would look like the 'wavy sea' depicted on an oscillograph, constantly moving between being driven and boredom.

This, however, by no means covers the entire domain of suffering. The reason that not only human life but *all* of life is largely suffering is to be found in the fact that life, or rather the will is constantly lacerating itself, consuming itself. On closer consideration, the world as representation is actually nothing other than an eternal cycle of such self-laceration "an inner conflict of the will to life with itself" (WWV I, p. 391). And it cannot be otherwise, since the will, insofar as "it is the absolute unity [...] has nothing outside itself with which it could quench its thirst, with which it could bring its restlessness to an end" (Simmel, 1907, p. 228). Schopenhauer extends the scope of the thought formulated by Hobbes, to the entire world of representation: for Schopenhauer all of nature becomes a *bellum omnium contra omnes* (cf. WWV I, p. 393). Everything in nature "possesses only what it has wrested from another", such that "a continual struggle for life and death is maintained" (WWV I, p. 364). The human being plays the precarious role of the first among equals in this struggle; he wears, as it were, the crown of thorns of creation, because is capable not just of physical, but also of "spiritual pain" (WWV I, 394). Now the capacity for compassion, understood as suffering-with (*Mit-Leiden*), also belongs to the realm of spiritual suffering. The pinnacle of compassion is reached when we not only put ourselves in the place of another by inferring the present suffering of another from one's own experiences of suffering, but when we intuitively grasp that in a metaphysical sense we are all one. We are only individualisations of the one will, parts of a whole by virtue of the *principium individuationis*, which makes us into individuals in space and time; a whole, which constantly lacerates itself by way of the incessant war that these parts wage against each other. This insight, which Schopenhauer condenses in the sentence 'tat tvam asi' ('this is what you are'), taken from far Eastern thought, on the one hand intensifies further our suffering. On the other hand, it also forms the basis for a morality of compassion, capable of alleviating the suffering of life by raising the ethical credo or imperative against the struggle of all against all: "*Neminem laede; imo omnes, quantum potes, juva* [Injure no-one; rather help all as far as you can, EB]!" (E, p. 137 et passim).

In the last instance Schopenhauer's ethics do not just aim at a reduction of suffering, but at its cessation. This noble goal can, however, only be realised by a radical negation of one's own life. Schopenhauer dreams of a kind of negative eschatology, that is, of the redemption of existence from existence through a "flowing away [*Zerfließen*] into the Nothing" (WWV I, p. 486),[13] effected by a negation of the will.

I.2 Nietzsche

The agonal character of life was presented most thoroughly by Nietzsche in his first book, *The Birth of Tragedy*. For this reason, and because Nietzsche's book on tragedy still stands clearly under the influence of Schopenhauer, in this section where I analyse the claim that life is suffering, I will limit myself to this work for my analysis of Nietzsche.

In his first work Nietzsche advances a kind of aesthetic metaphysics. It is metaphysical insofar as it holds onto the distinction between world of appearance and thing in itself, which Kant had introduced and Schopenhauer maintained – a distinction Nietzsche would later interpret as an expression of nihilism.[14] The Nietzschean thing in itself reminds us unmistakably of the will in Schopenhauer's metaphysics insofar as it bears a strong affinity with the blind will to life in its chaotic behaviour and inner diremption. At the same time, Nietzsche gives his fundamental metaphysical principle the name of a god: Dionysus. And this god is for Nietzsche the true creator of the world. Just as the Christian God (*qua* unity that is still three-in-one) represents a process, which one can interpret as a kind of dynamic relation of love, so Dionysus too, or the primordial One (*Ur-Eine*) must be grasped as a *mobile* unity. To understand it as a simple (*einfach*) unity would be a mistake. The movement that Nietzsche discerns within this

---

[13] This 'flowing away' is not to be taken as a negation of any substance, but rather as a redemption or release from the continuous will (cf. PuP II, p. 331). What after the dissolution of the will remains open (cf. PuP II, p. 331). An absolute nothingness cannot even be thought of.

[14] "He [Nietzsche, EB] views metaphysics from the 'optic of life'. The metaphysical reflections on Being are examined by Nietzsche in relation to their symptomatic value. Thus, the distinction between appearance and thing-in-itself are interpreted as the expression of a declining feeling of life; i.e. a form of life that does not feel at home in the sense-world and invents another world beyond appearance" (Fink 1960, p. 14–15).

unitary is grounded – other than with the trinity – in contradiction. Nietzsche writes of a "primordial contradiction and primordial pain [*Urwiderspruch und Urschmerz*] at the heart of the primordial One" (BT 6, KSA 1, p. 51).

This primordial contradiction can only be grasped in a mediate way from the human standpoint. For as the fundamental metaphysical principle, the primordial one is subordinate to the principle of individuation. Consequently, it is not a singular spatiotemporally determined being among others, but stands rather in an a priori relation to the world of representation (and thereby to the human being), which is born of the primordial pain (cf. BT 6, KSA 1, p. 39). Just like us, the world of multiplicity with which we daily interact, is the product of an agony become creative. Every single being is at bottom a copy of the painful disunity of the primordial One. We cannot, as mentioned, grasp the primordial immediately, yet we can nonetheless, by casting our eye on the world we live in and looking at (or within) ourselves, not only feel the originary pain, but also identify it as the ground and origin of our selves. In this way, we can experience that "[t]hat which wants to live in this horrifying constellation of things, that is, what must live, is in the ground of its being a copy of this primordial pain and primordial contradiction" (GSt, KSA 1, p. 768). Introspection reveals a self to us that is anything but unified. Instead it proves to be more of an occurrence: a struggle of different drives, all vying with one another for dominance, constantly raging within us.[15] Looking out on the world in turn "must strike our eyes, as 'worldly and earthly organs', as an insatiable greed for existence and an eternal self-contradiction in the form of time, that is, as *becoming*" (GSt, KSA 1, p. 768). But becoming knows no friends or foes; like the Schopenhauerian will, it wills only itself, and accordingly manifests itself as an endless process that takes the form of a constant giving and taking, a giving birth and taking of life, when viewed from the outside. The extremes of life and death are in the end just two sides of the same coin, that is, intrinsic elements of the One process of becoming. Nietzsche describes becoming with dramatic words, which could also have come from the pen of Schopenhauer: "Every moment devours the preceding, every birth is the death of countless beings, procreation life and murder are one" (GSt, KSA 1, p. 768). If we apply this knowledge, gained from contemplating the copy, to the primordial image, we get an image of the primordial contradiction, according to which it must be seen "as procreating and destroying – outside

---

[15] "Selfhood is by no means an instance outside the conflict of the drives, but rather *the* drive, that dominates the others and has made them submissive of them in order to achieve its goals" (Christians 2000, p. 322).

of time and becoming, *in* something *unitary* as eternal" (Fleischer 1988, p. 81). Becoming is the objectification of this primordial contradiction in space and time. The world is the copy of this primordial one, the outward turned primordial contradiction. There can be no doubt that in a world thus constituted, suffering belongs undeniably to life.

The metaphysics developed by Nietzsche in his first work is *aesthetic* insofar as it does not just explain the emergence and constitution of the world in this way, but also reflects on how this world (or rather: the metaphysically grounded, necessary suffering in the world) can be justified. And the justification to which Nietzsche in the end resorts is aesthetic in nature.

II Therapy

II.1 Schopenhauer: Negation of the Will

Neither Schopenhauer nor Nietzsche sees the possibility of separating suffering decisively from life. According to them, there is no way to eliminate suffering without at the same time eliminating life. Under these circumstances, the question that arises is whether suffering can be lived with or not. Put otherwise: Is there a way to justify life, despite its unavoidable character as suffering? As we have seen, for Schopenhauer an aesthetic justification does not come into consideration for ethical reasons. For him, the problem of suffering can only be solved by tackling the misery at its roots and eliminating it, so that it must be approached at the level of the will, which must be negated.

Even if an aesthetic justification of life is unacceptable for Schopenhauer, aesthetics nonetheless plays an important role in his reflections. For if we do manage to adopt an aesthetic attitude towards the world, in contemplating a work of art or a beautiful landscape for example, we experience for a stretch of time what it means to be relieved of the arduous business of willing and desiring. The world is now our representation in a different sense than before. In these moments it appears as a stage, as it were, on which there is a performance, which we follow with disinterested pleasure. For a certain stretch of time it is as if we are released from life and no longer completely caught up in the agonal course of events. A release from the world takes place, which feels like a redemption. The servant of the will to life is relieved of its daily labour and enjoys its midday rest, so to speak. Our empirical interests and needs are put on ice during this time, and that holds the promise of a profound rest and peace. Yet the aesthetic attitude cannot be adopted in a way that lasts, and the will, being the substrate of our existence, demands tribute sooner or later as long as we do not manage to negate it in a decisive way. Aesthetic experience can serve as a bridge to the negation of the will by helping us to anticipate what awaits those who succeed in negating the will. The prospect it offers is full of promise, nothing less than "that peace, which is higher than reason; that completely calm sea of the temperament, that profound serenity [*Ruhe*], that imperturbable confidence and cheerfulness [*Heiterkeit*]" (WWV I, p. 484). In other words, the end of suffering beckons. Another gateway to the negation of the will is the ethical experience of compassion discussed above. It is important at this point to bear in mind that Schopenhauer does not believe that an effective reduction of suffering in the world can be attained through compassion and compassionate deeds. Ironically, the compassionate person only increases suffering in the world by adding his suffering regarding suffering (i.e. his compassion) to that which already exists; so that the practice of compassion makes for an increase of suffering within the 'overall economy of unpleasure' in the world. If we let "compassion become a firm and steadfast disposition" and transform it "into justice and fellow love [*Menschenliebe*]", in the end we will suffer "with all other humans and all creatures capable of suffering" (Hauskeller 2003, p. 83). But no human can achieve this; one who practices compassion like this "suffers in the end more than he can endure, so that he finally turns from the world and negates the will, which all of life tenaciously affirms unto death" (Hauskeller 2003, p. 83). Such a person has found the path to redemption. Yet it concerns the entirely private path of personal negation of the will. He no longer has anything to do with the ethical business of compassion, which is fulfilled in compassionate or benevolent actions.

He lives his strict ascesis of the will alone with the goal of containing the will as much as possible. For where there is no will, there is no suffering. Schopenhauer's philosophy, born of ethical outrage, actually commends an attitude to life that understands morality not as an "end in itself", but merely as "a proven means [...] to something quite different, namely the goal of overcoming the world" (Hauskeller 2003, p. 83).

Overcoming the world fulfils what is at stake in all of this: the overcoming of suffering. In Schopenhauer's philosophy, the value of aesthetic and ethical experience cannot be valued highly enough, because we may ordinarily think of many things, but certainly not of negating our will, that is, the ground of our being. The will itself does its utmost to avoid this by "forbidding our intellect certain ideas, preventing certain lines of thought from arising" (WWV II, p. 233). The will takes our intellect by the reins and attempts to prevent it from realising itself as a potential source of resistance against the will. The struggle against suffering can only be won if we kill that in us which makes up the core of our life. The agonal character of life must be overcome through ascesis. This path or way out of suffering is marked by renunciation and promises itself to be to some degree painful. As in well known, Schopenhauer himself was neither a radical ascetic nor a saint. He knew only – and very well – the temporary negation of the will in the aesthetic-contemplative pose. In terms of his own life-practice, he was satisfied with that which he would not concede in theoretical terms: an aesthetic justification of life.

II.2 Nietzsche

II.2.1 Aesthetic Justification of Existence

Nietzsche claims that in his book on tragedy he had cast the ancient feeling for life in the right light as a "pessimism of strength" (BT Attempt 1, KSA 1, p. 12). The Greeks and especially the Greek work of art *par excellence*, ancient tragedy, serve Nietzsche as examples of an attitude to life that is in a position not only to accept the painful and tragic character of life, but is able to affirm it as the stimulant for a culturally superior form of life. Greek tragedy, this "fraternal bond" (BT 21, KSA 1, p. 140) between the crystal-clear, form-giving Apollinian and the dissolving, endlessly vital power of the Dionysian, is a model for a pessimism that is absolutely not negative and resigned by nature, but creative and affirmative in its expression: just as the rose breaks forth from the bush of thorns (cf. BT 3, KSA 1, p. 36), tragedy arises out of human suffering under the spell of individuation. Suffering provokes the work of art, and the work of art redeems from suffering. In tragedy the human being is brought face to face with its fate. We experience on the one hand our utter insignificance and frailty as singular, finite, moribund beings, while on the other a consoling feeling arises in us that we are immortal when we understand that "the life at the basis of things [...] is indestructibly powerful and pleasurable" (BT 7, KSA 1, p. 56). In tragedy there occurs a 'cross-over' speech of the same originary forces of nature that also struggle with one another in the human: "Dionysos speaks the language of Apollo, but in the end Apollo also speaks the language of Dionysos" (BT 21, KSA 1, 140). In tragedy a reconciliation of the two opposed primal drives is achieved, drives whose conflict ordinarily makes life so difficult for humans when it demands Apollinian clarity of them on the one side and they long for the feeling of totality in intoxication (*Rausch*) and a return to the Dionysian maternal womb on the other. Art succeeds in "bending those nauseating thoughts concerning the terrifying or absurd character of existence into representations that can be lived with" (BT 7, KSA 1, p. 57). Art is the bulwark against that which Schopenhauer's philosophy advocates: a "Buddhistic negation of the will" on the basis of an "ascetic, ill-negating mood" (BT 7, KSA 1, 56). In his *Tragödienschrift* Nietzsche comes to the conclusion that existence can be justified despite all suffering. He does, however, make an important qualification, when he writes that it is "only as aesthetic phenomenon that the existence of the world is eternally *justified*" (BT Attempt 5, 17, underlining, EB).

II.2.2 The Will to Power and the Overcoming of Suffering

The problem of suffering and the resigned pessimism or nihilism that comes out of it does not leave Nietzsche's thoughts, even after his book on tragedy. This can be taken as an indication that Nietzsche did not consider the problem solved yet, even by his approach in BT. Rather, he thinks about the possibilities of justifying the existence of the world and the individual in the world otherwise than just in aesthetic terms. In effect, Nietzsche's philosophical conception of the 'will to power' can be read as a contribution towards an ontological justification against the background of unavoidable suffering. This way of reading the Will to Power has been conducted by Bernard Reginster in his book *The Affirmation of Life*, and it merits particular attention. According to Reginster, it is important to give the problem of suffering its proper place in Nietzsche's programme of a transvaluation of all values. Whoever has the idea of rejecting life entirely because it necessarily involves suffering, like Schopenhauer does, must start from the position that the absence of suffering is a particularly important value. But is it really advisable to measure life against this standard of the absence of suffering? Is the absence of suffering really a value (or ideal worth striving for), or in other terms: is suffering necessarily an evil? It is precisely the application of specific (in in Nietzsche's eyes fatal) standards to life, like e.g. 'purpose', 'unity', 'being', that leads to negative judgements concerning the world (cf. NL 1887/89, KSA 13, 11[99], p. 48).

Reginster's interpretation of the 'will to power' is geared towards the insight that a transvaluation of values is needed above all with a view towards the evaluation of suffering. The will to power is according to Reginster "the will to the overcoming of resistance" (Reginster 2006, p. 131–132). The chief concern of the will to power lies in this overcoming of resistances: "It is, specifically, a desire for the *activity* of overcoming resistance" (Reginster 2006, p. 11). In this light, the particular goals that the will to power sets itself are not of any importance. The main thing is the exercise of power: the overcoming of resistances as such. Nonetheless, power is actualised only in engagements with determinate resistances, so that the will to power cannot attain satisfaction "unless the agent has a desire for something else than power". In this respect, the will to power has "the structure of a *second-order desire*". It is, then, considering both levels, "a desire for the overcoming of resistance in the pursuit of some determinate first-order desire" (Reginster 2006, p. 132). Conversely, suffering is considered by Reginster "in terms of resistance" (Reginster 2006, p. 133): We suffer in the face of resistances that stand in the way of our will-power. Suffering, as the "experience of dissatisfied longing or desire" (Reginster 2006, p. 176) is among the fundamental constants of our existence. Yet if we understand power with Nietzsche as a value of the highest order,[16] suffering loses its status as a principal objection against life. The decisive experience of overcoming resistances, the activity in which the will is at home with itself, would simply be impossible without the existence of resistances. Whoever values power must also value suffering:

> The doctrine of will to power radically alters our conception of the role and significance of suffering in human existence. If, in particular, we take power – the overcoming of resistance – to be a value, then we can see easily how it can be the principle behind a revaluation of suffering. Indeed, if we value the overcoming of resistance, we must also value the resistance that is an ingredient of it. Since suffering is defined by resistance, we must also value suffering. (Reginster 2006, p. 177)

The highest level of the affirmation of life, the Dionysian attitude to life can only be reached, as Nietzsche notes, if we reach the point where we

> understand the sides of existence that have hitherto been negated not only as *necessary*, but as desirable: and not just desirable in view of the sides [of existence] hitherto affirmed (as, say, their complements or prior conditions), but for their own sake, as the more powerful, more fruitful, *truer* sides of existence, in which its will expresses itself more clearly. (NL 1887/89, KSA 13, 16[32], p. 492)[17]

The justification of suffering is not completed by placing it into a conditional relation to happiness (of the satisfied will to power) according to the motto: 'No pain, no gain', but requires more: it requires a real transvaluation. Suffering must be valued for its own sake, which occurs when we consider it in its ontological relation to happiness (of the satisfied Will to Power), according to which suffering is an ingredient of the Good.

---

16 Reginster refers to the *Antichrist* (A 2, KSA 6, p. 170).
17 "[D]ie bisher verneinten Seiten des Daseins nicht nur als *nothwendig* zu begreifen, sondern als wünschenswerth: und nicht nur als wünschenswerth in Hinsicht auf die bisher bejahten Seiten (etwa als deren Complemente oder Vorbedingungen), sondern um ihrer selber willen, als der mächtigeren, fruchtbareren, *wahreren* Seiten des Daseins, in denen sich sein Wille deutlicher ausspricht."

As Reginster presents it, the transvaluation of suffering is decisive point for the overcoming of pessimism or nihilism. The will to power is in turn the principle of this transvaluation. In the end, however, a further fundamental transvaluation must be performed if the will to power is not going to become an objection to life. Becoming must be given primacy over Being (understood as that which always remains identical to itself). The will to power is not compatible with the ideal of Being. It is fulfilled in movement, in the overcoming of a resistance. But the successful completion of this movement leads to the frustration of the will to power. Its paradoxical fate is to bring together its frustration with its satisfaction. As Reginster writes:

> [T]he conditions of the satisfaction of the will to power do indeed imply its dissatisfaction. The overcoming of resistance eliminates it, but the presence of such a resistance is a necessary condition of satisfaction of the will to power. Hence, the satisfaction of the will to power implies its own dissatisfaction, in the sense that it necessarily brings it about. (Reginster 2006, p. 136)

A Dionysian philosophy of Becoming does not despair at the fact that the satisfaction of the will to power must always be achieved anew. Rather, in the dynamic will to power it recognises the engine, as it were, of an agonistically structured world, which it has resolved to affirm in all its facets.

II.3 *Amor Fati* as Rapprochement to Schopenhauer

At its core, pessimism is "the evaluation of the world as unworthy [*unwert*] of being lived in" (Stegmaier 2012, p. 205). A note written by Nietzsche in Autumn 1887 shows very clearly how for him pessimism is fused with nihilism:

> A nihilist is a human being who judges of the world as it is, that it ought *not* to be, and of the world as it ought to be, that it does not exist. In this view, existence (agency, suffering, willing, feeling) has no meaning [*Sinn*] [...]. (NL 1885/87, 9[60], KSA 12, p. 366)[18]

In the framework of Nietzsche's philosophy it is in fact difficult to draw a sharp line between pessimism and nihilism; it is more a matter of a transition of one into the other. The development of Nietzsche's thought shows how the problem of pessimism is increasingly absorbed into the broader problematic of nihilism.

---

18 "Ein Nihilist ist der Mensch, welcher von der Welt, wie sie ist, urtheilt, sie sollte *nicht* sein, und von der Welt, wie sie sein sollte, urtheilt, sie existirt nicht. Demnach hat dasein (handeln, leiden, wollen, fühlen) keinen Sinn".

One can even say that the problem of pessimism culminates in nihilism.[19] What is decisive for Nietzsche, however, is that the characteristic 'No' of nihilism does not have the last word. The possibility of overcoming nihilism (in which the overcoming of pessimism is contained) consists, as we have seen, in carrying out a transvaluation of values. Belief in old values must be renounced in order to make room for new values in their place, which make an affirmation of life possible.

Yet, another possibility of overcoming nihilism is considered by Nietzsche in *amor fati*. In the love of fate, *amor fati*, an all-embracing 'Yes' that abstains from all negation is expressed. Whoever makes *amor fati* into their maxim of life, allows themselves only a single form of no-saying, namely looking away (*Wegsehen*):

> Amor fati: Let that be my love from now on! I want to wage no war against that which is ugly. I do not want to accuse, I do not want even to accuse the accusers. Let looking away [*Wegsehen*] be my only form of negation! And, all in all: I want sometime to be just a Yes-sayer! (GS 276, KSA 3, p. 521)[20]

One who follows *amor fati* knows how to abstain from making negative judgements. Rather than to condemn something that they are not (yet) in a position to affirm, they prefer (for the time being) to look away; not, however, in a negating gesture, but rather in view of something else, to which they turn and which they are in a position to affirm.[21] It is certainly possible that they will also one day be in a position to look at and affirm what they previously overlooked, and it is Nietzsche's stated goal one day "to be just a Yes-sayer". That means, he wishes to replace judging with loving, and to be able in the end to love everything just as it is. One might perhaps add to Nietzsche's words, that he wants one day to be not even an 'overlooker'.

In the "*Dionysian Yes-saying* to the world as it is, without subtraction, exception or selection", which corresponds to the "highest state that a philosopher

---

19 "After book V of FW it seems to become clear to him [i.e. Nietzsche, EB] that nihilism is the logical consequence of pessimism [...], the difference in the degree of insight is then this: if pessimism is the evaluation of world as unworthy of being lived in, nihilism is the insight that there is nothing ('nihil') to the values according to which we have valued and which we have held in such high esteem" (Stegmaier 2012, p. 204–205).
20 "Amor fati: das sei von nun an meine Liebe! Ich will keinen Krieg gegen das Hässliche führen. Ich will nicht anklagen, ich will nicht einmal die Ankläger anklagen. *Wegsehen* sei meine einzige Verneinung! Und, Alles in Allem und Grossen: ich will irgendwann einmal nur noch ein Ja-sagender sein!"
21 This can also be another side of the same object.

can attain" (NL 1988, 16[32], KSA 13, p. 492), pessimism and nihilism are overcome. This all-encompassing love would be the realisation of the greatest that a human being can attain:

> My formula for greatness in human beings is *amor fati*: that one wants nothing to be other than it is, neither forwards nor backwards, in all eternity. Not just to endure what is necessary, much less to conceal it [...], but to *love* it ... (EH Smart 10, KSA 6, p. 297)[22]

The overcomer of nihilism wants nothing to be other than it is and thereby distinguishes himself in a fundamental way from the nihilist who judges life, who negates life precisely because it is not how he wants it to be. The nihilist, then, wants to have it otherwise than it is, and if that is not possible, he prefers not to have it at all, which is just another, extreme mode of wanting-to-have-it-otherwise.

In sum: Nietzsche's formula of 'amor fati' involves two decisive anti-nihilistic aspects: *In* Gay Sience *it emphasises 'looking away' as the only form of negation, and in* Ecce Homo, *not-wanting-to-have-it-otherwise. In this way, it proves to be* the *formula for the overcoming of nihilism insofar as judging and wanting-to-have-it-otherwise comprise the constitutive moments of nihilism.*

Now, not-wanting-to-have-it-otherwise is a remarkable philosophical concept, or to put it more cautiously: an astonishing philosophical wish, especially when it is issued by the philosopher of the 'will to power'. For what does it mean to want to have nothing otherwise, if not that one no longer wants (wills) anything? For willing can "be defined as a striving to change an Is-state into an Ought-state" (Weimer 1984, p. 45). But if everything is just as it ought to be, willing can no longer will. Does this mean that Nietzsche, at the end of his philosophical trajectory – taking *amor fati* as his last word – repudiates the will to power, which always wants to have more than it has, or always seeks out an obstacle in order to overcome it? In any case, willing itself is not sublated, for not-willing must also be willed. In other words: Even not-willing necessarily remains a willing. But perhaps this means that the will to power achieves its masterpiece in the paradoxical "willing not-to-will" (Stegmaier 2011, p. 195), i.e. in the overcoming of nihilism, as a willing that appears to go against its own nature, a willing that puts its own strength to the ultimate test. In any case, it is worth considering that with *amor fati*, i.e. the willing not-to-will (one of the paradoxical satori-formulae of Buddhism) Nietzsche comes closer to the thought of his educator

---

[22] "Meine Formel für die Grösse am Menschen ist amor fati: dass man Nichts anders haben will, vorwärts nicht, rückwärts nicht, in alle Ewigkeit nicht. Das Nothwendige nicht bloss ertragen, noch weniger verhehlen [...], sondern es *lieben* ..."

Schopenhauer than on would have thought possible, given his distance already inscribed in his work on tragedy from the pessimistic philosophy of the negation of the will.

References

Brock, Eike (2014): "Vom Schönmachen aller Dinge. Nietzsches Kunst der Transfiguration als antinihilistische Lebenskunst". In: *Nietzscheforschung. Jahrbuch der Nietzsche Gesellschaft.* Vol. 21. Berlin and Boston: De Gruyter, p. 197–209.
Brock, Eike (2015): *Nietzsche und der Nihilismus.* Berlin and Boston: De Gruyter.
Christians, Ingo (2000): "Selbst". In: Henning Ottmann (Ed.): *Nietzsche-Handbuch. Leben – Werk – Wirkung.* Stuttgart and Weimar: Metzler, p. 321–324.
Colli, Giorgio (1992): *Distanz und Pathos. Einleitungen zu Nietzsches Werken.* Frankfurt a.M.: EVA.
Fink, Eugen (1960): *Nietzsches Philosophie.* Stuttgart: Kohlhammer.
Fleischer, Margot (1988): "Dionysos als Ding an sich. Der Anfang von Nietzsches Philosophie in der ästhetischen Metaphysik der 'Geburt der Tragödie'". In: *Nietzsche Studien* 17, p. 74–90.
Hauskeller, Michael (2003): "Durch Leiden lernen. Schopenhauer zwischen Mitleid und Weltüberwindung". In: *Schopenhauer-Jahrbuch* 84, p. 75–90.
Lerchner, Thorsten (2010): *Der Begriff des "Charakters" in der Philosophie Arthur Schopenhauers und seines Schülers Philipp Mainländer.* Bonn: Diss. online, URN: urn: nbn: de: hbz: 5–22643.
Lütkehaus, Ludger (2003): *Nichts. Abschied vom Sein – Ende der Angst.* Frankfurt a.M.: Zweitausendeins.
Reginster, Bernard (2006): *The Affirmation of Life: Nietzsche on Overcoming Nihilism.* Cambridge, MA: Harvard University Press.
Rorty, Richard (1989): *Contingency, Irony and Solidarity.* New York: Cambridge University Press.
Ross, Werner (1997/98): *Der ängstliche Adler. Friedrich Nietzsches Leben.* Munich: Kastell.
Spierling, Volker (2002): *Arthur Schopenhauer. Zur Einführung.* Hamburg: Junius.
Stegmaier, Werner (2011): *Friedrich Nietzsche. Zur Einführung.* Hamburg: Junius.
Weimer, Wolfgang (1984): "Die ewige Wiederkehr des Gleichen bei Schopenhauer und Nietzsche". In: *Schopenhauer-Jahrbuch* 65, p. 44–54.

Razvan Ioan
Philosophical Physiology: Schopenhauer and Nietzsche

The main question of this essay is whether Nietzsche's use of physiology may be interpreted as a reaction to what Schopenhauer called 'philosophical' or 'true' physiology. In order to answer this question, it will first be necessary to show whether there are any similarities between Nietzsche's and Schopenhauer's 'physiologies'. Not wanting to neglect the differences (which, to a great extent, go hand in hand with Nietzsche's critique of metaphysics and which become manifest, in the realm of physiology at least, in their different accounts of the unity of the organism), the aim of this paper will be to show that, in spite of these differences, there are certain similarities, and that these are best evidenced in the continuity between Schopenhauer's notion of Platonic Ideas and Nietzsche's concept of drives, on the one hand, and in the way they both regard reason or the intellect as a product of the physical in human beings, on the other.

In order to suggest an answer to this question, this paper will include I) an account of what philosophical physiology means for Schopenhauer; II) a brief survey of the essential elements of Nietzsche's theory of drives; and III) an argument in favour of the hypothesis that Nietzsche's reaction to Schopenhauer's philosophy might have played an important part in the development of Nietzsche's concepts of physiology and drives. In other words: the aim of this paper is to show the extent to which the plurality of drives in Nietzsche's physiology is not as radically different from Schopenhauer's thought as one might assume. Nevertheless, this requires a reconsideration of the complexities that Schopenhauer is dealing with – complexities which remain only implicit in his philosophy due to his commitment to the metaphysical doctrine of the will.

The question guiding this research comes as a reaction to a number of Nietzsche commentators who have noticed a distinctive trait of his theory of drives. While a discussion on drives plays a role in the thought of both Kant and Schiller, for instance, they never refer to more than a limited number of drives (three in both cases). Nietzsche, however, speaks of a great multiplicity of drives and names more than a hundred throughout his works (Assoun 2006, p. 55; Kastafanas 2012, p. 8; Moore 2006, p. 72 and Parkes 1996, p. 250). The thesis supported in this paper is that this great number of drives in Nietzsche's philosophy can be seen as a result of his engagement with Schopenhauer.

I Schopenhauer's 'Philosophical Physiology'

The guiding thread of the first section is given by the question concerning the significance of philosophical physiology in Schopenhauer's oeuvre. Two elements will be the focus of our attention: 1) the place of the intellect and of Platonic Ideas in philosophical physiology, and 2) the nature of the unity that an organism displays. They will be the centre of attention not only because they are crucial to Schopenhauer's notion of physiology, but because, in the third section of this essay, it will be argued that they are essential to understanding Nietzsche's reaction to Schopenhauer.

First, it should be pointed out that the expression 'philosophical' or 'true' physiology is not very common in Schopenhauer's writings. It appears in the following context in his essay *On the Will in Nature*:

> True Physiology, at its highest, shows the spiritual (the intellectual) in man to be the product of the physical in him, [...] but true Metaphysics teaches us that the physical in man is itself mere product, or rather phenomenon, of a spiritual (the Will). (WN, p. 237)[1]

And it also features in the following phrase: "As long as it lasted, no philosophical Physiology was possible" (WN, p. 235). 'It' refers to

> that supposed Idea of Reason, the soul: that metaphysical being, in whose absolute singleness knowing and willing were knit and blended together in eternal, inseparable unity. (WN, p. 235)[2]

In order to better understand these passages, we must now turn to the analysis of Platonic Ideas and of unity.

I.1 The Intellect and Platonic Ideas

The foremost philosophical insight that colours the entirety of Schopenhauer's philosophy of science is his understanding of the relation between the will and the intellect. The relation consists in the primacy of the will over the intellect

---

[1] "Die wahre Physiologie, auf ihrer Höhe, weist das Geistige im Menschen (die Erkenntniß) als Produkt seines Physischen nach; [...] aber die wahre Metaphysik belehrt uns, dass dieses Physische selbst bloßes Produkt, oder vielmehr Erscheinung, eines Geistigen (des Willens) sei."
[2] "[D]ie Idee der Seele, dieses metaphysischen Wesens, in dessen absoluter Einfachheit Erkennen und Wollen ewig unzertrennlich Eins, verbunden und verschmolzen waren."

and has three crucial manifestations that may be labelled: a) metaphysical, b) epistemological, and c) methodological.

The metaphysical manifestation (a) is, of course, the cornerstone of Schopenhauer's philosophical system. Although it is not our aim to discuss it here in great detail, what must be mentioned is the radical distinction between the world seen as *will* and the world seen as *representation*, and the insufficiency of the perspective on the world given by the intellect. Since the will is the ground of all appearance, of all representation, an account of the world only in terms of representation can never be sufficient.

We have already mentioned that the metaphysical priority of the will over the intellect has important consequences for Schopenhauer's epistemology (b), for philosophy cannot be satisfied with a description of the world given by the intellect alone. Books II and IV of the First Volume of *The World as Will and Representation* are dedicated to a consideration of the world as will, and Schopenhauer probes the possibility of using knowledge of the body to gain access to the will. Traditional means of knowledge (reason or understanding) are dismissed as insufficient for knowing the will. This brings out, in sharp relief, the limits of intellectual knowledge that apply to all rational explanations – natural sciences included.

The third manifestation of the will-intellect relation features prominently in Schopenhauer's discussion of the methodology of natural sciences (c). According to Schopenhauer, natural sciences can be broken down into two categories: descriptive (or morphological) and etiological (WWV I, §17). Descriptive disciplines are characterised by an emphasis on classification of phenomena rather than causal explanations and Schopenhauer counts among them all the various sub-disciplines of natural history, in particular botany and zoology. Etiological disciplines, perhaps closer to what we would now understand as natural science, would include physics, chemistry and, most importantly here, physiology. They feature causal explanations for the phenomena they study. What is distinctive about Schopenhauer's take on these sciences is that etiological explanations are also considered insufficient. In WWV I, Schopenhauer raises the question of studying the generation of the individual and claims that the process, even if studied by physiology, has up to the present remained mysterious and "has so far eluded attempts at clear knowledge" (WWV I, p. 115). Etiological explanations are the most we could obtain from the intellect when we consider the world as representation, but they are incomplete. What is worse, they run the risk of being inadequate. Schopenhauer insists that a natural occurrence cannot be reduced to an account of the patterns displayed by cause and effect relations. Physics might tell us that whenever we throw a stone it will come back to earth and may describe very accurately the formula according to which this happens, but Schopenhauer claims physics can never fully grasp the natural force that makes the stone fall back to earth. The distinction that is being set up here is between natural laws (the etiological accounts given by the intellect and that are usually taken to constitute knowledge) and natural forces (immediate objectifications of the will). Natural forces cannot be explained, cannot have a cause (since they are outside the realm of the principle of sufficient reason) and are described as 'original' forces of nature:

> the original natural forces themselves, on the other hand, as immediate objectivations of the will (which, as thing in itself, is not subject to the principle of sufficient reason), lie outside the forms [...] that give validity and meaning to aetiological explanations and which, for this reason, can never lead to the inner essence of nature. (WWV I, p. 161)[3]

Within the phenomena that form the domain of inquiry of each and every science, investigators need to distinguish between etiological relations and the natural force that is active in the phenomenon being studied. In this context, it is crucial to notice that Schopenhauer does not want to reduce all active forces in the world to one original force. His metaphysics includes gradations of the will and these gradations of the will are its immediate objectifications; they manifest themselves in nature as natural forces. In physics the natural force needed for an explanation is gravity, while in physiology it is the "life force [*Lebenskraft*]" (WWV I, p. 146).

The natural forces that Schopenhauer speaks of are the empirical manifestation of the so called 'Platonic Ideas'. Schopenhauer employs this notion of 'Platonic Ideas' in order to account for the way in which the will is objectified in representation. Although this notion is essential to Schopenhauer's philosophy, it is also highly problematic. On the one hand, Platonic Ideas are part of the world as representation, which means they fall under the subject-object distinction that is the ground of all knowledge (WWV II, p. 210). On the other hand, though, Platonic Ideas stand above the Principle of Sufficient Reason. This means that these ideas are not things that we can encounter in empirical reality, but rather archetypes for the various objects in nature (WWV I, p. 154). As we have seen above, and in Schopenhauer's own terms, Platonic Ideas are immediate objectifications of the will, while objects in empirical reality are mediated objectifications. It can be argued that Platonic Ideas serve as intermediaries

---

3 "[D]ie ursprünglichen Naturkräfte selbst, als unmittelbare Objektivationen des Willens, der als Ding an sich dem Satz vom Grunde nicht unterworfen ist, [liegen] außerhalb jener Formen [...], innerhalb welcher allein jede ätiologische Erklärung Gültigkeit und Bedeutung hat und eben deshalb nie zum innern Wesen der Natur führen kann."

between the will and empirical reality. In this sense also, natural forces, as well as the character of animals or humans, are instantiations of Platonic Ideas:

> The intelligible character coincides with the Idea, or more specifically with the original act of will revealed in the Idea: to this extent, not only the empirical character of every person but also of every species of animal, indeed every species of plant, and even every original force of inorganic nature, can be seen as the appearance of an intelligible character, i.e. of an extra-temporal, indivisible act of will. (WWV I, p. 185–186)[4]

The character indicates the essence of the animal or human being in question; as an essence it is outside of time and space. The behaviour of an animal consists merely in the way in which external stimuli make the character manifest itself. If we were to know all of the stimuli or motives that act on an organism and at the same time understand its essence we would be able to always predict its behaviour.

> The motive, namely, is likewise effectual only under the presupposition of an inner drive [*Trieb*], i.e. of a determinate quality or constitution of will called its *character*; the motive in question only gives the latter a definite direction – individualizes it for the concrete case. (WWV II, p. 391)[5]

This brings us to the epistemological advantage of postulating the existence of Platonic Ideas. We must first remember that knowledge can only exist under the subject-object distinction (WWV I, p. 3). Given that Platonic Ideas fall under the subject-object distinction, there is the possibility that we may know them and therefore understand the world in its fullness.[6] But in order to better understand the role of Platonic Ideas in physiology, we must turn to Schopenhauer's treatise *On the Will in Nature*.

---

4 "Der intelligible Charakter fällt also mit der Idee, oder noch eigentlicher mit dem ursprünglichen Willensakt, der sich in ihr offenbart, zusammen: insofern ist also nicht nur der empirische Charakter jedes Menschen, sondern auch der jeder Thierspecies, ja jeder Pflanzenspecies und sogar jeder ursprünglichen Kraft der unorganischen Natur, als Erscheinung eines intelligibeln Charakters, d.h. eines außerzeitlichen untheilbaren Willensaktes anzusehn."

5 "Das Motiv nämlich wirkt ebenfalls nur unter Voraussetzung eines innern Triebes, d.h. einer bestimmten Beschaffenheit des Willens, welche man den *Charakter* desselben nennt: diesem giebt das jedesmalige Motiv nur eine entschiedene Richtung, – individualisirt ihn, für den konkreten Fall."

6 Readers of Schopenhauer will no doubt remember that aesthetic experience resides precisely in the contemplation of these Platonic Ideas. Nevertheless, an investigation of Schopenhauer's philosophy of art is not the direction that this essay will take.

What becomes apparent form the very preface to the second edition to the essay *On the Will in Nature* is that Schopenhauer has a dual purpose in mind. The first is to correlate (*bestätigen*) his metaphysical insights and the results of scientific observations and research.[7] The very first paragraph of the preface contains an optimistic account of the felicitous results of comparing Schopenhauer's metaphysics and the results of natural science (WN, p. 193 and also p. 215). The second goal is to criticise the way in which some of his contemporaries have performed their work in the field of science. Schopenhauer brands them materialists and is appalled by their desire to deny the existence of a life force, while attempting to explain organic nature by the mere play of chemical forces (WN, p. 194). In the introduction, Schopenhauer argues that natural scientists are poorly placed to have insight into natural forces because no matter how extensive their explanations of phenomena might be, there is a point where etiological explanation must cease. In perfect accordance with the arguments in WWV, the hiatus between will and intellect is based on the primacy of the will over the intellect, which will be understood as the will's servant. Natural forces are immediate objectifications of the will, and hence, prior to and independent of the intellect, and therefore inaccessible to it (WN, p. 218). What is strikingly different here, in opposition to the WWV, is the absence of the notion of Platonic Ideas. Indeed, the notion of Platonic Ideas does not feature prominently in the WN and does not play a major role in accounting for the metaphysical presuppositions of natural sciences. This omission is not without importance, and points to an unresolved issue in Schopenhauer's understanding of the premises of natural sciences. Although it is true that the intellect, taken as understanding (*Verstand*), is insufficient for understanding the world, is it the case then that the human mind, an expanded intellect,[8] is also insufficient? Must Platonic Ideas, which fall under the subject-object distinction and are therefore part of the human mind, also prove to be ultimately inadequate for grasping the world? In *The World as Will and Representation*, whenever Schopenhauer has to show what scientists do not understand, he always refers to natural forces (such as the *Lebenskraft*). We have already seen that natural forces are immediate objectifications of the will, i.e. Platonic Ideas, so it should be the case that it is the mind, or expanded intellect, that gives us a proper knowledge of the world. One might argue that although it is true that Schopenhauer offers examples of objectifications of the will, what he really is getting at is the existence of the will, the

---

7 For an in-depth discussion of what correlation (*Bestätigung*) means here, see Segala 2010.
8 Not considered, of course, only as Understanding (*Verstand*) but as will-less, pure consciousness – a pure contemplative awareness of the object by the pure subject of cognition.

metaphysical entity outside the grasp of Platonic Ideas. However, the will does not seem to play a role in Schopenhauer's account of science directly, but only through its immediate objectifications. In other words, scientists do not seem to be accused of misrepresenting or not knowing the will, but the various manifestations of the will – in the case of physiology, the *Lebenskraft*.

This line of reasoning might be countered by emphasising Schopenhauer's arguments in the *Will in Nature*.

> With me, that which is eternal and indestructible in man, therefore, that which constitutes his vital principle, is not the soul, but if I may use a chemical term its radical: and this is the Will. The so-called soul is already a compound: it is the union of the Will and the intellect (νους). This intellect is the secondary element, the *posterius* of the organism and, as a mere cerebral function, it is conditioned by the organism; whereas the will is what is primary, the *prius* of the organism, which is conditioned by the former. (WN, p. 236)[9]

Here, the scheme Schopenhauer constructs in order to account for physiology is tripartite: 1) the will, 2) the objectification of the will, i.e. the body or the organism, which is a phenomenon of the will, and 3) the intellect, which is the product of the physical.[10] What is interesting about this trichotomy for us now is, on the one hand, that the philosophical narrative offered here by Schopenhauer is one sided and, on the other, that the Platonic Ideas are missing. In relation to the first point, we must remember that subject and object are correlates for Schopenhauer, they depend on one another and it makes no sense to believe one can exist without the other.[11] The account above could have also been given from the subjective perspective and then the physical would have been the result of the faculty of representation, not the other way around. However, the view presented here is merely informative since, in dealing with natural sciences, we have already agreed to take up the objective view. Regarding the absence of the Platonic Ideas, we must first notice that the body is described as an objectification of the will without any further qualification. We already saw how in the first Volume of the WWV Schopenhauer draws a distinction between

---

9 "Bei mir ist das Ewige und Unzerstörbare im Menschen, welches daher auch das Lebensprincip in ihm ausmacht, nicht die Seele, sondern, mir einen chemischen Ausdruck zu gestatten, das Radikal der Seele und dieses ist der Wille. Die sogenannte Seele ist schon zusammengesetzt: sie ist die Verbindung des Willens mit dem *nous*, Intellekt. Dieser Intellekt ist das Sekundäre, ist das posterius des Organismus und, al seine bloße Gehirnfunktion, durch diesen bedingt. Der Wille hingegen ist primär, ist das prius des Organismus und dieser durch ihn bedingt."

10 Cartwright seems to agree when he writes that in the WN Schopenhauer took a "more direct approach" (2005, p. 113) and some exegetes seem to have also walked down this path, for instance Janaway 1989, p. 197 and Hamlyn 1980, p. 95.

11 For more on this topic see Janaway 1989, p. 293.

adequate or immediate objectifications of the will (the Platonic Ideas) and indirect objectifications (i.e. those that fall under the principle of sufficient reason). Therefore, in the text under consideration here, the type of objectification that Schopenhauer has in mind seems to be an indirect, inadequate one, i.e. one that falls under the principle of sufficient reason. The body does not stand for the Idea of the body but for the material instance present to our senses.

By minimising the impact of Platonic Ideas on the analysis of humans and of how physiology should work, the arguments of the WN only accentuate the critique of the intellect we saw in WWV. Nevertheless, my hypothesis is that the role of Ideas is crucial for coming to grips with Schopenhauer's philosophy of nature. The intellect, understood as more than the capacity for etiological explanation under the principle of sufficient reason, is essential for a full understanding of natural phenomena, because it is essential for understanding the manifestations of the will. In order to reinforce this point, we can also look at a passage from WWV I §24, where Schopenhauer argues that the explanatory principles of one region of nature cannot be transferred to another.

> People have been successful in reducing the many and manifold appearances in nature to particular original forces, and these successes have always brought real progress: people have taken a number of forces and qualities that were initially considered different, and derived them from each other (for instance, magnetism from electricity), thus reducing their number: aetiology will achieve its aim when it recognises all the original forces of nature for what they are, arranging them and establishing the way they operate, i.e. the rule by which, guided by causality, their appearances emerge in time and space and determine their positions with respect to one another. But original forces will always remain, the content of appearance will always be left over as an indissoluble residuum that cannot be reduced to form, and thus cannot be explained from something else in accordance with the principle of sufficient reason. (WWV I, p. 147)[12]

Since these principles or forces cannot be explained any further it is also impossible for there to be a more general principle which would subsume under it the

---

12 "Es ist gelungen, und gab, so oft es gelang, einen wahren Fortschritt, die vielen und mannigfaltigen Erscheinungen in der Natur auf einzelne ursprüngliche Kräfte zurückzuführen: man hat mehrere, Anfangs für verschieden gehaltene Kräfte und Qualitäten eine aus der andern abgeleitet (z.B. den Magnetismus aus der Elektricität) und so ihre Zahl vermindert: die Aetiologie wird am Ziele seyn, wenn sie alle ursprünglichen Kräfte der Natur als solche erkannt und aufgestellt, und ihre Wirkungsarten, d.h. die Regel nach der, am Leitfaden der Kausalität, ihre Erscheinungen in Zeit und Raum eintreten und sich unter einander ihre Stelle bestimmen, festgesetzt haben wird; aber stets werden Urkräfte übrig bleiben, stets wird, als unauflösliches Residuum, ein Inhalt der Erscheinung bleiben, der nicht auf ihre Form zurückzuführen, also nicht nach dem Satz vom Grunde aus etwas Anderm zu erklären ist."

laws of various regions of nature. In this sense, Schopenhauer is a strong anti-reductionist or holist with regard to natural forces (cf. WWV I, p. 161, p. 174 and p. 214).[13]

The arguments presented in this subsection can be summarised as follows: Philosophical physiology consists in understanding that without knowing Platonic Ideas, understood as the immediate objectifications of the will, we can never give a full account of organisms. Given that physiology is a scientific pursuit, this also implies the assumption that we take the objective point of view on the world: We consider our intellect to be the product of the physical in us.

I.2 The Unity of the Body

Schopenhauer's account of the sciences is not merely a neutral description of what their foundations ought to be, but a diagnostic tool in evaluating sciences from a philosophical perspective (Cartwright 2005, p. 112). In the case of physiology, Schopenhauer is quick to point out, both in *The World as Will and Representation* and in the *Will in Nature*, the lack of understanding by some physiologists of their object of study. He takes it as the philosopher's task to set scientists on the right path in their investigations and is highly critical of those who attempted to discard the notion of *Lebenskraft*.

In WN Schopenhauer is adamant that his great innovation, compared to the philosophical tradition, is the complete separation between intellect and will. Philosophers up to him had usually taken the will to be conditioned by and subjected to the intellect (WN, p. 236). This unjustified assumption did not leave unwelcome traces just in philosophy, but it affected natural science as well. Considering willing and knowing an "eternal, inseparable unity" made the appearance of philosophical physiology impossible (WN, p. 235). Schopenhauer criticises physiologists (and, more specifically, George Ernest Stahl) for believing that the rational soul builds for itself a body and directs all the inner organic functions without having any consciousness of these inner operations. This notion might seem absurd, but it stemmed from a real conundrum, namely the difficulties of explaining the unity displayed by the organism. In Schopenhauer's words: "a totality, a unity, a perfection and a rigidly carried out

---

[13] For accounts of Schopenhauer's anti-reductionist stance, see Janaway 1989, p. 178f. Holism means the belief that there are processes (in a secondary discipline) that are not obedient to the theoretical constructs of any primary discipline (Wilson/Lumsden 1991, p. 405). For a more detailed discussion of various types of holism and reductionism, see also Nagel 1979.

harmony in all its parts" (WN, p. 277, n. 1). Schopenhauer does not wish to forego the question of unity, but rather to offer a different account of its origin: it is not the intellect or the rational soul that creates a body for itself, but rather the will. This means that the unity of the organism is, for Schopenhauer, a metaphysical given. It is the manifestation of the *Lebenskraft*. The organising force at work here is the key notion of Schopenhauer's entire metaphysics. However, as we have seen in the discussion of the role of the intellect, the will does not directly objectify itself in organic entities. The archetypal forms (WN, p. 275) or the Ideas (WN, p. 277) play the role of intermediaries, given their status as immediate objectifications. This view of unity does, indeed, offer a different, perhaps more reliable account of the existence of an organic unity than the intellectualist approach, but it also leads Schopenhauer to some conclusions that may sound curious to contemporary ears: for instance his rejection of evolutionary theory (at least in the way Lamarck presented it). What matters more for the present argumentation, however, is the role that the notion of unity plays and the way Schopenhauer conceives it.

Indeed, the ability to give an account of the unity or cohesion of an organism is a major factor in evaluating the merits of a scientific theory and yet it cannot be the product of the scientific theory itself. Schopenhauer argues that the unity of the organism can be properly understood only metaphysically, i.e. as the product of the will. Schopenhauer disputes the premises that the unity present in organisms is the result of the rational soul, but he does not challenge the assumption that the unity is a metaphysical given. In other words, he does not believe that the unity may be a derivative one and that the cohesion present in the organism may be a *result*. Nevertheless, his philosophy still offers the premises for understanding unity as a result, such as will be the case in Nietzsche. The problems that Nietzsche saw in Schopenhauer's metaphysics are problems Schopenhauer himself saw and tried to tackle. This becomes clear when we consider the important role that the notion of Platonic Ideas played in Schopenhauer's system. Nevertheless, due to his commitment to the metaphysical doctrine of the will, Schopenhauer was unable to fully embrace the multiplicity of Platonic Ideas. Due to his metaphysical stance, Schopenhauer can only treat the multiplicity of Platonic Ideas and, consequently, of natural forces as derived from the unity of the will. Conversely, Nietzsche, by renouncing the notion of such a unitary will, develops an understanding of the world and of human beings grounded in a primary multiplicity: that of drives. But, as we have seen, this multiplicity is already present in Schopenhauer's philosophy.

The reader may have noticed that, in the passage on philosophical physiology, Schopenhauer speaks of the will producing the physical in man. This seems strange if we remember that the will is not subjected to the principle of sufficient reason and thus cannot be thought of under the category of causality. Therefore, the notion of production cannot take the same meaning it has when Schopenhauer claims that the physical in man produces the intellect. In fact, it seems there is hardly any way in which we can understand this. Unfortunately, Schopenhauer is not forthcoming with a clear way in which we could make sense of this. The will is necessarily outside the intellect and cannot be known by it. Ultimately, it seems we must be resigned to accept the mysterious nature of the will. It seems that we are forced to take note of the impossibility of offering a more adequate explanation on this point.

II Nietzsche's Theory of Drives

There is great deal of literature on the notion of drives and it is worth mentioning here some of the key accounts of drives. Paul Laurent Assoun speaks of *Trieb* as a "force operating in the subterranean space of the human Unconscious" (2006, p. 55), and argues that "there are instincts everywhere" for Nietzsche. Graham Parkes also identifies multiplicity as the key feature of Nietzsche's study of drives (1996, p. 250) and so does Gregory Moore (2006, p. 72). Drives are used to explain "broad patterns of behaviour" (Kastafanas 2012, p. 7) and the same author does not doubt the hermeneutic importance of drives; they are not only "explanatorily prior to affects" (Kastafanas 2012, p. 7) but also trigger affects (Kastafanas 2012, p. 8). Drives are embodied in organisms and are part of an organism (Kastafanas 2012, p. 9). What stands out, beyond the points of contention, is that the notion of drives fits the following description: drives form a plurality and explain our actions. In other words, the notion of drives serves to 1) group a variety of behaviours and actions (artistic, religious, moral, political) under one principle (call it drive or instinct) while acknowledging that there is a plurality of these explanatory principles; and 2) drives do not give up the claim to a form of realism. By realism, as opposed to conceptualism, is meant a commitment to the belief that the groupings mentioned above are not purely arbitrary. To the contrary, it is implied that there is good empirical and theoretical support for believing that assigning a drive to a group of actions explains something intrinsically true about those actions. One might be tempted to wonder whether such claims about Nietzsche's theory of drives imply that Nietzsche's theory of drives is a metaphysical construct. This, however, is not the case. While Nietzsche does make claims about drives that can be classified as ontological claims, drives are by no means eternal, immutable essences. As it has been argued by (Richardson 2004, p. 5), drives are the result of a process of change and evolution, just like anything else in reality. The claim that they are real does not imply that they are metaphysical in nature. The notion of drives does more than just group together or explain various affects or patterns of behaviour. Drives also have a normative aspect, i.e. they interpret or colour the world; they evaluate it and give partial perspectives (Kastafanas 2012, p. 8–9).

The point that must be discussed is what kind of unity the individual possesses, given that it is the sum of affects and drives. This is, for Nietzsche, one of the main tasks of physiology, as we can see in the fragment below:

> Point of departure from the *body* and physiology: why? – We gain the correct representation of the kind of the subject-unity we are, namely as regents at the summit of a commonwealth, therefore no "souls" or "vital forces [*Lebenskräfte*]" [...]. (NL 1885, KSA 11, 40[21], p. 638)[14]

The main thrust of the argument is Nietzsche's suggestion that the kind of unity we encounter in the study of the body is a derivative unity. He rejects not only the souls (*Seelen*) as a source of unity, as Schopenhauer has done in the *Will in Nature*, but also the *Lebenskräfte*. Given that he rejects Schopenhauer's notion of *Lebenskraft*, Nietzsche is left without a metaphysical notion that could account for the unity of the organism. As a consequence, he searches for an explanation of unity using a political metaphor. He does not speak the language of monarchy (as Schopenhauer does)[15] in describing the multiplicity of the body, but uses the word 'regents': suggesting a temporary unity that is the result of the interaction between the various elements constituting the body. This raises two questions: 1) what are the members of this commonwealth? and 2) how exactly is this multiplicity organised? Both questions can find an answer in the following fragment:

> As cells stand next to cells physiologically, so do drives next to drives. The most general image [*Bild*] of our nature is *an association* [Vergesellschaftung] *of drives* in perpetual rivalry and confederacy with one another. (NL 1883, KSA 10, 7[94], p. 274)[16]

---

14 "Ausgangspunkt vom *Leibe* und der Physiologie: warum? – Wir gewinnen die richtige Vorstellung von der Art unsrer Subjekt-Einheit, nämlich als Regenten an der Spitze eines Gemeinwesens, nicht also 'Seelen' oder 'Lebenskräfte'".
15 See the account of government offered in *Parerga and Paralipomena*, where Schopenhauer argues that a monarchical form of government is natural to men (PuP II, p. 271f.). Regardless of whether we believe that this is only a case of naturalistic fallacy, what is important for us is that Schopenhauer chooses to back his argument by giving examples of instances found in nature in which a multiplicity is organised in monarchical fashion.
16 "Wie Zelle neben Zelle physiologisch steht, so Trieb neben Trieb. Das allgemeinste Bild unseres Wesens ist *eine Vergesellschaftung von Trieben*, mit fortwährender Rivalität und Einzelbündnissen unter einander."

As was the case in the fragment we quoted above, Nietzsche is describing the idea of a plurality in political language. This time, however, he goes a bit further in his analysis and uses the notions of: association (*Vergesellschaftung*), confederacy (*Einzelbündnissen*) and rivalry (*Rivalität*). In this case, Nietzsche also mentions the components of the plurality: cells and, most importantly, drives. Analysing the politics present in Nietzsche's physiology would require a study of its own and is therefore beyond the scope of this paper. What is useful for our line of reasoning here, however, is to notice that the unity of the subject is a derivative unity. There is no metaphysical principle from which the unity is derived. That is the main reason why Nietzsche discusses politics in the case of physiology: he needs to show how the unity of the subject is merely the outcome of a self-organising multiplicity. In this sense, Nietzsche's view on the politics of physiology is very different from Schopenhauer's. In the account of government given in *Parerga and Paralipomena*, Schopenhauer argues that the body is similar to a monarchy: the brain is the ruling organ that coordinates the activity of the entire organism. There is no conflict between the parts of the organism and they all work together (cf. PuP II, p. 271f.).

III Philosophical Physiology

Considering Nietzsche's response to Schopenhauer best begins with an outline of the differences. Nietzsche is adamant in his critique and rejection of metaphysics. With regard to Schopenhauer, this amounts to a rejection of the metaphysics of the will. In the domain of physiology, this means that Nietzsche can no longer explain the unity of the organism by appeal to the will, as Schopenhauer did. All the natural forces that manifest themselves in an individual (physical, chemical forces, but also *Lebenskraft*) are no longer held together by a will that would direct everything in nature. This is the reason why Nietzsche needs to develop a politics of drives: the unity of the organism is no longer given by the will.

There is another important way in which the two are at odds. At first sight, it seems that both are engaged in a critique of science. Nevertheless, the nature of this critique is very different. In Schopenhauer's case, science is incapable of understanding the will or Platonic Ideas. Therefore, scientists who believe they can explain the entirety of nature simply with the help of scientific methods are misguided. Nietzsche's critique of science is of a different nature. While this is, in itself, a vast topic, Nietzsche never seems to imply that science is by necessity incomplete or inadequate because there is a metaphysical essence it cannot describe. While Nietzsche does criticise physiology or evolutionary theory for not properly understanding its object of study (GS 349, KSA 3, p. 585; GM II 12, KSA 5, p. 315–316), he does not imply that an adequate understanding is inaccessible to it. As a consequence of his rejection of metaphysics, Nietzsche cannot accept the direction of Schopenhauer's critique of science.

This account of the differences between Schopenhauer and Nietzsche should not obscure their points of contact. There is a sense in which Nietzsche's critique of the intellect approximates Schopenhauer's, insofar as they both argue that the intellect is a product of the body. Conscious thought, which appears to us as a unity, is the product of a pulsional, unconscious reality, made out of a multiplicity of drives or 'forces'. Nietzsche, more explicitly, and Schopenhauer, more elusively, understand that this plurality of forces must constitute the ground, the foundation for the emergence of the conscious, rational intellect. Schopenhauer's commitment to the metaphysics of the will may hide, at first glance, Nietzsche's debt to his immediate predecessor, but it cannot completely mask Nietzsche's engagement with Schopenhauer's critique of the intellect and his doctrine of Platonic Ideas. It must be acknowledged that Schopenhauer is more forthcoming in explicitly admitting the existence of a plurality of forces in the case of nature than in the case of human beings. Nevertheless, if the metaphysics of the will is done away with, as Nietzsche would have it, there is no reason to fail to recognise the multiplicity that constitutes human beings.

In order to understand the similarities between the two, we need to consider the role of reason or of the intellect from a physiological perspective. We saw that Schopenhauer's claim about true physiology is that it shows how the intellect is a result of the physical in man. The intellect is simply a product of the body or the organism. This is a recurring theme in Nietzsche (e.g. Z I: "On the Despisers of the Body") and he uses his account of physiology and of the drives in order to substantiate this claim.

> Body am I, through and through, and nothing besides; and soul is just a word for something on the body. [...] Behind your thoughts and feelings, my brother, stands a powerful commander, an unknown wise man – he is called self. He lives in your body, he is your body. (Z I Despisers, KSA 4, p. 39–40)[17]

The hypothesis of this paper is that key characteristics of Nietzsche's theory of drives, such as the multiplicity of drives, may be seen as a result of his critical

---

17 "Leib bin ich ganz und gar, und Nichts ausserdem; und Seele ist nur ein Wort für ein Etwas am Leibe. [...] Hinter deinen Gedanken und Gefühlen, mein Bruder, steht ein mächtiger Gebieter, ein unbekannter Weiser — der heisst Selbst. In deinem Leibe wohnt er, dein Leib ist er."

engagement with Schopenhauer's philosophical physiology. While criticising the notion of will, Nietzsche could be seen to be picking up on 1) the multiplicity of Platonic Ideas present in Schopenhauer, which he would then use to shape his own account of drives, and 2) Schopenhauer's argument that philosophical physiology shows us that the intellect is the product of the body.

References

Assoun, Paul-Laurent (2006): Freud and Nietzsche. London: Continuum.

Cartwright, David E. (2005): Historical Dictionary of Schopenhauer's Philosophy. Lanham, Maryland, Toronto and Oxford: The Scarecrow Press.

Hamlyn, D.W. (1980): The Arguments of Philosophers: Schopenhauer. London: Routledge & Kegan Paul.

Janaway, Christopher (1989): Self and World in Schopenhauer's Philosophy. Oxford: Clarendon Press.

Kastafanas, Paul (2012): "Nietzsche on Agency and Self-Ignorance". In: *The Journal of Nietzsche Studies* 43 (1), p. 5–17.

Moore, Gregory (2006): Nietzsche, Biology and Metaphor. Cambridge: Cambridge University Press.

Nagel, Ernest (1979): The Structure of Science: Problems in the Logic of Scientific Explanation. 2nd edition. Cambridge, MA: Hackett.

Parkes, Graham (1996): Composing the Soul: Reaches of Nietzsche's Psychology. Chicago: University of Chicago Press.

Richardson, John (2004): Nietzsche's New Darwinism. New York and Oxford: Oxford University Press.

Segala, Marco (2010): "Schopenhauer and the Empirical Confirmations of Philosophy". In: *Idealistic Studies* 40 (1/2), p. 27–41.

Wilson, Edward O./Lumdsen, Charles J. (1991): "Holism and Reduction in Sociobiology: Lessons from the Ants and the Human Culture". In: *Biology and Philosophy* 6 (4), p. 401–412.

Philipp Schwab
Critique of 'the System' and Experimental Philosophy: Nietzsche and Kierkegaard

In a letter from Copenhagen dated 11 January 1888, the Danish critic and scholar Georg Brandes refers Nietzsche to "one Nordic writer whose work would interest you" and who is said to be "one of the profoundest psychologists that have ever existed" (KGB III/6, Bf. 512). The writer Brandes is referring to is Søren Kierkegaard. A few weeks later, in his response dated 19 February, Nietzsche states that he plans during his "next journey to Germany [...] to study the psychological problem of Kierkegaard" (KGB III/5, Bf. 997).[1]

For reasons all too well known, this planned *Auseinandersetzung* never took place and most commentators regret that Kierkegaard was called to Nietzsche's attention too late.[2] Yet it is rather doubtful whether the late Nietzsche, given the extreme form of polemic he employs in his final manuscripts and letters, would in fact have valued Kierkegaard as an eminent psychologist. For overall, at least at first glance, Kierkegaard's and Nietzsche's philosophies seem to differ quite fundamentally, the most obvious point of difference being their respective relation to Christianity. Kierkegaard writes in his philosophical autobiography *The Point of View for My Work as an Author* that his "whole authorship relates to Christianity, to the problem: becoming a Christian" (SKS 16, p. 11; PV, p. 23). Accordingly, in *Practice in Christianity*, he describes his work as an "attempt again to introduce Christianity into Christendom" (SKS 12, p. 49; PC, p. 36). Indeed, the concept most widely associated with Kierkegaard is the notorious 'leap of faith' – although Kierkegaard in fact never uses exactly this expression (cf. McKinnon 1993). Nietzsche, by contrast, conceives of himself as the most radical *opponent* to the Christian tradition as a whole; and in the *Nachlass* we even discover a "Law against Christianity [*Gesetz wider das Christenthum*]" which seems to have originally been planned as a part of the *Anti-Christ* (A Epilogue, KSA 6, p. 254).

---

[1] I follow Middleton's translation here.
[2] Cf. e.g. Löwith 1991, p. 176. Recent research has shown that it is quite likely that Nietzsche had some knowledge of Kierkegaard prior to Brandes' letter, mainly through secondary sources, and that even certain passages in Nietzsche's works might be implicitly referring to Kierkegaard. Cf. the groundbreaking study by Brobjer 2003 and the more detailed account in Miles 2011, p. 268–278.

Thus, sharply put: For Kierkegaard, the problem of the 'present age' is a lack of *true* Christianity – while for Nietzsche, writing some 30 to 40 years later, the problem of *his* present age is that it still remains *too deeply* rooted in the Christian tradition.

Despite this fundamental difference, however, a closer look nonetheless reveals some quite striking similarities and parallels between the two thinkers,[3] a first parallel being already implied in the opposition just mentioned: Both Kierkegaard and Nietzsche diagnose a *crisis* of their present age, that is, a crisis of modernity. Even the terms by means of which they determine this crisis are rather similar: Kierkegaard speaks of an "age of levelling [*Nivellering*]" (SKS 8, p. 84; TA, p. 88); and Nietzsche's term for this crisis is, of course, Nihilism, which he takes to be 'a devaluation of all values'.[4]

The following reflections are based on the assumption that there are in fact at least three central aspects in which Kierkegaard and Nietzsche may be productively related to one another. Furthermore, I take it that in these three aspects Kierkegaard and Nietzsche shed some light on each other respectively.

First aspect: For both Kierkegaard and Nietzsche, thinking in the aftermath of German Idealism, traditional concepts and forms of philosophy become questionable and they both criticise established modes of thought. That this is already the case in Kierkegaard becomes especially evident when read in the light of Nietzsche's thought.

Second aspect: Both analyse the *existential* conditions and possibilities of the individual within the aforementioned crisis of modernity. Inverse to the first aspect, this 'existential' concern being already present in Nietzsche comes to light especially when read *vis-à-vis* Kierkegaard. Let me mention just one quotation to illuminate this point. In the second of his *Untimely Meditations* Nietzsche writes: "To what end the 'world' exists, to what end 'mankind' exists, ought not to concern us at all for the moment [...]; but do ask yourself to what end you, the

---

[3] Cf. on the following in some more detail, and with respect to ethics and ethical critique in both thinkers, Schwab 2013, here esp. p. 91–93. From recent research on both Kierkegaard and Nietzsche, cf. especially the valuable study by Miles 2011 as well as Grau 1997, Kellenberger 1997, Hannay 2000, Lippitt 2000, Longo 2007, Miles 2007, Hyde 2010, Kleinert 2013 and Miles 2013. For an overview of some of these works cf. Quist 2005, Sooväli 2009. Cf. the classical presentations of the matter by Löwith 1933, Jaspers 1955, p. 19–50 and Deleuze 2004, p. 6–13.

[4] Cf. NL 1887, KSA 12, 9[35], p. 350: "What does nihilism mean? *That the highest values devaluate themselves*". Cf. the similar passage already in NL 1885/86, KSA 12, 2[131], p. 131, and on this Heidegger GA 6.1, p. 36–37. 'Nihilism' is already taken to be the main point of comparison between Kierkegaard and Nietzsche by Löwith 1933.

individual, exist" (HL 9, KSA 1, p. 319).[5] Very similar expressions can easily be found throughout Kierkegaard's works.

Third aspect: Both Kierkegaard and Nietzsche do not merely *criticise* traditional modes of thought; they also, as a counter draft, develop *new* forms of philosophy. These new methods conceptualised by Kierkegaard and Nietzsche are essentially procedural and experimental drafts of thought. Thereby, in both thinkers, the respective experimental method points to an irreducibly *perspectival character* of cognition and existence, and it corresponds with the assumption that actuality is essentially *becoming* and does not offer a final and definite result. Thus, in both Kierkegaard and Nietzsche, the experimental form of thought is not to be (mis-)understood as a mere 'use' of 'literary or rhetorical devices'. Rather, it affects the very 'substance' of their respective philosophies.

On the backdrop of these general assumptions, I will in the following mainly elaborate aspects one and three in some more detail. On the one hand, I will focus on Kierkegaard's and Nietzsche's critique of that form of thought which dominates German Idealism – that is, the *system*. On the other hand, I set out to show that, and in which way, their respective experimental method of philosophy relates to or even directly emerges from this critique. In doing so, I intend to shed some light on the complex constellation of transition between German Idealism and post-idealistic modernity.[6]

I Kierkegaard

I.1 Critique of the System

In Kierkegaard, as is well known, the critique of 'the system' mainly represents a critique of *Hegel's* system. Concerning this critique, however, two 'external' factors have to be taken into account. Firstly, Kierkegaard's knowledge and thereby also his critique of Hegel are to a considerable extent mediated through the Danish Hegelians of the 1830s and 1840s.[7] This historical context is worth keeping in mind, as it puts some rather questionable aspects of Kierkegaard's

---

[5] Cf. on this passage Gerhardt 2006, p. 77. Brandes had already related this passage (significantly modified and without reference) to Kierkegaard. Cf. Brandes 1972, p. 14–15.
[6] On this topic and especially with respect to Kierkegaard, cf. Hühn 2009 and Schwab 2012, esp. p. 38–51.
[7] Cf. Stewart 2003 throughout.

critique of 'Hegel' into perspective. To name just one example: In the *Concept of Anxiety*, Kierkegaard's pseudonym Vigilius Haufniensis mocks "the ingenuity [*Aandrighed*] of heading the last section of the *Logic* 'Actuality'" (SKS 4, p. 324n; CA, p. 16n).[8] Commentators have consistently objected that Hegel's *Logic* does not conclude with a section on actuality. Rather, the discussion of actuality is to be found in the final section of the second part of the *Logic*, the *Wesenslogik*. In fact, Kierkegaard's pseudonym does not explicitly mention Hegel here, and the object of, or at least cause for, this critique appears to be the *Popular Lectures on Hegel's Objective Logic* by the Danish Theologian Adolph Peter Adler – which indeed does discuss 'actuality' in the final sections.[9]

The critique itself – i.e. that actuality is treated within logic – points to a second and, I assume, systematically even more important external factor. In 1841/42, Kierkegaard had travelled to Berlin and attended Schelling's lectures on *Philosophy of Revelation*. In referring to Schelling's second lecture from 18 November 1841, Kierkegaard enthusiastically writes in his notebook:

> I'm so glad to have heard *Schelling*'s 2nd lecture – indescribable. [...] [W]hen he mentioned the word "*actuality*" concerning philosophy's relation to the actual, the child of thought leaped for joy within me as in Elizabeth [cf. Lk. 1,41, PS]. After that I remember almost every word he said. Perhaps here there can be clarity. [...] Now I have put all my hope in Schelling [...]. (Not8:33; SKS 19, p. 235; KJN 3, p. 229)

Although Kierkegaard some weeks later stopped attending Schelling's lecture and was, in a whole, disappointed with the German's 'positive' philosophy, this very notion of *actuality* has a major impact on his later critique of Hegel.[10] In the second lecture Kierkegaard mentions here, Schelling develops the main distinction in his late philosophy, the distinction of *quid sit* and *quod sit*, of 'being-what' (*Washeit*) and 'being-that' (*Dassheit*). The *quid sit* is merely the sphere of thought, or of *possibility*. It determines – very briefly put – *what* something is, *if* it is (negative philosophy). However, *that* something is or exists cannot be deduced from mere thought. The being-that, actuality, is a facticity *beyond*

---

8 Cf. the more detailed elucidations on this in SKS 4, p. 317–318; CA, p. 8–9.
9 Adler only treats the first two (objective) parts of the *Logic* and, in accordance with Hegel, concludes the second part (*Logic of Essence*) with actuality. Cf. Adler 1842, p. 152–173, and on this SKS K4, p. 350 and Stewart 2003, p. 378–385.
10 Cf. Hühn 2009 and Hühn/Schwab 2013, Schwab 2014. Although the 'seed' of Kierkegaard's later critique of Hegel is already to be found in his dissertation *On the Concept of Irony*, Schelling's fundamental distinction between possibility and actuality apparently alters and sharpens Kierkegaard's perspective. Cf. my more extensive commentary in Hühn/Schwab 2013, p. 65–75 and Schwab 2014, p. 80–97.

thought (positive philosophy). Thus, it is an intermixture of spheres if actuality and existence are treated within the realm of pure thought, e.g. within logic.[11]

This, now, is exactly Kierkegaard's main point of criticism against Hegel. However, Kierkegaard radicalises and specifies the Schellingian motif in one decisive respect. In fact, he adopts it to the central topic of his thought as a whole, that is, the concrete existing individual in his or her singularity. Precisely the *individual's* existence – and *only* this existence – is, for Kierkegaard, that actuality which cannot be 'demonstrated' or 'analysed' in the sphere of possibility and pure thought. Furthermore, for Kierkegaard, individual existence as such withdraws from *any* form of scientific and systematic determination – even from 'positive philosophy'.

To illuminate this, I will now turn to one of Kierkegaard's central works, the *Concluding Unscientific Postscript*, published under the pseudonym Johannes Climacus. In one of the earlier sections of the book – the fourth of the "Possible and Actual Theses by Lessing" – Climacus elucidates his claim that a "system of existence [*Tilværelsens System*] cannot be given" (SKS 7, p. 114–120; CUP1, p. 118–125). Essentially, we can reconstruct three arguments for this claim from Climacus' elucidations.

Firstly, a system is always *conclusive* (*abgeschlossen/afslutted*). Climacus writes: "System and conclusiveness [*Afsluttethed*] correspond to each other" (SKS 7, p. 114; CUP1, p. 118). Existence, however, is essentially within time and thus within *becoming*, it is 'inconclusive'. For as long as we exist, there is no definite conclusion or final result to our existence.

Secondly, the system is necessarily in the sphere of the *universal* whereas individual existence is the *singular* or the *particular*, and thereby that which withdraws from being presented *as* universal. More precisely: The individual withdraws from being 'grasped' in a concept (*begriffen/begrebet*). This aspect is very clearly put in a journal entry from 1850: "[E]xistence corresponds to the individual, to the single individual, who lies outside of or is not subsumed into the concept" (NB14:150.a; SKS 22, p. 435; KJN 6, p. 440). So the bottom line of this 'singularity aspect' is the old formula *individuum est ineffabile*; the individual is 'unutterable'.[12]

---

11 Cf. Kierkegaard's notes, esp. Not11:2, Not11:3; SKS 19, p. 305–307; KJN 3, p. 303–305.
12 In the *Postscript*, this aspect is especially apparent in the first (possible) thesis by Lessing in which Climacus already determines the indirect form of thought (see below). Here, he describes the "double-reflection" of the "subjectively existing thinker": "In thinking, he thinks the universal, but, as existing in this thinking, as acquiring this in his inwardness, he becomes more and more subjectively isolated" (SKS 7, p. 73–74; CUP1, p. 73).

Thirdly, the existing individual is – as Climacus has it – essentially *interested* in his or her own existence. The individual relates *to* itself in the mode of interest *in* or *for* itself. In Climacus' and Kierkegaard's view, systematic thought, however, is necessarily objective in the first place and thus omits or *forgets* the existing individual. Systematic thought is, so to speak, 'disinterested' thought; it is 'indifferent' (*gleichgültig/ligegyldig*) to existence.[13]

For these three reasons – the aspect of becoming, the aspect of singularity and the aspect of interest – Climacus conceives of systematic thought as inappropriate with respect to existence. Yet this critique immediately poses the question as to whether there might be a *different* form of thought which could address existence more properly – for otherwise, we would apparently have to simply remain silent about existence at all.

I.2 Theory of Indirect Communication

This is where Kierkegaard's draft of experimental philosophy comes in. We see right away that *this* specific experimental philosophy has a clear concern: It will have to '*aim*' at concrete and individual existence. And with the three aspects of the critique of the system, we already have the 'criteria' for this form of thought: In one way or the other, it will have to 'respect' or even 'address' the inconclusiveness, the singularity and the 'self-interest' of existence.

This form of thought is, in Kierkegaard, called 'indirect communication'. Given this, it seems self-evident that Kierkegaard – or Climacus, or we ourselves as the interpreters – will have to say *what* indirect communication means or is specifically. However, at a closer look, this mode of thought – and, I assume, *any* form of indirect or experimental thought – poses a specific methodological problem: If we say what this form of thought *is*, we *define* it, and that is, we give a *direct* presentation of the *indirect*. Yet if the indirect is supposed to be an *essential* characteristic of this form of thought, we would, by defining it, abolish this characteristic, that is, we would *reduce* the indirect to the direct. Climacus himself – whom I take to present the strongest and most consistent account of the indirect method throughout Kierkegaard's *oeuvre* (cf. Schwab 2012,

---

[13] Again, this aspect is, in the *Postscript*, best displayed in the first (possible) thesis by Lessing: "Whereas objective [i.e. systematic, PS] thinking is indifferent to the thinking subject and his existence, the subjective thinker as existing is essentially interested in his own thinking" (SKS 7, p. 73; CUP1, p. 72–73). Cf. also an earlier passage in which Climacus says that the "scientific researcher" strives to become "objective, disinterested" (SKS 7, p. 30; CUP1, p. 21–22).

p. 80–147) – puts the matter pretty clearly: The "secret" of the indirect method "does not consist in [...] enunciating the double-reflection directly, since such an enunciation is a direct contradiction" (SKS 7, p. 74; CUP1, p. 74).

I cannot discuss this methodological problem here in full detail.[14] Basically, the 'solution' I suggest to this problem is that a 'first' and rather 'abstract' formulation is required which at the same time 'describes' the irreducible detour of the indirect *and* keeps it open. Fortunately, Kierkegaard himself provides us with such a formulation, although he by no means uses it as a consistent definition throughout his works. Yet in some instances, Kierkegaard and his pseudonyms say that indirect communication is a method that *works against itself*.[15] Apparently, this formulation does not define the indirect method in a strict sense nor does it yet describe it sufficiently. However, the working-against-itself is the 'basis', as it were, for any more specific explanation. It 'secures' the tension and procedural character of the indirect. For if we say that the indirect method 'is' working-against-itself in the first place, it is made clear from the very beginning that the indirect is by no means a *single* but rather a *double* movement. Within the tensed movement of the indirect, there is always a sort of recoil or backlash (*Rückstoß*) which prevents it from being grasped in a simple gesture as, say, a principle of philosophy in the strong (idealistic) sense. Thus, the indirect form of thought is a horizontal and circular movement as opposed to a vertical or transcendental movement. The recoil of the indirect defines neither a first starting point (or ground) nor a final result, rather, it deracinates its own movement from the very beginning. Yet in being circular, it is precisely not, as Hegel describes the movement of science in the *Logic*, a full circle which returns into itself and is thus completed (cf. SL II, TWA 6, p. 571–572). Rather, it is, in a verbal sense, a circl*ing* which necessarily and essentially remains incomplete.

If we look back at the 'criteria' taken from the critique of the system, the movement so far described apparently covers the criterion of inconclusiveness (and it thereby, I assume, in a certain sense, contours any experimental mode of thought). The working-against-itself or recoil of the indirect as such, does, however, not yet say anything about the singularity and the 'self-interest' of

---

14 Cf. on this systematic problem Schwab 2012, p. 9–37. Of course, a full picture of Kierkegaard's notion of indirect communication would have to closely investigate all of his texts dealing with this topic, even more so as they turn out to differ quite significantly from one another and none of them gives a 'definite' determination. Cf. my reconstruction in Schwab 2012, p. 67–441.
15 Cf. e.g. Kierkegaard's rather different uses of this notion in Papir 365:14, Papir 365:22; SKS 27, p. 397–398; JP 1:649, p. 275, p. 277, and SKS 13, p. 15n; PV, p. 9n, and, with respect to content, SKS 7, p. 73–74; CUP1, p. 73–74.

individual existence, and thus we have not yet said anything about the *specific* concern of Kierkegaard's thought. To introduce these two missing elements into the 'basic' double-movement of the indirect, I suggest distinguishing two essential aspects of the indirect method: the representational aspect (*Darstellungsaspekt*) and the appropriational aspect (*Aneignungsaspekt*).[16]

On the representational level, the working-against-itself of the indirect method appears to be a representation of the unrepresentable (*Darstellung des Undarstellbaren*); a structure we already find, within a very different framework, in romantic irony.[17] The indirect method *points*, as it were, to 'something' which withdraws from representation. If individual or singular existence is, as Kierkegaard has it, essentially *incommensurable* for thought, the only way of pointing to it is to *reflect* this incommensurability in the *form* of thought. And the indirect method does so precisely by marking or acknowledging that it is constantly missing or falling short of what it is aiming at. We might express this movement by saying that the indirect form of thought has to constantly 'revoke' or to 'undo' itself.[18] Apparently this is, again, the working-against-itself of the method, specified with respect to the *singularity* of existence.

On the appropriational level, we finally come closer to what seems to be semantically implied in the term 'indirect communication' itself. Kierkegaard does indeed consider the setting of a communicator who communicates to a receiver – albeit, I assume, *starting* with this relation would provide a far too

---

16 Cf. in more detail Schwab 2012, p. 20–30.

17 Cf. on Kierkegaard's relation to romantic irony and for further literature on the topic Schwab 2012, p. 484–501.

18 A prominent instance of this revocation as a working-against-oneself is to be found in the closing passages of the *Postscript*. After hundreds of pages, Climacus revokes the book, but not without calling to attention that writing a book and *then* revoking it is by no means the same as not writing a book at all (cf. SKS 7, p. 561–564; CUP1, p. 618–621). Furthermore, even the "First and Last Explanation" appended by Kierkegaard under his proper name *repeats* precisely this double movement, thereby explicitly referring to his works as a "doubly reflected communication": Kierkegaard formally acknowledges being the author of the pseudonymous works, but at the same time states that he himself has "no opinion about them except as a third party, no knowledge of their meaning except as a reader, not the remotest private relation to them, since it is impossible to have that to a doubly reflected communication", and, furthermore, he states that a "single word by me personally in my own name would be an arrogating self-forgetfulness that, regarded dialectically, would be guilty of having essentially annihilated the pseudonyms by this one word" (SKS 7, p. 570; CUP1, p. 626). Thus, in a double movement, the author's entrance is at the same time his exit. Cf. on these two passages, Schwab 2012, p. 142–146. Cf. on Kierkegaard's indirect communication *vis-à-vis* Wittgenstein, and, in one way or the other, relating to the revocation named, Conant 1989, 1993 and 1995.

narrow scope of what the indirect means in Kierkegaard.[19] Now in existential terms, for Kierkegaard, a certain problem is posed with any sort of communication: It includes the possibility of the receiver simply *following* the communicator by agreeing with him. For Kierkegaard, however, this would be fraudulent. The receiver, then, would not exist by himself and in his own right. Rather, he would come to be a derived existence, dependent on the communicator or the teacher. Thus, once more, the communicator has to 'work against himself'. He has to prevent the receiver from simply receiving a result by 'taking back' what he is saying. The result being omitted, the receiver is 'pushed' into some activity, into *Selbsttätigkeit* ('self-directed autonomy'). The communicator does not simply teach the receiver what he or she should do or how he or she should exist. On the contrary, the 'teacher' does not in fact teach anything at all, rather, he initiates *appropriation* (*Aneignung/Tilegnelse*). Hence, the working-against-itself is specified with respect to the self-interest of existence which cannot be delegated.

I.3 Praxis of Indirect Communication

Doubtlessly, this 'theoretical' presentation does not yet give a very clear and specific impression of how the indirect method works in Kierkegaard. At a closer look, this is by no means surprising: For if the indirect method is supposed to be a counter draft to the, allegedly, 'abstract' thought of the system, it cannot *itself* be sufficiently described in an abstract mode. Rather, it is one of the main features of this indirect method that it only truly works in a concrete *situation* – and thus we are referred to Kierkegaard's individual texts. I can only very briefly outline two exemplary settings of indirect communication here:

Kierkegaard's first pseudonymous book *Either/Or* presents, as is well known, two types of existence or life-views: the aesthetical and the ethical form.

---

19 More precisely, starting from the communicational (or appropriational) setting might easily lead to the understanding that the indirect method is exclusively valid or necessary with respect to *specific* situations or intentions. Yet I believe the more basic level of the representational aspect reveals that *any* form of thought addressing individual existence is *necessarily* indirect. This debate is complicated by the fact that certain accounts of the indirect method in Kierkegaard's works *themselves* reduce the indirect to a mere *means* of communication. The most prominent example is the retrospective account of the indirect as a 'deceiving into the truth' in Kierkegaard's *Point of View*. Cf. on this account, which I call the 'maieutico-teleological concept of indirect communication', Schwab 2012, p. 148–184. In the English literature, this matter is discussed with respect to the so called 'indispensability thesis'. Cf. esp. Aumann 2010.

This opposition itself is already quite characteristic of Kierkegaard's indirect method. In no case are we simply confronted with just *one* form of existence; rather, there is always a plurality of voices. In the Preface to *Either/Or*, the pseudonymous editor Victor Eremita points to a central feature of the book. He states that he himself considers it "a piece of good fortune" that the papers he is publishing do not simply come to a "conclusion"; for instance that the aestheticist might have convinced the ethicist to adopt his life-view or *vice versa* (SKS 2, p. 21; EO1, p. 13–14; cf. Schwab 2012, p. 502–506). Thus, the *result* is missing. Precisely this is one of the specific forms the indirect method takes, namely, the *aporia*. The reader is confronted with two (or more) opposing life-views and does not receive any direct hint as to which one he should choose: He is 'pushed' into appropriation, he has to by himself opt for one of them – or to dismiss them altogether and himself look for a further possibility of existence.

Another concrete form of the indirect method is the explicit *experiment*. This is, for instance, developed in the book *Repetition* which is in its subtitle called *A Venture in Experimenting Psychology*. This venture does not at all give a definition of what repetition *is*. Rather, it demonstrates several forms of repetition, without clearly or definitely stating which one of them is the 'true' form (cf. Schwab 2012, p. 512–527). Hence, on the very first page, this method is already made clear by the pseudonym Constantin Constantius:

> When I was occupied for a considerable time, at least on occasion, with the problem of repetition – whether or not it is possible, what meaning it contains, whether something gains or loses in being repeated – I suddenly had the thought: You can, after all, take a trip to Berlin; you have been there once before, and now you can prove to yourself whether a repetition is possible and what meaning it has. (SKS 4, p. 9; R, p. 131)

This passage – which even doubts the very possibility of the venture's own content, i.e. repetition – poses the *questions* the book will investigate, and it at the same time shows that an *answer* to these questions will not directly be given. In fact, the reader follows Constantin and the other pseudonym here – the 'young man' – through several passages of repetition without definite conclusion and is thus, once more, pushed into making his or her own choice.

Hence, to briefly conclude the Kierkegaard section: It should have become clear that Kierkegaard's method of indirect communication reflects and directly emerges from his critique of systematic thought insofar as the latter appears inappropriate with respect to concrete existence. From this perspective, it shows that there is a little bit more to 'indirect communication' than the word seems to imply: It does not merely mean saying 'something' in an indirect manner – which could *essentially* also be said directly.

II Nietzsche

II.1 Critique of the System and of Conceptual Thought

Turning to Nietzsche, I will try to show that, although the whole setting is different, a basic movement of thought is quite close to that unfolded in Kierkegaard. Yet unlike in Kierkegaard, the criticism of system and the meaning of experimental philosophy are, in Nietzsche, not related to just *one* central topic (i.e. concrete individual existence) but have a somewhat broader scope.

Beginning with the 'critique of the system', Nietzsche, especially in his published works, only in a few instances explicitly deploys such a critique. No doubt, this points to a 'historical' (*geschichtlich*) distance between the two thinkers: Whereas for Kierkegaard, the systematic philosophy of German Idealism still forms the 'natural' background to his thought (albeit as one to be criticised and 'overcome'), in Nietzsche's age, 'the system', in the strong sense of *singulare tantum*, is already taken to have been surrendered to the past.[20]

The most prominent passage displaying a 'critique of the system' in Nietzsche's works is the very short Maxim 26 in the *Twilight of the Idols*: "I distrust all systematisers and avoid them. The will to system is a lack of integrity" (TI Maxims 26, KSA 6, p. 63).[21] Accordingly, in the *Nachlass* and with respect to Schopenhauer, we find, in passing, polemics against the "absolute mendaciousness" and "counterfeit of a systematiser" (NL 1888, KSA 13, 15[10], p. 410). Yet only a few passages in Nietzsche's work serve to illuminate what this critique of the 'will to system' as a 'lack of integrity' amounts to, one of them being (albeit itself brief and with a rather narrow scope) *Daybreak* 318:

> *Beware of systematisers!* – Systematisers practice a kind of play-acting: in as much as they want to fill out a system and round off the horizon, they have to try to present their weaker qualities in the same style as their stronger – they try to impersonate whole and uniformly strong natures. (D 318, KSA 3, p. 228)[22]

---

[20] Other than one might expect, Nietzsche only very rarely discusses the issue of 'the system' in his critical debate with Schopenhauer, which often deals with related traditional terms from the 'metaphysical' tradition, e.g. morality or truth. Cf. only the two brief passages I mention in the following.
[21] There are several passages in the *Nachlass* which are forerunners to this maxim, some of them quite illuminating. Cf. NL 1887, KSA 12, 9[188], p. 450; NL 1887, KSA 12, 10[146], p. 538; NL 1887/88, KSA 13, 11[410], p. 189; NL 1888, KSA 13, 15[118], p. 477; NL 1888, KSA 13, 18[4], p. 53.
[22] "*Vorsicht vor den Systematikern!* – Es giebt eine Schauspielerei der Systematiker: indem sie ein System ausfüllen wollen und den Horizont darum rund machen, müssen sie versuchen, ihre

At a closer look, we can detect a *double* critique of the system here. On the one hand, Nietzsche seeks to uncover the originator's *personal* contribution to 'his' construction of the system. This aspect is already apparent from Nietzsche's rather frequent use of the word 'system*atiser*' as well as from the term '*will* to system'. Thus, the system as an assumedly 'objective' and 'rational' representation of (the essence of) what is, arouses suspicion of originating in rather 'subjective' and 'non-rational' elements, of being a 'translation' or '*sublimation*' of personal motives and drives.[23] In the following, I will refer to this aspect as the 'sublimation aspect'.

On the other hand, if we look at *what* the systematiser is said to be doing, we see that 'the system' in a certain sense points to a *reduction* of what there is, for the systematiser 'rounds off the horizon' to construct a system. This 'reduction aspect' is displayed more clearly in further passages from the *Nachlass*, perhaps most thoroughly in an entry from 1885 which at the same time covers the 'sublimation aspect':

> There are schematic minds, who hold a complex of thought to be *truer* if it can be inscribed into schemata or tables of categories drawn up beforehand. The self-deceptions in this field are countless: almost all great 'systems' are among them. The *fundamental prejudice* is, though, that it is inherent to the *true being* of things to be ordered, easy to survey, systematic; conversely, that disorder, chaos, the unpredictable can only make its appearance in a world that is false or incompletely known – in short, that it is an error – : – which is a moral prejudice, drawn from the fact that the truthful, reliable human being is a man of order, of maxims, and all in all tends to be something predictable and pedantic. And yet it cannot be demonstrated at all that the in-themselves of things follows this recipe for the model civil servant. (NL 1885, KSA 11, 40[9], p. 632)[24]

---

schwächeren Eigenschaften im Stile ihrer stärkeren auftreten zu lassen, – sie wollen vollständige und einartig starke Naturen darstellen."

23 This aspect is indicated in several other passages on the matter, mainly from the *Nachlass*. Most of these, too, have not been translated to date. Cf. esp. HH I 110, KSA 2, p. 110–111; NL 1882, KSA 10, 3[1], p. 62; NL 1883, KSA 10, 7[62], p. 262; NL 1884, KSA 11, 25[17], p. 16. Cf. also the related discussion of the 'construction of the system' in BGE 20, KSA 5, p. 34–35.

24 "Es giebt schematische Köpfe, solche, welche einen Gedankencomplex dann für *wahrer* halten, wenn er sich in vorher entworfene Schemata oder Kategorien-Tafeln einzeichnen läßt. Der Selbst-Täuschungen auf diesem Gebiete giebt es unzählige: fast alle großen 'Systeme' gehören hierhin. Das *Grundvorurtheil* ist aber: daß die Ordnung, Übersichtlichkeit, das Systematische dem *wahren Sein* der Dinge anhaften müsse, umgekehrt die Unordnung, das Chaotische, Unberechenbare nur in einer falschen oder unvollständig erkannten Welt zum Vorscheine komme – kurz ein Irrthum sei –: – was ein moralisches Vorurtheil ist, entnommen aus der Thatsache, daß der wahrhaftige zutrauenswürdige Mensch ein Mann der Ordnung, der Maximen, und im Ganzen etwas Berechenbares und Pedantisches zu sein pflegt. Nun ist es aber ganz unbeweisbar, daß das Ansich der Dinge nach diesem Recepte eines Muster-Beamten sich verhält."

Thus, the system is suspected of being a 'schematic' reduction or simplification and, at the same time, a distortion of the chaotic, unpredictable and polymorphic actuality or 'world'. Furthermore, with respect to the 'sublimation aspect', the systematiser's endeavour by no means arises from a pure 'will to truth'. Rather, it depends on a certain prejudice or 'interest' which itself remains unquestioned.[25]

The aspect of reduction becomes again clearer if we compare these rather brief and scattered statements on 'the system' to related topics more extensively dealt with by Nietzsche, most of all, the critique of conceptual thought. Already in *On Truth and Lie in an Extra-Moral Sense* (1873), Nietzsche describes the origin of concepts in mainly two respects: firstly, as a generalisation of individual experiences, and secondly, as a reduction of the unstable multiplicity or polymorphism (*Vielgestaltigkeit*) of reality:

> Every word immediately becomes a concept, inasmuch as it is not intended to serve as a reminder of the unique and wholly individualised original experience to which it owes its birth, but must at the same time fit innumerable, more or less similar cases – which means, strictly speaking, never equal – in other words, a lot of unequal cases. Every concept originates through our equating what is unequal. (TL 1, KSA 1, p. 879–880)[26]

Read in this light, it becomes apparent that Nietzsche's critique of the system relates to some aspects unfolded in Kierkegaard. First of all, Nietzsche's suspicion that system and concept 'schematically' reduce and distort individuality and becoming by means of generalisation relates to Kierkegaard's idea that, within a system, the individual's existential actuality is necessarily transformed into something universal, and thus reduced and missed. Furthermore, with respect to what I have called the 'sublimation aspect' in Nietzsche's critique of

---

[25] The same double 'uncovering' of reduction and sublimation is expressed in a short passage from 1887: "Logicising, rationalising, systematising as expedients of life./ Man projects his drive to truth, his 'goal' in a certain sense, outside himself as a world that has being, as a metaphysical world, as a 'thing-in-itself', as a world already in existence" (NL 1887, KSA 12, 9[91], p. 385). Cf. also the following passages, most of them not translated yet: NL 1884, KSA 11, 25[17], p. 16; NL 1884, KSA 11, 25[135], p. 49; NL 1884, KSA 11, 25[449], p. 132–133; NL 1886, KSA 12, 5[17], p. 191; NL 1887, KSA 12, 9[181], p. 445; NL 1887/88, KSA 13, 11[99], p. 46–47. Cf. also the related early quotation from Bagehot in *Schopenhauer as Educator* (SE 8, KSA 1, p. 420) and the corresponding note in NL 1873, KSA 7, 29[197], p. 710.

[26] "[J]edes Wort wird sofort dadurch Begriff, dass es eben nicht für das einmalige ganz und gar individualisirte Urerlebniss, dem es sein Entstehen verdankt, etwa als Erinnerung dienen soll, sondern zugleich für zahllose, mehr oder weniger ähnliche, d.h. streng genommen niemals gleiche, also auf lauter ungleiche Fälle passen muss. Jeder Begriff entsteht durch Gleichsetzen des Nicht-Gleichen."

the system, we also discover parallels to Kierkegaard: Both trace the system back to the thinker *who* thinks or 'constructs' the system; and both, albeit differently, criticise a certain 'forgetfulness' or 'self-deception' of this thinker who mistakes, as it were, himself for the universal.

Yet we also see quite significant differences in approach. The somewhat 'epistemological' aspect in Nietzsche's enterprise to 'reconstruct the construction', so to speak, of a stable reality is foreign to Kierkegaard's existential impetus. Accordingly, the 'multiplicity' assumedly reduced by conceptual and systematic thought has a far more narrow scope in Kierkegaard, referring exclusively to the *alterity* of individual existence, that is, to the individual's 'mineness' (*Jemeinigkeit*). Even more important is the *methodological* difference implied in this. Nietzsche most of all seeks to uncover the *origin* of conceptual and systematic thought. He does not simply *state* the incommensurability of the individual and the universal; rather, he *reconstructs* the process in which the distortion of singularity and polymorphism takes place. This approach of reconstruction in Nietzsche, I assume, points to his notion of experimental philosophy.

II.2 Critical Experimental Philosophy

In the following, I will try to show that there are in fact two movements of experimental philosophy in Nietzsche, a *critical* experimental philosophy and an '*affirmative*' experimental philosophy.[27]

The first and *critical* form of experimental philosophy relates quite directly to the critique of the system. Yet other than in Kierkegaard, it does not *emerge* from this critique. Rather, at closer examination, the critique of the system proves to be more of an *instance* of critical experimental philosophy and is itself essentially determined by it. The basic movement of this critical experimental philosophy has already been indicated above: Nietzsche criticises traditional forms of thought by reconstructing the process and the conditions of their formation.[28] This enterprise is, at least in the published writings, in the first instance undertaken in Nietzsche's 'middle period', starting with *Human, All Too Human*. The decisive methodological determination of the experimental critique

---

[27] Cf. the related distinction between 'critical' and 'visionary' experimental philosophy in Gerhardt 1988, esp. p. 173–174. On Nietzsche's experimental philosophy, cf. also Kaulbach 1980.
[28] Cf. on the following in some more detail Schwab 2011, p. 606–610 (regarding the 'tragic of cognition') and Schwab 2012, p. 102–106 (regarding the critique of morals).

(which I have hitherto used without further explication) is to be found in the later Preface to this book where Nietzsche describes his works as "a schooling in suspicion [*Schule des Verdachts*]" (HH I Preface 1, KSA 2, p. 13). This concept of suspicion has been made popular by Ricœur,[29] yet I think a close look at Nietzsche is necessary in this respect. For the very term 'suspicion' points to a *permanent* and *irresolvable* tentativeness and to the essentially *provisional* character of Nietzsche's critique. Ultimately, Nietzsche does not work with the stable opposition of *surface* and *ground*, or that of mere appearance and truth.[30] Rather, his critique takes the form of an *attempt* or a *venture*, it is a '*tempting*' (*versucherisch*) form of philosophy. Not at all by coincidence, the first aphorism within this project – that is, the first aphorism in *Human, All Too Human* – does not begin with a statement, but with a *question*.[31] In this aphorism, entitled "Chemistry of concepts and sensations" (*Chemie der Begriffe und Empfindungen*), Nietzsche asks:

> [H]ow can something originate in its opposite, for example rationality in irrationality, the sentient in the dead, logic in unlogic, disinterested contemplation in covetous desire, living for others in egoism, truth in error? (HH I 1, KSA 2, p. 23)[32]

Nietzsche's experimental operation from *Human, All Too Human* consists in *tentatively* turning around or reversing presumably qualitative differences and hierarchies, thus searching for the hidden trace which binds the allegedly 'higher' to the 'lower'. In this respect, Nietzsche's 'middle period' is already *genealogy*. The tentative, experimental character of this reversal becomes quite clear in Nietzsche's description of the 'free spirit': Nietzsche says that he "turns round whatever he finds veiled and through some sense of shame or other spared and pampered: He *puts to the test* what these things look like *when* they are reversed" (HH I Preface 3, KSA 2, p. 17; my emphasis). This line of experimental critique is not limited to the 'middle period'; rather, it persists until his late works: *Beyond Good and Evil* reintroduces the initial question quoted above from *Human, All Too Human* in aphorism 2 (cf. BGE 2, KSA 5, p. 16) and in this

---

29 Cf. the passage "Interpretation as Exercise of Suspicion" in Ricœur 1970, p. 32–36.
30 Which seems to be the way Ricœur understands Nietzsche, comparing him to Marx and Freud. Cf. Ricœur 1970, p. 33–34.
31 On the importance of the question marks in Nietzsche and on the problem inherent in some commentators simply stripping them off of Nietzsche's sentences, cf. the valuable comments in Conant 2005, p. 5–7.
32 "[W]ie kann Etwas aus seinem Gegensatz entstehen, zum Beispiel Vernünftiges aus Vernunftlosem, Empfindendes aus Todtem, Logik aus Unlogik, interesseloses Anschauen aus begehrlichem Wollen, Leben für Andere aus Egoismus, Wahrheit aus Irrthümern?"

work Nietzsche describes his method as a series of "dangerous Perhapses" (BGE 2, KSA 5, p. 17).

That this mode of critique is essentially *experimental* comes to light in Nietzsche's critique of morality. For Nietzsche does not simply *subvert* traditional morality. Rather, he underlines his critical interpretation *as* an interpretation. Ultimately, Nietzsche will always, in a *cyclical* movement, *cast back* suspicion upon his own mode of critique. This self-referential movement is, for instance, quite explicitly employed in *The Gay Science* 344, entitled "How we, too, are still pious" (*Inwiefern auch wir noch fromm sind*):

> But you will have gathered what I am driving at, namely, that it is still a *metaphysical faith* upon which our faith in science rests – that even we seekers after knowledge today, we godless anti-metaphysicians still take our fire, too, from the flame lit by a faith that is thousands of years old, that Christian faith which was also the faith of Plato, that God is the truth, that truth is divine ... (GS 344, KSA 3, p. 577)[33]

A similar movement is to be found in sections 24–27 from the third essay of the *Genealogy of Morality*. Here, Nietzsche unveils that his critique of the ascetic ideal is *itself* derived from and dependent on this very ideal (cf. GM III 24–27, KSA 5, p. 398–411; cf. also on this Stegmaier 1994, p. 194–206). I suggest reading these passages not in the first place as containing Nietzsche's 'positive morality of the critique of morality' but, rather, as the necessary 'working-against-itself' of the experimental philosophy, in this case, of the experimental critique. For indeed, Nietzsche cannot criticise the 'dogmatism' of traditional philosophy and at the same time *himself* employ a 'dogmatic' critique. Precisely by marking the perspective of the critique *as* a *perspective* – and by putting *this* perspective, too, into perspective[34] – Nietzsche's critique is experimental philosophy.

Looking back at the critique of the system, it becomes apparent that this critique as well is not a dogmatic subversion. For again, Nietzsche cannot, without falling short of the standard of his own critique, *positively* state or 'prove' that reality is 'in truth' unstable and schematically distorted by systematic thought. Rather, this critique, too, has to be formulated as a question: '*What if* a systematic and conceptual representation of reality amounts to its distortion?'

---

[33] "Doch man wird es begriffen haben, worauf ich hinaus will, nämlich dass es immer noch ein *metaphysischer Glaube* ist, auf dem unser Glaube an die Wissenschaft ruht, – dass auch wir Erkennenden von heute, wir Gottlosen und Antimetaphysiker, auch *unser* Feuer noch von dem Brande nehmen, den ein Jahrtausende alter Glaube entzündet hat, jener Christen-Glaube, der auch der Glaube Plato's war, dass Gott die Wahrheit ist, dass die Wahrheit göttlich ist ..."
[34] For a thorough account and discussion of 'perspectivism' in Nietzsche, also with respect to the development of this 'concept' throughout Nietzsche's work, cf. Conant 2005 and 2006.

II.3 Affirmative Experimental Philosophy and Nihilism

To now finally outline what one might call Nietzsche's 'affirmative experimental philosophy' – and, at the same time, his 'answer' to the question just posed, although by no means a *definite* answer – I will start from the final aphorism 34 of the first section of *Human, All Too Human*, entitled "In mitigation" (cf. HH I 34, KSA 2, p. 53–55). In aphorism 32, Nietzsche had developed the idea that all of our judgments and evaluations are based on incomplete knowledge and are, thus, necessarily unjust – in a way pointedly presenting the 'critical' project of his 'middle philosophy'. Nietzsche goes on to say: "We are from the very beginning illogical and thus unjust beings *and can recognise this*: this is one of the greatest and most irresolvable discords of existence" (HH I 32, KSA 2, p. 52). Based on this discord, Nietzsche in the final aphorism 34 then asks the question: "But will our philosophy not thus become a tragedy? [...] A question seems to lie heavily on our tongue and yet refuses to be uttered: whether one *could* consciously reside in untruth?" (HH I 34, KSA 2, p. 53–54). Although Nietzsche here (quite characteristic of the 'middle period') *denies* the tragic option in favour of a "free, fearless hovering over men, customs, laws and traditional evaluations of things" (HH I 34, KSA 2, p. 55), this option will return affirmatively in the later philosophy – and, thereby, as affirmative experimental philosophy.

This late experimental philosophy is, I assume, essentially linked to Nietzsche's project of the 'overcoming of nihilism', and more precisely, the *tragic* overcoming of nihilism. As to 'nihilism' itself, the term has, as virtually any central concept in Nietzsche, various meanings.[35] In the late writings, especially those from 1888, nihilism is basically identified with decadence, for instance with Christianity, Buddhism or Schopenhauer's philosophy. Here, the term refers to values which are essentially hostile to life (*lebensfeindlich*).[36] In the drafts to the first book of the *Will to Power* from summer 1886, however, Nietzsche develops a second and more complex notion of nihilism. In these entries and in the so called *Lenzer Heide Fragment* from spring 1887,[37] he sketches a history of European nihilism; and within this history, nihilism does

---

35 Cf. for a typology of Nietzsche's different uses of the term Kuhn 1992, esp. p. 8–9 and p. 237–255. Cf. on the following account of nihilism in more detail Schwab 2011, p. 596–605.
36 Cf. in the published (or finished) works GM II 21, KSA 5, p. 331; TI Skirmishes 21, KSA 6, p. 125; A 6, KSA 6, p. 172; A 20, KSA 6, p. 186; A 58, KSA 6, p. 247; EH BT 1, KSA 6, p. 310. Cf. on this Müller-Lauter 2000, esp. p. 289.
37 Cf. NL 1886/87, KSA 12, 5[71], p. 211–217. Cf. also NL, 1887/88, KSA 13, 11[99], p. 46–49. Cf. on this also Heidegger GA 6.1, p. 35–36, p. 45–77.

not simply *equal* Christianity as such but is rather understood to be a *consequence* of the devaluation of 'traditional' values. 'Nihilism' here refers to a *vacuum* of values in face of Christianity's decline.[38]

A third and highly interesting notion of nihilism which is sketched only in a few short passages will serve to illuminate the 'affirmative experimental philosophy'. In these entries, Nietzsche in a certain sense identifies his *own* position, as developed in the 'middle period', with nihilism. A passage from autumn 1887 lists several forms of nihilism (in the first instance, an active and a passive form), and here Nietzsche writes: "[T]hat there is no truth, that there is no absolute nature of things, no 'thing in itself'. This is itself a nihilism – even the most extreme one" (NL 1887, KSA 12, 9[35], p. 351).[39] Apparently, this is not something Nietzsche criticises; rather, it is a somewhat radicalised version of his very own position as we have seen in the 'middle period'. In fact, Nietzsche himself notes in one of the subsequent entries: "It is only late that one musters the courage for what one really knows. That I have hitherto, at the very root, been a nihilist [*von Grund aus bisher Nihilist gewesen bin*], I have admitted to myself only recently" (NL 1887, KSA 12, 9[123], p. 407). A further entry develops this new notion of the 'most extreme nihilism' in more detail:

> The most extreme form of nihilism would be that *every* belief, every considering-something-true, is necessarily false *because there simply is no* **true world**. Thus: a *perspectival appearance* [Schein] whose origin lies in us [...].
>
> That the **measure of strength** is given by the extent to which we can admit the merely *apparent character* [Scheinbarkeit], the necessity of lies, to ourselves without perishing.
>
> *To this extent, nihilism, as the* **denial** *of a truthful world, of a being, might be a divine way of thinking:* – – – (NL 1887, KSA 12, 9[41], p. 354)[40]

This 'most extreme form of nihilism' as a 'divine way of thinking', then, has to be *affirmed*. Read in this light, it shows that the 'overcoming of nihilism' in

---

[38] Cf. on this esp. NL 1885/86, KSA 12, 2[100], p. 109–110 and the three related entries NL 1885/86, KSA 12, 2[118], p. 120; NL 1885/86, KSA 12, 2[127], p. 125–126; NL 1885/86, KSA 12, 2[131], p. 129.
[39] Cf. on this and the following Volkmann-Schluck 1991, p. 194–203.
[40] "Die extremste Form des Nihilism wäre: daß *jeder* Glaube, jedes Für-wahr-halten nothwendig falsch ist: *weil es eine* **wahre Welt** *gar nicht giebt*. Also: ein *perspektivischer Schein*, dessen Herkunft in uns liegt [...]/ – daß es das **Maaß der Kraft** ist, wie sehr wir uns die *Scheinbarkeit*, die Nothwendigkeit der Lüge eingestehn können, ohne zu Grunde zu gehn./ *Insofern könnte Nihilism, als* **Leugnung** *einer wahrhaften* Welt, eines *Seins, eine göttliche Denkweise sein*: – – – ". Cf. also NL 1887, KSA 12, 9[60], p. 368; NL 1887, KSA 12, 10[22], p. 468; NL 1887, KSA 12, 10[192], p. 571.

Nietzsche by no means implies simply 'leaving behind' nihilism altogether, but instead it is to be understood as the '*self*-overcoming of nihilism' – and indeed we find this formula in the late *Nachlass*.[41] This self-overcoming, then, is at the same time essentially *tragic* and essentially *experimental*.[42] For the questions quoted above from *Human, All Too Human* – to what extent we can 'consciously reside in untruth', and whether 'philosophy will become a tragedy' – recur, but in the late work they are posed as a task and a challenge for tragic affirmation. Nihilism in the second meaning of a 'devaluation' of traditional values, resulting in a vacuum of values, apparently asks for the 'positing' of *new* values to fill this vacuum. This devaluation, however, had led Nietzsche, in his critical experimental philosophy, to the 'most extreme form of nihilism', the suspicion that there is no 'true world' which we could refer to in positing values. Thus, we are forced to posit values *in the face of* our knowledge that these are never simply and eternally 'true', but rather essentially rely on *interpretations* and are thereby necessarily unjust and provisional. We face the *impossibility* and at the same time *necessity* of positing values, a tragic collision which will never come to a final reconciliation. Affirming the 'most extreme nihilism', therefore, implies that the values we have to posit are *themselves* affected by *annihilation*. The tragic form of affirmation includes and affirms the possibility that values we posit are destroyed again; in fact, the tragic movement *is* the repeated creation and destruction of values, affirmed as inevitable. To this extent, the tragic positing of values is irreconcilably procedural and provisional – and in *this* sense 'experimental'.

Apparently, Nietzsche's 'critical' and his 'affirmative' experimental philosophy are closely intertwined: The experimental critique of traditional values leads to the 'hypothesis' of the 'most extreme form of nihilism', the suspicion that there is no 'true world' – and this, then, posits the task for an affirmation necessarily both tragic and experimental.

Finally, this constellation of nihilism, affirmation and experiment is also present in the only passage in which Nietzsche himself uses the term 'experimental philosophy':

---

41 Cf. esp. NL 1887, KSA 12, 9[127], p. 411; NL 1888, KSA 13, 13[4], p. 215, also NL 1887, KSA 12, 9[164], p. 432.
42 Cf. on this in more detail Schwab 2011, esp. p. 611–621. The reconstruction of the 'late' concept of the tragic in Nietzsche is complicated by two peculiarities: Firstly, Nietzsche only develops the idea in scattered and comparably few passages; secondly, he does so through a re-evaluation of his early *The Birth of the Tragedy*, thereby constantly shifting between re-interpretation, self-critique and development of a new concept.

> Philosophy, as I have hitherto understood and lived it, is a voluntary quest for even the most detested and notorious sides of existence. From the long experience I gained from such a wandering through ice and wilderness, I learned to view differently all that had hitherto philosophised: the *hidden* history of philosophy, the psychology of its great names, came to light for me. "How much truth can a spirit *endure*, how much truth does a spirit *dare*?" – this became for me the real standard of value. Error is *cowardice* ... every achievement of knowledge *follows* from courage, of severity toward oneself, from cleanliness toward oneself ... Such an experimental philosophy as I live anticipates experimentally even the possibilities of the most fundamental nihilism; but this does not mean that it must halt at a negation, a No, a will to negation. (NL 1888, KSA 13, 16[32], p. 492)[43]

★★★

Some very brief concluding remarks. The last sketch of the 'tragic movement' in Nietzsche should have indicated that 'experimental philosophy' by no means refers to mere playfulness. This is apparently true for Kierkegaard, too, as his indirect communication is, at the same time, 'seriousness': the 'ethical' attempt of philosophically doing justice to the conceptually unseizable singularity of individual existence.

There is no doubt that the purposes, questions, and, most of all, the *answers* in Nietzsche's and Kierkegaard's philosophies differ significantly: Nietzsche's tragic flux of creation and annihilation of values would, in Kierkegaard's view, amount to anachronistic paganism and a vital version of 'in despair willing to be oneself'. Conversely, Nietzsche would have refused Kierkegaard's hamartiological and negativistic analyses of 'becoming a self' through anxiety and despair as a symptom of late Christian decadence. However, it should have become

---

43 "Philosophie, wie ich sie bisher verstanden und gelebt habe, ist das freiwillige Aufsuchen auch der verwünschten und verruchten Seiten des Daseins. Aus der langen Erfahrung, welche mir eine solche Wanderung durch Eis und Wüste gab, lernte ich Alles, was bisher philosophirt hat, anders ansehn: – die *verborgene* Geschichte der Philosophie, die Psychologie ihrer großen Namen kam für mich ans Licht. 'Wie viel Wahrheit *erträgt*, wie viel Wahrheit *wagt* ein Geist?' – dies wurde für mich der eigentliche Werthmesser. Der Irrthum ist eine *Feigheit* ... jede Errungenschaft der Erkenntniß *folgt* aus dem Muth, aus der Härte gegen sich, aus der Sauberkeit gegen sich ... Eine solche Experimental-Philosophie, wie ich sie lebe, nimmt versuchsweise selbst die Möglichkeiten des grundsätzlichen Nihilismus vorweg: ohne daß damit gesagt wäre, daß sie bei einem Nein, bei einer Negation, bei einem Willen zum Nein stehen bliebe." For further relevant passages using the term 'experiment' cf. in the published works D 453, KSA 3, p. 274; D 501, KSA 3, p. 294; GS 7, KSA 3, p. 379–380; GS 51, KSA 3, p. 415–416; GS 319, KSA 3, p. 551; GS 324, KSA 3, p. 552; BGE 210, KSA 5, p. 142; GM III 9, KSA 5, p. 357. Cf. the mostly not yet translated passages in the *Nachlass* NL 1880, KSA 9, 3[6], p. 48; NL 1880, KSA 9, 6[356], p. 287; NL 1880, KSA 9, 6[442], p. 313; NL 1883, KSA 10, 7[261], p. 321; NL 1883, KSA 10, 16[56], p. 518; NL 1885, KSA 11, 35[43], p. 529–530; NL 1888, KSA 13, 24[1], p. 618.

clear that Kierkegaard and Nietzsche share a fundamental methodological approach: Both reject traditional ways of thinking and design a form of philosophy which is affirmatively experimental, inconclusive and which does not bring becoming to a final close. By contrast, they affirm a mode of thought which constantly reflects its own perspectival character and irresolvable tentativeness.

Naturally, this affinity with respect to philosophical form has correlations with respect to content. Given their strong respective notion of becoming, it is no coincidence that both Kierkegaard and Nietzsche reach out for concepts through which becoming does not merely result in disintegration or dissolution. Thereby, both develop *cyclical* determinations of thought: Nietzsche's 'eternal recurrence' in a certain sense answers to Kierkegaard's 'repetition'.[44] Accordingly, on an existential level, both share a paradoxical formula which encloses and binds together the tension of becoming and coherence: For both, existing is essentially the task *to become what one is*.[45]

References

Adler, Adolph Peter (1842): *Populaire Foredrag over Hegels objective Logik*. Copenhagen: C.A. Reitzel.
Aumann, Antony (2010): "Kierkegaard on Indirect Communication, the Crowd, and a Monstrous Illusion". In: Robert L. Perkins (Ed.): *The Point of View. International Kierkegaard Commentary*. Vol. 22. Macon: Mercer University Press, p. 295–324.
Brandes, Georg (1972): *Friedrich Nietzsche*. Translated by Arthur G. Chater. New York: Haskell House.
Brobjer, Thomas H. (2003): "Nietzsche's Knowledge of Kierkegaard". In: *Journal of the History of Philosophy* 41, p. 251–263.
Conant, James (1989): "Must We Show What We Cannot Say?". In: Richard Fleming/Michael Payne (Eds.): *The Senses of Stanley Cavell*. Lewisburg: Bucknell University Press, p. 242–283.
Conant, James (1993): "Kierkegaard, Wittgenstein and Nonsense". In: Ted Cohen/Paul Guyer/Hilary Putnam (Eds.): *Pursuits of Reason. Essays in Honor of Stanley Cavell*. Lubbock: Texas Tech University Press, p. 195–224.
Conant, James (1995): "Putting Two and Two Together: Kierkegaard, Wittgenstein, and the Point of View for Their Work as Authors". In: Timothy Tessin/Mario von der Ruhr (Eds.): *Philosophy and the Grammar of Religious Belief*. London: St. Martin's Press, p. 248–331.

---

44 Cf. on this Schwab 2013, p. 109–111. Cf. also Deleuze 2004, p. 6–13 and Kellenberger 1997.
45 In Kierkegaard, cf. e.g. the determination of the ethical in *Either/Or II*: The "ethical [in a person, PS] is that by which he becomes what he becomes" (SKS 3, p. 173–174; EO2, p. 178; cf. also SKS 3, p. 241–242; EO2, p. 253–254). In Nietzsche, the line "How One Becomes What One Is" is the subtitle to *Ecce Homo*.

Conant, James (2005): "The Dialectic of Perspectivism, I". In: *SATS – Nordic Journal of Philosophy* 6 (2), p. 5–50.
Conant, James (2006): "The Dialectic of Perspectivism, II". In: *SATS – Nordic Journal of Philosophy* 7 (1), p. 6–57.
Deleuze, Gilles (2004): *Difference and Repetition*. Translated by Paul Patton. London and New York: Continuum Press [French edition: PUF 1968].
Gerhardt, Volker (1988): "'Experimental-Philosophie'. Versuch einer Rekonstruktion". In: Volker Gerhardt: *Pathos und Distanz. Studien zur Philosophie Friedrich Nietzsches*. Stuttgart: Reclam, p. 163–187.
Gerhardt, Volker (2006): *Friedrich Nietzsche*. 4th edition. Munich: Beck.
Grau, Gerd-Günther (1997): *Vernunft, Wahrheit, Glaube. Neue Studien zu Nietzsche und Kierkegaard*. Würzburg: Königshausen und Neumann.
Hannay, Alastair (2003): "Nietzsche/Kierkegaard: Prospects for Dialogue?". In: Alastair Hannay: *Kierkegaard and Philosophy. Selected Essays*. London and New York: Routledge, p. 207–217.
Hühn, Lore (2009): *Kierkegaard und der Deutsche Idealismus. Konstellationen des Übergangs*. Tübingen: Mohr Siebeck.
Hühn, Lore/Schwab, Philipp (2013): "Kierkegaard and German Idealism". In: John Lippitt/ George Pattison (Eds.): *The Oxford Handbook of Kierkegaard*. Oxford: Oxford University Press, p. 62–93.
Hyde, John Keith (2010): *Concepts of Power in Kierkegaard and Nietzsche*. Farnham and Burlington: Ashgate.
Jaspers, Karl (1955): *Reason and Existence. Five lectures*. Translated with an introduction by William Earle. New York: The Noonday Press [first edition: Wolters 1935].
Kaulbach, Friedrich (1980): *Nietzsches Idee einer Experimentalphilosophie*. Cologne and Vienna: Böhlau.
Kellenberger, James (1997): *Kierkegaard and Nietzsche. Faith and Eternal Acceptance*. Basingstoke and London: Macmillan.
Kleinert, Markus (2013): "Kierkegaard and Nietzsche". In: John Lippitt/George Pattison (Eds.): *The Oxford Handbook of Kierkegaard*. Oxford: Oxford University Press, p. 402–420.
Kuhn, Elisabeth (1992): *Friedrich Nietzsches Philosophie des europäischen Nihilismus*. Berlin and New York: De Gruyter.
Lippitt, John (2000): "Nietzsche, Kierkegaard and the Narratives of Faith". In: John Lippitt/Jim Urpeth (Eds.): *Nietzsche and the Divine*. Manchester: Clinamen Press, p. 77–95.
Longo, Giulia (2007): *Kierkegaard, Nietzsche: Eternità dell'istante, istantaneità dell'eterno*. Milan: Mimesis Edizioni.
Löwith, Karl (1933): *Kierkegaard und Nietzsche oder philosophische und theologische Überwindung des Nihilismus*. Frankfurt a.M.: Klostermann.
Löwith, Karl (1991): *From Hegel to Nietzsche. The Revolution in Nineteenth Century Thought*. Translated by David E. Green. New York: Columbia University Press.
McKinnon, Alastair (1993): "Kierkegaard and the 'Leap of Faith'". In: *Kierkegaardiana* 16, p. 107–125.
Miles, Thomas P. (2007): "Kierkegaard and Nietzsche Reconsidered". In: *Kierkegaard Studies Yearbook*, p. 441–469.
Miles, Thomas P. (2011): "Kierkegaard and Nietzsche: Rival Visions of the Best Way of Life". In: Jon Stewart (Ed.): *Kierkegaard and Existentialism. Kierkegaard Research: Sources, Reception and Resources*. Vol. 9. Farnham and Burlington: Ashgate, p. 263–298.

Miles, Thomas P. (2013): *Kierkegaard and Nietzsche on the Best Way of Life. A New Method of Ethics*. New York: Palgrave Macmillan.
Müller-Lauter, Wolfgang (2000): "Über den Nihilismus und die Möglichkeit seiner Überwindung". In: Wolfgang Müller-Lauter: *Heidegger und Nietzsche. Nietzsche-Interpretationen III*. Berlin and New York: De Gruyter, p. 267–299.
Quist, Wenche Marit (2005): "Nietzsche and Kierkegaard. Tracing Common Themes". In: *Nietzsche-Studien* 34, p. 474–485.
Ricœur, Paul (1970): *Freud and Philosophy. An Essay on Interpretation*. Translated by Denis Savage. New Haven: Yale University Press [French edition: Seuil 1965].
Schwab, Philipp (2011): "Die tragische Überwindung des Nihilismus. Nietzsches 'Philosophie des Tragischen' von der *Geburt der Tragödie* bis zum Spätwerk". In: Lore Hühn/Philipp Schwab (Eds.): *Die Philosophie des Tragischen. Schopenhauer – Schelling – Nietzsche*. Berlin and Boston: De Gruyter, p. 575–621.
Schwab, Philipp (2012): *Der Rückstoß der Methode. Kierkegaard und die indirekte Mitteilung*. Berlin and Boston: De Gruyter.
Schwab, Philipp (2013): "Ethik und Ethikkritik. Philosophie der Existenz bei Kierkegaard und Nietzsche". In: Hans Feger/Manuela Hackel (Eds.): *Existenzphilosophie und Ethik*. Berlin and Boston: De Gruyter, p. 89–111.
Schwab, Philipp (2014): "'Das Reich der Wirklichkeit ist nicht vollendet'. Kierkegaard als Hörer Schellings und Kritiker Hegels". In: Axel Hutter/Anders Moe Rasmussen (Eds.): *Kierkegaard im Kontext des deutschen Idealismus*. Berlin and Boston: De Gruyter, p. 77–104.
Sooväli, Jaanus (2009): "Was ist das souveräne Individuum? Neuerscheinungen zu Nietzsche und Kierkegaard". In: *Nietzsche-Studien* 38, p. 477–485.
Stegmaier, Werner (1994): *Nietzsches "Genealogie der Moral"*. Darmstadt: Wissenschaftliche Buchgesellschaft.
Stewart, Jon (2003): *Kierkegaard's Relations to Hegel Reconsidered*. Cambridge: Cambridge University Press.
Volkmann-Schluck, Karl-Heinz (1991): *Die Philosophie Nietzsches. Der Untergang der abendländischen Metaphysik*. Würzburg: Königshausen und Neumann.

Elisabete M. de Sousa
Musical Controversies in Nietzsche and Kierkegaard

Søren A. Kierkegaard's and Friedrich Nietzsche's writings on music share the nature and fate of other texts they wrote, namely that the similarities can be striking, but the differences seem insurmountable. However, it is worth reflecting on a number of similarities and differences; in my view this will help us, not only to recognise a pattern of musical criticism that is prevalent in the nineteenth century – ever since the appearance in 1833 of *Ein Werk II*, the inaugural musical review by Robert Schumann (1811–1856) –, but it will also give us a new insight into some aspects of Kierkegaard's thought that seems to be present also in Nietzsche. I will begin by outlining the issues at stake in order to give an account of the knowledge Nietzsche might have had of Kierkegaard and, most particularly, of the chapter on the musical erotic in *Either/Or I* (1843). For this purpose I will give special attention to the intermediary role played by the Danish critic Georg Brandes. In the second part, I will give an overview of Kierkegaard's and Nietzsche's writings on music, highlighting the points of contact and of disagreement, and finally I will draw some conclusions heading towards future research.

One of the most striking similarities in the musical writings of these two philosophers is the fact that none of their elaborations on music can be pondered without taking into consideration the decisive factor that forms the backbone of their texts: at the heart of their musical writings lies the admiration for a composer whose work determines whatever they have to say about music in general or about a musical form or genre – Wolfgang Amadeus Mozart (1756–1791) in the case of Kierkegaard, and Richard Wagner (1813–1870) in the case of Nietzsche. And even when, in the case of Nietzsche, awe turns into vituperation against the fallen idol, Georges Bizet (1838–1875) becomes the new object of respectful appreciation and is submitted to the same model of criticism. In addition, both philosophers take as their point of departure for the presentation of their concepts and theories about drama (and naturally about the role of music in drama, and music as art in itself) not a description of music as art, or of a definite musical form or genre, but (a) specific musical composition(s): Mozart's *Don Giovanni* in the case of Kierkegaard, and in the case of Nietzsche, Wagner's *The Ring of the Nibelung* (as well as *Tristan and Isolde* and *Parsifal*) and also later, Bizet's *Carmen*. In other words, their philosophies of music as a medium and as a form of art are always produced under the perspective of a certain composer and, as a rule, the conceptualisation therein involved applies primarily to the production of that composer alone. This analogous pattern in the presentation of their ideas on music is all the more curious in Nietzsche's case, if we consider the two authors who do influence his thought on music, namely A. Schopenhauer (WWV I, § 52) and Richard Wagner (chiefly in his two major theoretical works, *Opera and Drama* and *The Artwork of the Future*). For neither Schopenhauer nor Wagner take a particular musical work as their point of departure and their theoretical work is not dependant on their awe and admiration for a particular composer. In fact, Schopenhauer tends to discuss music by analysing what is involved in the act of writing music, and quite paradoxically, he almost dispenses with concrete examples from actual musical compositions, and discusses the nature and scope of musical language resorting to fabricated examples. As for Wagner, as it is known, he commonly follows in his writings a paradigm of theoretical exposition of his own musical-dramatic ideas, and his commentaries on other composers tend to be used as a point of departure or as corroborative authority for his own proposals.

The works that can be of interest for a comparison between Nietzsche's and Kierkegaard's viewpoints on music are the following: the chapter entitled "The Immediate Erotic Stages or the Musical-erotic" in the first part of *Either/Or*, published by Kierkegaard in 1843 under the pseudonym Victor Eremita, and Nietzsche's "Richard Wagner in Bayreuth" (from his *Untimely Meditations IV*, 1876), as well as *The Case of Wagner* and *Nietzsche Contra Wagner*, both from 1888. Although *The Birth of the Tragedy* (1872) contains the most interesting contribution and the most challenging proposals for the role of music as a true art of the future, its genesis places the work out of the time boundaries that, as we shall see, apparently determine the possibility of Nietzsche having heard of Kierkegaard or read anything by him. Therefore, any discussion or reference to the content of that work will only be used here to measure the angle of deviation in Nietzsche's later musical texts.

Georg Brandes (1842–1927) is one of the key sources of Kierkegaard's reception in German-speaking countries between 1870 and the turn of the century, and his role as mediator between Kierkegaard and Nietzsche has been well acknowledged. Brandes' reputation as literary critic in Scandinavia, Germany and France is patent in the many translations of his works, and there is no doubt that he was widely read, given the numerous re-editions of his writings until the beginning of the twentieth century. Brandes usually chooses emblematic passages to comment and he frequently quotes the authors in question, thus providing vivid samples of their original texts and works. He typically approaches the work of an author by means of an analysis of the themes and stylistic traits, or strategies, that are dominant in the author's production, searching for an interpretation in what they say and how they say it, making frequent comparisons between works by predecessors or by contemporaries, and relying on complementary biographical details to complement the explanations he puts forward, and not the other way around; this is indeed a step ahead the common practice of his day. In Brandes' texts, Kierkegaard is always shown in the light of the German Romantics and of the reception of German Romanticism in Denmark, and this point, to my knowledge, tends to be omitted in comparative studies on Nietzsche and Kierkegaard that rely on the Danish critic. Furthermore, such studies typically leave out aesthetics and focus only on ethical and religious issues, and music is never mentioned. Hence, the impact Brandes might have had in Nietzsche's reception of Kierkegaard in what concerns music should be re-evaluated. In the following I intend to re-evaluate the role of Brandes, as well as reconsider the importance of Schopenhauer's reception in musical circles. Indeed, among historians of music, especially the Wagnerians, the years between the 1840s and 1860 are considered to be dominated by the rise and consecration of Wagner, and the ensuing confrontation of his theories with Eduard Hanslick's. Most often, writings on musical practice and criticism on this period leave loose threads concerning the reception of Schopenhauer's musical thought, and tend to take for granted Wagner's acknowledgement that he first read Schopenhauer between the autumn of 1854 and the following summer, following the second edition of *The World as Will and Representation*, which would then mean that before that date he had no knowledge at all of Schopenhauer's thought.

The champion in providing evidence to prove that Nietzsche had read or at least had read *about* Kierkegaard is Thomas Brojber. Brojber has conducted a thorough investigation of Nietzsche's archive and works, digging out information and clues that offer new guidance in Nietzsche's readings and his reception of Kierkegaard, opening up horizons of research that have in some ways remained precluded, owing to the assumed inexistence of any knowledge about Kierkegaard's writings on Nietzsche's part. In his essay "Notes and Discussions, Nietzsche's Knowledge of Kierkegaard" (2003), Brojber considers Nietzsche's statement in a letter to Brandes dated 19 February 1888, concerning his intention to deal with "Kierkegaard's psychological problem" (Brobjer 2003, p. 252) and his works in his next trip to Germany. He also underlines Nietzsche's confession that it would be of use to him. However he does so, not as a proof that until that date Nietzsche had no knowledge whatsoever of Kierkegaard, but as an indication that what he already knew about him required a deeper study. Brobjer also explains that Nietzsche could have had access to other works which would have provided him with "five full pages of quotations from Kierkegaard and about fifty pages about him" (Brobjer 2003, p. 253). Yet, Brobjer finds it unlikely that

Nietzsche ever read Brandes monographic study on Kierkegaard which the latter had expressly recommended to Nietzsche in his answer to the letter mentioned above. Nonetheless, Brobjer believes that Nietzsche could have read at least one of the several reviews of this work. There were six in total and four of them in journals that are mentioned by Nietzsche at some time, and this because of the popularity attained by Brandes' *Søren Kierkegaard*. Moreover, Brobjer has no doubts about Nietzsche having read Hans Lassen Martensen's work in three volumes *Die Christliche Ethik*. A first edition had been published in 1871, followed by an improved edition in 1873 (Verlag von Rudolf Besser), and another edition in 1878 (Gotha), and subsequently, the work was reprinted many times. However, if it is true that Martensen's discussion and critique of "Kierkegaard's position as the most extreme form of ethics and religion" (Brobjer 2003, p. 256) should already be taken into account to interpret some passages in Nietzsche's works, namely in *Daybreak* (Brojber 2003, p. 255–256), such discussion is, however, of little use for his later writings on music. The same applies to Nietzsche's reading of Harald Höffding's *Psychologie in Grundrissen auf Grundlage der Erfahrung* (1887); if Nietzsche's pencilling and margin notes highlighting Höffding's statement "This is why, for Kierkegaard, the possibility of repetition is the fundamental ethical problem" (Brobjer 2003, p. 259) make proof of Nietzsche's awareness of possible implications with his own idea of "eternal recurrence", and although this is of obvious importance for this particular topic within what we could call Nietzschean ethics (Brobjer 2003, p. 258), it is not useful for my purpose now.

Brobjer assumes without any doubt that Nietzsche read Brandes' work *Die romantische Schule*, which is the second volume of the four-volume work *Die Hauptströmungen der Literatur des neunzehnten Jahrhunderts*, supposedly, in an edition from 1887. In addition, Nietzsche would have read the studies "Émile Zola", "Goethe und Denmark" and "Ibsen" from *Moderne Geister* published in 1882 (Brojber 2003, p. 261). However, *Hauptströmungen* had initially been published between 1872 and 1876, and it was so popular that, immediately after the 1st edition, there followed a long series of re-editions in different publishing houses that lasted until 1901. In this work, the evidence Brandes finds about music in Kierkegaard's thought, and specifically about the essay on the musical-erotic and Mozart's *Don Giovanni*, is too general to provide any consistent link between the writings on music of the two philosophers. On the other hand though, as pointed out by Brojber, and later by Thomas P. Miles in an article on the misappropriations by analysts who have compared Kierkegaard's and Nietzsche's thought on ethics, Nietzsche probably had a fairly exact idea about Kierkegaard's use of pseudonyms, including his simultaneous admission and revocation of their use in *Concluding Unscientific Postscript to Philosophical Frag-*

ments. In section XI of Brandes' *Hauptströmungen*, entitled "Romantic Reflexion and Psychology", there is indeed a long excerpt from the *Postscript*, followed by a detailed commentary, where Brandes clearly stresses the deep psychological twist Kierkegaard gave to the use of pseudonyms – a literary device that had become typical during the German and Danish romantic periods (Brandes 1872–1876, vol. 2, p. 185–199). Other aspects focused in this work include: Kierkegaard's commentaries in *The Concept of Irony* on Friedrich Schlegel's *Lucinde* and on romantic irony (Brandes 1872–1876, vol. 2, p. 72, 74, 80, 86), which are intertwined in Brandes' analysis of the work, together with a long quotation from *The Concept of Irony* (Brandes 1872–1876, vol. 2, p. 68–69); considerations on Kierkegaard's orthodox political thought and religious fanaticism in later life (Brandes 1872–1876, vol. 2, p. 17); Kierkegaard's appropriation of Friedrich Schelling and Franz Baader (Brandes 1872–1876, vol. 2, p. 24); Kierkegaard's view on sickness compared to Novalis' (Brandes 1872–1876, vol. 2, p. 217–218); and Ludwig Tieck's influence (via his novel *William Lovell*) in the epistolary structure of "The Seducer's Diary" and in the determination of the character of Johannes, the Seducer (Brandes 1872–1876, vol. 2, p. 51). Although Brandes dedicates a twenty-page section to the "Relation to the musical and to music" (Brandes 1872–1876, vol. 2, p. 132–152), there is one sole remark about Kierkegaard, made *en passant*, where Brandes suggests that Kierkegaard's famous concluding sentence "hear, hear, hear Mozart's Don Giovanni" (SKS 2, p. 92; EO1, p. 103), is in fact an indirect quotation of the last line of the opening scene of a work by Tieck, *Die verkehrte Welt* (Brandes 1872–1876, vol. 2, p. 146–147).

However, had Nietzsche read *Søren Kierkegaard*, Brandes' monographic study on the philosopher, he would have found more information on Kierkegaard's ideas on music and in particular on his relation to Mozart, which might have supported the hypothesis I outlined above. Brandes' study was initially published in 1877 in Copenhagen and a year later the German translation came out in Leipzig (Barth). This 1878 translation was broadly publicised and a series of preview extracts appeared in the *Beilage zur Allgemeinen Zeitung* (Munich) in October 1878, as well as a laudatory review by the translator, Adolf Strodtmann (1829–1879). In the original Danish edition Brandes' monography has one hundred and fifty-five pages, with a four-page introduction, and is divided into twenty-eight numbered sections. The initial five sections deal with Kierkegaard's childhood and adolescence, as well as the relation to his father; section X is dedicated to his engagement and the last three sections focus Kierkegaard's late years and his battle against the Danish Church – this is approximately one third of the book. The second third of the book discusses *Either/Or* (sections IX, X–XIII, XVI–XX); and the remaining third is dedicated to the rest of Kierkegaard's work, mainly until 1846 and the Corsair Affair, which is also dealt with in detail. Of relevance to my purpose, and bearing in mind what might have caught Nietzsche's attention, if he had the occasion of reading this essay, we find in section XI, two pages dedicated to the description of Kierkegaard's admiration for Mozart (Brandes 1889, p. 324–325). In these two pages, Brandes claims that by means of his unconditional praise of Mozart and his unreserved admiration for the composer, Kierkegaard was able to stand out as a critic and to put forward his ideas and his ideal of art, and by being Mozart's "servant", "offerer" and "priest" he had made an "hymn in his honour". A few pages later Brandes compares the expression of Kierkegaard's enthusiasm for Mozart to Bettina's eulogy of Beethoven in *Goethes Briefwechsel mit einem Kinde*, as well as to Hoffmann's reports on composers in *Kreisleriana*. Then he introduces the key concepts of the chapter of the musical-erotic showing how, according to Kierkegaard, in Mozart's opera form and content interpenetrate each other thereby turning this work into a classic. In *Don Giovanni* the most abstract idea – that Brandes labels "the most universal" (Brandes 1899, p. 328) – meets the most abstract music, taken by Brandes as the medium that is further away from reality. Brandes also explains how Kierkegaard's view, according to which "primordial sensuality" is the most abstract idea, plays a crucial role in his conception of Mozart's *Don Giovanni* as constituting the most perfect unity between that idea and its corresponding form and medium (Brandes 1889, p. 328). Brandes expresses a deep admiration for Kierkegaard, especially because he does not believe him to be "very musical". He even states that he wonders whether any other eulogy can be found as "profound and enthusiastic" as Kierkegaard's that "is not common aesthetic theory, but a transcription and explanation of music" (Brandes 1889, p. 29). To support his statement, Brandes quotes the famous paraphrase of the overture which, as I have demonstrated elsewhere (Sousa 2009, p. 160–162), is heavily inspired in Richard Wagner's essay "De l'Ouverture" (1841).[1] Kierkegaard incorporates much of Wagner's essay and develops the imagery used by him for his own commentaries on the overture of *Don Giovanni*. The passage chosen by Brandes shows Kierkegaard displaying all his linguistic and stylistic skills in terms of vivid descriptions, clearly outdoing Wagner's text:

> The overture begins with a few deep, earnest, even notes; then for the first time we hear infinitely far away an intimation that is nevertheless instantly recalled, as if it were premature, until later we hear again and again, bolder and bolder, more and more clamorous, that voice which at first subtly, demurely, and yet seemingly in anxiety, slipped in but

---

[1] "De l'ouverture" was initially published in *Revue et Gazette de Paris*, 8 and 10 January 1841, p. 17–19 and 28–29 respectively.

could not press through. So it is in nature that one sometimes sees the horizon dark and clouded; too heavy to support itself, it rests upon the earth and hides everything in its obscure night; a few hollow sounds are heard, not yet in motion but like a deep mumbling to itself. Then in the most distant heavens, far off on the horizon, one sees a flash; it speeds away swiftly along the earth, is gone in an instant. But soon it appears again; it gathers strength; it momentarily illuminates the entire heaven with its flame. The next second, the horizon seems even darker, but it flares up more swiftly, even more brilliantly; it seems as if the darkness itself has lost its composure and is starting to move, just as the eye in this first flash has a presentiment of a great fire, so the ear has a presentiment of the total passion in that dwindling stroke of the violin bow. There is an anxiety in that flash; it is as if in that deep darkness it were born in anxiety – just so is Don Giovanni's life. (SKS 2, p. 116–118; EO1, p. 129–130)

Brandes concludes by saying that although Kierkegaard's approach is not technical, his insight into Mozart's music would also have allowed him to understand Wagner, something we know well that he did. Before ending the section with another quote, namely the paraphrase with the famous sentence "*hør, hør, hør Mozarts Don Juan*" (SKS 2, p. 92; EO1, p. 103), Brandes claims that Kierkegaard's piece on *Don Giovanni* attains its climax in the lyric; and that the previous two sentences suggested an epidictic intention in Kierkegaard's text:

In love as he is with the thought of an unconditional authority, he resounds the thankful drive of his heart in making Mozart such an authority, and gives free rein to his inclination to a humble and imploring submission. Less than judging Mozart, he wants then to bring attention to him, make room for him, open the doors ajar to him and announce: the Cesar [*Kejseren*]. (Brandes 1889, p. 329f.)

If Nietzsche ever read this (or a citation of it), it would be strange that he did not feel curious to read more – all the more so, since it describes the same admiration that Nietzsche expressed for Wagner in his earlier writings. In "Richard Wagner in Bayreuth" completed in April 1876, four months before the first edition of the Festival where the *The Ring of the Nibelung* was performed for the first time, much of the initial praise bestowed to Wagner in *The Birth of the Tragedy* is still present, although it is known that the two would diverge in thought and opinion and split their ways after the 1876 festival. In *The Birth of the Tragedy*, Nietzsche had claimed that the contemporary gradual awakening of the Dionysian spirit was an accomplishment of German music, and he had assigned to Wagner the role of inheritor of Bach and Beethoven in this path of glory (BT 19). Four years later, Wagner's music is "philosophy in sounds", and *Tristan and Isolde* is the "*opus metaphysicum* of all art" (RWB 8, KSA 1, p. 479), a statement that goes further than the previous mention in *The Birth of the Tragedy*, where *Tristan and Isolde* is described as "the reign of sounds presented before us as a plastic world" (BT 21, KSA 1, p. 134). However, in *Richard Wagner in Bayreuth*, Nietzsche showed signs of ambivalence, especially in the criticism directed at the tyrannical effect of the will to power and glory that invaded Wagner, making him sacrifice his work at the expense of the public's taste (RWB 8, KSA 1, p. 473). But despite stressing Wagner's undermining excess and ambition, Nietzsche still ranks the composer highest among his contemporaries, and the tone of the text is far from the polemics and vituperation of his later writings. Wagner is still seen as the true heir and renovator of the Greek cultural heritage, and as the true interpreter of conceptions of life and art, of history and philosophy, of aesthetics and criticism that had run aground. Furthermore, Wagner is still qualified as dithyrambic dramatist, and at the same time as actor, poet and musician, while judged to be capable of standing out as the universal dramatist, the only one that can launch the rebirth of the tragedy, thus transforming modern men into tragic men (RWB 4, KSA 1, p. 448 and 467). The musical drama is the highest form of dramatic expression, the influence of Schopenhauer is still seen as a positive factor that allows Wagner to create a language that no longer thinks by means of isolated concepts, but by means of poetical images which, instead of denoting feelings or states of nature, directly represent each of those feelings or states of nature (RWB 10, KSA 1, p. 502f.). This is of relevance, since we know that what Nietzsche retracts in his later writings, by means of invective and denunciation, is exactly what in *Richard Wagner in Bayreuth* is said about Wagner's relation to Greek aesthetics: the renewal of the arts and philosophy, Wagner's multiple roles as dramatist, composer, stage and musical director, the philosophical content of his musical dramas, Schopenhauer's presence, and Wagner's musical language.

This brief survey shows to what extent Nietzsche's musical criticism is criticism of Wagner's music. Nietzsche shares this way of approaching music – i.e. via the musician – with Kierkegaard's stance in the long chapter on the musical-erotic. However, this does not mean that Kierkegaard's essay on music and Nietzsche's writings can be the object of a comparison intended to draw analogies point by point, because there are too many differences from a musical, literary and dramatic point of view. And yet, there are certain aspects that manifest a strong resemblance, as I will now show. The chapter on the musical erotic comprehends a long introduction which presents the fundamental topics, followed by an unnumbered section devoted to the three stages of the musical erotic. The theory of the stages of desire constitutes the most speculative part of the chapter and it is based on three characters of Mozart's operas (Cherubino, Papageno and Don Giovanni) which are dealt with as proto-mythical representations of desire. Three numbered subsections treat more circumscribed points concerning *Don Giovanni*: in the first section ("The Elementary Originality of the Sensuous Qualified as Seduction") one of the topics is the comparative analysis between the Faust legend and the Don Juan myth, with an emphasis on the role of Christianity and the spirit in its appearance and determination, as well as the role of the demonic in each case, and the contrast with Greek psychical love. This section ends with the appeal to hear not to see, consubstantiated in the paraphrase of the champagne aria mentioned above. The second section ("Other versions of Don Juan Considered in Relation to Musical Interpretation") is a comparative study of Mozart's opera and Molière's *Don Juan*, with reference to the Danish *vaudeville* by J.L. Heiberg (1791–1860) – a vaudeville based on Molière's play. The third section ("The Inner Musical Construction of the Opera") is the actual analysis of the opera-overture, the main characters, as well as the lyric, epic and other dramatic elements that deserve attention in *Don Giovanni*. However, a number of topics that are featured in the introduction are re-elaborated along the four sections that I have very briefly described, namely, the following: an unconditional praise and admiration of Mozart; the definition of masterpiece (one where form and content are so thoroughly permeated that it becomes pointless, and impossible, to tell one from the other); the actual process of becoming a classic work of art and a classic creator ever since Homer (the *felicitas* when the perfect form meets the perfect subject matter, thus making eternal recollection possible). Also of relevance are the following claims: *Don Giovanni* stands higher than any other work of art because, firstly, it fulfils the two principles just mentioned (SKS 2, p. 48; EO1, p. 56), and secondly, because the perfect medium meets the perfect idea, since music is the only medium capable of representing the most abstract idea (that is, primordial sensuality), and the most abstract idea one can conceive is primordial sensuality (SKS 2, p. 55; EO1, p. 64). In order to support this last claim, there is a seven-page long contrastive study of the nature and limits of verbal language and musical language (SKS 2, p. 61–66; EO1, p. 71–77) with the split between the two languages lying in the claim that music is the only language (and medium) that expresses the immediate in its immediacy. And finally, one still finds room for the criticism of the production of effects in the performance of musical works that stir up emotions dangerously. The discussion of these ideas is recurrent along the chapter with variable extension and intension, and while the elaborations are apparently debated to justify the narrator's praise of Mozart, what is constantly at stake is representation and presentation of concepts, actions and feelings in music, taken as medium, and how this representation and presentation co-exist in performance.

This cluster of questions is also, to a certain extent, at the core of Nietzsche's critique, although *The Case of Wagner* and *Niezsche Contra Wagner* are more problematic to compare with Kierkegaard's essay than *Richard Wagner in Bayreuth* – in particular due to the fragmented structure of the former and their polemical character expressed in the epigraph of *The Case of Wagner: ridendo dicere severum*. But despite their dense rhetoric – which also serves Nietzsche's confessed purpose to prove that the composer is a representative of *décadence* and not of a new age – it is worth commenting a few common features. These elements are both present in Kierkegaard's essay and (although in an obviously diverse context) in many moments of Nietzsche's new remarks on Wagner's decadence, which show a totally different approach to Wagner from what we find in *The Birth of the Tragedy* and *Richard Wagner in Bayreuth*. Both for Kierkegaard and Nietzsche musical language (and orchestration) is seen as a result of an aesthetic view of sensuality, which in Nietzsche becomes the distinguishing factor between Bizet and Wagner. For Nietzsche, Christianity is the basis of the "unhealthy" concept of sensuality developed by Wagner (CW 3, KSA 6, p. 15–16) and this is why he condemns Wagner's 'opera of salvation'; and for Kierkegaard, Christianity is also problematic since it introduces a form of sensuality into the world that determines the demonic in the character of Don Juan, and hence, in Mozart's opera (SKS 2, p. 81–84; EO1, p. 92–95). Both philosophers discuss immediate representation and the issue of the ineffable versus the monumental, as well as the search for effects and the ensuing dangers. Furthermore, they both discuss the prevalence of drama in the musical texture of opera and musical drama as well as the presence of elements from dramatic arts in opera – especially acting skills in the case of Nietzsche against Wagner (CW 11, KSA 6, p. 37–39) and the epic and the lyric in the case of Kierkegaard (SKS 2, p. 121–123; EO1, p. 133–135). They both deal with the success and public recognition of the musician, but whilst Nietzsche accuses Wagner of relinquishing to public taste, Kierkegaard canonises Mozart founding his immortality on eternal recollection. Therefore, we can conclude that there is at least a common set of questions at the core of the Nietzsche's and Kierkegaard's thought which constitutes the actual axis of the writings that I have briefly commented here. I believe this to justify further research so as to find possible linking threads between the two philosophers.

Despite the inexistence of any further evidence regarding Nietzsche's reading of Kierkegaard's work, what I have outlined here provides enough proof that the relations between the two should at least be the object of deeper investigation. Though I do believe that some German musical periodical containing reference of Kierkegaard's reception of *Don Giovanni* may have reached the young Nietzsche, another possible path to take would be Schopenhauer. In fact, in the case of Nietzsche's musical writings, besides Wagner, the other key thinker is obviously Schopenhauer, whose thought permeates Nietzsche's analysis of Wagner's music. In the case of Kierkegaard's essay, many of his statements make much more sense once we read them in relation, not only to the

German Romantics, but also Schopenhauer. However, this hypothesis is usually discarded for two reasons: the first is that Kierkegaard's journals and notebooks only refer to Schopenhauer in 1854; and the second is the question of the undetermined delay in the reception of *The World as Will and Representation*. And yet, as the Hongs write:

> [Kierkegaard] must have heard of Schopenhauer as early as 1837, inasmuch as his teacher and close friend Professor Poul M. Møller in his treatise *On Immortality*, which Kierkegaard read thoroughly, mentions Schopenhauer as the philosopher who had drawn most clearly the implications of the "nihilistic aspect of modern pantheism" (*Efterladte Skrifter*, Copenhagen: 1856, V, p. 99). (Hong/Hong 1967, p. 631)

This seems to me all the more likely, since at this time there was a lot of talk about Schopenhauer's name in the Copenhagen intellectual milieu, because of general indignation concerning the circumstances that prevented his essay "Ueber das Fundament der Moral" from being the recipient of the prize awarded by Royal Norwegian Society for Science in 1838. A second essay, "Ueber die Freiheit des menschlichen Willens" would be awarded by this same society a year later and both essays would be published in 1841 under the title *Die beiden Grundprobleme der Ethik*. This edition, as well as a first edition of 1819 of *The World as Will and Representation* reached Copenhagen and are listed in the Royal Library's catalogue, which is now, as it was then, the University Library. All this took place during the genesis of *Either/Or*. In a time when Schopenhauer's philosophy had not reached the fame of some fifteen years later, Kierkegaard could have done with him just like he did with Wagner (and Berlioz, and Schumann, and Liszt) and the enormous quantity of novels by Arnim, Tieck and Eichendorff: appropriation by copying or adaptation of whatever he found of use to consolidate his own views, leaving the source unmentioned. Therefore, knowing with more precision the reception of Schopenhauer in Scandinavia in the late 1830s would definitely help, especially reviews on the *Preiseschriften* mentioned above or accounts of the discussions of the time. Another field of research, that shouldn't be neglected, lies in the many German musical periodicals published between the 1830s and 1850s, particularly in the area of Leipzig and Berlin, an area where the most influential musical critics of the time congregated. These periodicals might have been read by the young Kierkegaard in his early twenties and during the period of his infatuation with Mozart and at least until the writing of the chapter on the musical erotic, which he did in Berlin coinciding with Franz Liszt's epochal series of concerts between December 1841 and March 1842. But they could also have been read by Nietzsche in his formative years. Indeed these periodicals may provide a clue that can explain something which otherwise is apparently destined to remain a series of coincidences.

References

Brandes, Georg (1872–1876): *Die Hauptströmungen der Literatur des neunzehnten Jahrhunderts. Vorlesungen, gehalten an der Kopenhagener Universität*. 6 vols. Translated into German by Adolf Strodtmann. Berlin: Duncker.

Brandes, Georg (1899): "Søren Kierkegaard". In: *Samlede Skrifter*. Copenhagen: Gyldendalske Boghandels Forlag, p. 249–418.

Brobjer, Thomas (2003): "Notes and Discussions, Nietzsche's Knowledge of Kierkegaard". In: *Journal of the History of Philosophy* 41 (2), p. 251–263.

Hong, Howard V./Hong, Edna V. (1967): *Kierkegaard's Journals and Papers*. Bloomington and London: Indiana University Press.

Sousa, Elisabete M. (2009): *Formas de Arte: A Prática Crítica de Berlioz, Kierkegaard, Liszt e Schumann*. Lisbon: CFUL.

José Miranda Justo
Time and Freedom in Kant and Kierkegaard: Towards a Better Understanding of the Affinities between Kierkegaard and Nietzsche

Nietzsche's 'eternal recurrence' – just like Kierkegaard's notion of 'repetition' – raises important problems concerning time and freedom. Firstly, while the 'eternal recurrence' supposedly takes place in time, it also transforms the straightforward line of time into a circle, or a succession of circles. Secondly, if everything comes back again in the same way as it had happened before, there are serious reasons to doubt whether there is any space left for (human) freedom. And yet, if we emphasise the ethical dimension opened up by Nietzsche when dealing with the idea of the eternal recurrence, we find that neither the existence of linear time or freedom is necessarily contradicted through the idea of 'recurrence'. As a matter of fact, in a fragment from 1881 we read:

> Do not look toward distant unknown salvations and *blessings* and *forgiveness*, but live in a way that we would want to live again, and live *thus* in eternity! Our task approaches us in every second. (NL 1881, KSA 9, 11[161], p. 503)[1]

The imperative contained in this fragment allows us to interpret Nietzsche's 'eternal recurrence' as the suspension of any trivial conception of time and hereby invites us to think of freedom – and the possibility of free deliberation regarding the way of conducting one's life – as an unavoidable moment in existence. We can find similar lines of thought in Kant's discussion of the Third Antinomy in his *Critique of Pure Reason* and in Kierkegaard's (i.e. Johannes Climacus') thoughts on the problem of 'coming into existence' in the *Philosophical Fragments*. In this sense, the following attempt to contrast Kant and Kierkegaard on the topics of time and freedom is intended as a preliminary remark for a future study on the relation between Nietzsche's 'eternal recurrence' and Kierkegaard's notion of 'repetition'.

---

[1] "Nicht nach fernen unbekannten Seligkeiten und *Segnungen* und *Begnadigungen* ausschauen, sondern so leben, daß wir nochmals leben wollen und in Ewigkeit *so* leben wollen! – Unsere Aufgabe tritt in jedem Augenblick an uns heran."

However, the aim of this paper is not the analysis of possible traces of Kant's practical philosophy and his philosophy of religion in Kierkegaard's thought. Neither is its aim to assess their importance. This task has already been developed with relevant results by various scholars such as Ronald M. Green, who stands out with his work on *Kierkegaard and Kant. The Hidden Debt* (1992), joined by some of the essays collected in a more recent volume, *Kant and Kierkegaard on Time and Eternity* (2011). What I will attempt to do here, though, is to present some conceptual elements in order to outline a relation which – as far as I can judge – has been neglected; namely the relation between the way in which Kant posits the problem of freedom in the discussion of the Third Antinomy of Pure Reason (KrV B 560f.) and the theme of freedom, as introduced by Kierkegaard in a few passages from his *Philosophical Fragments*.

In the first part of this paper, I start by underlining the critical role that Kant assigns to the form of time when he discusses the antinomies; and then I highlight what could be called a 'suspension of time' in the solution of the third antinomy. In the second part of the paper, I will try to show how Kierkegaard locates the problem of freedom in relation or dependence to the problem of time, so that, in the end, one could argue that he is dealing with what in his *Philosophical Fragments* is also a suspension of time – directly related to the categories of eternity and the instant. Indeed, it would be impossible to understand Climacus' approach to freedom without taking into account the idea of the 'suspension of time'.

Considering the different styles of thinking of these two authors, the asymmetry between the two parts of my paper cannot be avoided. The first part is ruled by the systematic nature of Kant's text, and it might be seen as purely descriptive. The second part attempts to follow the motion of the deliberate non-systematic manner of Kierkegaard's thought, and will inevitably be more interpretative.

I

It is well known that the discussion (and the solution) that Kant applies to the antinomies of pure reason in the second division of the "Transcendental Dialectics" is fundamentally grounded in the consideration that the antinomies of reason derive from the spatially and temporally bounded character of experience. The thesis and antithesis of each of the four antinomies aim to obtain an integral completeness, while the spatial-temporal boundaries of experience do not allow it.

I will now follow the way in which Alexis Philonenko in *L'Œuvre de Kant* introduces the problem of time within the context of the discussion of the antinomies. Philonenko takes as an obvious point of departure the assumption that "it is [...] the idea of unconditioned totality that, by being objective, will provide the theme of the antinomies" (Philonenko 1989, p. 267). He then makes this formulation explicit when he writes that this has to do with "defining the world as totality, reaching both positively and negatively" (Philonenko 1989, p. 267) what in Kant's words is "the absolute totality [...] of the synthesis of the conditions of all possible things in general" (KrV B 434). The general transcendental illusion – as opposed to the partial appearance brought about at the level of paralogisms – begins exactly at this point. Thus Kant writes:

> when the conditioned is given, the entire sum of conditions, and consequently the absolutely unconditioned (through which alone the conditioned has been possible) is also given. (KrV B 436)[2]

As Philonenko underscores, this principle is rooted in general logic: "if the conclusion is given, then it will be possible to trace logically the way back to the premises" (Philonenko 1989, p. 268). It is at this precise point that Philonenko introduces an important remark on time that we will now transcribe in its full length:

> Yet [...], by doing thus, reason will take the consideration of time as useless, which is however the means and the mediation of the whole regressive synthesis, and even of a progressive synthesis: it [i.e. reason] only needs to place the conclusion in order to demand the principle – far from being the effective middle term, time will merely be a negligible circumstance: "[...] in conformity with the idea of reason, past time, as condition of the given moment, is necessarily thought as being given in its entirety" [KrV B 439, JJ]. Hence, by putting aside time as mediation and synthesis, reason will rise to the unconditioned. (Philonenko 1989, p. 268)

Following this line of thought: it is precisely because time as 'mediation' and 'synthesis' is placed at the margin of the process, that reason can assume the pretension of rising to the unconditioned. An alternative to this would be to consider time as a mere but also inevitable circumstance that prevents reason from reaching its intentions. In this case reason will doubt about itself. In other words, from its dogmatic side, reason will consider time to be *negligible*; from its sceptical side, reason will consider time as "an insurmountable, though aimless

---

2 "[W]enn das Bedingte gegeben ist, so ist auch die ganze Summe der Bedingungen, mithin das schlechthin Unbedingte gegeben, wodurch jenes allein möglich war."

obstacle" (Philonenko 1989, p. 268). By taking each of these sides, one will reach the formulation of the theses and of the antitheses of each of the antinomies, and one will delude the true transcendentality of the method, which "sees in time neither something negligible, nor an obstacle, but instead, a method of determination, at the level of principles" (Philonenko 1989, p. 268).

Philonenko's analysis is an obvious consequence of the relevance given to time as "the universal form of matter" and to the "categorial constitution of time as the form of all possible experience" (Philonenko 1989, p. 157) within the context of his own reading of the Transcendental Deduction. But his analysis also seems to derive from the reading of a passage in the first paragraph of the "Antinomy of Pure Reason", that is, from Kant's elaborations on the "System of Cosmological Ideas". It is here that Kant launches the foundations of his critical assessment of the antinomies, and he does so by developing an argumentation that is ultimately based on time (KrV B 436–440).

After asserting that "[t]he transcendental ideas are thus, in the *first* place, simply categories extended [*erweiterte*] to the unconditioned", and as such, have to organise themselves in a table arranged according to the headings of the categories themselves, Kant then claims that not all categories are fitted for such employment, "but only those in which the synthesis constitutes a *series* of conditions subordinated to [...] one another, and generative of a [given, JJ] conditioned" (KrV B 436).[3] While establishing a rigorous distinction between regressive synthesis and progressive synthesis, Kant points out, immediately after, that the cosmological ideas deal with the totality of the regressive synthesis, proceeding *in antecendentia* and not *in consequentia*. Time, says Kant, "is in itself a series, and indeed the formal condition of all series" (KrV B 438), and "[t]he transcendental idea of the absolute totality of the series of conditions of any given conditioned [...] refers only to all *past* time" (KrV B 438–439). Therefore, he can later affirm that: "in conformity with the idea of reason, past time, as condition of the given moment, is necessarily thought as being necessarily given" (KrV B 439).[4] This consideration of time becomes then a solid base for what comes next: the analysis of what simultaneously happens on the side of space.

---

3 "Also werden *erstlich* die transscendentalen Ideen eigentlich nichts, als bis zum Unbedingten erweiterte Kategorien sein [...]. *Zweitens* aber werden doch auch nicht alle Kategorien dazu taugen, sondern nur diejenige, in welchen die Synthesis eine *Reihe* ausmacht, und zwar der einander untergeordneten (nicht beigeordneten) Bedingungen zu einem Bedingten."
4 "Die Zeit ist an sich selbst eine Reihe (und die formale Bedingung aller Reien) [...] Folglich geht die transscendentale Idee der absoluten Totalität der Reihe der Bedingungen zu einem gegebenen Bedingten nur auf alle vergangene Zeit. Es wird nach der Idee der Vernunft die ganze verlaufene Zeit als Bedingung des gegebenen Augenblicks notwendig als gegeben gedacht." (KrV B 438–439).

Nevertheless, in the third part of Section 9, "The Empirical Employment of the Regulative Principle of Reason, in Respect of All Cosmological Ideas", i.e. the section that is directly concerned with the problem of freedom, under the heading: "Solution of the Cosmological Idea of Totality in the Derivation of Cosmical Events from their Causes" (from B 560 to B 586), Kant develops a very special approach to the problem of time, whereby time is dependent on the distinction of the sensible and the intelligible. This allows him to keep the balance and the co-possibility of 'natural causality' (*nach der Natur* or *nach den Naturgesetzen*) and 'causality through freedom'.

This treatment of the problem of time, which sends time back to the domain of sensible experience and excludes it from the domain of the intelligible, is immediately noticeable from the moment in which Kant introduces the notion of freedom in cosmological sense:

> By freedom, on the other hand, in its cosmological meaning, I understand the power of beginning a state *spontaneously*. Such causality will not, therefore, itself stand under another cause determining it in time, as required by the law of nature. Freedom, in this sense, is a pure transcendental idea, which, in the first place, contains nothing borrowed from experience, and which, secondly, refers to an object that cannot be determined or given in any experience [...]. (KrV B 561)[5]

It is a general law of experience and of the mere possibility of experience that everything has a cause and that such cause has a cause, and this makes the field of experience into a sum of the merely natural (*Inbegriff blosser Natur*). Yet, Kant adds:

> Since in this way no absolute totality of conditions determining causal relation can be obtained, reason creates for itself the idea of a spontaneity which can begin to act of itself, without requiring to be determined to action by an antecedent cause in accordance with the law of causality. (KrV B 561)[6]

Kant proceeds straight away to ground the 'practical concept' of freedom on the 'transcendental idea of freedom', describing the former in the following terms:

---

[5] "Dagegen verstehe ich unter Freiheit im kosmologischen Verstande das Vermögen, einen Zustand *von selbst* anzufangen, deren Kausalität also nicht nach dem Naturgesetze wiederum unter einer anderen Ursache steht, welche sie der Zeit nach bestimmte. Die Freiheit ist in dieser Bedeutung eine reine transscendentale Idee, die erstlich nichts von der Erfahrung Entlehntes enthält, zweitens deren Gegenstand auch in keiner Erfahrung bestimmt gegeben werden kann".

[6] "Da aber auf solche Weise keine absolute Totalität der Bedingungen im Kausalverhältnisse herauszubekommen ist, so schafft sich die Vernunft die Idee von einer Spontaneität, die von selbst anheben könne zu handeln, ohne dass eine andere Ursache vorangeschickt werden dürfe, sie wiederum nach dem Gesetze der Kausalverknüpfung zur Handlung zu bestimmen."

"*Freedom in the practical sense* is the will's independence of *coercion* through sensuous impulses [Freiheit im praktischen Verstande *ist die Unabhängigkeit der Willkür von der* Nötigung *durch Antriebe der Sinnlichkeit*]" (KrV B 562). Human *arbitrium* – "will" in Kemp Smith's translation – is thus "*arbitrium liberum*", for "sensibility does not necessitate its action [of the will, JJ]. There is in man a power of self-determination, independently of any coercion through sensuous impulses" (KrV B 562).

Nevertheless, the most important part of the argumentation for the possibility of freedom derives from the specification of the 'dynamic' character (as opposed to the 'mathematical' character in the first two antinomies) of the concepts of reason involved in the last two antinomies and, particularly, in the third (KrV B 563–564). Sequentially to this specification, Kant, while insisting on the refusal of the 'absolute reality of the phenomena', that is, the refusal of the vision, according to which 'phenomena are things in themselves', will introduce the idea of an 'intelligible cause', namely when he states the following:

> If, on the other hand, appearances are not taken for more than they actually are; if they are viewed not as things in themselves, but merely as representations, connected according to empirical laws, they must themselves have grounds which are not appearances. The effects of such an intelligible cause appear, and accordingly can be determined through other appearances, but its causality is not so determined. While the effects are to be found in the series of empirical conditions, the intelligible cause, together with its causality, is outside the series. Thus the effect may be regarded as free in respect of its intelligible cause, and at the same time in respect of appearances as resulting from them according to the necessity of nature [...]. (KrV B 564–565)[7]

Kant is able, therefore, to distinguish between two sides (*Seiten*) of the causality of a being (*Wesen*) that has a faculty which is not an object of sensible intuition:

> the *causality* of this being can be regarded from two points of view. Regarded as the causality of a thing in itself, it is *intelligible* in its *action*; regarded as the causality of an appearance in the world of senses, it is *sensible* in its *effects*. We should therefore have to form

---

7 "Wenn dagegen Erscheinungen für nichts mehr gelten, als sie in der Tat sind, nämlich nicht für Dinge an sich, sondern bloße Vorstellungen, die nach empirischen Gesetzen zusammenhängen, so müssen sie selbst noch Gründe haben, die nicht Erscheinungen sind. Eine solche intelligible Ursache aber wird in Ansehung ihrer Kausalität nicht durch Erscheinungen bestimmt, obzwar ihre Wirkungen erscheinen, und so durch andere Erscheinungen bestimmt werden können. Sie ist also samt ihrer Kausalität außer der Reihe; dagegen ihre Wirkungen in der Reihe der empirischen Bedingungen angetroffen werden. Die Wirkung kann also in Ansehung ihrer intelligiblen Ursache als frei, und doch zugleich in Ansehung der Erscheinungen als Erfolg aus denselben nach der Notwendigkeit der Natur angesehen werden".

both an empirical and an intellectual concept of the causality of the faculty of such a subject, and to regard both as referring to one and the same effect. (KrV B 566)[8]

The subject thus characterised reveals a distinctive trait that is of paramount interest for our purposes: "Now this acting subject would not, in its intelligible character, stand under any conditions of time; time is only a condition of appearances, not of things in themselves" (KrV B 568). And Kant makes it clear that, although it is true that this intelligible character cannot be immediately known, it is still possible to be thought of. He then writes:

> In its intelligible character [...] this same subject must be considered to be free from all influence of sensibility and from all determination through appearances. [...] And consequently, since natural necessity is to be met with only in the sensible world, this active being must in its actions be independent of, and free from all such necessity. (KrV B 569)[9]

Now it is Kant himself who shows us the possibility of simultaneity of both sensible and intelligible causes in the domain of experience. Such possibility is applied to man in as much as s/he is "one of the appearances of the sensible world [*eine der Erscheinungen der Sinnenwelt*]" (KrV B 574). Now: man is

> to himself, on the one hand phenomenon, and on the other hand, in respect of certain faculties, a purely intelligible object, since its action cannot be ascribed to the receptivity of sensibility. (KrV B 574–575).[10]

These faculties are understanding and reason, and in the subsequent section Kant deals chiefly with the latter, since,

> in particular, we distinguish [reason] in a quite peculiar and especial way from all empirically conditioned powers. For it views its objects exclusively in the light of ideas [...]. (KrV B 575)[11]

---

[8] "so kann man die *Kausalität* dieses Wesens auf zwei Seiten betrachten, als *intelligibel* nach ihrer Handlung, als eines Dinges an sich selbst, und als *sensibel*, nach den Wirkungen derselben, als einer Erscheinung in der Sinnenwelt. Wir würden uns demnach von dem Vermögen eines solchen Subjekts einen empirischen, imgleichen auch einen intellektuellen Begriff seiner Kausalität machen, welche bei einer und derselben Wirkung zusammen stattfinden."
[9] "Nach dem intelligiblen Charakter desselben [...] würde dasselbe Subjekt dennoch von allem Einflusse der Sinnlichkeit und Bestimmung durch Erscheinungen freigesprochen werden müssen, und [...] so würde dieses tätige Wesen, so fern in seinen Handlungen von aller Naturnotwendigkeit, als die lediglich in der Sinnenwelt angetroffen wird, unabhängig und frei sein."
[10] "[S]ich selbst freilich einesteils Phänomen, anderenteils aber, nämlich in Ansehung gewisser Vermögen, ein bloß intelligibler Gegenstand, weil die Handlung desselben gar nicht zur Rezeptivität der Sinnlichkeit gezählt werden kann."
[11] "[V]ornehmlich wird die letztere [die Vernunft, JJ] ganz eigentlich und vorzüglicherweise von allen empirischen Kräften unterschieden, da sie ihre Gegenstände bloß nach Ideen erwägt".

At this point Kant takes up once again the topic of practical reason mentioned above, emphasising that the 'ought' (*sollen*) "expresses a kind of necessity and of connection with grounds which is found nowhere else in the whole of nature" (KrV B 575). He then elaborates this idea and writes:

> [t]his ought expresses a possible action the ground of which cannot be anything but a mere concept [...]. The action to which the ought applies must indeed be possible under natural conditions. These conditions, however, do not play any part in determining the will itself, but only in determining the effect and its consequences in the [field of, JJ] appearance. (KrV B 575–576)[12]

Moreover, reason:

> frames to itself with perfect spontaneity an order of its own according to ideas, to which it adapts the empirical conditions, and according to which it declares actions to be necessary, even although they have never *taken place*, and perhaps never will take place. And at the same time reason also presupposes that it can have causality in regard to all these actions [...]. (KrV B 576)[13]

In relation to the problem that is at stake for us now, namely the place and role of time in this whole argumentation, Kant will argue that:

> The action, in so far as it can be ascribed to a mode of thought as its cause, does not *follow* therefrom in accordance with empirical laws; that is to say, it is not *preceded* by the conditions of pure reason, but only by their effects in the [field of, JJ] appearance of inner sense. Pure reason, as a purely intelligible faculty, is not subject to the form of time, nor consequently to the conditions of succession in time. The causality of reason in its intelligible character does not, in producing an effect, *arise* or begin to be at a certain time [...]. (KrV B 579)[14]

---

[12] "Dieses Sollen nun drückt eine mögliche Handlung aus, davon der Grund nichts anderes, als ein bloßer Begriff ist [...]. Nun muß die Handlung allerdings unter Naturbedingungen möglich sein, wenn auf sie das Sollen gerichtet ist; aber diese Naturbedingungen betreffen nicht die Bestimmung der Willkür selbst, sondern nur die Wirkung und den Erfolg derselben in der Erscheinung."

[13] "[Die Vernunft, JJ] macht sich mit völliger Spontaneität eine eigene Ordnung nach Ideen, in die sie die empirischen Bedingungen hinein passt, und nach denen sie sogar Handlungen für notwendig erklärt, die doch nicht *geschehen* sind und vielleicht nicht geschehen werden, von allen aber gleichwohl voraussetzt, dass die Vernunft in Beziehung auf sie Kausalität haben könne".

[14] "Die Handlung nun, sofern sie der Denkungsart als ihrer Ursache beizumessen ist, *erfolgt* dennoch daraus gar nicht nach empirischen Gesetzen, d.i. so, daß die Bedingungen der reinen Vernunft, sondern nur so, daß deren Wirkungen in der Erscheinung des inneren Sinnes *vorhergehen*. Die reine Vernunft, als ein bloß intelligibles Vermögen, ist der Zeitform und mithin auch den Bedingungen der Zeitfolge nicht unterworfen. Die Kausalität der Vernunft im intelligiblen Charakter *entsteht nicht*, oder hebt nicht etwa zu einer gewissen Zeit an".

And further down we can also read:

> But of pure reason we cannot say that the state wherein the will is determined is preceded and itself determined by some other state. For since reason is not itself an appearance, and is not subject to any conditions of sensibility, it follows that even as regards its causality there is in it no time-sequence, and that the dynamical law of nature, which determines succession in time in accordance with rules, is not applicable to it. (KrV B 581)[15]

Kant will then conclude this section of the Antinomy by reiterating the illusion of the third antinomy and by highlighting (using the moderate style that he always attributes to reason) that

> [w]hat we have alone been able to show, and what we have alone been concerned to show is that [...] causality through freedom is at least *not incompatible with* nature. (KrV B 586)[16]

II

In order to evaluate the connection that Kierkegaard establishes between freedom and time in the *Interlude* that separates the fourth and fifth chapters of his *Philosophical Fragments*, we must first review the topic of freedom and recall the argument presented by Climacus concerning the alternative between freedom and necessity. Both the topic of freedom and the alternative relation between freedom and necessity are discussed in relation to the topic of 'coming into existence' (*Tilblivelse*), which – as it becomes clear in the fourth section of the *Interlude*, entitled "The Apprehension of the Past" – is a temporal category.

Climacus begins with a question: "How is that changed which comes into existence, or what is the change (κινησις) of coming into existence?" (SKS 4, p. 273; PF, p. 73). This question already suggests the need to distinguish this particular type of change from all other types of change. And this is so because, for Climacus: "All other change presupposes the existence of that in which change is taking place, even though the change is that of ceasing to be in existence"

---

[15] "Aber von der Vernunft kann man nicht sagen, daß vor demjenigen Zustande, darin sie die Willkür bestimmt, ein anderer vorhergehe, darin dieser Zustand selbstbestimmt wird. Denn da Vernunft selbst keine Erscheinung und gar keinen Bedingungen der Sinnlichkeit unterworfen ist, so findet in ihr, selbst in Betreff ihrer Kausalität, keine Zeitfolge statt, und auf sie kann also das dynamische Gesetz der Natur, was die Zeitfolge nach Regeln bestimmt, nicht angewandt werden."
[16] "[D]aß Natur der Kausalität aus Freiheit wenigstens *nicht widerstreite*, das war das einzige, was wir leisten konnten, und woran es uns auch einzig und allein gelegen war."

(SKS 4, p. 273; PF, p. 73). However, when it comes to 'coming into existence', it is understood that it does not take place this way,

> for if that which comes into existence does not in itself remain unchanged in the change of coming into existence, then the coming into existence is not *this* coming into existence but another [...]. (SKS 4, p. 273; PF, p. 73)

The problem Kierkegaard is addressing here is obviously the problem of incarnation, where 'coming into existence' is a change that actually does not change in essence that which comes into existence: "This change, then, is not in essence [*Væsen*] but in being [*Væren*] and is from not existing to existing" (SKS 4, p. 273; PF, p. 73). Climacus concludes his reasoning with the following statement:

> such a being that nevertheless is a non-being is possibility, and a being that is being is indeed actual being or actuality, and the change of coming into existence is the transition from possibility to actuality. (SKS 4, p. 274; PF, p. 74)

Matching possibility and actuality inevitably involves the discussion of the problem of necessity. Yet, Climacus introduces the question of necessity in a very peculiar manner:

> Can the necessary come into existence? Coming into existence is a change, but since the necessary is always related to itself in the same way, it cannot be changed at all. All coming into existence is a suffering [*Liden*], and the necessary cannot suffer, cannot suffer the suffering of actuality [...]. (SKS 4, p. 274; PF, 74)

Thinking necessity thus implies thinking an unperturbed and imperturbable continuity: "the only thing that cannot come into existence is the necessary, because the necessary *is*" (SKS 4, p. 274; PF, p. 74). Or in another formulation: "necessity [...] is not a qualification of being, but of essence, since the essence of the necessary is to be" (SKS 4, p. 274; PF, p. 74). However, thinking necessity would imply a *regressus* fundamentally distinct from what we noticed in Kant, since this would now be a question of finding not a cause, but – in Hegelian terms – a ground [*Grund*]. Conversely, thinking the 'coming into existence' implies what Climacus designates as *suffering*, i.e. a passivity facing actuality, or in other words, a modification – even though the reason for that very modification may lie in what actually comes into existence.

This is why Climacus introduces the idea of freedom as follows:

> The change of coming into existence is actuality; the transition takes place in freedom. No coming into existence is necessary – not before it came into existence, for then it cannot come into existence, and not after it has come into existence, for then it has not come into existence. (SKS 4, p. 275; PF, p. 75)

It seems important to note that the meaning of the topic of freedom in Kierkegaard/Climacus is more than merely epistemological. Although it is true that Ronald Green's study does not establish a direct link between the problem of freedom in Kierkegaard's *Philosophical Fragments* and Kant's discussion of the third antinomy, he does indicate the importance of the concept of freedom in Kierkegaard in relation to other instances of Kant's work. Green acknowledges the fact that those very principles of Kantian practical philosophy (already present in the first *Critique*) must have influenced Kierkegaard's thought on freedom. He thus quotes a specific passage from Climacus' *Postscript* "that recalls Kant's understanding of freedom as our unique access to the realm of intelligible reality", which in Green's opinion,

> suggests the centrality of freedom for Kierkegaard's religious position [...]. "Freedom", says Climacus, "is the true wonderful lamp; when a man rubs it with ethical passion, God comes into being for him." (Green 1992, p. 149)

In effect, freedom, for Kierkegaard, is not only the freedom of God to incarnate; it is also the basis for the ethical choice, the 'choice of oneself' in *Either/Or*, as well as for the non-determinist understanding of sin – a problem prevailing in many of Kierkegaard's more religious writings. Now, what I would like to highlight in this context is precisely the *theoretical* prevalence of the notion of freedom – as it is introduced in the *Philosophical Fragments* – over those other functions that the notion of freedom performs in other contexts. Despite the impossibility of demonstrating it here in detail, it is important to remark that the problem of the opposition between necessity and freedom is discussed precisely within this context and that without such discussion the notion of freedom would not achieve the status of a true philosophical concept, capable of sustaining all the other functions ascribed to it.

What follows now is an attempt to show two aspects of Kierkegaard's thought that are comparable to what we have described above in Kant: firstly, that the discussion of the opposition between necessity and freedom comes from a certain conception of time, and secondly, that the idea of freedom involves a suspension of the *regressus* applicable to causality. The suspension of this *regressus*, in its turn, implies the suppression of any considerations on time. This last point, however, leads us to the notion of 'belief'.

On the one hand, Climacus considers that

> [e]verything that has come into existence is *eo ipso* historical, for even if no further historical predicate can be applied to it, the crucial predicate of the historical can still be predicated – namely, that it has come into existence. (SKS 4, p. 275; PF, p. 75)

However, in the subsequent paragraph he adds that: "the historical is the past" (SKS 4, p. 275; PF, p. 76). And later, in the section entitled "The Apprehension of the Past", he writes:

> The distinctively historical is perpetually the past [...], and as something bygone it has actuality, for it is certain and trustworthy that it occurred. But that it occurred is, in turn, precisely its uncertainty, which will perpetually prevent the apprehension from taking the past as if it had been that way from eternity. Only in this contradiction between certainty and uncertainty, the *discrimen* of something that has come into existence and thus also of the past, is the past understood. [...] Any apprehension of the past that thinks to understand it thoroughly by constructing it has only thoroughly misunderstood it. (SKS 4, p. 278–279; PF, p. 79)

Hence, it becomes clear that, on the one side, the comprehension of coming into existence depends on the category of time, namely on the exact mode of understanding the historical as past. But it also becomes clear, on the other side – and to put it in Kantian terms – that there is a 'form of time' which is radically different from any arbitrary construct, and which regulates the intellectual apprehension of the phenomenon of coming into existence. We may recall here that, as Climacus later will say, "the coming into existence cannot be sensed immediately" (SKS 4, p. 280; PF, p. 81).

And yet, in the aftermath of the discussion of the opposition between necessity and freedom, Climacus writes the following:

> Nothing coming into existence comes into existence by way of a ground [*Grund*], but everything by way of a cause [*Aarsag*]. The intervening causes are misleading in that the coming into existence appears to be necessary; the truth about them is that they, as having themselves come into existence, *definitively* point back to a freely acting cause. As soon as coming into existence is definitively reflected upon, even an inference from natural law is not evidence of the necessity of any coming into existence. (SKS 4, p. 275; PF, p. 75)

The necessity of the causes is a deceiving appearance because the causes that are here at stake are ultimately something that *came* into existence, and, if they came into existence, they must belong to the sphere of freedom; thus, when investigating the cause of the causes, we are led to decide "definitively" for a cause that acts freely, that is to say, with total independence from natural necessity.

And further on, in a passage in which we are led to believe that Climacus is especially referring to incarnation, he writes:

> The more special historical coming into existence comes into existence by way of a relatively freely acting cause, which in turn definitively points to an absolutely freely acting cause. (SKS 4, p. 276; PF, p. 76)

In other words, coming into existence, which as we saw is "*eo ipso*, historical", depends on a cause or a set of causes that act freely, though only in a relative manner, because once what came into existence is viewed from its historical side, it has somehow 'naturalised itself', i.e. it has integrated sequenced temporal connections, and therefore it allows for the backward movement of the *regressus*, in search of the cause of the causes, and so on and so forth. Yet, coming into existence must also be viewed from another perspective, namely from the perspective that, according to Climacus, reunites the instant and eternity, i.e. the single instant when coming into existence takes place and the eternity that coming into existence means. From this point of view, the *regressus* is definitively suspended, and the cause that can be thought for the coming into existence will now be considered as acting in an absolutely free manner.

This "absolutely freely acting cause" compels Climacus to include in his argumentation the idea of "belief" or "faith [*Tro*]" (SKS 4, p. 281; PF, p. 81), and, in accordance, he adds that:

> it is now readily apparent that belief is not a knowledge but an act of freedom, an expression of will. It believes the coming into existence and has annulled in itself the incertitude that corresponds to the nothingness of that which is not. (SKS 4, p. 282; PF, p. 83)

This 'belief' clearly does not fit in the domain of sensible experience, and in this sense, it signifies, just like the 'intelligible' in Kant: *a suspension of any considerations within the domain of time*, while simultaneously admitting two kinds of causality, a natural, historical causality (in the case of objects that are not part of the domain of the coming into existence), and a causality through freedom (in the case of coming into existence, and very particularly, the case of incarnation). But *incarnation*, as it is known, is a matter where the proximity between Kant and Kierkegaard is radically... *suspended*.

References

Green, Ronald M. (1992): *Kierkegaard and Kant. The Hidden Debt*. New York: SUNY.
Green, Ronald M. (2011): *Kant and Kierkegaard on Time and Eternity*. Macon: Mercer University Press.
Philonenko, Alexis (1989): *L'Œuvre de Kant. La philosophie critique*. Vol. 1. Paris: Vrin [first edition: 1969].

Danielle Cohen-Levinas
A Critique of the Aesthetics of German Idealism: Reflections on Nietzsche's Rupture with Wagner

I

With the exemption of mathematical and/or cosmological speculations, the dialogue between philosophy and music has been rather tense and apprehensive if not non-existent. In the best case, it has been charged with metaphysical content. There is a rational explanation for this, which has to do with the fact that throughout the period known as Romanticism, philosophy found herself complying with the necessity of achieving an ideal *System* that included aesthetics, and this meant that philosophy had to find a place for music within this overall system. German Idealism needed to put music in the correct place within the system. In many cases, though, this was done at the margins of a true philosophical practice, without being able to fulfill a rigorous conceptual work within the artistic world. Kant refers to it without restraint. Hegel admits it with embarrassment and integrates music into his system of fine arts by resuming Plato's thoughts on the mimetic process between *mousikè* and *logos*; Schopenhauer exaltedly explains music through the will; Nietzsche will see a key for inverting the relation between *Dichten* and *Denken*; and Heidegger will interpret the rupture between Nietzsche and Wagner as the necessary turning point in the History of Being.

Music haunts philosophy. It is as if the Greek concept of *melos*, meaning the abstraction of human speech represented through the melodic structure, were inaudibly at play in the practice of thinking. Just like a sound touches the *prosa oratio*, becoming to *logos* what music is to hearing, or colour is to eyesight: music is the *ethos* of philosophy. For philosophy, music represents a realm of resistance and is considered a threat. Two episodes tell us the story of this threat: the first episode is Plato's expulsion of the tragic poet, of the myth-tellers and practically of all music (except for the music that followed the Pythagorean code) from the *Republic*. The second is Nietzsche's rupture with Wagner – which can be seen as the reversal of Platonism. In any case, what is rejected and what inevitably returns is what the Greeks called *hé mousiké* or *ta mousika*, or to be more precise, the dialogue, which in Plato's writings corresponds to the dramatic and mimetic forms. *The Laws* is presented as the most beautiful of the tragic poems. It is, thus, music considered as a tragic speech, or moreover the tragic speech prolonging itself in music which would disrupt the order of being-in-a-community. That is why Heidegger, in an additional note to his conference in Berlin from 1938 entitled "The Age of the World Picture" where he criticises the notion of value, will not hesitate to present Nietzsche's rupture with Wagner as an example of this, giving this rupture full philosophical significance.

> Because Nietzsche's thinking remains imprisoned in value representation, he has to articulate what is essential for him in the form of a reversal, as the transvaluation of all values [*Umwertung aller Werte*]. Only when we succeed in grasping Nietzsche's thinking independently of value representation will we come to a standing-ground from which the work of the last thinker of metaphysics becomes a task assigned to questioning, and Nietzsche's antagonism to Wagner becomes comprehensible as the necessity of our history [*Notwendigkeit unserer Geschichte*]. (Heidegger GA 5, p. 102)

This is an astonishing view on what Heidegger calls "our history". From this perspective, 'history' has followed music's destiny, it has become its ally and has failed to dissolve itself in it. Because of his differences with Wagner, Nietzsche, according to Heidegger, avoided the worst: the end of philosophy. In other words, the end of metaphysics managed to escape from the seizure of the power of thought by a *theatrecracy* disguised as metaphysics without logos. On the other hand, though, would it be even conceivable to approach the work of the last thinker of metaphysics without music? Is it not in order to develop his critique against Christian morality that Nietzsche, in his *Birth of Tragedy*, exaggeratedly recourses to Dionysus? Christian consciousness is sublimated by an enigmatic deployment of *melos*, and in particular, by the use of a Wagnerian leitmotif which leads us to a microscopic reading of the form and the system which Wagner himself was trying to overcome. The myth defended here by Nietzsche is subjected to a temporal and textual blurring: What can be ascribed to *mythos* and what can be ascribed to *logos* in Wagner's music? In any case, it seems, at least in Nietzsche's early writings, that *logos* is preceded by *mythos*. When the opposite is the case, when *logos* precedes *mythos*, we are confronted with a mirror-movement, a circular movement which is both musical and philosophical, a movement from which philosophy will not emerge unscathed. But which postulate is Heidegger's allusion based on? Probably on the idea that a musical thought or musical phraseology – however much involved or caught it may be in the ellipsis of inversion and reversal of values – cannot but obstruct our access to Nietzsche's metaphysical thoughts, and more precisely to the determination of being as *will to power* and *eternal recurrence*.

In his *Nietzsche* lectures, Heidegger distinguishes between philosophy as such, the famous *dichterische*, and *Dichtung*, which strictly speaking and however *denkerisch* (thoughtful) it might be, is never philosophical. It is clear that, for Heidegger, only Hölderlin managed to achieve at the same time *denken* and *dichten*. But Nietzsche certainly also saw the possibility of uniting *denken* and *dichten* in Wagner's *Tristan and Isolde*.[1] That is why, just like Heidegger had done with Hölderlin, Nietzsche never interprets Wagner from a romantic perspective – which is not less paradoxical if we consider the extent to which *Dichtung* is at the core of the concerns of Romantic composers, such as Schuman, who will write the lieder cycle *Dichterliebe*.[2] Conversely, Wagnerian *Dichtung* can be seen as an attempt to overcome or to break from the Hegelian confines; this is certainly how Nietzsche saw it.

I believe that this issue clarifies Nietzsche's definition of nihilism, paraphrased by Heidegger as "the degradations of the until now highest values [*die Entwertung der bisherigen obersten Werte*]" (Heidegger GA 5, p. 222). It also clarifies the figure of *Zarathustra*, who presents himself in the form of songs, verses, parabolas, enigmas, prophet's discourses and is not alien to the dimension of *Dichtung*. One finds here that speech is turning to music and when Nietzsche refers to his book *Zarathustra* in *Ecce Homo*, he does so in order to present it as a dithyramb – Wagner's favourite figure or leitmotif. The model is, thus, not so different from the tragic poem in Plato's *Laws*, even if the relation is ambiguous. Indeed, once we question Nietzsche's writing style in his *Zarathustra*, we are inevitably led to question Plato's writing and to understand that the Wagnerian writing of *Tristan and Isolde* is located exactly at the intersection point between the two.

It is at this point that Heidegger's remark regarding the task to question history (which is also a question about being, since for Heidegger being is nothing but the history of being) comes into play. Nietzsche's rupture with Wagner is therefore not anecdotal, such as some have wanted to believe. Neither is it motivated by resentment or a personal disappointment; at stake are philosophical and political issues. Indeed, Heidegger, who did not pay great attention to music, would not have focused his attention on a mere quarrel. And yet, in the section "Six Basic Developments in the History of Aesthetics" from his *Nietzsche* lectures, not only does he mention Nietzsche's rupture with Wagner, but he shows its relevance for our understanding of the meaning of

---

[1] Action in three acts based on a poem by Richard Wagner, composed between 1857 and 1859, performed on 10 June 1865 at the Royal Theatre of Bavaria, under the direction of Hans von Bülow.

[2] Composed in 1840, the *Dichterliebe* is a cycle of 16 melodies based on poems by Heinrich Heine.

intoxication and its relation to philosophical thought. According to Heidegger, the bond between the two, intoxication and thought, constitutes the embodiment of an essential aesthetical state; it is the representation or configuration of the 'will to power'. However, for Heidegger, artistic knowledge is nothing but a *tekhne* in the Greek sense of the word, which means to say that it does not carry any intellectual reflection or conceptual thought. Only tragic thought – and certainly music – requires this absence of conceptuality. That would explain why philosophy had to abandon it – as if by forgetting tragic thought and music it could exist and affirm its autonomy. One will have to wait for the metaphysical moment – the moment where great art comes to an end – in order for the question of the musical and of *Dichtung* to return to the surface of philosophical reflection. At this moment, the hegemony of fundamental concepts by Plato and Aristotle affecting the question of *episteme*, of experience and of the sensitive behaviour of the individual, will be challenged. But what *tekhne* will be able to escape this form of hegemony that already seems to take on a political significance? Which disastrous poetics is Nietzsche judging, as he tries to liberate philosophy from an almost deadly fascination? Is it the problem of *phainesthai*, of showing-itself according to *eidos*; is it the determination of beauty as *ekphanestaton*, as the pinnacle of appearance; or is it the poetic purpose of *tekhne* which opens itself to the metaphysical domain of subjectivity? Where should we situate Wagner, whose entire work is constructed as an audacious response to the decline of art and to the deterioration (*Abfall*) of its essence? The target is, thus, Hegel, because Wagner's entire project, the *Gesamtkunstwerk*, aims to follow an art project in spite of Hegel's diagnosis and verdict which presupposed the death of modern art, i.e. the death of Romanticism. There was only one Wagner who could have embarked wholeheartedly into such an aesthetical enterprise, searching to restore that great Greek form of art, namely tragedy. On the other hand, in Wagner's time, between 1850 and 1860, such a project had to remain unique to Wagner. Indeed, in his attempt to save Great Art – something which Nietzsche welcomes in *The Birth of Tragedy* – Wagner was not only transforming the arts through a new receptiveness to form which was accomplished through the ideal of *Dichtung*, i.e. the absolute alliance between melody and poetry, which in music is called *arioso continuo*. He also implicitly subscribed to the emergence of a religious, and hence political form of art, an art whose vocation was to *religere*, to point towards a community of the people (*Volksgemeinschaft*) and towards a social life such as had been conceived by Attic tragedy. In this way, according to Heidegger who was very critical to the 'total work of art', Tragic and Romantic myths were summoned to the same process of increasing barbarisation, because Wagner's *tekhne* was not the true *Dichtung* of Hölderlin:

> Theoretically, music is to be a means for achieving effective drama; in reality, however, music in the form of opera becomes the authentic art. Drama possesses its importance and essential character, not in poetic originality, i.e., not in the well-wrought truth of the linguistic work, but in things pertaining to the stage, theatrical arrangements and gala productions. Architecture serves merely for theatre construction; painting provides the backdrops, sculpture portraits the gestures of actors. Literary creation and language remain without the essential and decisive shaping force of genuine knowledge. What is wanted is the domination of art as music, and thereby the domination of the pure state of feeling – the tumult and delirium of the senses [...]. (Heidegger GA 6.1, p. 101–102)

Conceding that Heidegger did not understand much of Wagner's music, we can still acknowledge the validity of his analysis concerning the overemphasis on aesthetics. This affective hyperbole has the effect of producing an emphatic concupiscence between the subject and the work of art itself; here, the subject/spectator is drawn into a total and obscure passive form of listening, which is the opposite of what is achieved by great art. For Heidegger, the shaping (*Gestaltung*) in great art, contrary to the sophisticated and hysterical lack of measure from *Tristan and Isolde* for instance, is virile from end to end. Following this line of thought to the end, we come to the conclusion that Wagner takes music to a nihilistic culmination or *acme*. To be sure, one must insist on one point which is without doubt the most essential of all: according to Heidegger, music (as opposed to poetry) is not capable of achieving what he calls *Gestaltung*. The difference between the poetical and the musical experience determines Heidegger's relation to writing: on the one side, the reading of Hölderlin, and on the other, the process of a theatre that privileges "the domination of art as music [*die Herrschaft der Kunst als Musik*]" (Heidegger GA 6.1, p. 102). If Nietzsche is extremely *dichterisch* in his *Zarathustra*, Wagner, conversely, is supremely nihilistic in his *Tristan and Isolde*. It is all a question of presentation (*Darstellung*). In the first case, the presentation is adequate, in the other it is decadent, because once theatre enters into the picture there is *mimesis*, passive identification and disappropriation. However, this does not mean that Heidegger condemns *all* types of music. Like Plato, he makes a distinction between active and passive music, virility and femininity. This division is the same that was practiced by the Greeks: it conserves the 'right' forms (Dorian or Phrygian) and excludes the 'bad' ones (Lydian); it selects the 'good' instruments (such as string instruments) and rejects the 'bad' ones (such as the flute, the *aulos*); it privileges simple rhythms over complex ones.

According to Heidegger, the "necessity of our history" (Heidegger GA 5, p. 102) was to reject the lethargy, the narcotic fascination and the ecstasy of affects and effects. But, does this mean that the last metaphysician, Nietzsche, is the one who gives rise to a conception of the musical that is not and cannot be related in any way to the sphere of affects? Must we believe that the Wagnerian heritage corresponds to a form of music-idolatry that necessarily leads to the display of nihilism, to the dissimulation of the truth of art, and hence, to the dissimulation of philosophy? If music cannot be translated into Greek or German, in which language can it be said or done? Presumably, Nietzsche is the philosopher who broke not only with Wagner, but also with the romantic identification with Greece, Germany and myths. By affirming, as he does in *Ecce Homo:* "I am in Greek, and not just in Greek, the *Anti-Christ*" (EH Books 2, KSA 6, p. 302), by reiterating, as he did so many times, that he was 'Latin' or 'Roman', Nietzsche was grasping the modernity of music and engaging in the quest for a conception of musical time and musical language that did not coincide anymore with what we have learnt from the history and culture of metaphysics. One could argue that by liberating itself from language, music was able to distance itself more and more from the logic of mimesis *vis à vis* philosophy, for which it had been excluded for centuries and confined to tautology – almost to the point of madness.

With his *Sprechgesang* (spoken singing), Schoenberg inaugurates in his monodrama *Pierrot Lunaire* (1912–1913) a new modality of the relation between text and music, whereby music distances itself deliberately from *Dichtung* and moves slowly towards *Sprache* (speaking) and *Sage* (saying). Also in music a new path had been found, the one leading to the exit, not only from metaphysics, but also from Wagnerian nihilism.

II The Image-Less Word

In contrast to the passive reception of affects and figures, Schoenberg introduced the idea of perception: the perception of something we call 'sound'. The Schoenbergian revolution, as well as being grounded on the dialectic reversal of the tonal system and its excess in Wagner's chromaticisms and enharmonics, was also based on certain postulates which nevertheless remained mute. Such as, for instance, the possibility of conceiving sound as a phenomenon and not as a code; a phenomenon that reveals itself and retreats at the very moment it reveals itself as such. Only Nietzsche could have echoed the critical aesthetic dimension represented by that very 'in-audibleness', a critique that targeted German Idealism and its unchanging character, capable of ruining precisely what it aims to celebrate. With Schoenberg, music ceased to be thought of in relation to its philosophical and political determination, subjected to the fatality of decline and decay and to the representation of nationalist affects. Far from dwelling on the Wagnerian cleft from whence the ruin of philosophy had started to be announced, far from restricting himself to a historical determination of how to access an expression of truth, Schoenberg knew how to make music *sound* differently: namely by liberating it from the coatings of affections, by shifting the consonance/dissonance relation to a tonal register, instead of a pitch register, which is what determines the melody or figure. In brief, Schoenberg's composition programme was to go back to the inexplicable, unimaginable, unconceivable, inimitable and unpronounceable. As he wrote it in a letter to Kandinsky dated 24 January 1911: "art belongs to the *unconscious!*" (Schoenberg/Kandinsky 1980, p. 21).

Serial composition forbids all figuration. This rupture within the melodic identity shows very clearly that the place in which the unconceivable (*infigurable*) is conceived is a non-place: "but in the desert you are invincible", says Moises in Schoenberg's opera. The unconceivable is, thus, pure shifting, pure movement and passage from Moises' (Aaron's) mouth, to the voice of the burning bush (the choir), and to the words that speak (Moises). The only phenomenal presence is given by the Tablets of Law, which is a way to reintroduce *Bildung* or the imagery from the total exile of tonality. *Moises and Aaron*[3] is a lyric opera constructed on a single tone row. But this row or series is combined, from the very beginning, with versions or derived forms of itself, and does not occur in its original form. In the same way, the flow of the text itself cannot be represented in any determined way, or as following one subject alone. The text is instead borne by an inexhaustible acoustic combination, appealing directly to us, rather than referring us to an allegorical, poetical or narrative comprehension. The pathos of freedom in the sense of the self-determination of the I is not required by the world of figural appearances. Here, what activates our attention to the extreme is the absolute experience of hearing. For Schoenberg, this experience is without any doubt the highest manifestation of a total defection of nihilism and its corresponding transmutations in the Neo-Classical and Romantic aesthetic movements which pervaded music in Europe. Under 'defection' it is important that we understand a radical transformation at the core of the hierarchical structures and parameters of the language of sound. With Schoenberg this transformation reached a point of non-return: an inaudible structure embodied by infinite variations of all the elements composing this gigantesque work, which, in a certain sense, constitutes a negative form of Greek tragedy. For its form does not fall back on anything, except for a lack: a breach, an impossibi-

---

[3] Schoenberg started this Opera in 1933 but never finished it. He put music to the first two acts, but the 3rd only has the text.

lity, a suspended word, an alteration of time itself: "*O Wort, du Wort, das mir fehlt!*".[4]

It is the task of music to recount this lack, the lack of words, or the lack of *logos*. Its task is to carefully *disfigure* the temporalisation of the infinite combinations so as to not reconfigure it, for fear of making the positivity of the figural and the message appear at the surface of the notation. While German musical Idealism strived towards the idea of an originary unity which would prevail over and against any scission, Schoenberg endeavours to achieve the inverse movement. With *Moises and Aaron*, he shows that the separation or rupture is what is always already inscribed at the core of the original structure. Its development in time and becoming, movement and space is a form of exile with no return towards an immemorial unity that never took place. A certain narration can be born from this immemorial absence. But it is a form of narration in which what is said and revoked does not lie in the sounds, but rather emerges in between the sounds. The nihilistic figure has thus fallen into the *Mitte* – as if it had been absorbed by it. What is told is precisely what is not said.

Schelling had already envisaged an access to what escapes our knowledge by listening to a thought; the thought of the original being. This form of listening, which according to Nietzsche became a passion for the origin, was much more than just a means to attain knowledge. Similarly, though, Nietzsche himself, after his initial admiration for Schopenhauer and Wagner and turning away from Romanticism and Idealism, would try to find in music a sonorous existence (*ein tönendes Dasein*) that would form a unity with philosophy and poetry. In this sense, Schoenberg's unfinished *Moises and Aaron*, can be seen as a response to Nietzsche's intuitions. For, in spite of his Jewish spiritual orientation, Schoenberg places the question of the Law transmitted by Moises at the core of a problematic which is certainly difficult to apprehend, namely the renewal of the lyrical genre after Wagner.

Thus, the idea of modernity defended by Schoenberg is represented by a composition that captures a reflection of the sacred which had already become inaccessible in the sense that the present time could no longer relate to it. This paradox is particularly significant if we consider that the unfinished character of Schoenberg's *Moises and Aaron* can be interpreted as being 'a response' to Gershom Scholem's theological intuitions. Scholem was a contemporary and friend of Walter Benjamin, who defended his belief that in a time of decline, of extreme precariousness of humanity over and against an increasing process of de-humanisation, the only aesthetic that can still redeem a remnant of huma-

---

4 "*Oh word, word, that I lack!*" (End of the 2nd act of Schoenberg's *Moises and Aaron*).

nity, the only aesthetic that can still conserve a fragment of utopia and a promise of joy is an aesthetic of the fragment, an aesthetic of the unfinished. It is what Benjamin calls the 'ruins' or the allegory as a form of discontinuity between representation (what is visible) and the Idea (what is non-representable). The fragment of the utopia is like the negative of a given representation: a representation without image, without message – with an *unnamable name*.

Adorno, developing further this idea, considers that Schoenberg's opera brings to light an antinomy that is intrinsic to art. For Adorno, the utopia of modern art lies in this very antinomy, which is to be seen as a radical and non-reconciliatory way of diverting the question of the aura in order to supplant it by the sheer force of the non-representable and unimaginable. According to Adorno, the actual presence of a religious dimension within the musical work overturns the hypothesis of the aura, which is substituted by the radicality of a musical language that goes beyond any signifying language and sends us back to the divine Name that reveals itself without being said or told, without being named. By revealing the power of the work without disclosing it, the meaning of the Name – both precise and concealed – endows music, not with an irreducible *aura* as Benjamin says, but with a non-mediated form of the 'absolute'. As Adorno puts it: "music finds the absolute immediately" (Adorno 1978, p. 254). But, at the very precise moment in which we begin to participate in the musical experience, the experience itself becomes unattainable, "at the moment of discovery it becomes obscured, just as a too powerful light dazzles the eyes, preventing them from seeing things that are perfectly visible" (Adorno 1963, p. 254). If the essence of music is the mystery of the Name of what cannot be named because it is unknown to us, it also is what allows us to put an end to the lie of representation. That is also why musical language is not reducible to a conceptual signification, but calls for a mimetic dimension – which is a recurrent theme in Adorno's thought.

Within mimetic practice, musical language (understood as the experience of being out of place, confronted by language, concepts, narration and everything belonging to the art of saying and signifying) becomes friction and rapture, fragmented into shreds of meaning. Both music and language allure each other in this intimate nomadic movement through which they resemble the unfinished. At the moment in which one of them touches the absolute, the condition of which is to remain unattainable, the other responds with a clinical logic. But what can be said about an art that unites the relative and the absolute? Adorno's response is itself a mimetic attempt and demands that art itself respond to its own deficiencies. Failure brings music and language together: "It is by distancing itself from language that its resemblance to language finds its fulfilment" (Adorno 1978, p. 255).

We can now almost foresee from Schoenberg's *Moises and Aaron*, understood as following Nietzsche's legacy after his rupture with Wagner, a form of aesthetics that cannot be thematised, although this does not mean that it is totally void of content. This is the paradox, because the absence of a theme, the non-thematic is also a disturbing manifestation of incompleteness itself. What can be thematised can be delimitated; it is historical from back to front, such as all those works of art that follow a logic of closure. History itself, taken as a symptom of a symbolic code, cannot account for those time effects that come from the necessity of something that is beyond our own temporality. For they install a moment of indecisiveness, a doubt, something that is almost historical, a harrowing and tragic vision of modernity that music transmutes into dissonances without resolution. Conversely, the utopia Benjamin refers to has a melancholic, nostalgic nature and offers an alienating representation of history. But, by subverting the aura-logic, the utopia itself recovers its intrusive and disruptive force and is able to reverse the disenchantment provoked by the loss of an ideal aura. With *Moises and Aaron*, Schoenberg develops the non-theme of the failure of language and of the way in which each word defeats itself. The truth of the work of art, just as the truth of history cannot be said in words. The reason why the word is always missing has to do with the nature of words. Language takes place always already after the event. Thus the fall, the catastrophe, the ruin. Following the model of Adam, the word of signifying language reproduces itself infinitely. Once we want to name a thing, from the very moment in which we want to stick a name to an experience, we need to say it incessantly, and we need to say it again and again to infinity together with other words. This impossibility of saying or naming a thing once and for all is the reason why we can only achieve our aim by distorting it: distorting both the thing and the word. Whatever we say, whatever we announce, pronounce or proclaim, we never have perfect knowledge of the truth of the words. Once they constitute a piece of knowledge, they have already lost their relation to 'things'. Music, on the contrary, as a form of the Name is full of the 'thing'. Musical experience is not knowledge or mastery of *logos*, an accumulation of words and voices with the teleological vocation of waiting for the Name.

In *Moises and Aaron*, this whole accumulation seems to be in a free fall. It falls within the notes, within the gaps of the silent intervals and is witness of a fragmented knowledge. Music is here a sublime gesture of a deposition. In this way something emerges that is more essential than the totality of all the words. Indeed, the critique of German Idealism inaugurated by Nietzsche proves to be very influential within the domain of aesthetics. By distancing himself from the idea of art as an *organon* (Schelling), Schoenberg is able to re-establish the will to the unimaginable and non-representable as a new way of experiencing of our relation to the world. Schoenberg follows the path opened up by Nietzsche and, without saying it, defies the idea of the saviour, Christian God. The only God who recognises aesthetic thought to be a philosophical thought is not a mythological God, i.e. a god that can be represented. If there is a God, He is more like like the will to power in Nietzsche or the will to *desacralisation* in Schoenberg.

References

Adorno, Theodor W. (1978): *Musikalische Schriften I–III*. In: *Gesammelte Schriften*, vol. 16. Frankfurt a.M.: Suhrkamp.

Schönberg, Arnold/Kandinsky, Wassily (1980): *Briefe, Bilder und Dokumente einer außergewöhnlichen Begegnung*. Jelena Hahl-Koch (Ed). Salzburg and Vienna: Residenz Verlag.

Leonel Ribeiro dos Santos
The 'Will to Appearance' or Nietzsche's Kantianism According to Hans Vaihinger

I Defying the Improbable

The following essay aims to evoke one of the first explicit interpretations of *Nietzsche as a Philosopher*; one which, though nearly forgotten, would still appear to defy the improbable. Indeed, despite the deafening and all but courteous criticism of Kant and Kantian philosophy echoing from Nietzsche's most renowned writings, Hans Vaihinger (1852–1933) was able to recognise, not only the philosopher in Nietzsche, but also a previously ignored Kantian genealogy deep within the core of his programme – namely, within the *topos* of the 'will to appearance' (*Wille zum Schein*). But of course, this insight was only possible because Vaihinger had discovered a previously undisclosed dimension of Kant's thought, perhaps even a different Kant altogether.

Vaihinger was perhaps one of the first thinkers to recognise the philosophical substance and significance of Nietzsche's work, and the very first of few to recognise not only Nietzsche's debt to Kant, but also a profound and essential affinity between their thought; an affinity that went unnoticed for a long time, let alone recognised by Nietzsche himself, especially if we consider the more mature phase of his thought. Beyond, and in spite of Nietzsche's words against Kant and his philosophy, Vaihinger succeeds in discerning in the author of *The Anti-Christ* a true Kantian thinker. A Kantian thinker influenced perhaps by 'another Kant', perhaps even the 'authentic Kant', whom Vaihinger himself had discovered. This is the Kant who had demonstrated the fundamental and positive role of fiction in all creations of the human mind, regarding not only science, metaphysics or art, but also (and especially) morality and religion; in brief: the Kant of the "as if [*als ob*]" (Vaihinger 1911, p. 771–790).

If we approach Nietzsche's best known texts (excluding some of the more expressive statements from the first phase of his writings from the late 60s and early 70s), we are bound to observe nothing but aggressive anti-Kantian sentiments. However, in some *Nachlass* notes from 1872–1873, Kant is portrayed as a thinker who, by means of his *Critique of Pure Reason*, put an end to the intentions and illusions of science, thus leaving free space for the emergence of "a new kind of philosopher-artist, capable of creating a work of art of aesthetic value" (NL 1872/73, KSA 7, 19[38], p. 431). For Nietzsche, *this* Kant represents a pioneer as well as a precursor of his own aesthetic metaphysics insofar as the

Critique of Pure Reason had preceded him in "taming the instinct of knowledge" and making way for the "reinforcement of moral and aesthetic instincts":

> A necessity of civilisation drives Kant: he wants to *save* a field *from knowledge*: that is where the roots of everything most noble and most profound – art and ethics – are to be found [...]. (NL 1872/73, KSA 7, 19[34], p. 427)[1]

Years later, however, this depiction of Kant as *"the philosopher of tragic knowledge"* who had tamed the "instinct of knowledge [*Wissenstrieb*]", and yet refrained from founding "a new metaphysics" (NL 1872/73, KSA 7, 19[35], p. 427–428) – ends up being definitively buried and forgotten under the image of a moralist whom Nietzsche subjects to the most unfounded and vile accusations. It is these accusations that give rise to the doubt as to whether Nietzsche even bothered to read the writings of Kant, which he so harshly attacked. It is no use to assume that those first considerations, positive and promising as they may be, succeed in compensating for the raw hostility of his later judgment. For it is Nietzsche himself who, in 1886, attempts to write a "self-critique" of his early writings, where he regrets not having had the courage to express his new ideas in his own true language, having instead resorted to the language of Schopenhauer and Kant, although he was expressing something contrary to their spirit and taste (BT Attempt 6, KSA 1, p. 19). Therefore, only by contradicting the self-representation that Nietzsche made of himself can we re-enact and re-establish his real genealogy: to which we may apply, no doubt, Kant's observation regarding his own interpretation of Plato, according to which we are frequently in a position of understanding and interpreting an author much better than he himself did (KrV B 370).

Returning to Vaihinger's discoveries of Nietzsche as a philosopher and Nietzsche as a Kantian thinker, however, let us begin by stating that neither one nor the other were early, much less were they simultaneous discoveries. One might ask: was it the attention devoted to Kant's 'as if' that enabled Vaihinger to discover the philosophical dimension of Nietzsche's work? Or was the discovery of Nietzsche as a philosopher that had an impact on the discovery of Kant's 'as if'? In fact, neither of these is the case. The first hypothesis proves unfounded, since in his book on Nietzsche (1902), neither the 'will to appearance' nor fiction stand out as being particularly relevant themes for Vaihinger. Certainly, the theme of appearance (*Schein*) is present, but only with reference to Schopen-

---

1 "Eine Kulturnoth treibt Kant: er will ein Gebiet *vor dem Wissen retten*: dorthin legt die Wurzeln alles Höchsten und Tiefsten, Kunst und Ethik".

hauer's doctrine of the subordination of the understanding and its representations to the will, and in relation to Nietzsche's subsequent transformation of the concept of 'truth' under the influence of Darwinism. Rather than the 'will to appearance' or fiction, the topics that come to the fore in the text are the 'will to live' (*Wille zum Leben*) and the 'will to power' (*Wille zur Macht*). Likewise, the second hypothesis – i.e., that which posits a possible influence of Vaihinger's discovery of Nietzsche as a philosopher after the discovery of the importance of the 'as if' in Kant's philosophy – must also be discarded; for in the first edition of his Nietzsche book, Vaihinger never considers any possible relation between Nietzsche and Kant as being important for his interpretation. A reference to Nietzsche's anti-Kantianism does not appear until a short paragraph in the brief appendix to the third edition of 1905. In other words, it seems that Vaihinger draw his attention to the existence of a kinship between Nietzsche and Kant quite later. On the other hand, his discovery of the importance of Kant's 'as if' occurred much earlier than his discovery of Nietzsche as a philosopher. In the late essay in his intellectual autobiography, "How the 'As If' Philosophy was Born" ("Wie die Philosophie des Als Ob entstand"), Vaihinger informs us that the third Historical Part of his work *The Philosophy of the As If* (i.e. the interpretation of the passages in Kant dealing with the *Als Ob*) had been produced between 1877 and 1879. However, the final version of that section (or parts of it) probably appeared after 1906, i.e. after Vaihinger was afflicted by blindness which impeded him from lecturing at university. He presumably wrote the "Appendix on Kant and Nietzsche" during this final phase, concluding the work on the text in the spring of 1911.

II Vaihinger's Discovery of Nietzsche as a Philosopher

In the preface to the first edition of *Nietzsche as a Philosopher*, Vaihinger feels no reluctance in admitting his very late discovery of the philosophical significance of Nietzsche's work. One such opportunity may have arisen at a conference he held in late July 1899.This concurs with Vaihinger's words in the preface to the second edition of *The Philosophy of the As If* (1913), where he reveals that his encounter with Nietzsche's philosophy was experienced as a new and refreshing event. Indeed, it was in this encounter that he discovered a fundamental kinship between his and Nietzsche's philosophical perspectives, which he attributes to their mutual sources of inspiration: Schopenhauer and Lange. Vaihinger writes:

> Back then, around 1898, something new arose in my spiritual horizon, the acquaintance with Nietzsche's writings [...] Herein lay a fountain of purely fresh water; herein lay ideas which were independent from traditional problems and formulations, and these revolutionary ideas which very often coincided with my own – something which I discreetly indicated in my work *Nietzsche as a Philosopher*. (Vaihinger 1918, p. III–IV)[2]

Even though, as has been asserted above, Vaihinger's reading of Nietzsche played no role in the genesis and conception of his notion of 'as if', it did influence him by confirming the pertinence both of that conception and reinforcing his decision to publish his work, over three decades after its earliest composition. Vaihinger himself confirms this in his "Vorwort des Verfassers" to the first edition of *The Philosophy of the As If*:

> When, in the late 90s, I read Nietzsche (from whom I had previously strayed, misled as I was by second-hand and false expositions), I acquiesced, to my own amazement, a profound kinship between our whole comprehension of life and the world, partly leading back to the same sources: Schopenhauer and F.A. Lange. From the moment I met Nietzsche, this great liberator, I decided to publish, still during my lifetime, the work which by then lay in my drawer, destined to be an *Opus Postumum*. For now could I hope that the point I had reached – the doctrine of false yet necessary representations – would be understood; for this very doctrine is to be found in Nietzsche. In him, most certainly as but one of the many tones inherent to his rich polyphonic nature, whereas in me, as an exclusive (and yet all the more clear, consequent and systematic) principle. A special appendix (p. 771–790) describes the coincidences regarding this matter. The greater part of Nietzsche's developments concerning this problem result from his last phase; and yet, it is noteworthy that his fundamental assertions on this matter proceed from the same period – the 70s – in which this work was produced. (Vaihinger 1918, p. XIV–XV)[3]

---

[2] "Um jene Zeit, ca. 1898, trat ein Neues in meinen geistigen Horizont ein, die Bekanntschaft mit den Schriften Nietzsches. [...] Hier war ein ganz frisches Quellwasser, hier waren Ideen, unabhängig von den traditionellen Fragestellungen und Formulierungen – und diese revolutionären Ideen deckten sich in vielen Punkten mit den meinigen: in meiner Schrift 'Nietzsche als Philosoph' habe ich das leise angedeutet."

[3] "Als ich Ende der 90Jahre Nietzsche las, dem ich bis dahin, durch falsche sekundäre Darstellungen abgeschreckt, fern geblieben war, erkannte ich zu meinen freudigen Erstaunen eine tiefe Verwandtschaft der ganzen Lebens- und Weltauffassung, die teilweise auf dieselben Quellen zurückgeht: Schopenhauer und F.A. Lange. Damals, als ich Nietzsche, diesen grossen Befreier, kennen lernte, fasste ich den Entschluss, mein im Pulte liegendes Werk, dem die Rolle eines *Opus Postumum* zugedacht war, doch noch bei Lebzeiten erscheinen zu lassen. Denn ich durfte nun hoffen, dass der Punkt, auf den es mir ankam, die Lehre von den bewusstfalschen, aber doch notwendigen Vorstellungen, eher Verständnis finden werde, da er auch bei Nietzsche sich findet: freilich bei ihm nur als einer der vielen Töne seiner reichen, polyphonen Natur, bei mir als ausschliessliches Hauptprinzip, aber vielleicht darum auch klarer, konsequenter, systematischer. Ein besonderer Anhang (S.771–790) legt die Koinzidenzen in diesem Punkte dar. Die

In 1902, in the first edition of his *Nietzsche as a Philosopher*, Vaihinger deems it necessary to situate Nietzsche's philosophy; and he does so by placing him in opposition with other philosophical positions. Nietzsche thereby becomes an '*anti*' philosopher: anti-metaphysical, anti-spiritualist, anti-absolutist, anti-teleological, anti-hedonist, anti-egoist, anti-utilitarian, anti-Christian, anti-romanticist, anti-democratic, anti-liberal, anti-humanist, anti-nationalist and anti-German. This list can be divided into seven 'main tendencies', described as follows: anti-moralism, anti-socialism, anti-democratism, anti-feminism, anti-intellectualism, anti-pessimism and anti-Christianity (Vaihinger 1902a, p. 28–37). In his appendix to the third edition, Vaihinger adds two further characteristic tendencies which, in fact, are no more than a specification of the anti-metaphysical tendency: Nietzsche is now also characterised as

> not just anti-platonic, but also *anti-Kantian*; and certainly one of the most sagacious and unfair of Kant's opponents. Kant transformed the objects of ancient metaphysics from knowable beings into unknowable "things-in-themselves". But this doctrine also is opposed to Nietzsche's sense, just as Nietzsche's sense is opposed to it. To Nietzsche, this doctrine is but a camouflaged metaphysics, and therefore he fights in it the same way he fights almost all other Kantian positions. In Plato and Kant, as in nearly all other metaphysicians, Nietzsche discerns the defenders of ideas such as the Unconditional and the Absolute; and it is against these ideas that he aims the arrows of his satire. (Vaihinger 2002, p. 46)[4]

Let us observe some aspects of Vaihinger's interpretation of Nietzsche as a philosopher. First of all, he feels the need to address the objections which at the time impeded the recognition of the philosophical value of Nietzsche's writings; the objection, for example, that Nietzsche was no more than a fashion writer, soon to be replaced by a different fashion writer; or that his thought exhibited the lack of systematicity and even incongruence, typical of such writers; or that his writings were the work of an ill mind. It was generally accepted that

---

meisten Ausführungen Nietzsche's über dies Problem stammen aus seiner späten Zeit; aber es ist bemerkenswert, dass Nietzsche's grundlegende Äusserungen hierüber aus derselben Zeit stammen, aus den 70er Jahren, in denen auch die vorliegende Schrift entstanden ist."

4 "Nietzsche ist aber nicht bloß Antiplatoniker, er ist auch *Antikantianer*. Und zwar einer der schärfsten und wohl auch ungerechtesten Gegner Kants. Kant hat die Objekte der alten Metaphysik aus erkennbaren Seienden in unerkennbare 'Dinge an sich' verwandelt. Aber auch diese Lehre ist gegen Nietzsches Sinn, und Nietzsches Sinn ist gegen sie. Diese Lehre ist ihm nur verkappte Metaphysik, und so kämpft er gegen sie, wie auch fast gegen alle anderen Positionen Kants. In Platon und Kant, wie überhaupt in den Metaphysikern sieht Nietzsche Vertreter der Idee des Unbedingten, des Absoluten, und gerade gegen diese Ideen richtet er die Pfeile seines Spottes."

Nietzsche could be considered a brilliant writer who seduced his readers by means of his poetic, rhetorical and symbolic style, as well as the critical, unsystematic, fragmentary and even contradictory character of his work. However, only reluctantly could it be accepted that he deserved to be considered a true philosopher. Nonetheless, around the same time, other essays emerged that laid claim to the philosophical aspect of Nietzsche's work and thought (Eisler 1902, Rittelmeyer 1903). While rejecting the aforementioned prejudices, Vaihinger attempts to identify the nucleus of Nietzsche's vision of the world, as well as to understand it both genetically and in its peculiar coherence, convinced that a work which had caused such a powerful impact must possess an underlying, unified message. By the end of his book, Vaihinger feels entitled to conclude that, despite its aphoristic form and its unsystematic appearance, Nietzsche's thought forms a logically coherent whole that proceeds with immanent necessity from a fundamental principle and finally constitutes an enclosed circle. According to Vaihinger, this only becomes apparent once one understands the kernel of Nietzsche's thought; to be sure, even his apparently most paradoxical assertions may be understood as consequences of that fundamental principle (Vaihinger 1902a, p. 102–103).

Vaihinger makes some interesting remarks concerning Nietzsche's peculiar, aphoristic, lyrical and symbolic style. Without wanting to minimise his originality, he does point to some thinkers with whom Nietzsche is akin in some aspect or other of his thought, be they antique, renaissance, modern or even contemporary authors. In this last case, three names are emphasised: Schopenhauer, Darwin and Lange (whom, as we shall see, Vaihinger himself considers to be decisive with respect to his own intellectual development). Above all, Vaihinger identifies the fundamental principle from which the whole of Nietzsche's vision derives, namely, Schopenhauer's doctrine of the will, which suffers a positive inversion under the influx of Darwinism. Thus, the pessimism which characterises Schopenhauer's philosophy of the will becomes, through Darwin's mediation, the optimistic philosophy of life and the 'will to live' (*Wille zum Leben*) that characterises the second period of Nietzsche's writing. This, in turn, would soon evolve into his philosophy of the "will to power" (*Wille zur Macht*), which dominates the third phase of his thought (Vaihinger 1902a, p. 52–55).

According to Vaihinger, it is Schopenhauer's thought that prevails throughout the three phases of Nietzsche's work: the primacy of the will over the intellect; the intellect conceived as an organ of life subordinated to life and will; the consequent relativisation of the intellect, science and truth; the idea that the world represented by the understanding is but a phenomenon of a deceptive appearance, and that, in truth, nothing is real. But this pessimistic Schopenhauerian background is then combined with Darwin's principle of the original energy of instincts, which commands the struggle to live. It is this Darwinian principle, taken as a form of metaphysical vitalism, which then transforms Schopenhauer's pessimism into an optimistic worldview. Life's struggle for existence has a meaning: the production of the fittest and the strongest. Therefore, not all deceptive representations of the intellect, of which Schopenhauer spoke, are equally valid – or, in other words, these are not equally destitute of value. The Darwinian notions of selection and the struggle for existence allow us to distinguish two main groups of illusive representations; namely, on the one hand, those which promote life and, on the other, those which are harmful to life. There is a selection between them, and only those that promote life survive. It is these that men call 'truths'. Nietzsche's anti-intellectualist orientation, thus, culminates in a powerful inversion of the traditional concept of truth. Appearance is at the service of the will to live, and deception and illusion lose their negative sense and acquire a positive value as organs promoting life, that is, as instruments of power (Vaihinger 1902a, p. 83–84).

III From the Discovery of Nietzsche as a Philosopher to the Discovery of a Kantian Nietzsche

A noteworthy aspect in Vaihinger's account is the affinity he establishes between his own fictionalist vision and certain essential aspects of Nietzsche's vision of the world. Not that this affinity implies a complete identity between the two positions. This affinity is explained by Vaihinger as proceeding from a common intellectual genealogy; that is, from influences which left an identical mark but were apprehended differently by both authors: Schopenhauer, Darwin, Lange and, of course, Kant.

As far as his relation to Lange is concerned, Vaihinger emphasises how he found in Lange a fertile symbiosis between Schopenhauer and Kant (whose philosophy had already exerted a decisive influence on him). Referring to the publication of the second edition of Lange's *History of Materialism* (1874/75), Vaihinger confesses to have found in Lange a guide, a master, a thinker who was on the right path towards the methodological problem of fictions and from whom he received the stimulus to further deepen this problem (Vaihinger 1921, p. 197).

Furthermore, Vaihinger considers Lange to be the true pioneer of the 'return to Kant' movement which evolved in Germany in the last quarter of the nineteenth century. In a note to his late autobiographical essay, he interprets the different paths followed by that movement, claiming himself to be the protagonist of at least one of them:

> Departing from the neo-Kantianism of F.A. Lange, one could choose two different paths: either one which more accurately developed Kant's point of view, by leading to a closer and more faithful investigation of Kant's teaching – which was done by Cohen; or one which combined Lange's neo-Kantianism with empiricism and positivism. This was operated by my *philosophy of the 'as if'*, which, in turn, also leads to a deeper investigation of Kant's *as if* theory. (Vaihinger 1921, p. 197)[5]

In the first edition of *The Philosophy of the As If*, Vaihinger uses an excerpt from one of Lange's personal letters as epigraph for his own work. In this excerpt, Lange declares he is "convinced that the topic emphasised in that work would, one day, become the cornerstone of the philosophical theory of knowledge". Further, one of the sections contained in the third part of the work, devoted to "historical confirmations" of the *Als Ob* doctrine, is dedicated to Lange: "Friedrich Albert Langes 'Standpunkt des Ideals'" (Vaihinger 1911, p. 753–771). In this part of the text, Vaihinger indicates the Kantian origins of Lange's philosophy – even if Lange himself did not always acknowledge such influence.

The young Nietzsche had also recognised the influence which the first edition of Lange's work had exerted on his philosophical development. This is stated in a letter to Hermann Muschacke dated November 1866:

> The most substantial philosophical work of the last decade is undoubtedly the History of Materialism by Lange; a work to which I could devote a long eulogy. Kant, Schopenhauer and this book by Lange – I need nothing else. (KSB 2, p. 184)[6]

Back then, the Kant who interested Nietzsche – or the Kant he was able to see – was the one projected either by his reading of Schopenhauer, or by his reading of Lange.

As has already been shown, Vaihinger makes no positive allusion to the relation between Kant and Nietzsche in the first edition of his book on Nietzsche.

---

[5] "Vom Neukantianismus eines F.A. Lange aus konnten zwei verschiedene Wege eingeschlagen werden, entweder konnte der Kantischen Standpunkt auf Grund genaueren Eindringens in die Kantische Lehre schärfer und treuer herausgearbeitet werden, dies geschah durch Cohen. Oder man konnte den Neukantianismus Langes mit dem Empirismus und Positivismus in Verbindung bringen. Dies ist durch meine Philosophie des Als Ob geschehen, die aber ebenfalls auf ein gründlicheres Eindringen in die Kantische Als-Ob-Lehre führt."

[6] "Das bedeutendste philosophische Werk, was in den letzten Jahrzehnten erschienen ist, ist unzweifelhaft Langes, Geschichte des Materialismus, über das ich eine bogenlange Lobrede schreiben könnte. Kant, Schopenhauer und dies Buch von Lange – mehr brauche ich nicht."

The brief reference to Nietzsche's anti-Kantianism appears only in the third edition of the book (1905). Consequently, one may assume that only after this date did Vaihinger discover such a relation, and that he did not clarify it until the re-elaboration phase of his work *The Philosophy of the As If* – which, as was demonstrated, was concluded in the spring of 1911. How, then, did this change in perspective, which led to the discovery of a Kantian Nietzsche, occur?

We can only conjecture. Vaihinger, of course, notes a certain affinity of topics, which he interprets as proceeding from the aforementioned mutual influences. In the meantime, however, some of Nietzsche's early writings were published. One in particular, *On Truth and Lie in an Extra-Moral Sense*, would be promptly commented by Vaihinger in his appendix to his work of 1911 and may be considered the *organon* of Nietzsche's thought: a true 'discourse of method' to what one could consider a transcendental metaphorology. In that essay – and in response to the question "What is truth after all?" – Nietzsche writes:

> An army of moving metaphors, metonymies, anthropomorphisms, a sum of human relations which have been poetically and rhetorically sublimated, transposed, adorned, and which, after having been long used, now tend to appear in the eyes of a people as firm, canonical, binding: truths are illusions which we forget as such, metaphors which were once used and have lost their sensible force, coins which have lost their face and are no longer considered as coins, rather as mere metal. (TL 1, KSA 1, p. 880–881)[7]

Given that in 1900 Vaihinger had written an essay proposing that Kant be considered not just a metaphysician but also a metaphorician (Vaihinger 1900, p. 158 and 1902b, p. 117), when he read Nietzsche's essay, he could not but view the two thinkers as being linked by a common philosophical root. Indeed, in his appendix, two other sources of inspiration for Nietzsche appear alongside Schopenhauer and Darwin; namely, F.A. Lange and Kant. Vaihinger underscores the decisive role of Lange's work on Nietzsche's reception of Kant (Nietzsche now being explicitly recognised as a member of the *Als Ob* family of philosophers). Certainly, it is worth recalling that it was Kant who unveiled the transcendental illusions of reason and characterised the ideas of reason as reason's own fictions or inventions (*Dichtungen der Vernunft*); it was also he who, under the recurrent formula of the *Als Ob,* granted fictional judgment a vast territory in his own phi-

---

[7] "Was ist also Wahrheit? Ein bewegliches Heer von Metaphern, Metonymien, Anthropomorphismen kurz eine Summe von menschlichen Relationen, die, poetisch und rhetorisch gesteigert, übertragen, geschmückt wurden, und die nach langem Gebrauche einen Volke fest, canonisch und verbindlich dünken: die Wahrheiten sind Illusionen, von denen man vergessen hat, dass sie welche sind, Metaphern, die abgenutzt und sinnlich kraftlos geworden sind, Münzen, die ihr Bild verloren haben und nun als Metall, nicht mehr als Münzen in Betracht kommen."

losophy. That which, according to Vaihinger, best links Nietzsche and Kant is thus the theme of fiction – i.e. the doctrine of consciously false yet necessary representations. Nietzsche approached this theme in terms of the 'will to appearance'; a notion he opposes to the 'will to truth', which, according to him, had long since dominated western thought.

In his appendix on Kant and Nietzsche, entitled "Nietzsche and his Theory of Consciously Willed Appearance (The Will to Appearance) [*Nietzsche und seine Lehre vom bewusstgewollten Schein ('Der Wille zum Schein')*]", Vaihinger embraces the task of showing how the idea of fiction shapes the whole of Nietzsche's philosophy. Likewise, he uses the third part of the work to illuminate how the 'as if' doctrine shaped Kant's work right up until his last reflections in the *Opus Postumum*. The result of this new reading is that Nietzsche is placed in the vein of neo-Kantianism discovered by Lange and followed by Vaihinger himself. In his own peculiar style, therefore, Nietzsche would not only be a Kantian who did not recognise himself as such, but also a Kantian not recognised as being such by his contemporaries. For the first time, the Kantian – or even neo-Kantian – origin of Nietzsche's doctrine is recognised as well as emphasised through an appreciation of Lange's influence. Vaihinger writes:

> Until now, this Kantian – or, if one prefers – neo-Kantian origin of Nietzsche's doctrine has been utterly neglected. [...] Nietzsche does indeed possess a lot of Kant, certainly not of that Kant in school books, [...] rather of Kant's spirit, the authentic Kant: the one who saw appearance to its deepest roots and yet, having seen it in its depth, also consciously saw and recognised its usefulness and necessity. (Vaihinger 1911, p. 772)[8]

Vaihinger's appendix follows the theme of appearance and a variety of associated concepts (e.g. illusion, perspectivism, 'as if', metaphor and lie) through the development of Nietzsche's thought. Here Vaihinger reveals Nietzsche's proximity to Kant, which he repeatedly emphasises with exclamations such as: "entirely Kantian! [*ganz Kantisch!*]". The appendix ends with an idea suggested by some of Nietzsche's writings from the late period (one of his most ostensibly anti-Kantian stages): the idea of an "'as if' metaphysics". This idea faced the following question: what part does illusion or appearance play in the totality of

---

8 "Man hat diesen Kantischen, oder wenn man lieber will, Neukantischen Ursprung der Nietzscheschen Lehre bisher vollständig verkannt. ... Nietzsche hat tatsächlich sehr viel von Kant, freilich nicht von dem Kant, wie er in den Schulbüchern steht [...], sondern vom Geiste Kants, des echten Kant, der den Schein bis in seine tiefsten Wurzeln durchschaut, aber auch die Nützlichkeit und Notwendigkeit des durchschautem Scheins mit Bewusstsein erkennt und anerkennt."

occurrences that make up the world, and how should one value those occurrences that necessarily produce illusion? Within one such programme, illusion or appearance would no longer be conceived as a mere logic of human thought, but as the logic of the world, as the very game that being plays with itself. It would thus be aesthetic creation and poetical illusion that would enable us to catch a glimpse of the being as an eternal representation and forgery. The will to appearance, illusion and deception would therefore reveal itself as possessing more metaphysical depth than the will to truth of scientists and metaphysicians. Thus, Vaihinger concludes,

> From this point of view, appearance should no longer be pitied and fought by philosophers (as it has been until now), rather it should be asserted, desired and justified, inasmuch as appearance is useful, valuable and, at the same time, presents itself as being aesthetically untouched. We have a "need for perspectivism". (Vaihinger 1911, p. 778)[9]

This surprising similarity between Nietzsche and Kant not only offers fertile ground for the hermeneutics of their respective philosophies, but also suggests the need for a re-evaluation of the relation between them. Indeed, this is a relation that requires greater critical attention if we are to gain a better understanding of the way in which Nietzsche's programme answers (through continuity, antithesis and further insight) Kant's own programme. Indeed, what joins the two philosophers is the way in which each of them values poetical fiction and, consequently, recognises the importance of poetics of fiction as the fundamental task of the creative activity of the mind (Santos 2012, p. 197–203).

IV Vaihinger's Kant and Nietzsche's Kant

Vaihinger's interpretation of Nietzsche allows us to establish not only a dual relation between Nietzsche and Kant, but also a triangular relation linking Kant, Nietzsche and Vaihinger himself. That which binds them together is fictionalism: the idea of consciously fake, yet necessary illusions or appearances. The philosophical significance and originality of Vaihinger's reading of Kant is clearly confirmed by the breadth of its influence in the 1910s. Although this influence waned in the 1920s and Vaihinger's work came to be severely criticised

---

[9] "Von diesem Standpunkt aus ist der Schein nicht mehr wie bisher von den Philosophen zu beklagen und zu bekämpfen, sondern der Schein ist, soweit er als nützlich und wertvoll, sowie als ästhetisch einwandfrei sich herausstellt, zu bejahen, zu wollen und zu rechtfertigen. Der 'Perspektivismus' ist uns 'notwendig'."

as an inadequate interpretation of Kant (Cassirer 1913, p. 40–45, Adickes 1927), he has more recently once again come to be recognised as an important reader of Kant (Ceynowa 1993, Santos 2007, 2008 and 2012, La Rocca 2011). Although the notion of the 'as if' is unable to exhaustively unpack Kant's philosophy, one must nevertheless accredit Vaihinger with having discovered and emphasised this truly fundamental aspect of Kant's thought.

However, in recognising this genealogical relation, what do we stand to gain with respect to our understanding of Nietzsche's and Kant's philosophy? Instead of the Kant viewed as a 'theorist of knowledge' or 'metaphysician', we now find ourselves with an aesthete – that is, a fictionalist and conjecturalist Kant. What, then, does this tell us about Nietzsche? How could he have been so plainly mistaken, to the point of identifying in Kant nothing but an enemy?

There is, in fact, an archaic relation linking Nietzsche to Kant and his philosophy; a relation which, despite its subsequent repression and denial, should not be neglected. Returning to Nietzsche's *On Truth and Lie*, which presents its readers with a sketch of a transcendental metaphorology, one might say that it fulfils a suggestion given by Kant himself; namely, in §59 of his *Critique of Judgement*, where Kant calls for an investigation into the fundaments or metaphorical assumptions which underlie philosophical concepts themselves. However, although Kant thought this task deserved "deeper investigation" (KU, p. 352), it was one he failed to undertake. In TL, it is then almost as if Nietzsche wanted to answer the challenge posed by Kant. So, whilst it remains impossible to conclusively prove Kant's influence on Nietzsche's belief that the *Metaphertrieb* constitutes one of man's fundamental instincts, such a hypothesis should not be discarded (Santos 1994, p. 66–68). Nietzsche had read Kant's third *Critique* around 1868 and had worked on one of its main themes: teleology; indeed, Nietzsche intended to write a dissertation entitled *The Teleology since Kant* [Die Teleologie seit Kant]. In a letter to Vischer dated January 1871, he confesses: "Among all the latest philosophers, I studied with special predilection Kant and Schopenhauer. They have certainly earned my good faith in the last two years" (KSB 3, p. 177).

From the preparatory notes Nietzsche made for the aforementioned dissertation (which was never actually brought to completion), it becomes clear that he learnt from Kant that, beyond their explanatory or scientific power, philosophical concepts and systems are also endowed with an aesthetic sense and value. Nietzsche even writes that "just like optimism, teleology is but an aesthetic product" (BAW 3, p. 375). Nonetheless, Nietzsche's early interpretation of Kant is of greater importance (Santos 1993, Giordanetti 2011). In these writings, Kant is considered a philosopher who anticipates the emergence of a simultaneously tragic and artistic view of the world. Here Nietzsche argues that it is with Kant that philosophical consciousness first transcends itself in the aesthetic experience of reason's and nature's inherent teleology; in this way, then, science is overcome by "mytho-poietical forces" and by a "mythical instinct" (NL 1872/73, KSA 7, 19[62], p. 439).Whether Nietzsche read this out of the *Critique of Judgement* itself, or whether he was led to this conclusion through the mediation of Schopenhauer and Lange (as Vaihinger contends), there is no doubt that his early writings clearly represent a veritable return to Kant. Nietzsche can therefore be read as developing one of the most fundamental (though often underappreciated) dimensions of Kant's thought, which would in turn be taken up once again by his contemporary Vaihinger, though in a work which, due to its late publication, Nietzsche would not have been able to read. So, when Nietzsche asserts in TL that truth is "an army of moving metaphors" and contends that

> we believe we know something about things themselves, [...] though, in truth, we possess nothing but metaphors of things, which in no way correspond to their respective primordial essentialities (TL 1, KSA 1, p. 879),[10]

he is, perhaps unwarily, continuing reason's critical self-interrogation. As Nietzsche illustrates, when reason becomes self-aware and judges its own mode of proceeding, it should question not only the boundaries of knowledge and the status of metaphysics, as Kant did, but also the nature of its own language – *philosophical language* – and thus coming to realise that "the philosopher, too, is caught in the web of *language*" (NL 1872/73, KSA 7, 19[135], p. 463).

Translated from Portuguese by Fernando M.F. Silva; revised by James Pearson

References

Adickes, Erich (1927): *Kant und die Als-Ob Philosophie*. Stuttgart: Fr. Frommanns Verlag.
Cassirer, Ernst (1913): "Erkenntnistheorie nebst den Grenzfragen der Logik". In: *Jahrbücher der Philosophie* 1, p. 4–45.
Ceynowa, Klaus (1993): *Zwischen Pragmatismus und Fiktionalismus. Hans Vaihingers "Philosophie des Als Ob"*. Würzburg: Königshausen & Neumann.
Dörflinger, Bernd/Kruck, Günter (Eds.) (2011): *Über den Nutzen von Illusionen. Die regulativen Ideen in Kants theoretischer Philosophie*. Hildesheim: Olms.
Eisler, Rudolf (1902): *Nietzsche's Erkenntnistheorie und Metaphysik*. Leipzig: H. Haacke.

---

10 "Wir glauben etwas von den Dingen selbst zu wissen, [...] und besitzen doch nichts als Metaphern der Dinge, die den ursprünglichen Wesenheiten ganz und gar nicht entsprechen."

Giordanetti, Piero (2011): *L'avventura della ragione. Kant e il giovane Nietzsche*. Hildesheim: Olms.
La Rocca, Claudio (2011): "Formen des Als-Ob bei Kant". In: Bernd Dörflinger/Günter Kruck (Eds.): *Über den Nutzen von Illusionen. Die regulativen Ideen in Kants theoretischer Philosophie*. Hildesheim: Olms, p. 29–46.
Rittelmeyer, F. (1903): *Friedrich Nietzsche und das Erkenntnisproblem*. Dissertation: Leipzig.
Santos, Leonel Ribeiro dos (1993): "Retorno ao mito. Nietzsche, a música e a tragédia". In: *Philosophica* 1, p. 89–111; reprinted as: "O retorno ao mito, ou a herança kantiana de Nietzsche". In: Leonel Ribeiro dos Santos (1994): *A razão sensível. Estudos Kantianos*. Lisbon: Colibri, p. 117–140.
Santos, Leonel Ribeiro dos (1994): *Metáforas da razão ou economia poética do pensar kantiano*. Lisbon: JNICT/F.C. Gulbenkian.
Santos, Leonel Ribeiro dos (2007): "Hans Vaihinger: O Kantismo como Ficcionalismo?". In: Leonel Ribeiro dos Santos (Ed.): *Kant: Posteridade e Actualidade*. Lisbon: Centro de Filosofia da Universidade de Lisboa, p. 515–536.
Santos, Leonel Ribeiro dos (2008): "Las ficciones de la Razón, o el Kantismo como Ficcionalismo. Una reapreciación de *Die Philosophie des Als Ob* de Hans Vaihinger". In: *Devenires. Revista de Filosofía y Filosofía de la Cultura* IX, No. 18, p. 25–52.
Santos, Leonel Ribeiro dos (2012): *Ideia de uma Heurística Transcendental. Ensaios de Meta-Epistemologia Kantiana*. Lisbon: Esfera do Caos.
Vaihinger, Hans (1876): *Hartmann, Dühring und Lange. Zur Geschichte der deutschen Philosophie im XIX. Jahrhundert. Ein Kritischer Essay*. Iserlohn: J. Baedeker.
Vaihinger, Hans (1900): "Kant – ein Metaphysiker?". In: *Philosophische Abhandlung. Christoph Sigwart zu seinem 70. Geburtstag von einer Reihe von Fachgenossen gewidmet*. Tübingen: Mohr, p. 133–158.
Vaihinger, Hans (1902a): *Nietzsche als Philosoph*. Berlin: Reuther & Reichard.
Vaihinger, Hans (1902b): "Kant – ein Metaphysiker?". In: *Kant-Studien* 7, p. 110–117.
Vaihinger, Hans (1911): *Die Philosophie des Als Ob. System der theoretischen, praktischen und religiösen Fiktionen der Menschheit auf Grund eines idealistischen Positivismus. Mit einem Anhang über Kant und Nietzsche*. Berlin: Reuther & Reichard.
Vaihinger, Hans (1918): *Die Philosophie des Als Ob. System der theoretischen, praktischen und religiösen Fiktionen der Menschheit auf Grund eines idealistischen Positivismus. Mit einem Anhang über Kant und Nietzsche*. Leipzig: Meiner.
Vaihinger, Hans (1921): "Wie die Philosophie des Als Ob entstand". In: Raymund Schmidt (Ed.): *Die Deutsche Philosophie der Gegenwart in Selbstdarstellungen*, vol. 2. Leipzig: Meiner.
Vaihinger, Hans (2002): *Nietzsche als Philosoph*. New edition from the 3rd enlarged edition 1905 (Berlin: Reuther & Reichard), with a "Nachwort" by G. Bleick. Norderstedt: PortaWestfalica.

About the Authors

Frederick Neuhouser is Professor of Philosophy at Barnard College, Columbia University. He is the author of four books: *Rousseau's Critique of Inequality* (2014); *Rousseau's Theodicy of Self-Love: Evil, Rationality, and the Drive for Recognition* (2008); *Actualizing Freedom: Foundations of Hegel's Social Theory* (2000); and *Fichte's Theory of Subjectivity* (1990). He is currently working on a project on the idea of social pathology in 18th-, 19th-, and 20th-century social philosophy.

Herman W. Siemens is Associate Professor in Modern Philosophy at Leiden University and is President of the Friedrich Nietzsche Society of Great Britain. He is a chief editor and contributor to the ongoing Nietzsche Dictionary project, based at the Radboud University of Nijmegen and Leiden. He has published widely on Nietzsche and is co-editor of the 2008 volume *Nietzsche, Power and Politics* (De Gruyter). He now directs a research programme funded by the NWO (Netherlands Organisation for Scientific Research): "Between Deliberation and Agonism: Rethinking Conflict and its Relation to Law in Political Philosophy". He is also a Research Associate of the Universidad Diego Portales (Chile), the University of Pretoria (South Africa) and the Universidade de Lisboa (Portugal).

João Constâncio teaches in the Philosophy Department at the New University of Lisbon. He is director of the research projects of the 'Nietzsche International Lab' on "Nietzsche and the Contemporary Debate on the Self" and "The Plurality of the Subject in Nietzsche and Fernando Pessoa". He is the author of *Arte e niilismo, Nietzsche e o enigma do mundo* (2013), and has published several articles on Nietzsche, including "On Consciousness: Nietzsche's Departure from Schopenhauer", in *Nietzsche-Studien* 40 (2011). He has also edited, with M.J. Branco, *Nietzsche on Instinct and Language* (De Gruyter, 2011) and *As the Spider Spins: Essays on Nietzsche's Critique and Use of Language* (De Gruyter, 2012).

Maria João M. Branco is a Post-Doc researcher at the Instituto de Filosofia da Linguagem (Universidade Nova de Lisboa, Portugal). She has worked and published several articles on Nietzsche and Aesthetics and is currently developing her investigation on the relations between philosophy and music. She is co-editor of *Nietzsche On Instinct and Language* (De Gruyter, 2011) and *As the Spider Spins, Essays on Nietzsche's Critique and Use of Language* (De Gruyter, 2012). She is a member of the Seminario Permanente Nietzscheano – Centro Interdipartimentale Colli-Montinari di Studi su Nietzsche e la Cultura Europea (Università di Pisa, Lecce, Padova, Firenze) and of the GIRN (Groupe International de Recherches sur Nietzsche).

Thomas Kisser is Philosophy Lecturer for the 'Aisthesis Studiengang' at the Ludwig-Maximilians-University in Munich. He is an expert in Spinoza and German Idealism and has worked for the Critical Edition of Schelling's writings based in Munich. He is author of *Selbstbewusstein und Interaktion: Spinozas Theorie der Individualität* (1998), and some of his publications as editor include: *Metaphysik und Methode: Descartes, Spinoza, Leibniz im Vergleich* (2010), *Bild und Zeit* (2011), *Angst. Dimensionen eines Gefühls* (2011).

Carlos João Correia is Associate Professor at the University of Lisbon. Some of his books include: *Sentimento de Si e Identidade Pessoal* (2012), *A Religião e o Sentido da Vida. Paradigmas Culturais* (2011), *Mitos e Narrativas*, (2003) and *Ricoeur e a Expressão Simbólica do Sentido* (1999). He has also published various articles and is the chief editor of several works in the field of Aesthetics and Philosophy of Art. He is Director of the International eJournal of the Centro de Filosofia of the University of Lisbon: philosophy@lisbon.

Katia D. Hay is a Post-Doc researcher at the University of Lisbon, where she was awarded a 6-year grant from the FCT (Fundação para a Ciência e a Tecnologia) for a project on Nietzsche, laughter and language. She has mainly worked on 19th-century Philosophy and Aesthetics. She is author of *Die Notwendigkeit des Scheiterns. Das Tragische als Bestimmung der Philosophie bei Schelling* (2012) and has published various articles in books and journals. She is member of the Centro de Filosofia of the University of Lisbon and of the Collège d'études juives et de philosophie contemporaine at the University Sorbonne, Paris IV.

Eike Brock is Lecturer for Philosophy at the Ruhr University Bochum. He is also a Research Fellow at the Institute for Philosophical Research of Hannover (FIPH). His work is mainly focused on Nietzsche, Nihilism, Cultural Philosophy, Philosophy of Existence, narrative Philosophy and Literature. He has recently published *Nietzsche und der Nihilismus* (De Gruyter, 2015).

Razvan Ioan is currently completing a dissertation on the theme of "The Turn to the Body in Modern Philosophy: Spinoza and Nietzsche", at Leiden University. He is member of the Nietzsche Workgroup in Leiden/Nijmegen and also participates in the Nietzsche Dictionary project (NWB). He has a number of publications, such as "The Politics of Physiology" in *Nietzsche as Political Philosopher*, ed. by M. Knoll (De Gruyter, 2014).

Philipp Schwab is a Postdoctoral Scholar at the Department of Philosophy and Committee on Social Thought, University of Chicago (DAAD, invitation Robert B. Pippin). He is the Scientific Coordinator of a project on editing Schelling's Erlangen Lectures and has published widely on Kierkegaard, German Idealism, Post-

Idealism and 19th- and 20th-century philosophy. He is author of: *Der Rückstoß der Methode. Kierkegaard und die indirekte Mitteilung* (De Gruyter, 2012). He is also co-editor of *Die Philosophie des Tragischen. Schopenhauer – Schelling – Nietzsche* (De Gruyter, 2011) and co-editor of the Journal *Schelling-Studien* and the book series *Beiträge zur Schelling-Forschung* (Alber Verlag).

José Miranda Justo is Associate Professor at the Faculty of Humanities of the University of Lisbon. He is also member of the Research Centre for Philosophy at the University of Lisbon (CFUL) where he headed the projects "Subject and Passivity" and "Translation of Kierkegaard's Works". He has translated Hamann, Herder, Humboldt, Kierkegaard, Nietzsche and Adorno among other authors. He is also co-editor of two collections of essays on Kierkegaard. Some of his recent publications include: *Aesthetic Experience and Artistic Creativity: Knowledge, Affects, Imagination and Language* (2014) and "Kierkegaard: Unity or Singularity?" in *Rivista di Filosofia Neo-Scolastica* 3–4 (2013).

Elisabete M. de Sousa gained her PhD at the University of Lisbon in 2002 with a dissertation on 19th-century Musical Criticism, entitled *Forms of Art: the Practical Criticism of Berlioz, Kierkegaard, Liszt and Schumann*. She is now developing a postdoctoral project on Kierkegaard at the University of Lisbon. She is member of the Permanent Seminar on Kierkegaard Studies. Her publications include several articles on Richard Wagner and Kierkegaard, Mozart and Kierkegaard and on the idea of virtuosity in Kierkegaard's thought, and on his aesthetical thought. She is co-editor of several books, such as *Kierkegaard and The Challenges of Infinitude* (2013).

Danielle Cohen-Levinas is an 'ancienne élève' of the Conservatoire National Supérieur de Musique and Philosophy Professor at the Sorbonne University in Paris, where she has founded the 'Centre d'esthétique, musique et philosophie contemporaine' and the 'Collège d'études juives et de philosophie contemporaine'. She is associate-researcher at the Archives Husserl de Paris at the Ecole Normale Supérieure and editor director of Éditions Hermann. She has written many articles and, essays, and has published various collections dedicated to different philosophical themes. Some of her works include: *L'impatience des langues* (2010, co-written with Gérard Bensussan); *Le siècle de Schoenberg* (2010); *Emmanuel Levinas et le souci de l'art* (2010) and *L'Opéra et son double* (2013).

Leonel Ribeiro dos Santos is Full Professor at the Department of Philosophy of the University of Lisbon and currently Visiting Professor at the UFSC (Florianópolis, Brazil). He is researcher and Coordinator of Research at the Centre of Philosophy of the University of Lisbon (CFUL). He is editor (1993–2000), and Director (2000–2012) of the philosophical journal *Philosophica* (Lisbon). His main publications include *Metáforas da Razão ou Economia Poética do Pensar Kantiano* (1989 and 1994); *A razão sensível. Estudos kantianos* (1994); *Linguagem, Retórica e Filosofia no Renascimento* (2004); *O Espírito da Letra. Ensaios de Hermenêutica da Modernidade Regresso a Kant: Ética, Estética e Filosofia Política* (2012).

Index

Adler, Adolph Peter 226
Adorno, Theodor W. 7, 279, 298
aesthetics/aesthetic/aesthetical 2–3, 7, 104–105, 122, 190, 192, 197, 199–202, 212, 231–232, 248, 251, 253, 255, 271, 275–283, 292–293
affect (Affekt) 69, 79–81, 83, 87–89, 107, 113, 177, 180, 218–219, 275–276
affirmation/affirmative 5, 26–28, 38, 45, 48–49, 62, 93, 113, 128, 151, 178–179, 183, 191, 201, 203, 205, 236, 239–241, 243
– self-affirmation 26–27, 30, 31, 33, 70–74, 92–93, 130, 139, 151
agon/agonal 55–58, 95, 197, 199–200
Altizer, Thomas J.J. 157
amor fati 5–6, 116, 138, 191, 204–206
animal 3, 23–25, 28, 32–33, 75, 84, 87, 97, 127, 133, 159, 212
anxiety 242, 251–252
Apollo/Apollinian 4, 118, 120–121, 132, 201
appearance (Erscheinung/Schein) 24, 26, 41, 76–77, 85, 101, 118–120, 122–127, 129–131, 144, 149–150, 194–195, 197, 209–210, 212, 215–216, 234, 237, 240, 260, 263–266, 269, 274, 277, 282–284, 287–288, 291–292
Aristotle 163, 274
art (see also music) 4–5, 7, 19, 100, 105–109, 111, 120–124, 128, 164, 190, 199, 201, 212, 246–247, 251–254, 274–276, 279–280, 282–283
Aumann, Antony 231

Beach, Edward A. 165
becoming 30, 37–38, 61, 105, 119, 123, 134, 151, 176, 178–180, 183–184, 198–199, 204, 223, 225, 227–228, 235, 242–243, 254, 278
– becoming what one is/to become what one is 158, 179, 243
being 24, 30, 37, 38, 43, 77, 80, 82, 86, 116-117, 120–123, 132, 139, 144, 149–151, 160–165, 176, 179, 185, 191, 194–195, 200, 202, 204, 209, 226, 234, 240, 267–268, 271–273, 278–279, 292

– human being 28, 30, 44, 60, 67, 69–71, 84, 87–88, 97, 155, 163, 189, 193–208, 212, 217–222, 234
– living being/s 11–15, 19, 21–23, 129, 192
– primordial being 118, 123, 129, 162, 176, 181
Benjamin, Walter 7, 94, 278–280
Bernstein, Jay 35, 40, 43, 45
biology/biological 11–13, 15, 17–19, 23–24, 75, 181
Bizet, Georges 246, 255
body (see also physiology) 6, 46, 49, 76, 78, 80–81, 106, 113, 121, 126, 132, 162–165, 172, 178, 194–195, 210, 214–217, 219–222
bondsman (see master/slave)
Bourdieu, Pierre 116
Brandes, Georg 6, 223, 225, 246–252
Brink, Bert van den 67, 71
Brobjer, Thomas 6, 223, 248–249
Buddha 155
Buddhism/Buddhist/Buddhistic 191, 201, 206, 239

Christianity/Christian 28–29, 31–33, 35, 38–39, 135, 154, 157, 159, 197, 223–224, 238–240, 242, 254–255, 272, 281
Cicero 154
Climacus 227–228, 230, 258–259, 266–270
compassion 196, 200
Conant, James 230, 237–238
conceptual/conceptualisation 1–2, 4, 68, 73, 81, 88, 90, 100, 104–105, 107–111, 149, 154, 161, 181, 233, 235–236, 238, 247, 259, 271, 274, 279
conscience 27–28, 46, 185
– bad conscience 3, 19, 24–30, 32, 61, 83
consciousness 12–14, 16, 26–27, 29, 32, 59, 61–63, 69–70, 81, 88, 93, 96, 108, 116–117, 122, 125–126, 130, 133, 140–142, 146–147, 149–151, 160–162, 164–166, 176, 192, 213, 216, 221, 272, 294
– false consciousness 16, 59, 61–62
– self-consciousness 3, 12–19, 25, 29, 45, 69–75, 93–94, 96, 115, 129, 145, 149–150, 161, 164–166

critique 4, 6, 7, 40, 46–47, 49–54, 59, 62, 63, 70, 71, 79, 82, 111, 130, 183, 215, 220–221, 224–226, 228, 233, 235–238, 240, 249, 254, 271, 276, 280
– of (positive) law 3, 35, 46, 49–50, 53, 64
– of (the) system 2, 6, 125, 223, 225–229, 232–236, 238
– of metaphysics 208, 220
– of morality 2, 47, 236, 238, 272
– self-critique 63, 241, 283
Cuppitt, Don 157

Dahlhaus, Carl 107
Darwin, Charles 8, 22, 287–288, 290
Darwinian 83, 287–288
decadence 68, 97, 110, 112, 239, 242, 255
Deleuze, Gilles 70, 93, 115, 118, 152, 156, 224, 243
desire 14–16, 26, 67, 69, 70, 75–79, 81, 86–87, 93, 95, 158, 163–166, 170–171, 173, 179–180, 182–184, 202–203, 213, 237, 253
Dionysian 4, 61, 118–121, 129–130, 132, 139, 201, 203–205, 252
Dionysus 119, 159–160, 164–165, 197, 272
Doniger, Wendy 162
drama (see also tragedy) 4, 61, 111, 118, 123, 130, 152, 246, 253, 255, 275
Drive (*Trieb*) 2, 4–6, 21, 28, 39–40, 42, 46, 49, 66–67, 76, 78–91, 93, 125–126, 128, 134, 136, 141, 145–146, 170, 176–177, 180–185, 198, 201, 208, 212, 218–222, 234–235, 252
– multiplicity of drives 6, 80–82, 176, 182, 208, 217, 221
Durand, Gilbert 161

Engels, Eva Maria 134
Entzweiung 3, 12, 42–43, 55
'eternal recurrence' 7, 243, 249, 258, 272
error 47, 116, 134, 168, 172, 192, 234, 237, 242
existential 189, 224, 230, 235–236, 243
experiment/experimental 6, 181, 225, 228–229, 232–233, 236–243

failure 11, 14–17, 71, 173, 279–280
Fichte, Johann Gottlieb 1–2, 4, 115–117, 139–143, 145–147, 149–152
fiction 8, 181, 282–284, 288, 290–292

force (*Kraft*) 5, 23, 31, 38, 49, 54–55, 57–58, 60–61, 67, 78–79, 83, 89, 92–93, 116, 118, 126, 135–165, 171, 176–180, 183, 201, 211–213, 215–221, 240, 275, 279–280, 290
Foucault, Michel 66, 79–80, 83, 91
freedom 7, 12, 14–18, 26, 38, 40–41, 47, 49, 52, 68–75, 90, 95–96, 100–101, 107–108, 113, 116–118, 125, 143, 148–151, 169–173, 176, 178, 182–185, 258–259, 262–263, 266–270, 277
future 5, 26, 61, 97, 101–102, 136, 173–174, 182, 184, 247

Geiger, Ido 39
Geist (see spirit)
genealogy/genealogical 58–59, 61–64, 130, 132, 137–139, 237, 282–283, 288, 293
Gerhardt, Volker 47–48, 90, 225, 236
God 2, 5, 27–28, 32–33, 36, 39–41, 44, 48, 130, 154–163, 165, 167, 169, 173, 193, 197, 238, 268, 281
Goethe, Johann Wolfgang von 117, 249
Green, Ronald M. 259, 268
ground (*Grund*) 5, 40, 48, 49, 63, 73, 115, 118–120, 122, 132, 137, 139–141, 143–144, 146, 151, 157, 158, 180, 190, 193, 195, 198, 200, 210–211, 221, 229, 237, 240, 262, 263, 265, 267, 269, 272, 289, 292

Habermas, Jürgen 138
Hegel, Georg Wilhelm Friedrich 1–4, 11–16, 18–19, 21–23, 32–36, 38–46, 49–50, 52–55, 58–60, 62–64, 66–74, 78, 82, 84, 90, 93–96, 100–101, 104–112, 156–158, 161, 225–227, 229, 271, 274
Hegelian 4, 20, 53, 55, 66–67, 70, 74–75, 84, 90, 92–94, 96, 100, 157–158, 225, 267, 273
Heidegger, Martin 7, 154, 156, 159, 196, 224, 239, 271–275
Heraclitus 37, 132
Hill, Gareth S. 161
history 5, 7, 27–28, 30–31, 72, 82, 96, 101, 103, 109–110, 127–128, 131–132, 136,

154, 156, 160–161, 166, 171–176, 210, 239, 242, 253, 271–273, 275–276, 280
Hobbes, Thomas 66, 70, 79–80, 196
Hobbesian 69, 72, 87
Hölderlin, Friedrich 41–42, 273–275
Honneth, Axel 66, 69, 71, 79, 83, 91
Hühn, Lore 225–226
humanity 84, 97, 127, 174, 278

Idealism/German Idealists 1–2, 4, 6–7, 100, 102–104, 117, 127, 160, 224–225, 233, 271, 276, 278, 280
illness (see also pathology; sickness) 3, 11–12, 19, 23–32, 34, 102, 172–173
illusion 70, 118–119, 125–128, 134, 260, 266, 282, 288, 290–292
image (Bild) 12, 38, 117–118, 120, 122–124, 126–127, 144, 150–151, 163, 198, 219, 253, 279, 290
individuality 4, 93, 118–121, 123, 127–128, 130, 139, 143, 148, 235
– principium individuationis 196
instinct 24–26, 28, 31–32, 82, 84, 86–87, 89, 96, 125, 127, 133, 218, 283, 288, 293–294
irony 164, 230, 250

Kant, Immanuel 1–2, 7–8, 38, 40, 42, 45, 50, 100, 103–105, 121, 141, 160–161, 194, 197, 208, 258–268, 270–271, 282–284, 286, 288–294
Kastafanas, Paul 208, 218–219
Kierkegaard, Sören 1–2, 6–7, 223–233, 235–236, 242–243, 246–251, 255–256, 258–259, 266–268, 270
knowledge 4, 15, 29, 48–51, 55, 61, 85, 103–104, 122, 130, 136, 138–142, 145, 150–151, 167, 169–171, 173, 181–182, 192, 210–213, 238–239, 241–242, 270, 274–275, 278, 280, 283, 289, 293–294
Kojève, Alexandre 73, 75, 92

Lange, Friedrich A. 8, 284–285, 287–291, 294
law (*Gesetz*) 2–3, 35–64, 74, 142, 144, 146, 148, 211, 216, 223, 239, 262–263, 265–266, 269, 278
Lerchner, Thorsten 195–196

life affirmation/life-affirming/life-affirmative 3, 5, 26, 36, 49, 62, 128, 178, 203, 205
– sublated life (*aufgehobenes Leben*) 3, 11
logos 167, 271–272, 278, 280
lord (see master/slave)
love 33, 42–44, 46, 52, 54–58, 60, 64, 69, 76–78, 87, 89, 92–95, 182, 197, 200, 205–206, 254
lyrical 278, 287

Mallet, Marie-Louise 101, 108
Marx, Karl 20–21, 30, 237
master/slave 3, 22, 31, 35, 40–41, 52–53, 60, 68, 71–73, 83, 89–90, 95, 133, 137
– lord/bondsman 17–18, 40, 68
McKinnon, Alastair 223
metaphysics 8, 110, 143, 156, 180, 191, 194–195, 197, 199, 208–209, 211, 213, 217, 220–221, 272, 276, 282–283, 286, 291, 294
Miles, Thomas P. 223–224, 249
modernity 2, 54, 68, 96, 110, 112, 138, 183, 224-225, 276, 278, 280
Moingt, Joseph 157
Moore, Gregory 218
morality/morals (see also critique of morality and slave morality) 29, 35–39, 42, 43, 45–49, 54–56, 61, 64, 115–116, 137–139, 145, 169, 192, 195–196, 200, 233, 238, 272, 282
– overcoming of morality 36, 46, 58
Mozart, Wolfgang Amadeus 246, 249–256
multiplicity (see also drives) 4, 6, 54, 59, 80–83, 88–89, 91, 95, 105, 127–128, 176, 198, 217–222, 235–236
music (see also song) 4, 6–7, 100–113, 119–120, 130–131, 246–255, 271–280
– musical language 105, 247, 253–255, 276, 279
mythological 112, 160, 162, 164, 167, 181, 281
– myth/mythos 122, 130–132, 159–160, 163, 167, 254, 271–272, 276, 294

Narcissus 163
nature 21, 24, 30, 36–38, 41–42, 45–46, 49, 54, 57–58, 116, 120, 124–125, 132, 156–157, 159, 165, 177, 181, 195–196,

201, 209, 211–216, 219–221, 253, 262–263, 265–266, 294
– state of nature 69, 71–72, 95
nausea/nauseating 190, 201
necessity 7, 17, 19, 41, 48–50, 61, 63, 126, 133, 139–140, 149, 171, 174, 220, 240–241, 263–269, 271–272, 275, 280, 283, 287, 291
negation 5, 38, 53, 63, 106, 113, 139–140, 157, 184, 190, 197, 200–201, 205–207, 242
nihilism/nihilistic 2, 28, 32, 48–49, 53–55, 57–58, 61–64, 97, 128, 138, 144, 155–156, 182–183, 197, 202, 204–206, 224, 239–242, 273, 276–277
– self-negation 12, 184
noble 67, 95, 137–138, 197, 283
nothingness 31–32, 157, 165, 171, 183, 197, 270

(the) One 36, 42, 45, 46, 56, 60, 62, 64, 123, 127, 129, 149, 151, 170, 196, 198
– primordial One 119, 122–124, 126, 128–129, 132, 197–198, 199
organism 17, 19, 21–23, 25, 67, 116, 126, 85, 120, 127, 131, 208–209, 212, 214, 216–221
– organic 22–23, 26, 85, 132–134, 136, 177, 213, 216–217
Ottmann, Henning 83
overcoming (see also morality) 13, 36, 43–44, 47, 56, 58, 75, 79, 131, 200, 202–206, 239–240
– self-overcoming 3, 11, 37, 63, 78, 84, 87, 139, 241
Owen, David 90

pain/painful (see also suffering) 29, 58, 77–78, 84–85, 121–124, 129, 159, 170, 185, 196, 198, 201, 203
Parkes, Graham 208, 218
Pascal, Blaise 156–157, 159
past 5, 21, 126, 144, 167, 174–176, 180–185, 233, 260–261, 269
pathology (see also illness) 3, 11–18
Persephone 163
perspectivism 136, 143, 238, 291–292
Philonenko, Alexis 260–261
physiology 6, 49, 54, 170, 208–212, 214–217, 219–222

Pindar 158
Pinkard, Terry 74
Pippin, Robert B. 74–75, 82, 94, 297
Plato 102–104, 158, 167, 191, 238, 271, 273–275, 283, 286
Plutarch 156, 159
Pöggeler, Otto 41
progress/progressus 23, 68, 71–73, 96, 131–132, 178, 215

reason 4, 6, 38–42, 52, 110, 113, 137–138, 146, 160–161, 166, 176, 178, 193, 195, 200, 208, 210, 259–266, 290, 294
– principle of sufficient reason 140, 142, 211, 215, 218
recognition 3, 15–17, 60, 66–77, 79–80, 84, 89–97, 143, 147, 179
redeem/redemption 5, 118, 123, 125, 129, 197, 199–201, 278
Reginster, Bernard 26, 29, 202–204
repetition 23, 232, 243, 249, 258
ressentiment 31, 83, 116, 137–138, 152, 183–184
revaluation/re-evaluation (see transvaluation)
Richardson, John 67, 181, 218
Ricœur, Paul 237
Romantic/Romanticism 105, 169, 230, 248, 250, 271, 273–274, 276–278

Sallis, John 101, 108–109
satisfaction 14–15, 17, 20, 30, 69–73, 75, 86, 93, 194–195, 202, 204
Schelling, Friedrich Wilhelm Josef 1–2, 5, 104, 154, 156, 158–165, 167–185, 226, 250, 278, 297
Schellingian 159, 170, 175, 227
Schmidt, Jochen 125
Schoenberg, Arnold 276–278, 280–281, 298
Schopenhauer, Arthur 1–2, 5–8, 27, 80, 96, 105, 117, 125, 162, 176, 179, 189–202, 206, 208–222, 233, 235, 247–248, 253, 255–256, 271, 278, 283–285, 287–290, 293, 296–297
Schopenhauerian 84, 190, 198, 287
Schulz, Walter 160
Schumann, Robert 246, 256, 298

self (see affirmation, consciousness, negation, overcoming)
senses 101–104, 110–113, 215, 263, 275
- sensation 108–109, 110, 112, 142, 146, 183, 237
- sensibility 35, 40–42, 103, 105, 110–112, 263–264, 266
- sensible 104, 106–107, 109, 262–264, 270, 290
- sensitive 103, 179, 183, 274
sickness (see also illness) 26, 27, 32, 112, 172, 190, 250
Siep, Ludwig 66–67, 69, 74
Simmel, Georg 48, 194, 196
slave (see also master/slave) 47, 62, 68, 137
- slave morality 35, 61, 137
- slave revolt 60, 138
social 3, 16–19, 36, 46, 54, 66–75, 82–83, 87–96, 133, 138, 143, 274
- social contract 69–70, 72, 90, 95
- social life 87–88, 133, 143, 274
song 109, 111, 130, 159, 273
- singing 119, 276
species 11–13, 19, 22–23, 68, 84, 97, 185, 212
Spinoza, Baruch de 41, 116, 149
Spinozistic 41, 59, 84
spirit (*Geist*) 2–3, 11–20, 24, 28, 40, 69, 72, 82, 109, 113, 127, 137, 154, 163, 165, 177, 185, 242, 252, 254
- free spirit/s 55, 62–63, 173, 237
Stegmaier, Werner 102, 104, 204–206, 238
Steiner, George 156
struggle 14, 16–17, 60, 67–73, 81–84, 87, 91, 93, 95, 115–116, 129, 134–135, 176, 178–180, 182, 196–198, 200–201, 288
- struggle for recognition [see recognition] 70, 77, 84, 91, 93–96
suffering (see also pain/painful) 5, 24, 29–32, 121, 123, 125, 129, 159, 189–204, 267
system/systematic (see also critique of the system) 2, 6, 15, 18, 22, 40, 100, 148, 160, 164, 166, 171–174, 190, 210, 217, 225, 227, 231, 233–236, 259, 271–272, 276, 285, 293
- unsystematic/ non systematic 7, 259, 287

temporality 184, 280
- temporal [including transitory] 30, 105, 118, 128, 212, 259, 266, 270, 272
tragedy/tragic 33, 97, 118–123, 125, 128–132, 139, 158–159, 184, 190, 194–195, 197, 201–202, 207, 236, 239, 241–242, 253, 271–275, 277, 280, 283, 293
transitory (see temporal)
transvaluation/revaluation/re-evaluation (*Umwertung*) 5, 59, 202–205, 241, 272, 292
truth (see also will to truth) 13, 40, 51–52, 72, 119–121, 130, 134–136, 146, 167–168, 171–172, 231, 233, 235, 237–238, 240, 242, 269, 275–277, 284, 287–288, 290, 294
- untruth 239, 241

unity 4, 6, 19, 22, 37–38, 56, 59–60, 81–82, 91, 111, 118–123, 125, 127–128, 130, 136, 139–140, 147, 151, 162, 172, 176–177, 179, 196–197, 202, 208–209, 216–217, 219–221, 251, 278

Vaihinger, Hans 7–8, 282–294
value/s 5, 13, 17, 20–21, 25, 27, 31, 33, 37, 41, 47–48, 52–54, 58–59, 62–64, 76, 83–88, 96, 105, 133, 138, 145, 155–156, 197, 200, 202–203, 205, 224, 239–242, 272–273, 282, 288, 293
Voltaire 154

Wagner, Richard 4, 7, 110–113, 246–248, 252–256, 271–276, 278, 280, 298
(free) will 24, 115–116, 147
- will to appearance (*Wille zum Schein*) 282–284, 290–292
- will to power (*Wille zur Macht*) 2–5, 22, 31, 54, 66–68, 75–89, 93–96, 131, 133–134, 137–139, 191, 202–204, 206, 253, 272, 274, 281, 284, 287
- will to truth (*Wille zur Wahrheit*) 172, 235, 291–292
Williams, Robert R. 1, 69–70, 74–75, 93, 95

Zarathustra 56, 137, 154, 184, 190, 273, 275

www.ingramcontent.com/pod-product-compliance
Lightning Source LLC
Chambersburg PA
CBHW050853160426
43194CB00011B/2139